CAUSING ACTIONS

Causing Actions

PAUL M. PIETROSKI

OXFORD
UNIVERSITY PRESS

OXFORD

UNIVERSITY PRESS

Great Clarendon Street, Oxford OX2 6DP

Oxford University Press is a department of the University of Oxford.
It furthers the University's objective of excellence in research, scholarship,
and education by publishing worldwide in

Oxford New York

Athens Auckland Bangkok Bogotá Buenos Aires Calcutta
Cape Town Chennai Dar es Salaam Delhi Florence Hong Kong Istanbul
Karachi Kuala Lumpur Madrid Melbourne Mexico City Mumbai
Nairobi Paris São Paulo Singapore Taipei Tokyo Toronto Warsaw

and associated companies in Berlin Ibadan

Oxford is a registered trade mark of Oxford University Press
in the UK and in certain other countries

Published in the United States
by Oxford University Press Inc., New York

British Library Cataloguing in Publication Data

Data available

Library of Congress Cataloging in Publication Data

Data available

ISBN 0–19–825042–8

1 3 5 7 9 10 8 6 4 2

Typeset by Hope Services (Abingdon) Ltd.
Printed in Great Britain
on acid-free paper by
Biddles Ltd.,
Guildford and King's Lynn

to the memory of my father
who taught me that action reveals belief.

PREFACE

Reasons are causes, and reasons do not have arational descriptions. Yet how can this be so, given that reasons often have effects—like bodily motions—whose occurrence can be explained in arational terms?

I used to think about this strand of the mind–body problem differently: since rationalizing causes often have effects whose occurrence can be explained in arational terms, reasons must also have arational descriptions; and at least in humans, reasons must be complex biochemical events of some sort. From this perspective, the question is how biochemical events could have the properties that mental events do have. But I now think this is the wrong question to ask, in part because it seems unanswerable. We need not and probably cannot show how certain 'impersonal' causes—events describable without reference to a thinking subject of those events—could *be* mental causes. Borrowing a metaphor from Sellars, I suspect that causes visible in the manifest image are not there to be seen in the scientific image. This presents us with an intellectual problem: how can we maintain that reasons are *sui generis* in this sense, without falling into an objectionable dualism? But I think we can make progress on answering this question; whereas I see little prospect for attempts to identify reasons with events describable in impersonal terms.

In 1992, I started to develop the kind of non-Cartesian dualism presented here; and three times, I have been rescued from rushing too quickly into a book-length treatment. First, a conversation with Martin Davies helped me get over a misguided aversion to Frege's notion of sense, which I now rely on. A year or so later, I was asked to write a critical notice of John McDowell's book *Mind and World*; and although this postponed other work for a while, I learned much about the issues at stake. Finally, at an important juncture, I reread Jennifer Hornsby's book *Actions*. This led me to identify and abandon some of my assumptions about actions, with considerable ramifications for my views about mental causation. Then, for better or worse, it came to seem that it really was time to take on a sustained writing project.

That is, I went on sabbatical. My thanks to McGill University for releasing me from teaching and administrative duties in 1996–7, and to my then future colleagues at the University of Maryland for their hospitality. SSHRCC and FCAR provided welcome financial support during my time in Canada. Chapters 1 and 4 are revised versions of essays published in, respectively, *Mind* (107 (1998): 73–111) and *British Journal for the Philosophy of Science* (46 (1995): 81–110). My thanks to Oxford

University Press for permission to reproduce this material. Chapter 2 is a revised version of an essay previously published in *Mind and Language* (11 (1996): 331–62); portions of 'Mental Causation for Dualists', also published in *Mind and Language* (9 (1994): 336–66), appear in Chapters 5 and 6. My thanks to Blackwell Publishers Ltd. for permission to reproduce this material.

Various friends and colleagues deserve more credit than they will get by being mentioned here. Martin Davies provided encouragement and insight, in his characteristic way. Georges Rey got me to think about *ceteris paribus* laws ten years ago; and the first three sections of Chapter 4 come from a joint paper. I am grateful to Georges for letting me use our work in this manner, and for many discussions about views at odds with his own. Two reviewers for the press helped me see a range of interconnected difficulties with an earlier version of the manuscript; Chapters 5 and 6, in particular, are very different as a result of their generous comments. My intellectual debts to Donald Davidson and Jerry Fodor will, I hope, be obvious from the text. This book descends (very indirectly) from a dissertation; and the surviving parts bear the mark of my supervisor, Robert Stalnaker. Newer parts have been influenced by my experience with two other teachers, Noam Chomsky and Judith Thomson.

In the course of thinking about the material presented here, I have benefited from more discussions than I can remember. With apologies to those forgotten, let me recognize: Nick Adamson, Louise Antony, Kent Bach, Mark Baker, Alex Barber, John Bigelow, David Brink, Andy Brook, Brian Garret, Brendon Gillon, Norbert Hornstein, David Hunter, Richard Larson, Ernie Lepore, Joe Levine, Peter Ludlow, Storrs McCall, Clare McRae, Karen Neander, Rob Stainton, Manuela Ungureanu, Juan Uriagarecka, and Chris Viger. David Davies and Jim McGilvray merit special thanks for years of regular support/scepticism, of the sort one just hopes for from those around the hall. Finally, my greatest debt is to Susan Dwyer, who has heard more about mental causation than any rational being would care to hear. Sue provided friendly criticism and rich conversation. But even more importantly, she has been a constant partner and source of happiness.

CONTENTS

Introduction

On 13 April 1865, John Wilkes Booth shot Abraham Lincoln. It happened in a theatre near the White House, at about 10.13 p.m. Booth wanted to kill Lincoln in retaliation for his treatment of the South during the civil war. So upon learning that the President would attend a play that night, Booth (an actor who knew the layout of the theatre) decided to hide near the President's box and wait for an opportunity to get inside. At some point, the Secret Service guard left his station to get a better view of the stage. Booth saw his chance, got into position, and fired his pistol.

American history texts usually contain some such account of the events that led to Lincoln's death. Taken at face value, the brief account just given offers a description of Booth's action, and an intentional explanation of that action. This explanation reveals why Booth acted as he did, by providing information that makes his reason for action apparent, even if we find the reason insufficient (and the action deplorable). Following Davidson (1963, 1967a, 1971) and many others, I hold that rationalizing explanations cite causes, and that actions are events. An intentional explanation of a person's action cites a mental cause of the event that is his action. When we speak of mental *causes*, we may be speaking of various things: events, like Booth's coming to see that he had an opportunity to kill Lincoln; states, like Booth's desire to kill Lincoln; or perhaps other entities, like the fact that Booth wanted to kill Lincoln. But I will focus primarily on events, which have the effects they do, in part because of prevailing background conditions.

Given that actions have mental causes, a variety of considerations make two further claims very tempting: paradigmatic actions are bodily motions; and the mental causes of human actions are certain biochemical events in our brains. On this view, Booth's action of pulling the trigger was a motion of his trigger finger; and when we say 'Booth saw his chance', we are citing a biochemical cause of that finger motion. But I think these further claims are false. My principal aim is to defend an alternative conception of intentional explanation, according to which actions typically cause bodily motions, and the mental causes of our actions are not biochemical events of any sort. (Let me say at the outset that I have been influenced by Hornsby (1980, 1997), in elaborating and modifying certain aspects of Davidson's view.)

I

My plan is to argue first that events like Booth's action of pulling of the trigger cause events like the motion of Booth's trigger finger. With this conclusion in place, I develop a conception of intentional explanation that leaves it open whether (human) mental events are really biochemical events, or whether a non-Cartesian form of dualism is true. Finally, I contend that the latter option is better, all things considered. Along the way, the following theses will be defended: among a person's mental events are his *tryings*—events that typically cause bodily motions, and are caused by (the acquisition of) beliefs and desires; paradigmatic actions are tryings; an intentional explanation usually cites a belief or desire that causes an action/trying that causes a bodily motion; and human mental events are causes distinct from, although they supervene on, biochemical events. In this sense, both reasons and actions belong to a distinctively mental domain. To explain a person's action is (at least in the first instance) to explain a mental episode of trying. Some of these claims may initially sound paradoxical. So it may be helpful to provide a less telegraphic overview.

Chapter 1 begins with a puzzle that arises in giving a semantics for action sentences. I think Davidson was basically right about the logical forms of sentences like 'Booth shot Lincoln' and 'Booth pulled the trigger'; they involve quantification over events, like shootings and pullings. Given this analysis and some further facts, it follows (perhaps surprisingly) that the event of Booth's shooting Lincoln was distinct from the event of Booth's pulling the trigger. But as Davidson noted, there are powerful reasons for saying that 'the shooting' and 'the pulling' can be used to describe a single action. I argue that the best resolution of this puzzle, which has implications for several issues in semantics and action theory, treats event descriptions like 'his shooting of Lincoln' as ambiguous: they can be used in referring to actions/tryings, or to complex events (processes) that begin with an action and end with some effect of the action (cf. Thomson 1977). The shooting and the pulling are distinct complex events; but there was one action, which caused Booth's finger motion, which caused the motion of the bullet.

It may seem odd to begin a study of intentional explanation with a puzzle about action sentences. But this provides a good forum for expositing and testing the coherence of my views about actions. Moreover, in discussing intentional explanations of why *Booth pulled the trigger*, one would like to know how the italicized sentence is related to Booth's action. The puzzle reminds us that this relation is not obvious. Talk of events also raises the question of what events are; but I do not want to begin with a criterion of individuation for events. Such criteria are tendentious, and I want to explore (not prejudge) issues about which event descriptions describe the same events. Davidson's event analysis, however, can be defended on independent grounds. The conception of events implicated in ordinary speech is quite rich. So we can usefully begin by saying that events are what sentences that quantify over events quantify over. I say a little more in subsequent chapters. But the idea, familiar in the analytic tradition, is to use semantics as a prolegomenon to metaphysics.[1]

That said, the meanings of action sentences do not settle the questions of interest here. While the semantics is highly suggestive, further argument is needed to show that actions cause bodily motions. And a full defence of the claim that actions are tryings requires an account of tryings. Eventually, I offer a functional account (similar to O'Shaughnessy (1973, 1980)), in terms of how tryings are nomically related to beliefs and desires. In the interim, I operate with a pretheoretic notion of trying. In particular, I assume that every trying has a *content*—a propositional specification of its success conditions.

In this respect, a trying is like the acquisition of a belief (which can be true or false) or a desire (which can be satisfied or not). For familiar reasons, contents appear to be more finely grained than states of the mind-independent world. Suppose Booth once met a nice man called 'Abe', who later became president. Then intuitively, Booth could have believed that Lincoln was in the theatre, without believing that Abe was in the theatre, even though Lincoln *was* Abe; and Booth could have tried to shoot Lincoln without trying to shoot Abe. This leads to the cluster of puzzles associated with the semantics of propositional attitude ascriptions. I approach the question of what contents are via these puzzles.

In Chapter 2, I defend a version of Frege's view: epistemic verbs like 'believe' ('want' and 'try') express relations between thinkers and *senses* of sentences; 'that P' is a device for referring to the sense of 'P'; and verb phrases like 'try to shoot Abe' contain a clause relevantly like 'that he shot Abe'. But unlike Frege, I hold that terms embedded in 'that'-clauses have their customary referents. Even in the sentence 'Booth believed that

---

[1] I do not deny that many events are changes (see Lombard 1986). We typically, and perhaps always, see instances of causation as cases in which one change brings about another. And it is tempting to say that events are changes of state in an object. (As I typed these words, my fingers moved, keys went down, and text appeared on my screen; as my fingers changed states, this caused changes of state in the machine.) But some events, like vigils, may not be changes; and some occurrences may not be changes in any object (see Steward 1997; Strawson 1959). In Ch. 3, I address the relation of events to states more explicitly. Some philosophers will find talk of events suspect, absent a substantive account of what it is for there to be *one as opposed to two* of them (see Quine 1969; cf. Brody 1980). Perhaps as Davidson (1969) suggests, E = F iff E and F have the same causes and effects, where E and F are events that have causes and effects. But we can assess arguments for or against neuralism without a reduction of events to other entities. Indeed, such arguments should influence our views about the nature of events.

Lincoln was a tyrant', the referent of 'Lincoln' is the man Lincoln. On my view, the complementizer 'that' is a meaningful expression: the referent of 'that P' depends on the referent of 'that', which depends on the sense of 'P' (cf. Davidson 1968). This preserves the attractive features of Frege's view, while avoiding many objections to it. And remaining objections can be met, I contend, if one lets the sense of a referring expresssion depend on the context.

Since intentional explanations often involve 'that'-clauses, we want a clear view of what such clauses mean. But my interest in Fregean semantics is not limited to its clarificatory role. In Chapter 3, I extend the account of attitude ascription to explanation: the fact that P explains the fact that Q, iff the sense of 'P' explains the sense of 'Q'. This fits well with the common view that explanation is a relation between facts, if we follow Frege in taking facts to be the senses of true sentences. And given the event analysis, the senses of many true sentences can be construed as *ways of thinking about events*. The sense of 'Booth shot Lincoln', I claim, is a way of thinking about the event of Booth's shooting Lincoln.

If explanation often holds between ways of thinking about particular events, this invites the thought that causation (insofar as it is a relation between events) is the transitive *extensionalization* of explanation. To a first approximation: if C is the Φ-ish event, and D is the Ψ-ish event, and the fact that the Φ-ish event occurred explains why the Ψ-ish event occurred, then C caused D (no matter how these events are thought about, or described); and if C caused D, which caused E, then C caused E. Of course, not every explanation involves ways of thinking about events related as cause to effect. We must restrict attention to explanations *of an appropriate sort*. If 'appropriate' is a mere synonym for 'causal', the proposed sufficient condition may not be very interesting. But, I argue, one can avoid vicious circularity; and this bears on the question of whether our tryings and their mental causes are biochemical events. To see why, we need to step back and consider a central aspect of the mind–body problem.

2

Minds affect the world, at least in the sense that mental events cause non-mental events. Booth's decision to shoot Lincoln changed the course of history. In the summer of 1914, European leaders came to believe that a Bosnian Serb had killed the Austrian Archduke; these mental events had dramatic effects. Or to take a fictional example, there were causal consequences of Othello's coming to believe that Desdemona loved Cassio. Like Iago, most of us believe that affecting a person's thoughts will affect what that person does; and this belief influences our own actions when dealing with others. Behaviour may not be the only somatic manifestation of the mental. For example, stress effects and placebo effects suggest that certain beliefs can affect a person's health. But the paradigmatic cases of mental causation are those in which a person's mental events cause her actions, which have a host of non-mental effects.

In my view, many bodily motions are already effects of actions. Shifting to a non-violent example, suppose Nora reached for her umbrella because she came to believe that it was raining. I think the acquisition of her belief caused an action/trying that caused a bodily motion, which caused the motion of the umbrella. Nonetheless, mental causes of actions can still be distal causes of bodily motions, which have non-mental effects. (I will not try to define 'mental', since our intuitions will be more secure than any definition. Nora's noticing the weather is a mental event, while the motion of her umbrella is not. If some mental events like pains are not intentional, so be it; though I am not concerned with such events.)

Indeed, it is a truism that bodily motions often have mental causes. But the truism is in tension with other plausible claims. Human bodily motions are typically caused by muscle contractions, which are caused by certain biochemical events that in turn have other biochemical causes, and so on—until one comes to events of sensory transduction, whose proximal causes lie outside the body in question. These facts appear to leave no room for mental causes. Correspondingly, they also make it seem that a bodily motion with mental causes would be overdetermined, like the death of a victim both shot and poisoned. But ordinary bodily motions should not be assimilated to paradigmatic cases of overdetermination. If I wave my hand, the motion of my hand does not seem to be the result of two independent (but coordinated) causal processes. This intuition is bolstered by counterfactual considerations. My hand would have remained motionless had relevant neuromuscular pathways been severed. So while there are clearly mental causes, it is not clear *how there can be* mental causes.[2]

One might think the mystery is easily solved: each mental cause of a human bodily motion B *is* a biochemical cause of B; or as it is sometimes put, our mental events just are certain neural events. Call this thesis 'neuralism'. (One could speak of 'biochemicalism'; but following philosophical

---

[2] I take as given, in light of Davidson (1963, 1967*b*, 1971) and more recent development of his arguments (e.g. Mele 1992), that there are no conceptual barriers to treating reasons as causes. One might deny that there are any mental causes; though if anyone but a philosopher denied having thoughts, or said that his thoughts never affected his body, this would be taken as a sign of madness. And in my view, evidence of mental causation abounds: people reach for umbrellas when it is raining; they drive to airports shortly before friends are due to arrive; they fill in circles on standardized tests; etc. (see Fodor 1975, 1987; Rey 1997). But my goal is not to convince sceptics that mental events have non-mental effects. I want to know how mental causation is possible, given facts that seem to exclude its possibility. I return to this point in Sect. 4 below.

custom, I will use 'neural' broadly to include changes in nervous systems that are not literally changes in neurons. For example, neuralism is compatible with the existence of mental causes that are—or are in part—changes in the level of hormones that affect action potentials.) Neuralism has many attractions. In particular, if mental causes *are* neural causes, there is nothing puzzling in the fact that certain bodily motions have mental *and* neural causes. Indeed, I understand neuralism in terms of the puzzle it is supposed to dispel. So for the most part, I will not distinguish between the following two claims: mental events are identical with certain neural events; and mental events are constituted by neural events, where 'constitute' is understood so that constituted events are not *causes distinct from* their constituting events.

Correspondingly, neuralism is true if mental events are fusions of biochemical events; and this is a point worth pausing over. Assume that we have an adequate grasp of which predicates count as mental and which as neural. This lets us speak of at least some mental events and neural events without settling questions of identity a priori. But neuralists need not say that mental events satisfy predicates like 'has action potential p'. Put crudely, neuralism should be understood as a thesis that is compatible with mental events being relatively large and complex biochemical events. This makes appeal to mereology tempting, and perhaps unavoidable. So let us grant that some events are mereological fusions of other events, and that a fusion of neural events also counts as a neural event. In the context of debates about mental causation, this is to grant that if a part *p* of an event fusion F has an effect *e*, then F is not a cause of *e* distinct from *p*. That is, there is nothing puzzling in the fact that a fusion *and* some part(s) of the fusion caused a given effect. But this seems right. If we learned that some mental event was a fusion F of events that could be described in the language of neuroscience, there would be no further question about how some event caused by the parts of F (perhaps in coordination) could have a mental cause.[3]

This is *not* to say that neuralism is true if mental events are constituted by neural events in some way or other, with talk of mereological fusions being just one example of such a constitution relation. For it is crucial that event fusions are not *causes distinct from* their parts. And the mere fact that mental events are constituted by neural events in *some way or other* does not guarantee that mental events are not causes distinct from neural

---

[3] Davidson (1970) claims that all causes are covered by strict physical laws. So on the assumption that strict laws are stated in terms of predicates satisfied by events involving *very* small objects, the following is a natural gloss of Davidson's claim: C caused E only if C and E are both mereological sums of events, such that the parts of C are related to the parts of E by strict physical laws. (See Hornsby (1985), who argues that many event fusions will lack a kind of unity that genuine *causes* exhibit.)

events. There is a sense in which supervenient entities are constituted by subvenient entities; and the mental supervenes on the non-mental. But as we shall see, it does not follow that mental events are not causes distinct from non-mental events. And if one defines 'constitute' so that constituted events cannot be causes distinct from their constituting events, then event dualists will deny that mental events are constituted (in this demanding sense) by non-mental events.

On the other hand, talk of fusions may not capture the *only* notion of 'constitution' that will support neuralism. Perhaps there is an intermediately strong notion, such that constituted events are neither fusions of their constituting events nor causes distinct from their constituting events. But one cannot just assume that mental events bear some such metaphysical relation to events that satisfy untendentiously neural predicates. Absent an *account of how* constituted events can be causes that are not distinct from their constituting events, the main virtue of neuralism—viz. its simple explanation for why a bodily motion can have mental 'and' neural causes—has been lost. By way of comparison, suppose an event dualist appealed to an intermediately weak notion of being distinct, such that mental causes can be distinct from neural causes without overdetermining any effects of neural causes. One would want to hear more about this notion of distinctness; for therein lies the account of mental causation.

In short, one makes choices about where to do the hard work on the mind–body problem. Historically and theoretically, the following choice has been particularly important: should one adopt the simple account of mental causation, and embrace the consequences of saying that each human mental event is (or at least fails to be distinct from) some biochemical event; or should one eschew these consequences, and defend another conception of mental causation? From this perspective, to say that mental events *are* neural events is to say that mental events are related to certain neural events in a way that obviates the need for any further *account* (like the one I am proposing) of how an effect of those neural events can have mental causes. If mental events are identical with the relevant neural events, or fusions of them, no such account is needed. And one is free to characterize other notions of constitution, given which constituted events are not causes distinct from their constituting events. *Perhaps* mental events are constituted by neural events in some such sense. But the word 'constitution' is not a talisman that protects against objections to both neuralism and dualism; it labels work that needs doing.

One might claim that mental events are related to biochemical events, much as biochemical events are related to physical events; where 'physical' is interpreted in a demanding sense, characterized by reference to our best theories in physics.[4] But biochemical events may not be fusions of physical events. One cannot assume otherwise, claim that mental events are neural events in the same sense that neural events are physical events, and declare this an account of mental causation. Nor can one assume, without begging questions against event dualists, that mental events are just one more species of 'macro' event in a hierarchy of events that can in principle be described in physical terms. Even if biochemical events are constituted by (but not fusions of) physical events, defending this view may require a conception of causation like the one I will be urging here; and this conception might not be sufficiently motivated, without the independent support of reflection on mental causation. So one cannot make the puzzle of mental causation go away, simply by pointing to other macro causes. Mental causes may be special, at least epistemically, and perhaps ontologically. (I return to these issues in Chapters 5 through 7.)

Event dualists will say that mental causes fail to be biochemical causes, in any sense of 'be' that avoids the need for a substantive account of how an event can have mental causes *and* neural causes. There are reasons, to which I return, for adopting this view. That is, there are reasons for taking on the question of how a bodily motion can have distinct mental and neural causes, as opposed to the questions that neuralists must take on. But it is hard to see the force of objections to a view, absent any alternative; and it can seem that postulating non-neural mental causes must lead to disaster. Given that mental events are inner causes of bodily motions, it can seem that Cartesian dualism and neuralism exhaust the options; and Descartes' picture of mental causation is unacceptable. Moreover, as Lewis (1966) and Armstrong (1968, 1970) note, the inner causes of bodily motions discovered by our best science are biochemical. So a challenge to neuralism requires at least some outline of a non-Cartesian alternative.

---

   [4] While our current theories are incomplete, and no doubt partly mistaken, assume that the standard model of particle physics is essentially correct: there are particles (and associated fields) of at least many of the posited kinds—quarks, electrons, photons, etc.; there is a stock of such particles (or a stock of more primitive entities to which quarks and such are reducible) out of which every material object in the universe is composed; and these fundamental particles have properties that are (or provide the reductive base for properties that are) at least importantly *like* the properties ascribed by the standard model, e.g. mass and charge. The fundamental particles and their interactions are governed by laws; and if these laws are not strict, at least they form a *closed* system, in that any apparent exceptions are explicable from within the system, i.e. by citing the fact that certain fundamental particles have certain fundamental properties. This provides at least a starting point for a characterization of physical events: any event involving only fundamental objects and properties, and any fusions of such events. It seems unlikely that any corrected version of the standard model will include reference to mentality. My aim is to defend a thesis which entails that mental events are not physical events in this demanding sense. (If 'physical' is characterized in a less demanding sense, e.g. as anything occurring in spacetime, event dualists may be able to grant that mental events are physical; see Crane and Mellor 1990.)

3

Returning now to my claim at the end of Section 1, suppose that: in general, event C caused event E if a fact suitably related to C explains (in an appropriate way) a fact suitably related to E; a fact suitably related to a particular event *c* explains a fact suitably related to a particular event *e*; and a fact suitably related to a third event *g* also explains a fact suitably related to *e*. Then *c* and *g* are both causes of *e*, since the occurrence of *e* (i.e. the fact that *e* occurred) is twice explained. But the relation between *c* and *g* is left open. If *e* is the motion of Booth's finger, the occurrence of *e* can be explained in neuroscientific terms, without recourse to the intentional idiom. Yet the occurrence of *e* can also be explained as the result of some action/trying, whose occurrence can be explained in overtly rationalizing terms. I will argue that *e* is not overdetermined in any objectionable sense, even if its mental causes are distinct from every neural cause of *e*, given that Booth's mental events (including his tryings) supervene on his neural events. And as we shall see, this supervenience thesis does not entail neuralism.

Elaborating this story requires work. In particular, it requires at least: a reply to overdetermination objections; a non-reductive account of *why* the mental supervenes on the non-mental; and a defence of the claims that causation can (without vicious circularity or implausibility) be characterized in terms of explanation. But the idea is not that mental causes fill gaps between certain neural causes of bodily motions. It is rather that the occurrence of a single event can be twice explained, even if the explanations do not share a common ontology of events. We cite causes in giving reasons for actions, and in giving impersonal explanations of various non-mental phenomena.[5] The latter style of explanation can be applied to

---

[5] I return to the distinction between rationalizing and impersonal explanations in Ch. 5. But let me say a few words here. A person's behaviour can often be revealed as a sensible course of action, given her goals and assumptions; while the behaviour of mere objects cannot be explained in this fashion. (I use 'behaviour' broadly; persons, plants, and protons all behave in various ways.) One might explain why Nora dropped a brick, by saying: Nora dropped the brick, because she wanted the brick to break, and believed the brick would break (when it hit the floor) if dropped. When dropped, the brick falls to the floor with a certain acceleration. One can explain why the brick falls as it does by citing the law of gravity. But the law does not reveal the brick's motion to be a sensible course of action, given certain goals and assumptions; the law tells us something about the arational workings of the world to which we belong. Similarly, events that occur inside a person's body can cause motions of that body, without the internal causes being reasons. Given any bodily motion B, one can in principle explain why B occurred without rationalizing anything. One can offer the same *kind* of impersonal explanation for why B occurred that one offers for why a brick falls to the floor, or for why a person shivers when cold: it happened because of external forces and/or internal causes that are not among the person's reasons for acting. But Nora's hand opened, because Nora wanted to drop the brick. This raises the question of whether rationalizing causes can be described in impersonal (e.g. biochemical) terms. To

persons—in the form of physics or neuroscience—since (necessarily) persons have bodies. But persons are individuals of a special sort; and differences between rationalizing and impersonal explanations may correspond to different styles of *individuating* causes of bodily motions. This may preclude the possibility that these explanations involve thinking about the same events in different ways. Instead of identifying mental events with neural events, we may have to recognize different (correct) ways of characterizing *as a series of events* what happens inside persons. The world affects us, and we affect it. Events inside us figure in causal chains that include events external to us. One can describe some such causal chains using impersonal terminology. But often one describes such chains in rationalizing terms. And rationalizing causes may not be describable in impersonal terms.

In Chapters 4 to 7, I argue that this picture offers a coherent and motivated alternative to neuralism, given the conclusions of Chapters 1 to 3. But while it is useful to frame the issue in terms of event identities, my claim is that advancing theses about the nature of mental events is *not* the best way to resolve puzzles about mental causation. We do better by critically examining our views about causation and explanation (cf. Burge (1989, 1992, 1993), Rudder-Baker (1995)). For example, a common view is that every genuine cause C has an effect E, such that the event pair <C, E> instantiates a conditional generalization of the right sort, where generalizations couched in intentional terms fail to be of this sort. Given some minimal assumptions, it follows that every intentional cause has a nonintentional description. Davidson (1970) advances a version of this view, requiring that singular causal claims be backed by *strict* laws of nature. It is unclear that every cause is covered by a law of any interesting sort. But in any case, many scientific explanations invoke laws that are hedged by *ceteris paribus* clauses.

There is a puzzle about how a hedged law can be non-vacuously true. But as I argue in Chapter 4, this puzzle can be resolved. Instead of imposing a necessary condition on causation, I offer a sufficient condition for explanation. Roughly, F_1 explains F_2 if F_1 is an instance of the fact that an event of type T_1 occurred; F_2 is an instance of the fact that an event of type T_2 occurred; and *ceteris paribus* if a T_1-event occurs, then a T_2-event occurs. The less rough proposal will exclude certain instances of T_1 and T_2 as relevant instances of the hedged law. And I argue that familiar objections to traditional covering-law models of explanation can be avoided, given my proposal about *ceteris paribus* laws. I also take the following to be a *ceteris paribus* law: if a person who wants Ψ to be the case comes to

use another Sellarsian metaphor: are causes visible in the manifest image visible in the scientific image?

believe that Φ-ing will make Ψ the case, then she will try to Φ.[6] So the
that someone acquired a certain belief can explain why she tried to do
something. Similarly, the fact that she tried to do something can explain
why her body moved. The fact that Nora's arm rose may well be explained
by the fact that Nora raised her arm; where Nora's action (of raising her
arm) *is* the event of Nora's trying to raise her arm. And, I suggest, tryings
and bodily motions often instantiate *ceteris paribus* laws; if Nora tries to
raise her arm, her arm typically rises. (This is not to say, however, that we
always appeal to laws in *giving* intentional explanations.) In any case, suppose the onslaught of a belief explains the occurrence of a trying, and this
explains why some bodily motion occurred. Then if causation is the extensionalization of explanation, mental events satisfy a sufficient condition
for being causes *whether or not mental events are neural events*. This will let
us see how acquiring a belief can cause a trying, and in turn a bodily
motion, even if neuralism is false.

Let me note that the proposed sufficient condition for event causation
is closely related to Fodor's (1989) account of why mental properties are
causally relevant (despite being supervenient): a property T_1 is causally
relevant, if it is projected by a causal law, i.e. if for some property T_2, it is
a causal law that events with T_1 are followed by events with T_2; and there
are (hedged) causal laws that project mental properties. Fodor goes on to
suggest that cp laws have to be 'mediated by' physical mechanisms, while
confessing to uncertainty about what this means. Given some such further
claim, one can try to argue for Davidson's conclusion without his necessary condition on causation. For perhaps mental causes are covered by
hedged laws, and only physical events are covered by hedged laws. But
event dualists will challenge the latter assumption.[7] And interestingly,
Fodor (1989: 156) ends his paper as follows:

[I]f we *can't* get both the causal responsibility of the mental and an argument for
physicalism, then it seems to me that we ought to give up the argument for physicalism. I'm not really convinced that it matters very much whether the mental is
physical; still less that it matters very much whether we can prove that it is.
Whereas, if it isn't literally true that my wanting is causally responsible for my
reaching . . . then practically everything I believe about anything is false and it's
the end of the world.

---

[6] This is a simplification. The person might *intend* to Φ when some condition C obtains.
But then the person will try to Ψ, *ceteris paribus*, if she comes to believe that C obtains (see
Ch. 3).

[7] As Fodor (1989: 159, n. 18) says, if you want to get physicalism out, you have to put
physicalism in—say, in the form of 'the independent assumption that the mechanism of
intentional causation is physical'. Segal and Sober (1991) challenge Fodor's account; but
see Sect. 4.2 of Ch. 5 below.

Cataclysmic rhetoric aside, I agree with this ordering of priorities; and one can substitute 'neural' for 'physical'. Indeed, one might see my account of mental causation as an attempt to develop Fodor's proposal as part of a view according to which neuralism *undermines* the idea that we do things for reasons. But one cannot reject neuralism, maintain that there are mentalistic *ceteris paribus* laws, and then just assume that pairs of events covered by *ceteris paribus* laws are related as cause to effect. Defending this assumption is where I think the hard work lies; though I think the needed work can be done.

With this possible account of mental causation in hand, one can better appreciate the various reasons for rejecting neuralism. Given an alternative, a weighty burden of proof lies with those who say that intentional explanations cite the same causes (thought about in different ways) as certain impersonal explanations. I think neuralism actually threatens the idea that reasons are causes by identifying mental events with events characterizable without reference to *persons*. Identifying reasons with impersonally characterized events threatens our view of ourselves as agents whose actions are *free*. And if mind–brain identity theories repeatedly invite charges of epiphenomenalism (see Heil and Mele 1993), this suggests that such theories have not really helped to show how minds can affect the world.

In Chapter 5, I also argue against neuralism more directly. Following Hornsby (1981) and others, I contend that while mental events are spatially located, their location is typically less determinate than that of any biochemical event. This reinforces a claim I hinted at above: intentional explanations individuate causes in a way that makes mental events poor candidates for identification with events not individuated in rationalizing terms. Neuralism also has the implausible consequence that certain biochemical events have propositional contents. (Othello's coming to believe that *Desdemona loved Cassio* was an event with the content expressed by the italicized sentence; see Chapter 3. So if this mental episode was some biochemical event B, then B had the same content.) In the appendix, I focus on how this saddles neuralists with the unenviable task of explaining how a biochemical event *could* be semantically evaluable in this sense; whereas event dualists can and should avoid this project, which turns out to be the ambitiously reductionistic project of providing a so-called naturalistic theory of content. (If we think of the mind–body problem as having causation and content strands, adopting neuralism in response to the former makes responding to the latter harder—and perhaps impossible.)

4

Often, disagreement in philosophy concerns what one should be trying to do. So let me end this introduction with a few remarks about what I am trying to do, and why. Given the number of topics I connect—action sentences, Fregean thoughts, *ceteris paribus* laws, and so on—it will come as no surprise that I agree with Sellars (1963): the aim of philosophy is 'to understand how things in the broadest possible sense of the term hang together in the broadest possible sense of the term'. But time is short, and so we don't discuss just *any* things. (We leave out talk of sealing wax, of cabbages, and kings.) Motivation for philosophical inquiry is usually rooted in *puzzles*: questions for which every imaginable answer seems wrong, especially when such questions concern the nature of persons, whose nature it is to think. And certain facts come to seem less puzzling, I claim, given the proposed conception of how the topics under discussion hang together.

In particular, the proposal lets us see how mental events can cause bodily motions, even given that such motions have neural causes. This is not the only puzzling fact about thinkers. In the appendix, I briefly address the related question of how error is possible, given that beliefs are in some sense representations of the environment. (How can a thinker *re*present that which is not the case? Yet if error is impossible, it seems that there is no interesting notion of mental content.) And the hardest questions about minds are not about causation or content. But I leave the topic of consciousness to braver souls, hoping that it is (at least largely) independent of the issues addressed here. Providing, motivating, and defending an alternative to neuralism is hard enough although a successful defence of event dualism as an account of mental causation may have implications elsewhere in the philosophy of mind.

It is worth being explicitly clear, however, about the *kind* of question to which my proposal is a purported answer. Nozick (1981) provides a model of the kind of project I have in mind. So let me set mental causation aside, for the moment, to consider why one might want a theory of knowledge. A central puzzle of epistemology is that we know anything, given facts of the sort adduced by sceptics. You know that you are currently reading a page of text. But certain modal facts appear to exclude the possibility of such knowledge. Things would seem as they do now if you were being deceived by a clever demon or a nefarious neurosurgeon (who envatted your brain a short while ago). You don't know that you're not being deceived. So how can you know that you are reading a page of text?

This problem has a familiar form: it is the case that P; but it is also the case that Q; and it is hard to see *how it could be the case* that P, given that Q. One response to such problems is to deny P and/or its apparent excluder Q. But it strikes me as obvious that we often know things, despite our fallibility. Like Moore (1925), I see no prospect for a convincing proof that knowledge is impossible based on premisses connecting fallibility to the impossibility of knowledge. For I don't see how such premisses could be more compelling than ordinary knowledge claims. And any valid sceptical argument can be rephrased as a *reductio* of some tendentious epistemic thesis. Similarly, it is hard to imagine premisses more compelling than (but which entail the denial of) the claim that people are fallible, even if recognizing our fallibility makes it hard to see how knowledge is possible.[8]

It is equally unlikely that one can establish the possibility of knowledge, using only premisses a sceptic would accept. But if one is convinced that knowledge is possible, one doesn't need a proof to that effect, unless one is trying to convince someone else. If the goal is to understand how P, one need not *make* anyone believe that P. (If some people deny that anyone knows anything, so be it; one is not obliged to convert the infidels.) Moreover, the existence of actual sceptics is irrelevant. Sceptical arguments would not cease to be bothersome if it were discovered that the alleged sceptics were joking, or that it is psychologically impossible to maintain scepticism. An argument can reveal a tension *in one's own thinking*, even if everyone agrees that the conclusion is false. By my own lights, deceivable people know things. An argument can show me that I do not see how my views on this score can be compatible.

Put another way, I may be *inclined* to think that sceptical possibilities exclude knowledge, even if I know otherwise. A good response to scepticism will address this inclination, by making explicit some tacit assumptions about knowledge that I judge (all things considered) to be

---

[8] Tensions can take the form of an outright contradiction between seemingly obvious propositions. But more often one has the sense that P and Q do not cohere, even though one cannot yet formulate the trouble-making background assumptions. Still, some people may see no puzzle, even after informed reflection. (Consider how most of us would react to the question of how water can flow downhill, given that steam rises—or how fish can swim, given that turnips can't. What assumptions would lead one to see *problems* here? In the former case, perhaps mistaken views that a course in chemistry would correct; in the latter case, who knows?) It is hard to argue that one *ought* to be puzzled by something: where I see a paradox, you may see an obvious mistake. And one cannot demand that others see a tension, so they can be shown how to resolve it. But even if the rest of us cannot *make* others feel certain tensions, it does not follow that *our* predicament stems from an irrational overindulgence of metaphysics. I emphasize this point, because my views here are in line with those of Burge (1993) and Rudder-Baker (1995), who urge that we emphasize our confidence in mental explanation over metaphysical principles that make mental causation into a mystery. And fairly or not, these philosophers have been charged with adopting the following overly relaxed attitude: it would be silly to deny, on metaphysical grounds, that mental events have effects; so don't worry, be happy (see Kim 1995). Antony (1995: 160) lampoons those who 'see no problem about reconciling our folksy conviction that what we *think* matters to what we *do*, with our more tutored views about the structure of reality and the nature of causation'; and this attitude is equated with offering 'deflationary' responses to 'philosophical puzzles about mental causation', by emphasizing explanation instead of causation. Perhaps this makes me a deflationist. But to offer a response is already to recognize the puzzles. And defending deflationism requires effort that the unworried would never expend. I return to these issues in Ch. 7.

mistaken—even though I am favourably disposed towards these assumptions, when they remain unstated (or when I do not focus on their implications). It may be a piece of common sense *that* fallibility does not exclude knowledge. But to show oneself *why* fallibility does not exclude knowledge, one needs to show that one's inclination to think otherwise is rooted in a conception of knowledge that is partly misguided (and misguiding). So a good account of knowledge will make it clear how fallible agents can know things, by revealing aspects of our conception of knowledge that dispose us towards puzzlement. This will remove a reason for thinking that knowledge is impossible, and in that sense explain how knowledge is possible.

Intellectual tensions are themselves puzzling things. How can one fail to see how P is possible (given an apparent excluder Q) if one sees that P is actual? Nonetheless, we sometimes experience such tensions; one's beliefs can exhibit a failure to 'hang together' that is literally queasy-making, when the lack of integration is noticed. This phenomenon is not peculiar to philosophy, or even to science broadly construed. Novelty stores often sell toys that pose the challenge of showing how something actual is physically possible. (The ring can be separated from the post, but how?) And I assume that removing tensions in one's thought is a valuable activity, once we turn from toys to puzzles concerning the nature of persons: how can our actions be free (and morally evaluable), given a world governed by natural laws; how is experience possible, given that subjects exist in a world composed of physical objects; how is knowledge possible, given that knowers are fallible?

Like Nozick, I think philosophical theories are best viewed as attempts to clarify and answer such questions.[9] Theories of knowledge should be assessed, in part, by how well they help resolve the tension revealed by scepticism. Similarly, if philosophers say that mental events are (not) biochemical events, I think such claims should be assessed according to how well they help resolve the tensions associated with mental causation. The question is not *whether* mental events have non-mental effects, or *whether*

---

[9] Wittgensteinians will say that *theorizing* is the wrong response to such questions; and 'theorizing' may be the wrong word for the kind of response I have in mind. In any case, I try to defend some claims that help show why certain facts about the mental are compatible with apparently conflicting facts. Perhaps philosophical theses are best viewed as tools for escaping from confusions, not as straightforwardly factual claims (like 'The cat is on the mat'). But one can say, to borrow a Quinean metaphor, that each portion of a person's cognitive web is meaningful by virtue of being part of a system of beliefs that serves as the person's overall conception of her world. And recognition that thesis T has helped one resolve puzzles may well be a good reason for retaining T in one's cognitive web, though revision to such aspects of one's web may be driven more by 'housekeeping' considerations than by observation (cf. Carnap's (1950) suggestion that, in one sense, metaphysical questions call for pragmatic decisions about how to speak—and how to carve up the work).

we have false beliefs. (They do.) The question is *how there can be* mental causation, given various facts about persons. But the form of such questions at least suggests the form of helpful answers.

Faced with a tension between P and an apparent excluder Q, an obvious strategy is to search for a condition C, such that C is sufficient for P; one can see how C could obtain, given Q; and seeing that C is sufficient for P helps one see that some tempting assumptions (which entail the incompatibility of P and Q) are false. From this perspective, one wants a sufficient condition for knowledge, such that: one can see how this condition can obtain, even given sceptical possibilities; and stating this condition helps one expose and reject tempting claims that would render knowledge incompatible with fallibility. Similarly, I want a sufficient condition for being a cause of a bodily motion, such that: one can see how mental events can satisfy this condition, even though all bodily motions have neural causes; and the resulting proposal helps us see why we found mental causation to be puzzling in the first place.

In the case of epistemology, many theorists have urged us to abandon the assumption that knowledge is closed under entailment. For then one can grant that a subject S can fail to know that Q (e.g. that she is not being deceived), even if S knows that P and that P entails Q. So one might look for a theory—a sufficient condition for having knowledge—according to which knowledge is not closed under entailment.[10] Sceptics are unlikely to accept any such theory. But that does not matter if the goal is not to convince sceptics. Similarly, those who deny the existence of mental causes are unlikely to accept my proposed sufficient condition for mental causation. But if the aim is to resolve a tension for those who grant that there are mental causes, then what matters is whether that audience finds the proposal plausible and helpful in resolving the tension. Discovering such a theory is hard enough. For given my pretheoretic intuitions, I will find many theories implausible and/or unhelpful.

That said, I may (and often should) revise my intuitions in light of an otherwise plausible theory. Not *all* of my pretheoretic judgements about what counts as knowledge (right action, causation, etc.) will conform to any simple theory; and as discussions of reflective equilibrium suggest, there is epistemic value in having judgements such that one can provide a relatively simple systematization of them. More importantly, it would be absurd to deny that the value of resolving puzzles ever justifies revision to one's judgements, if such judgements are manifestations of an overall conception that (by one's own lights) contains some internal tensions. Still, I cannot always give up an intuition, just because doing so would let me

---

[10] See Dretske 1970; Goldman 1986. Nozick discusses this point at length. Perhaps one can argue that knowledge is closed under entailment after all; see Lewis (1997). But that is another issue.

achieve cognitive harmony. That is why intellectual tensions are persistent. Nor should one be cavalier in rejecting pretheoretic views. The goal is to see how one's views fit together, perhaps with minor revision. So it is self-defeating to reject intuitions too quickly. I want not just any coherent set of beliefs, but a coherent set of beliefs that is recognizably *mine*.

On this view, philosophical theorizing is not an attempt to define terms (like 'know' and 'cause'), or to systematize intuitions. Nor is the goal to provide a theory of concepts if these are taken to be mental representations that thinkers typically use in categorization. The aim is to resolve intellectual tensions. A person's intuitions will *constrain* which theories she will and should find to be acceptable ways of resolving tensions. Reflective thinkers will and should reject some sufficient conditions for knowledge (or mental causation) as too revisionary.[11] Moreover, in emphasizing what Nozick calls 'domestic' rather than 'foreign' policy—fixing one's own beliefs, as opposed to proselytizing—one need not deny the relevance of others' intuitions. If my intuitions are idiosyncratic, I should take seriously the possibility that my intuitions are distorted. One wants to address tensions that others also experience, in a way that others would also find plausible. Finally, to emphasize the role of puzzles is not to deny that one aims at truth in philosophy. Resolving tensions in one's overall conception of the world is part of making one's beliefs fit the facts.

Once again, a philosophical account of mental causation should provide a sufficient condition for being a mental cause of a bodily motion, such that this condition helps us see how bodily motions have both mental and neural causes. (That is, a good theory should provide at least this much.) My proposal combines event dualism and a conception of causation as the transitive extensionalization of explanation. I argue that this is preferable, all things considered, to neuralism. A crucial component of my view is that actions typically cause bodily motions. So let me now turn to the argument for this claim.

---

[11] A theory can tell us something about our concept of knowledge (and what knowledge is). But intuitions are not best viewed as *data*, in the way that speakers' intuitions serve as data for theories in linguistics; although if a theory relieves a tension for individuals who felt it—and not because the theory has some arational soothing effect—that tells in favour of the theory. Stich and Laurence (1994) rightly ask what philosophers are doing when offering theories, such that intuitions are germane to theory choice, but the goal is not to describe intuitions (or reveal an innate competence *à la Chomsky*). But solving puzzles can be an intellectually respectable activity; see e.g. Kuhn (1970). Note that *neccesary* conditions for knowledge (causation, etc.) are not required; the issue will be whether some sufficient condition is plausible (and plausibly satisfied in relevant cases). So a philosophical theory need be a traditional *analysis* of anything.

I

Actions as Inner Causes

According to a traditional view of mind–body relations, when a person raises her arm, the rising of her arm is caused by a volition—a mental act of willing, which is the person's (autonomous) contribution to the causal order. In this chapter, I motivate and defend a version of this traditional view; though following O'Shaughnessy (1973, 1980) and Hornsby (1980), I speak of *tryings* instead of volitions. When a person (intentionally) moves some part of her body, the motion of her body is an effect of her action, which is an event of trying to do something. This thesis is defensible; and our best semantics of action sentences requires it, I argue, given some strong intuitions about actions.

1. A Puzzle for Davidsonians

My strategy is to show that Davidson's (1967*a*) event analysis engenders a puzzle, the best resolution of which involves the claim that paradigmatic actions are tryings that cause bodily motions. So let me begin by introducing the event analysis and some apparently conflicting intuitions about actions.[1]

1.1

Davidson offers an attractive account of entailments like those among:

   (1) Booth shot Lincoln
   (2) Booth shot Lincoln with a pistol
   (3) Booth shot Lincoln on 13 April 1865
   (4) Booth shot Lincoln with a pistol on 13 April 1865.

Sentence (4) entails (2) and (3), both of which entail (1). These facts demand explanation. For simplicity, ignore considerations of tense. Let us also ignore compositionality *within* adjunct phrases like 'with a pistol',

---

[1] Here and throughout, I reserve 'action' for particular events, not things (potentially) done by different people at different times and places.

and represent such phrases in our metalanguage with unanalysed predicates like 'with-a-pistol'. Then according to Davidson, the logical forms of (1–4) are:

(1a) ∃e[Shoot(e, Booth, Lincoln)]
(2a) ∃e[Shoot(e, Booth, Lincoln) & With-a-pistol(e)]
(3a) ∃e[Shoot(e, Booth, Lincoln) & On-13-April-1865(e)]
(4a) ∃e[Shoot(e, Booth, Lincoln) & With-a-pistol(e) & On-13-April-1865(e)],

where something satisfies 'Shoot(e, Booth, Lincoln)' iff it is a shooting of Lincoln by Booth. The inference from (2) to (1) is thus represented as an instance of the valid form '∃e[Φ(e, a, b) & Ψ(e)], so ∃e[Φ(e, a, b)]'; and similarly, *mutatis mutandis*, for the other entailments.

On this view, (1–4) involve quantification over events. Given that Booth shot Lincoln exactly once, a single event satisfies 'Shoot(e, Booth, Lincoln)'. This event, which satisfies the adjunct phrases 'with a pistol' and 'on 13 April 1865', is the truth-maker for (1–4). Similar reasoning applies to

(5) Booth pulled the trigger
(6) Booth pulled the trigger with his finger
(7) Booth pulled the trigger on 13 April 1865
(8) Booth pulled the trigger with his finger on 13 April 1865.

According to the event analysis, the logical forms of (5–8) are:

(5a) ∃e[Pull(e, Booth, the trigger)]
(6a) ∃e[Pull(e, Booth, the trigger) & With-his-finger(e)]
(7a) ∃e[Pull(e, Booth, the trigger) & On-April-13-1865(e)]
(8a) ∃e[Pull(e, Booth, the trigger) & With-his-finger(e) & On-13-April-1865(e)].

But while this nicely explains the relevant entailments, it also presents something of a quandary.

Assume that Booth pulled the trigger of the pistol in question exactly once. Then a single event satisfies 'Pull(e, Booth, the trigger)'. This event, which is the truth-maker for (5–8), satisfies the adjunct phrases 'with his finger' and 'on 13 April 1865'. Yet Booth did *not* pull the trigger with a pistol. That is,

(9) ¬∃e[Pull(e, Booth, the trigger) & With-a-pistol(e)].

So the event that makes (5–8) true does not satisfy 'with a pistol'; but the event that makes (1–4) true *does* satisfy this adjunct phrase. Hence, the event that makes (5–8) true is not the event that makes (1–4) true.

Similarly, Booth did *not* shoot Lincoln with his finger. That is,

(10) ¬∃e[Shoot(e, Booth, Lincoln) & With-his-finger(e)].

So the event that makes (1–4) true does not satisfy 'with his finger'; but the event that makes (5–8) true *does* satisfy this adjunct phrase. Hence, the event that makes (1–4) true is not the event that makes (5–8) true. That is, the event that satisfies 'Shoot(e, Booth, Lincoln)' is *not* the event that satisfies 'Pull(e, Booth, the trigger)'. Only the shooting is With-a-pistol, and only the pulling is With-his-finger.[2]

Nonetheless, there are good reasons for saying that Booth's action of shooting Lincoln *was* Booth's action of pulling the trigger. I return to the theoretical motivations for this view. But intuitively, once Booth pulled the trigger, he needed to do nothing else in order to shoot Lincoln. So while Booth pulled the trigger and (thereby) shot Lincoln, this is not a report of two actions performed by Booth on the fateful day. Anscombe (1957) offers the example of a man who operates a pump by moving his arm, thereby replenishing the water supply in some house. In this case, it seems that a single action can be described in several ways—as a replenishing, a pumping, and a moving. So a natural thought is that actions (like all events) can be described in many ways, and that speakers can describe a *single* action by using 'Booth's shooting of Lincoln' or 'Booth's pulling of the trigger'. Indeed, this is Davidson's (1971) own view. Yet it is hard to see how nominalizations of (1) and (5) can serve as descriptions of the same action, given that actions are events, if (1) and (5) have different events as their truth-makers.[3]

I want an account that lets us maintain all three of the following claims without conflict: the event analysis is correct; Booth's action of pulling the trigger was an event identical with Booth's action of shooting Lincoln; but given the event analysis (and some facts about the truth conditions of sentences involving adjuncts), the event of Booth's pulling the trigger is distinct from the event of Booth's shooting Lincoln. In Section 2, I propose such an account, which I go on to use in the course of arguing that paradigmatic actions are causes of bodily motions. But one might resist this whole line of thought by rejecting at least one of the three claims above. So let me say a little more (in Sections 1.2–1.4) about why I find these aspects of the puzzle individually compelling.

---

[2] Taylor (1985) uses a similar example, attributed to Christopher Arnold, in a slightly different context. Taylor also shows why the entailments exhibited in (1–8) are not adequately explained by appealing to a *series* of logically binary predicates ('shoot', 'shoot-with-a-pistol', etc.) related by meaning postulates.

[3] I ignore gerund phrases used (not as event descriptions, but) in a propositional sense: in '*the tolling of the bell* surprised Tom' the italicized phrase can be roughly synonymous with (and as opaque as) 'that the bell tolled' (see Vendler 1967; Bennett 1988). A complicating factor is that when a so-called perfect event nominal like 'the destruction' is in common use, the corresponding imperfect nominal ('the destroying') sounds odd; but this point is tangential to my present concerns.

1.2

I endorse the event analysis, because it systematically explains a wide range of semantic facts. Davidson focused on entailments like those exhibited in (1–8); but there are other important sources of evidence for his treatment of action sentences. Parsons (1990) amasses a considerable body of further data, some of which I summarize here. For example,

(11) After the singing of the National Anthem, Nora bought a hotdog

seems to be true iff an event of Nora's buying a hotdog occurred after the event that satisfies the definite description. Davidsonians can also (at least begin to) account for the validity of arguments like: when Nora cuts onions, she sneezes; Nora cut onions; so she sneezed. Suppose that there is a sneezing by Nora whenever there is a cutting of onions by Nora, and that there was a cutting of onions by Nora. It follows, as a matter of logic, that there was a sneezing by Nora.

The event analysis also suggests an attractive treatment of perceptual idioms like

(12) Nora heard Fido bark.

Note that (12) differs from the propositional attitude report 'Nora heard that Fido barked'; in (12), 'bark' is untensed, and substituting coreferential expressions for 'Fido' seems to preserve truth. So following Higginbotham (1983) and Vlach (1983), one might well take the logical form of (12) to be

(12a) $\exists e \exists f[\text{Hear}(e, \text{Nora}, f) \,\&\, \text{Bark}(f, \text{Fido})]$.

That is, there is a hearing by Nora of a barking by Fido. A similar analysis can be given for 'Nora watched Nick sign the letter.' Moreover, we can explain the ambiguity of

(13) Nora heard Fido bark in her apartment

if 'in her apartment' can modify the hearing or the barking, as indicated in:

(13a) $\exists e \exists f[\text{Hear}(e, \text{Nora}, f) \,\&\, \text{Bark}(f, \text{Fido}) \,\&\,$
        $\text{In-her-apartment}(e/f)]$.

Either reading entails the corresponding reading of 'Nora heard something in her apartment'. Those who reject the event analysis owe an alternative explanation of such facts; see also Section 2. For other arguments, see Taylor (1985), Schein (1993), Herburger (forthcoming), Pietroski (1999, forthcoming *a*, *b*).

One might challenge the 'identificationist' claim that Booth's action of pulling the trigger was his action of shooting Lincoln, especially given the event analysis. If the pulling was With-his-finger but not With-a-pistol, while the shooting was With-a-pistol but not With-his-finger, perhaps there are two (related) actions here. Why not reject contrary intuitions in the light of a well-confirmed semantic theory? Moreover, shootings and pullings seem to have different spatio-temporal properties: the shooting of Lincoln was not over until the bullet entered Lincoln, while the pulling of the trigger ended before the bullet left the gun. Correspondingly, the shooting involves the motion of a bullet, in a way that the pulling does not. These 'anti-idenificationist' intuitions become even clearer if we focus on the following contrast:

> (14) Booth killed Lincoln on 13 April, but Lincoln did not die until 14 April.
> (15) Booth shot Lincoln on 13 April, but Lincoln did not die until 14 April.

Sentence (14) is anomalous in a way that (15) is not. Thomson (1971), Thalberg (1972), and others have taken this to show that a killing is not over until the victim dies. Similarly, while Booth shot Lincoln in Ford's Theater, Lincoln died in a boarding house across the street. So it seems wrong to say that Booth killed Lincoln in Ford's Theater. The killing and the shooting have different spatio-temporal properties; only the latter event occurred in Ford's Theater on 13 April. Once this is granted, there is little reason to deny that the shooting and the pulling are distinct events. It should come as no surprise if semantic arguments lead to the same conclusion. So one might argue that there is no puzzle to resolve, since the semantic arguments just add to the case for denying that some *one* action was: Booth's pulling of the trigger; his shooting of Lincoln; the killing of Lincoln; etc.

Nonetheless, the intuition remains that Booth's action of killing Lincoln and Booth's action of pulling the trigger are not *two* actions, but one. And this intuition coheres with others. Following Davidson (1971), I think that Booth's action of killing Lincoln did indeed occur on the day before Lincoln died, in a theatre that Lincoln left while still alive. For Booth did *his* bit on 13 April in Ford's Theater, and Booth's action was *his* contribution the causal order. Lincoln would have died just the same had Booth ceased to exist after pulling the trigger. Indeed, anything that happened after Booth moved his trigger-finger would seem to be at most an *effect* of Booth's causal contribution. As Davidson puts it, there is an important sense in which we 'never do more than move our bodies: the rest is up to nature' (1971: 59). If this is correct, the time and place of Lincoln's death do not constrain the time and place of Booth's action in the way that anti-identificationist arguments suggest.

On this view, a person's actions are never *individuated* by effects of his bodily motions, although a person's actions can often be *described* by reference to such effects. An action occurs (entirely) where the actor is. When the actor has ceased to do his bit, the action is over. If we think of events as changes in objects, actions seem to be changes *in persons*. Booth's actions are events in which *he* undergoes some change. But if the killing of Lincoln was not over until Lincoln died, it is hard to view this event as a change in Booth. Moreover, a person's actions are *in his control* in a way that effects of his actions are not. It was up to Booth whether or not to act as he did; but it was not up to Booth that Lincoln would die, or even that the bullet would leave the pistol. Once Booth did his bit, the rest (i.e. the motion of the bullet into Lincoln, and Lincoln's death) was due to natural processes that were external to Booth and beyond his control. This suggests that the action of killing Lincoln, which occurred where Booth was when he shot Lincoln, was Booth's action of pulling the trigger.

Correlatively, in explaining actions, we aim to explain the occurrence of events that constitute the (rationalizable) contributions of persons to causal history. An intentional explanation of why Booth acted as he did would have been an equally good explanation of *Booth's* causal contribution, even if Lincoln had survived his wound, or even if the pistol had jammed. So it seems that an *intentional* explanation of why Booth killed Lincoln is not an explanation of (the occurrence of) an event that ended when Lincoln died. Rather, actions are the points at which we persons effect changes in a world that otherwise carries on quite nicely without us. If I throw a ball in outer space, the ball may still be in motion when I die; but *my* causal contribution—the event explained by citing my reasons for throwing the ball—consists in moving my body in a certain way for just a little while. (Dretske (1988) notes that a kicker has done his bit even before leg meets ball; leg travels through space awhile, after being launched.) A person is responsible for the effects of his actions. But this suggests a distinction between actions and their effects. So we should not individuate actions in terms of events that persons bring about via forces and facts beyond their control.

At this point, one might introduce talk of basic actions and non-basic actions, where the former are changes in persons, and the latter are partly individuated by (person-external) effects of basic actions. Using these terms, there was one basic action, such that by virtue of performing it: Booth pulled the trigger, shot Lincoln, and killed Lincoln, where the pulling, shooting, and killing are three (distinct but related) events, all of which are among Booth's non-basic actions. Clearly, there is something right in this suggestion; and it accords with one aspect of ordinary usage, in treating pullings and shootings as actions of a sort. But I think talk of non-basic actions reformulates the puzzle in misleading terms. We still need to see how Booth's (basic) action of shooting Lincoln can *be* Booth's (basic) action of pulling the trigger, given that the events satisfying 'Shoot(e, Booth, Lincoln)' and 'Pull(e, Booth, the trigger)' are distinct.[4]

Moreover, if actions are the distinctively personal causal contributions of persons, then so-called non-basic actions are not actions—much as koala bears are not bears. Defending this claim requires the rest of this chapter. But the event that satisfies 'Shoot(e, Booth, Lincoln)' is what it is. *Calling* it a non-basic action does not make it an event of the same species as the relevant change in Booth, which occurred before the bullet left the gun. I will argue that (basic) actions are tryings, which are importantly unlike events individuated by effects of bodily motions. So I eschew talk of non-basic actions. In any case, we face a puzzle. While identificationist claims about actions are motivated, it remains unclear how such claims *can* be true. Given the semantic and spatio-temporal arguments, even Davidsonians should grant that Booth's shooting of Lincoln was an event distinct from Booth's pulling of the trigger.

1.4

One might think the puzzle stems from a general feature of predication, and thus poses no special problem for Davidsonians. So let me conclude this section by saying why I disagree. Consider

> (16) Nora swam the channel quickly
> (17) Nora crossed the channel slowly.

If Nora crossed the channel by swimming it in record time, (16) is true; and arguably (17) is true, since even a record swim would be much slower than typical ways of crossing the channel. According to the event analysis, the logical forms of (16–17) are:

> (16a) $\exists e[\text{Swim}(e, \text{Nora, the channel}) \,\&\, \text{Quick}(e)]$
> (17a) $\exists e[\text{Cross}(e, \text{Nora, the channel}) \,\&\, \text{Slow}(e)]$.

---

[4] Cf. Goldman (1970). One might think that 'Booth's action of shooting Lincoln' is like 'Nora's daughter', as used when Nora has two daughters: context can determine which daughter the speaker is referring to on a given occasion; so perhaps context can determine whether a speaker is referring to Booth's basic or non-basic action. But even if 'action' is true of some non-basic actions, the event satisfying 'Shoot(e, Booth, Lincoln)' is not a basic action. We still need to see how 'Booth's action of shooting Lincoln' can be used in referring to a basic action (such that in virtue of performing it, Booth shot Lincoln). Similarly, one cannot solve the puzzle simply by saying that context determines whether the referent of 'Booth's shooting' is Booth's action or some other event (not an action) partly individuated by Lincoln's death.

It would be a mistake to argue that (16–17) have distinct truth-makers, or that Nora's swimming was not her crossing, on the grounds that the swimming was quick while the crossing was slow. For as Davidson (1967*a*) notes, a parallel argument based on adjectival modification is clearly unsound. Something can be a big ant *and* a small animal; it can be big for an ant, yet small for an animal. This tells us something about the semantics of attributive (or comparative) adjectives like 'big'. A plausible view is that, relative to context C, 'big' is true of things that are big for a Φ; where Φ is a comparison class determined in C, and C includes the fact that 'big' modifies a particular word, like 'ant' or 'animal'. But this does not tell against identifying the big ant with the small animal. That would leave one creature too many.

Davidson does not expressly apply this paradigm to the puzzle we have been considering. But one might advance the following view: an event can be With-a-pistol *for a shooting*, yet not be With-a-pistol *for a pulling*; while the same event is With-his-finger *for a pulling*, yet not With-his-finger *for a shooting*. This would let one maintain that a single event was the truth-maker for sentences (1–8) above. As Taylor (1985) notes, however, the claim that 'big' is to 'small' as 'quick' is to 'slow' feels like a good analogy, whereas extending the analogy to 'with a pistol' and 'with his finger' feels strained. The claim that *every* adjunct phrase is comparative in this way seems gratuitous. (For example, I see no reason to say that an event can be On-Monday for a swimming, yet not On-Monday for a crossing.) So anyone adopting this kind of response to our puzzle owes a *principled* account of how (and how far) to extend the analogy with comparative adjectives.[5] But I know of no such account. Hence, like Taylor, I think the argument of Section 1.1 provides good reason for distinguishing the shooting and the pulling. The question is how to reconcile this distinction with the claim that Booth's action of shooting Lincoln was his action of pulling the trigger.

---

[5] Moreover, if all adjunct phrases are like 'big'/'small', one cannot ever argue against proposed event identities by using the event analysis in conjunction with intuitions about the truth conditions of sentences involving adjuncts. (It would be strange for Davidsonians to thus sever metaphysical and semantic issues.) Taylor also mentions two other examples, due to David Wiggins and John Foster. Nora's action of walking uphill can be her action of signalling (to Nick) that the coast is clear. But the walking is uphill, while the signalling is not; and it hardly helps to say an event can be uphill for a walking without being uphill for a signalling. Similarly, if a pool player sinks the 7-ball and the 9-ball on the same shot, his action is at once a sinking of the 7 and a sinking of the 9. But the sinkings have different properties; and here it is not even clear how to apply the response considered in the text. Parsons (1990) offers another kind of example: if Nora pays with a cheque, her paying is With-a-cheque, but her writing (of the cheque) is not; and this seems to preclude identifying the paying with the writing.

2. Grounding Complex Events

The proper response to the puzzle presumably lies in the fact that actions typically have a concertina of effects, and that we can refer to an action in part by referring to one of its effects (see Feinberg 1965). The question is how best to employ this familiar observation. My proposal combines two ideas that have been developed by other authors. First, the basic event analysis can and should be elaborated in terms of thematic roles, like Agent and Patient. Second, some events have other events as *parts*; in particular, certain events have actions (and some of their effects) as parts. As we shall see, both identificationist *and* anti-identificationist intuitions have a place in the event analysis if one construes the notion of 'Agent' in terms of a relation that actors bear to complex events that have actions as parts.

2.1

Recall that Davidson (1967*a*) would take the logical form of (1) to be (1a):

(1)   Booth shot Lincoln
(1a) ∃e[Shoot(e, Booth, Lincoln)],

where (1a) is glossed as, 'There is a shooting of Lincoln by Booth'. (I continue to ignore tense.) But one might suspect that (1a) fails to reveal all the semantic structure in (1). Taking Davidson's gloss of (1a) as a cue, and following Castañeda (1967), one might hold that the logical form of (1) is

(1b) ∃e[Agent(e, Booth) & Shooting(e) & Patient(e, Lincoln)].

For if (1) is true: Booth did something; there was a shooting; and something happened to Lincoln. These facts are easily explained if (1b) is the logical form of (1) where 'Shooting' is true of certain events (like the shooting of Lincoln by Booth) the thematic predicates are true of ordered pairs consisting of an event and a participant in that event. Saying what it is to be an Agent is part of my task. But intuitively, the Agent of an event is its salient *initiater*, while the Patient is the person or thing saliently *affected*. Appeals to thematic structure have proven fruitful, not just in semantics, but in linguistic theory more generally.[6] Parsons (1990), Schein (1993), and Herburger (forthcoming) offer a range of arguments for thematic 'separation', as indicated in (1b); see also Davidson (1985),

---

[6] Haegeman (1994) provides an overview. One must distinguish the metalanguage predicate 'Shooting', which is the object language gerund, from the object language progressive (as in 'Nora was shooting the rifle when the aliens landed'). The meaning of the latter is presumably determined by the meaning of 'shoot', which is true of Shootings, and the progressive marker 'ing'. See Parsons (1990) for a proposal.

Pietroski (forthcoming *a*, *b*). In particular, Schein argues persuasively that only a thematically elaborated event analysis can provide a satisfactory treatment of certain plural constructions (like, 'Three adults taught every child two new games'). So I propose to take this development of the basic event analysis as given, returning below to questions about how thematic categories are related to grammatical categories like 'subject' and 'object'.

By itself, appealing to thematic roles does not solve our puzzle. If anything, the difficulty for Davidsonians is sharpened if we gloss 'Booth shot Lincoln' and 'Booth pulled the trigger' as

(1b) ∃e[Agent(e, Booth) & Shooting(e) & Patient(e, Lincoln)]
(5b) ∃e[Agent(e, Booth) & Pulling(e) & Patient(e, the trigger)].

For even without considering adjuncts, one might want to distinguish the shooting from the pulling, on the grounds that these events have different Patients. If this were the *only* reason for denying that Booth's shooting was his pulling, one might view thematic elaboration as unfriendly to Davidson's original proposal. (Moreover, thematic individuation of events leads to difficulties that I want to avoid here; see Schein 1993: 94–6.) But the arguments based on adjuncts and spatio-temporal properties are still available, and they are untouched by appeal to thematic roles. Nonetheless, I think the puzzle can be resolved, given the right account of what it is to be the Agent of an event.

2.2

The right account, I suggest, involves a common anti-identificationist thought: some events are *parts* of others. Consider the toppling of a line of dominoes. This event has parts; and some of its parts (the topplings of individual dominoes) are *caused* by other parts. One can speak here of a process. But taking processes to be complex events will simplify matters. Say that event D *grounds* event E if D and E occur; D is a (perhaps improper) part of E; and D causes every event that is a proper part of E but is not a part of D. Every event grounds itself. But more interestingly, the toppling of the first domino grounds the complex event that is the toppling of the whole line of dominoes.[7]

---

[7] I do *not* say that for every event E, there is another event consisting of E and all (or even some) of its causes. The grounded event must occur (exist); and Hornsby (1985) offers reasons for scepticism about unrestricted fusion theses about events. But some events are grounded by others, and I think we have sortal terms for such events: 'pulling', 'shooting', etc. Thomson (1977) offers a detailed theory of what it is for one event to be part of another. My discussion of these matters owes much to hers, although Thomson endorses a fusion thesis about which I remain agnostic. At present, I am not primarily interested in the metaphysics of events—or constraints that a notion of parthood must satisfy, in order to play a certain role in various metaphysical projects. I just want to use an intuitive notion of

Suppose Booth's pulling of the trigger and his shooting of Lincoln are distinct complex events: only the shooting has parts that begin after the trigger has gone back. This is not to deny that the complex events overlap. But speaking of parts captures the idea that a shooting of Lincoln (unlike a pulling of the trigger) involves a projectile traversing space and entering Lincoln. And one can capture anti-identificationist intuitions, by saying that action sentences quantify over complex events. Consider:

(18) $\exists$e[Agent(e, Booth) & Shooting(e) & Patient(e, Lincoln) & With-a-pistol(e)]

(19) $\exists$e[Agent(e, Booth) & Pulling(e) & Patient(e, the trigger) & With-a-pistol(e)].

If the domain of quantification includes complex events, the shooting and the pulling can be distinct events. So the shooting can be With-a-pistol while the pulling is not; hence, (18) can be true while (19) is false. This leaves many details, like the semantics of 'with', to be worked out. (If 'Booth shot Lincoln with his finger' is false, an event is not With-a-finger just because a finger was used in the course of the event. A subtler notion of instrumentality, sensitive to the Patient, is needed.) But it is plausible that an account along these lines can capture the sense in which the shooting differs from the pulling. The trick is to see how, given such an account, Booth's action of pulling the trigger can still *be* his action of shooting Lincoln.

This is where appeal to thematic roles comes in. Suppose the following thesis is roughly correct: Agent(e, N) $\leftrightarrow$ $\exists$a[grounds(a, e) & action(a, N)]; N is the Agent of event e, just when e is grounded by an action of N.[8] Then (1b) is true just when (1*) is true:

parthood to indicate a relation that seems to obtain between the events we quantify over in using action sentences (whether or not this relation has independent interest). Given a more technical notion designed to address metaphysical questions, perhaps 'grounds' could be defined differently, so that a process can be grounded by an event that is not literally part of the process (cf. Steward 1997).

[8] Hedging seems unavoidable. Hart and Honoré (1959) note that a second party can 'break the chain' of responsibility between a first person's action and its effects. Nora did not burn the forest if her campfire (which would have spread) is all but extinguished by a passer-by, who then comes to think that burning the forest would be fun after all—and so rekindles the fire. But second parties are not essential to the general point. If (at 1 p.m.) Nora sets an alarm (for 2 p.m.) to remind her of an appointment, it seems odd to say that Nora is the Agent of an event that has as parts *both* her action of setting the alarm *and* her action of leaving for the appointment. In any case, Nora's later action is not a *mere* effect of her earlier action. She responds to the alarm as she does because of her beliefs and desires, while the alarm goes off without further contribution by Nora. Perhaps no event can have as parts two actions, one of which causes the other. But I may need the notion of an 'unbroken' event, to account for second interventions by actors: Agent(e, N) $\leftrightarrow$ $\exists$a[grounds(a, e) & action(a, N) & unbroken(e)]. For ease of presentation, however, I ignore this complication. A more important complication (to which I return) concerns sentences like 'The rock broke the window', where the subject performs no action.

(1b) ∃e[*Agent(e, Booth)* & Shooting(e) & Patient(e, Lincoln)]

(1*) ∃e{∃a[*grounds(a, e)* & *action(a, Booth)]* & Shooting(e) & Patient(e, Lincoln)}.

The idea will be that the grounders of complex events satisfy the conception of action that motivates identificationist claims. But for now, the important point is that 'Booth's shooting of Lincoln' is ambiguous if this nominalization of 'Booth shot Lincoln' is associated with quantification over *two* event positions.

For in that case, the event description could be used in referring to the complex event *e* (which is With-a-pistol, has Lincoln as its Patient, etc.); or the action *a* that grounds *e* (where *a* has whatever further features it has). In speaking about the shooting of Lincoln by Booth, one could be referring to either of two events, which can be represented with the following descriptions:

∃!e{∃a[grounds(a, e) & action(a, Booth)] & Shooting(e) & Patient(e, Lincoln)}

∃!a{∃e[grounds(a, e) & action(a, Booth)] & Shooting(e) & Patient(e, Lincoln)}.

There is room for disagreement about whether (1*) is a more detailed representation of the sentence's true logical form, or whether it combines the genuine representation of logical form in (1b) with an important truth about what it is to be the Agent of an event. So there is room for disagreement about whether the ambiguity is genuinely semantic, as opposed to a pragmatic ambiguity that arises because of speakers' (tacit) knowledge about Agents. While I won't try to resolve these issues now, I return to them.

Initially, one might have been attracted to a simpler view of how Agents and actions are related: Agent(e, N) iff action(e, N). Indeed, something like this principle seems to be at work in our puzzle. Given that Booth is the Agent of a certain shooting, it follows from the simple view that the shooting is one of Booth's actions. And from here, the road to paradox is short. Semantic and spatio-temporal considerations strongly suggest that Booth is the Agent of a complex event that involves the motion of a bullet. If the shooting is one of Booth's actions, then actions include events with parts that are changes external to actors; and this seems wrong, for the reasons surveyed in Section 1.3 above. I think the trouble lies in the inference from the claim that Booth is the Agent of a shooting to the claim that the shooting is an action. This inference is not licensed by:

Agent(e, N) ↔ ∃a[grounds(a, e) & action(a, N)].

Let me be explicit about this crucial point. Since 'Agent' is a quasi-technical notion of semantic theory, and 'action' is a quasi-technical notion in the philosophy of thought, the relation between Agents and actions need not be trivial. If the relation is as I suggest, we can deny that a person's actions include events with parts external to her. For we need not say that a person's actions include all the events of which she is the Agent. Once we reject the simple view, we can also speak of *the* action that grounds a complex event. As Davidson (1971: 49) says, at least some actions must be 'primitive' in that they 'cannot be analysed in terms of their causal relations' to other actions. In my terminology, if event e has an Agent, e is grounded by an action not grounded by any other action. For a person makes finitely many contributions to history, even if her contributions have infinitely many distinct effects. It does not follow that the *only* action that grounds a complex event is its primitive grounder. But there is no reason to say that Booth's shooting of Lincoln is grounded by his (non-basic) action of pulling the trigger *and* by some more basic action. If a is the primitive grounder of e, then a grounds every grounder of e. Any event that a grounds (apart from itself) has effects of a as parts. And one will not track the causal contributions of persons with the notion of 'action' if actions include events that have *effects* of other actions as parts.

2.3

To summarize: if Booth shot Lincoln, $\exists e[\text{Agent}(e, \text{Booth}) \& \text{Shooting}(e) \& \text{Patient}(e, \text{Lincoln})]$; if the connection between Agency and action is as suggested, $\exists e\{\exists a[\text{action}(a, \text{Booth}) \& \text{grounds}(a, e)] \& \text{Shooting}(e) \& \text{Patient}(e, \text{Lincoln})\}$. Since 'Booth's shooting of Lincoln' is associated with quantification over *two* event positions, it can be used in referring either to the complex event e (which is With-a-pistol, but is not an action), or to the action a that grounds e. So let us introduce subscripts as follows:

Booth's$_E$ shooting of Lincoln was not his$_E$ pulling of the trigger; only the$_E$ shooting was With-a-pistol; only the$_E$ pulling was With-his-finger; and neither complex event was an action; but Booth's$_A$ shooting of Lincoln was his$_A$ pulling of the trigger; though the$_E$ shooting was not the$_A$ shooting, and the$_E$ pulling was not the$_A$ pulling. Identificationists are right about actions, while anti-identificationists are right about something else, viz. the complex events, grounded by actions, that satisfy sortal terms like 'shooting'.

If 'shooting' is only true of complex events, Booth's$_A$ shooting of Lincoln was not an event that satisfied 'shooting'. So one cannot insist on the truth of claims like 'his shooting *was* his action', while holding fixed the assumption that his shooting was an event that satisfied 'shooting'. And one can use nominalized action sentences to refer to events (like Booth's$_E$ shooting of Lincoln) that are not actions. But these are small costs to pay for preserving the event analysis *and* the internalist conception of action. One might worry that this leaves no unambiguous and non-technical way of referring to actions. We should be unsurprised, though, if ordinary language lacks devices for referring exclusively to the distinctively personal causal contributions of persons; and in my view, talk of events that *ground* shootings is not overly technical. Moreover, I argue below that (paradigmatic) actions do fall under the familiar sortal 'trying'.

Anti-identificationist intuitions also get their due. Note that

(14) Booth killed Lincoln on 13 April, but Lincoln did not die until 14 April

is false, if *every* part of an on-13-April event must occur on 13 April. Given this assumption, $\neg\exists e\{\exists a[\text{action}(a, \text{Booth}) \& \text{grounds}(a, e)] \& \text{Killing}(e) \& \text{Patient}(e, \text{Lincoln}) \& \text{On-13-April}(e)\}$, since the$_E$ killing had parts that had not yet occurred on 13 April. Similarly, the$_E$ killing had parts that did not occur *in* Ford's Theater. Nonetheless, the$_A$ killing occurred on 13 April in Ford's Theater. On any view, we typically refer to actions by using sortals like 'pulling' and 'shooting'. So if such terms are true of complex events, identificationists should welcome the anti-identificationist's favoured events. But these events are grounded in actions, about which identificationists are right. So identificationist and anti-identificationist intuitions are not in tension. They come as a package.

3. Moving Bodies

Distinguishing complex events from their grounders preserves identificationist intuitions about actions, in the face of anti-identificationist considerations. But what sort of event *is* an action? Again, on my view, Booth's action of shooting Lincoln does not satisfy the event sortal 'shooting'. Yet if Booth's action was not a$_E$ shooting (or a$_E$ pulling), what was it? Figure 1.1, in which squares represent parts of the overlapping complex events, may render the question vivid (cf. Thomson 1977). A common suggestion is that actions are bodily motions—or at least that many bodily motions are actions. But I know of no good *argument* for this thesis, except that it can be hard to think of a coherent alternative; and as we will see, there is reason for seeking an alternative. My plan, though, is to sneak up on the ontological question. First, I want to consider the apparently valid inferences:

(20) Nora melted the chocolate, so the chocolate melted.
(21) Nora moved her finger, so her finger moved.

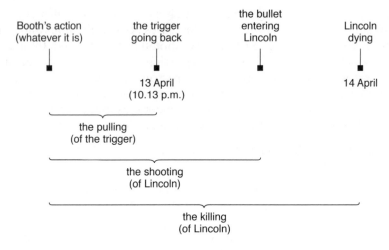

FIG. I.I

For the best account of such entailments suggests that when Nora moves her finger, the event of Nora's moving her finger is grounded by an action that causes the event of her finger's moving (i.e. the motion of her finger). That is, when we move our bodies, our actions *cause* our bodily motions.[9]

3.1

The inferences in (20) and (21) are examples of a more general pattern. For a wide class of tensed verbs 'V', competent speakers find the following (truth-preserving) inferences compelling: Nora V_T ——, so ——V_I; where subscripts indicate transitive/intransitive forms of the verb. In

(22) Nora *raised*$_T$ her arm/glass/flag, so her arm/glass/flag *rose*$_I$,

we still have transitive and intransitive forms of the same verb, I assume, despite the phonetic variation. But talk of moving fingers and raising arms is likely to trigger metaphysical views, which will muddy our semantic intuitions. So for now, let us focus on

(23) Nora *melted*$_T$ the chocolate.   (24) The chocolate *melted*$_I$.

---

[9] In what follows, I draw heavily on Hornsby (1980); but Hornsby does not frame the issue in terms of grounded events (and this obscures a gap in her argument). Davis (1979) offers a similar account of actions. Other useful discussions include: Thomson (1971, 1977); Thalberg (1972, 1977); O'Shaughnessy (1973, 1980); Lombard (1985); Costa (1987); Wilson (1989); Ginet (1990); Parsons (1990); Francken and Lombard (1992). Many features of my account can be found in one or more of these proposals.

(Other verbs that fit this pattern include: 'shattered', 'broke', 'boiled', 'froze', 'sank', 'increased', 'emptied', 'opened', 'closed', 'hanged', 'felled', etc.; see Parsons (1990) for discussion.) Given the thematically elaborated event analysis, the logical form of (23) would seem to be:

(23a) $\exists e[\text{Agent}(e, \text{Nora}) \ \& \ \text{Melting}_T(e) \ \& \ \text{Patient}(e, \text{the chocolate})]$.

If (23a) is true, then given the proposed gloss of 'Agent(e, Nora)':

(23*) $\exists e\{\exists a[\text{grounds}(a, \ e) \ \text{action}(a, \ \text{Nora})] \ \& \ \text{Melting}_T(e) \ \& \ \text{Patient}(e, \text{the chocolate})\}$.

So one can use 'Nora's melting$_T$ of the chocolate' in referring to Nora's$_E$ melting$_T$ of the chocolate or Nora's$_A$ melting$_T$ of the chocolate (a complex event or its grounder). Either way, however, the melting$_T$ differs from the melting$_I$. The melting$_I$ is a change *in the chocolate*. Nora brought about this change, but only with the help of nature. For the melting$_I$ occurred after Nora did her bit—say, putting the chocolate in a hot pot. So the melting$_I$ is not Nora's action; and neither is the melting$_I$ a complex event grounded by her action. Rather, there are three events: the melting$_I$, the$_A$ melting$_T$, and the$_E$ melting$_T$. The first two are parts of the third; the second grounds the third; and the$_A$ melting$_T$ *caused* the melting$_I$.

In (24), the chocolate is represented as the thing saliently *affected*, and not the salient initiator of the melting$_I$. So I assume that the logical form of (24) is

(24a) $\exists f[\text{Melting}_I(f) \ \& \ \text{Patient}(f, \text{the chocolate})]$.

This does not yet explain why (24) follows from (23). So let us say that F *terminates* E—or that E *terminates in* F—if events F and E occur; F is a (perhaps improper) part of E; and F is an effect of every proper part of E that is not a part of F. And suppose that a melting$_T$ of y terminates in a melting$_I$ of y:

Melting$_T$(e) & Patient(e, y) iff
$\exists f[\text{Terminates-in}(e, f) \ \& \ \text{Melting}_I(f) \ \& \ \text{Patient}(f, y)]$.

A consequence of this thesis, to which I return, is that every melting$_I$ of y is also a melting$_T$ of y. Or in the formal mode, every melting$_I$ satisfies the metalanguage term 'Melting$_T$', since every event terminates itself. More importantly for present purposes, given a melting$_T$ of y, it follows that there is a melting$_I$ of y. So the truth of (23a) ensures the truth of (24a). And this semantic relation between the transitive and intransitive construction is plausibly reflected in the syntactic structure of the former.

A traditional idea is that the relevant verbs, which exhibit the entailment pattern 'x V_T y, so y V_I', are fundamentally intransitive; and their sole argument is that of Patient. On this view, the surface form of (23)

masks an underlying syntactic form that includes a hidden verb: [Nora [#
[melt [the chocolate]]]]; where '#' assigns the role of Agent. Following
Baker (1988), I assume that the overt intransitive verb *incorporates* with
the hidden verb, forming a unit that (for many purposes) behaves like a
single verb that takes two arguments: [Nora [#-melt$_i$ [t$_i$ [the chocolate]]]];
where 't$_i$' is the trace of 'melt'. And

> (23b) $\exists e\{Agent(e, Nora)\ \&\ \exists f[Terminates\text{-}in(e, f)\ \&\ Melting_I(f)\ \&$
> Patient(f, the chocolate)]\}

provides a plausible interpretation of the underlying syntax. The inference
from (23b) to (24a) is an instance of the valid form: $\exists e\{\Phi(e, x)\ \&$
$\exists f[\Psi(e, f)\ \&\ \Theta(f)\ \&\ \Omega(f, y)]\}$; so $\exists f[\Theta(f)\ \&\ \Omega(f, y)]$. In (23b), Nora is represented as the Agent of the 'e-position' event the melting$_T$, not the
melting$_I$. If (23b) is true:

> (23*) $\exists e\{\exists a[grounds(a, e)\ \&\ action(a, Nora)]\ \&$
> $\exists f[Terminates\text{-}in(e, f)\ \&\ Melting_I(f)\ \&\ Patient(f, the\ choco\text{-}$
> late)]\}.

So (23) is true iff one of Nora's actions grounds an event that terminates
in a melting$_I$ of the chocolate.[10]

I return to the details of this proposal, saying why it is preferable to a
more familiar causative analysis of constructions like (23). But let me
emphasize that if (23*) is true, Nora's action caused the melting$_I$.
Similarly, if Nora raised$_T$ the flag, the flag rose$_I$; and Nora's action is distinct from the rising$_I$ of the flag, which is caused by her action. As Hornsby
(1980) notes, actions are reported by using the transitive form of verbs in
this class. One says what Nora did, by saying: she melted$_T$ the chocolate;
she raised$_T$ the flag; etc. One does not say what Nora did, by saying: the

---

[10] Alternatively, one might take the logical form of (23) to be

> (23c) $\exists e\{Agent(e, Nora)\ \&\ \exists f[Terminates\text{-}in(e, f)\ \&\ Melting_I(f)\ \&\ Patient(e, the$
> chocolate)]\}

on the grounds that Nora and the chocolate should be represented as participants in the
same event. And (23c) follows from (23a), given that every melting$_T$ terminates in a
melting$_I$: Melting$_T$(e) iff $\exists f[Terminates\text{-}in(e, f)\ \&\ Melting_I(f)]$. The inference from (23c) to
(24a) is not formally valid. But (23c) and (24a) are sentences of predicate logic; and one
might argue that the inference from (23) to (24) is still truth-preserving in natural language,
especially in light of Chomsky's (1995) claims about the syntactic structure of natural languages. But these details need not concern us here (see Pietroski (forthcoming *a*) for defence
of a Chomskian decomposition, *pace* Fodor (1970); Fodor and Lepore 1998, forthcom-
ing)). A third view would be that the logical form of 'Y melted' is 'Δ melted$_T$ Y', where 'Δ'
is an unvoiced subject. On this view, 'Y melted' entails that something melted Y, but if there
is an entailment here, I do not think it is *semantic*. (Contrary intuitions may stem from our
faith that every event has a cause.) Similarly, I doubt that the verb in 'Y melted' assigns *two*
thematic roles.

chocolate melted$_I$; the flag rose$_I$; etc. And at least where the relevant Patient is some chocolate or a flag, it seems that Nora's action caused the event specified with the intransitive form.

3.2

Let us now consider

(25) Nora moved$_T$ her finger.　　　(26) Her finger moved$_I$.

The logical form of (26) is

(26a) $\exists f[\text{Moving}_I(f) \,\&\, \text{Patient}(f, \text{her finger})]$.

Treating 'move$_T$' like 'melt$_T$', the logical form of (25) is (25b), which is the decomposition of (25a):

(25a) $\exists e[\text{Agent}(e, \text{Nora}) \,\&\, \text{Moving}_T(e) \,\&\, \text{Patient}(e, \text{her finger})]$
(25b) $\exists e\{\text{Agent}(e, \text{Nora}) \,\&\, \exists f[\text{Terminates-in}(e, f) \,\&\, \text{Moving}_I(f) \,\&\, \text{Patient}(f, \text{her finger})]\}$.

Given (25b), (26a) follows trivially; this explains why (26) follows from (25). If (25b) is true, Nora is the Agent of the 'e-position' event—the moving$_T$, not the moving$_I$. So given (25) and the proposed gloss of 'Agent(e, Nora)': $\exists e\{\exists a[\text{grounds}(a, e) \,\&\, \text{action}(a, \text{Nora})] \,\&\, \exists f[\text{Terminates-in}(e, f) \,\&\, \text{Moving}_I(f) \,\&\, \text{Patient}(f, \text{her finger})]\}$; an action of Nora's grounds an event that terminates in a moving$_I$ of her finger.

This strongly suggests that if Nora moved$_T$ her finger, then Nora's action *caused* the moving$_I$ of her finger. Her action caused the finger motion, just as Nora's action causes the melting$_I$ of the chocolate. A similar treatment of 'raised$_T$' suggests that if Nora raised$_T$ her hand, her action caused the rising$_I$ of her hand—just as her action caused the rising$_I$ of a flag if Nora raised$_T$ a flag.[11] Alas, showing that actions cause bodily motions is not quite this easy. While I want to treat 'move' fully on a par with 'melt', one might adopt another view, given that every event grounds (and terminates) itself: if Nora moved$_T$ her finger, her action grounds an event that terminates in the moving$_I$ of her finger; but perhaps Nora's action *is* the moving$_I$ of her finger, and not *a cause of* the moving$_I$ of her finger.

Before arguing against this view, it will be useful to contrast my semantic proposal with a more familiar variant that *rules out* the possibility of

---

[11] While I focus on verbs that appear in both transitive and intransitive constructions, I suspect that similar points apply to all transitive action sortals (see Lombard (1986), and the references in n. 9). If Nora lifted her finger, Nora's action grounds a complex event that terminates in an effect of her action.

identifying Nora's action with her finger motion. One might have said that the logical form of (23), repeated here along with (24), is (23pca):

(23)   Nora melted$_T$ the chocolate   (24) The chocolate melted$_I$
(23pca) $\exists e\{$Agent(e, Nora) & $\exists f[$Cause(e,f) & Melting$_I$(f) & Patient(f, the chocolate)]$\}$.

From (23pca), it follows that: $\exists f[$Melting$_I$(f) & Patient(f, the chocolate)]. This is the logical form of (24). So the 'pure causative analysis' of (23) explains why (23) entails (24). Parsons (1990) defends this account, noting that many other theorists have had essentially the same view; and my proposal is a variation on Parsons'. Hornsby (1980) also urges the pure causative analysis. On this account, (23) says that Nora is the Agent of an event that *causes* a melting$_I$ of the chocolate, whereas on my view, (23) says that Nora is the Agent of an event that *terminates in* a melting$_I$ of the chocolate. This can seem like a distinction without a difference. If (23) is true, Nora's action did cause the melting$_I$; and Nora is the Agent of her actions (since every action grounds itself). But it need not be part of the *meaning* of (23) that Nora is the Agent of *a cause of* the melting$_I$.

This matters when we turn to (25–6), with (25pca) being the hypothesized logical form of (25):

(25)   Nora moved$_T$ her finger   (26) Her finger moved$_I$
(25pca) $\exists e\{$Agent(e, Nora) &
        $\exists f[$Cause(e,f) & Moving$_I$(f) & Patient(f, her finger)]$\}$.

From (25pca), it follows that: $\exists f[$Moving$_I$(f) & Patient(f, her finger)]. So the pure causative analysis neatly explains why (26) follows from (25). It also follows from (25pca) that Nora is the Agent of an event that causes the moving$_I$ of her finger. But one might dispute this, holding that (25) can be true when Nora's action *is* the moving$_I$ of her finger. In fact, one might cite the internalist conception of action in arguing for an asymmetry between 'melt' and 'move': the melting$_I$ of the chocolate is external to Nora (beyond her control, etc.) in a way that the moving$_I$ of her finger is not.

That is, given the availability of my proposed variant on the pure causative analysis, one cannot argue that actions cause bodily motions *simply* by offering the pure causative analysis of verbs like 'melt', and then noting that 'move' belongs to the relevant class of verbs. This is not to deny that semantic arguments can play a role here. On the contrary, other things being equal, we should treat 'melt' and 'move' on a par semantically; for these verbs seem to be on a par syntactically. So I am suspicious of the claim that Nora's action causes a melting$_I$ in (23), while her action is a moving$_I$ in (25). But these considerations are not yet decisive.

3.3

Of course, if the pure causative analysis is correct, that would secure the case for treating actions as causes of bodily motions. But I think the pure causative analysis is less plausible, *qua* semantic theory, than my proposed variant of it. Let me briefly say why. In Section 4, I offer some other (semantic and non-semantic) arguments for not identifying actions with bodily motions.

Note that the explanations of relevant entailments do not require reference to causation (or termination). Suppose we analysed (23) abstractly as (23-R_c):

   (23)   Nora melted$_T$ the chocolate
   (23-R_c) $\exists e\{\text{Agent}(e, \text{Nora}) \ \& \ \exists f[\text{Melting}_I(f) \ \& \ R_c(e,f) \ \&$
           $\text{Patient}(f, \text{the chocolate})]\}$,

where R_c is some relation that holds between an event of which Nora is the Agent and the melting$_I$ of the chocolate. The relation R_c will have *something* to do with causation, hence the subscript; for it must 'fit' with the notion of being an Agent, which has something to do with causation. In general, R_c must be such that if x melted$_T$ y, then x is the Agent of an event that bears R_c to a melting$_I$ of y; and similarly for other verbs in this class. But it does not follow that R_c is the relation of causation. It could be the relation *causes-or-is* (where Nora is the Agent of her actions), or the relation *terminates in* (where Nora is the Agent of those events, many of which are complex, grounded by her actions). On either view, the moving$_I$ of Nora's hand would bear R_c to itself, if the moving$_I$ is one of Nora's actions.[12]

With this in mind, suppose Nora melted$_T$ the chocolate by moving$_T$ a lens between the chocolate and the sun. And consider the following instance of our initial puzzle:

   (27)   Nora melted$_T$ the chocolate with her lens
   (28)   Nora moved$_T$ the lens with her hand
   (29)   Nora melted$_T$ the chocolate with her hand
   (30)   Nora moved$_T$ the lens with her lens.

I take it that (27–8) can be true, while (29–30) are not. This is a problem, if the logical form of

---

[12] As many authors have noted, one can account for the entailments without saying that the English word 'cause' figures in the logical form of sentences like (25). One can use a technical notion 'cause*' whose extension differs from that of 'cause'. So the basic analysis cannot be refuted, by describing odd cases in which Nora's action caused the melting$_I$ of the chocolate, though it seems wrong to say that Nora melted$_T$ the chocolate. But if one can replace 'cause' with a technical variant, one can replace 'cause' with other causal notions, given compensating adjustments to the extension of 'Agent(e, N)'.

'Nora V_T ———' is: $\exists e\{$Agent(e, Nora) & $\exists f[$Cause(e, f) & V_I-ing(f) & Patient(f, ———)]$\}$. For no treatment of adjuncts will be satisfactory. Since the melting$_I$ and the moving$_I$ differ, it is tempting to say that the adjuncts in (27–30) modify the caused events, i.e. the events in the 'f-position'. But as Parsons (1990: 164–5) notes, the instrumental 'with . . .' modifies the caus*ing* event on the pure causative analysis. For 'with . . .' modifies what Nora did, not what happened to the chocolate/lens. Moreover, 'the chocolate melted$_I$ with her lens/hand' and 'the lens moved$_I$ with her lens/hand' are barely intelligible; yet the intransitive verbs easily take modifiers, as in 'the chocolate melted$_I$ slowly on Monday'. (Similarly: if Nora closed$_T$ the door with her foot, the door closed$_I$, but not with her foot.)

So there seem to be *two* events: Patient(e1, the chocolate) & With-her-lens(e1) & ¬With-her-hand(e1); Patient(e2, the lens) & ¬With-her-lens(e2) & With-her-hand(e2). This suggests that e1 and e2 are complex events with different end points: e1 is a melting$_T$ of the chocolate, e2 is a moving$_T$ of Nora's lens. But then e1 does not *cause* the event f1 that is the melting$_I$; e1 terminates in f1, which is caused by the action that grounds e1. And e2 does not cause the event f2 that is the moving$_I$; e2 terminates in f2, which is caused by the action that grounds e2. Nora's action of melting$_T$ the chocolate may be her action of moving$_T$ the lens. But the instrumental 'with . . .' does not modify a causing event (*pace* Parsons); it modifies a complex event—or if you prefer, a process that begins with the relevant action and terminates with the event specified by the intransitive verb.

Since Nora is the Agent of her actions, it is true that

(23pca) $\exists e\{$Agent(e, Nora) & $\exists f[$Cause(e,f) & Melting$_I$(f) & Patient(f, the chocolate)]$\}$.

And *if* this were the logical form of 'Nora melted$_T$ the chocolate', the logical form of (27) would be

(27pca) $\exists e\{$Agent(e, Nora) & $\exists f[$Cause(e,f) & Melting$_I$(f) & Patient(f, the chocolate)] & With-her-lens(e)$\}$.

But I do not think that any cause of the melting$_I$ is With-her-lens.[13] If

---

[13] The complex melting$_T$ terminates in, but does not cause, the melting$_I$. If one appeals to a complex event that terminates sooner (say the moving$_T$), other examples will reproduce the objection in the text. See Francken and Lombard (1992) for related discussion. Wilson also discusses these issues from a Davidsonian perspective. But he holds that an Agent who buttered the toast performed an act that buttered the toast; and he says that there is 'nothing odd' about the sentence 'Sirhan performed an act that killed Kennedy' (1989: 46). I disagree, even if we grant (*pace* Thomson 1977) that Sirhan performed an act of killing Kennedy. On my view, acts don't kill, Agents do; acts don't perform actions that ground complex events that culminate in deaths. I return (in Sect. 5) to special cases in which event nominals (that do *not* describe actions) appear as subjects, e.g. 'The explosion broke the window'.

Nora's action is With-her-lens, then by parity of reasoning, it should also be With-her-hand. Yet if Nora's action is With-her-hand, then:

(29pca) $\exists$e{Agent(e, Nora) &
$\exists$f[Cause(e,f) & Melting$_I$(f) & Patient(f, the chocolate)] &
With-her-hand(e)}.

And *if* (27pca) were the logical form of (27), then (29pca) would be the logical form of (29). Since this incorrectly predicts that (29) is true, the pure causative analysis does not give the correct logical forms.

4. Locating Actions in the Head

I have claimed that actions are grounders of complex events like shootings and pullings. This resolves the initial puzzle. As we just saw, it also introduces an (independently desirable) twist on the traditional semantics of so-called causative constructions. But the truth of such constructions does not semantically *require* that actions be inner events. There is conceptual room for the claim that (many) actions are bodily motions. So in this section, I offer some arguments against this claim (Section 4.1), some arguments for identifying actions with tryings (Section 4.2), and replies to a cluster of objections (Section 4.3).

4.1

No one thinks that Nora's actions include the melting$_I$ of her chocolate. But if the moving$_I$ of Nora's finger is one of her actions, why *isn't* the melting$_I$ of Nora's chocolate one of her actions as well? One might reply that the melting$_I$ is external to Nora and beyond her control, in a way that her finger motions are not. But upon reflection, this distinction is neither clear nor principled.

It is worth remembering that many bodily motions are not actions. Even setting reflexes aside, a person can move$_T$ some part of her body as she might move$_T$ a piece of furniture. Consider

(31) Nora moved$_T$ her left hand with a pencil (that she held in her right hand)
(32) Nora raised$_T$ her left arm with a pulley (that she operated with her right arm).

If (31) is true, Nora's action caused the moving$_I$ of her left hand; and the truth of (32) does not tempt us to identify Nora's action with the rising$_I$ of her left arm. The moving$_I$ and rising$_I$ are like the melting$_I$—events that occur in nature, after the Agent has done *her* bit. So a bodily motion is not intrinsically the kind of event that satisfies the internalist conception of action. But if some bodily motions are not actions, those who say that some bodily motions *are* actions owe an account of the relevant difference.

The obvious—and perhaps only—reply lies with appeal to causal history. In one sense, I favour such appeals: some bodily motions are caused by actions; others (like reflexes) are not. But an alternative, and initially tempting thought is that actions are bodily motions with an intentional etiology. This suggestion is scotched, however, by examples of 'deviant' causal chains. Frankfurt (1978) discusses a paradigm case: Smith believes that spilling his drink will signal that it is time to begin a crime; Smith comes to believe the time has come; but this makes Smith nervous, which causes his hand to shake, and his drink spills. The shaking$_I$ of Smith's hand is not an action, yet it has an intentional etiology. One can try to say what it is for bodily motions to be caused (by mental events) 'in the right way'. But as Frankfurt (ibid. 69) notes, one thereby concedes that 'actions and mere happenings do not differ essentially in themselves at all'; and this is hardly intuitive. Moreover, I do not know of any satisfactory account of causal deviance. No such account is needed if bodily motions are never actions. On this view, Smith's case is odd, because the shaking$_I$ of his hand is not caused by an action/trying. And while examples like (31–2) may not readily spring to mind, the causal chains are not deviant. They seem on a par with ordinary cases of moving$_T$ chairs and raising$_T$ flags, in which an action causes the motion of an object.

One can say that in (31–2) some other unspecified bodily motion is Nora's action. But then at least some uses of 'move' are like 'melt', in that the relevant moving$_I$ is caused by an action of the Agent in question. A striking example of this point is

(33)   Nora$_i$ moved$_T$ her$_j$ finger

where the italicized subscripts indicate that 'her' is *not* referentially dependent on 'Nora'. It is natural to hear 'Nora moved her finger' as meaning that Nora moved her own finger. But this interpretation is not mandatory. If Nora moved$_T$ Sally's finger, Nora's action caused the moving$_I$ of Sally's finger. So if Nora's action causes the relevant bodily motion in (31–3), the simplest hypothesis is that when an Agent moves$_T$ *any* finger, her action causes the finger motion in question.[14]

---

[14] Perhaps 'Nora moved$_T$ her finger' is ambiguous, and not just because 'her' may or may not be linked to 'Nora', with a reading that covers only cases of moving one's body in the usual way. (In conversation, Richard Larson noted that 'Sally moved$_T$ her finger, and Nora did too' sounds strained, if Sally moved$_T$ her finger in the usual way and then Nora moved$_T$ Sally's finger; though I find it less strained as an answer to 'Who moved$_T$ Sally's finger?') But given the proposal in the text, I see no reason for saying that 'move$_T$' is

In short, instead of insisting that history determines which bodily motions are actions, one can identify actions with certain causal antecedents of the relevant bodily motions. And there is independent reason for saying that many actions occur inside persons. Suppose Nora is asked to divide 390 by 13, and (after a pause) answers '30'. Nora *did something* before answering; she performed a division. This action occurred in her head. We can do many things without moving$_T$ our bodies: *figure out* the answer to a riddle; *prove* a theorem; *determine* whodunnit; *read* the paper; etc. This does not show that actions are never bodily motions. But it reminds us that actions can and do occur beneath the skin. (While a reader's eyes move$_I$, actions of reading are not eye motions; and even if Nora moves$_T$ internal parts of her body when she calculates, this shows that actions need not be peripheral bodily motions.)

Further evidence that actions cause bodily motions stems from a puzzle case discussed by Hornsby (1980). Suppose Nora wants to contract$_T$ the muscles in her forearm—either to show them off, or to make a point about the effects of actions. Nora knows that when she clenches$_T$ her fist, her muscles contract$_I$. So Nora clenches$_T$ her fist. It is also true that Nora contracted$_T$ her muscles. So her action can be described as the$_A$ clenching$_T$ of her fist or the$_A$ contracting$_T$ of her muscles; given identificationist intuitions, the$_A$ clenching$_T$ *is* the$_A$ contracting$_T$. But the clenching$_I$ of Nora's fist *was caused by* the contracting$_I$ of her muscles. (Again, I assume that contractings$_I$ are contractions.) So it cannot be that Nora's action of clenching$_T$ her fist is the clenching$_I$ *and* that Nora's action of contracting$_T$ her muscles is the contracting$_I$. Indeed, if Nora performed just one action and that action is the clenching$_I$ of her fist, then Nora's action of contracting$_T$ her muscles is caused by the contracting$_I$ of Nora's muscles.

Even if one is willing to live with this result, the fact remains that 'contract' is like 'melt' and 'move'. If Nora contracted$_T$ her muscles, her muscles contracted$_I$. So on the version of the event analysis developed here, the transitive construction is true iff $\exists e\{\text{Agent}(e, \text{Nora}) \ \& \ \exists f[\text{Terminates-in}(e, f) \ \& \ \text{Contracting}_I(f) \ \& \ \text{Patient}(f, \text{her muscles})]\}$. This treatment is unavailable if Nora's action is the clenching$_I$ of her fist. For in

---

ambiguous (like 'bank'), with direct and indirect *causation* readings (cf. Vendler 1967). This alleged distinction has proven hard to make out. Moreover, suppose Nick *thinks* that he is looking at Sally, and that Nora moved$_T$ Sally's finger by remote control; but in fact, Nick is looking at Nora, who moved her own finger. If Nick utters (33), his *claim* seems true; yet if 'moved' has an indirect reading, Nick presumably used it. Perhaps the indirect reading is true, whenever $i = j$ and the direct reading is true. But then the indirect reading does not require indirection; it is like the univocal reading of 'move$_T$' discussed in the text. This does not prove that there is no second reading, though given the possibilities for confusion here, one wants clear motivation for the second reading. Wilson (1989) claims that 'move' (or at least 'movement') is ambiguous, but I don't think his reasons apply to other verbs, like 'raise', that provide equally good reason for taking actions to be causes of bodily motions.

that case, the 'e-position' event—the$_E$ contracting$_T$ of her muscles—cannot be an event whose grounder is Nora's action and whose terminator is the contracting$_I$, unless there is backwards causation. On the other hand, one can avoid any hint of backward causation, by saying that Nora's action *causes* the contraction of Nora's muscles, which in turn causes the clenching$_I$ of Nora's fist (see Figure 1.2).

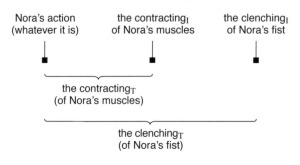

FIG. 1.2

One might assimilate such cases to those in which Nora raises$_T$ her left arm with her right arm. So perhaps the clenching$_I$ of Nora's fist is an effect of the$_A$ contracting$_T$, and Nora's action is her muscle contraction. But if some actions are not *peripheral* bodily motions, one owes a reason for insisting that other actions are peripheral. Suppose Nora clenched$_T$ her fist in order to grasp some object. If actions are ever bodily motions, Nora's action is the clenching$_I$ of her fist. The clenching$_I$ is caused by a contraction of Nora's muscles. So if Nora's actions include some muscle contractions, one owes a reason for not identifying Nora's action with the relevant contraction of her muscles *whenever* Nora clenches$_T$ her fist.

To appreciate the force of this challenge, consider a third case in which Nora tries to clench$_T$ her fist while her hand is held open. Nora's muscles will begin to contract$_I$. Indeed, Nora seems to do her bit, just as when she clenches$_T$ her fist. If her fist fails to clench$_I$, it seems that Nora still made *her* causal contribution, much as if she squeezed her finger against the trigger of a jammed pistol. Put another way, if Nora's action is a clenching$_I$ when she clenches$_T$ her fist, then her action is a different kind of event when her fist fails to clench$_I$; but intuitively, the consequent of this conditional is false, since *Nora's* causal contribution seems the same in both cases. So again, we have reason to say that Nora's action causes the clenching$_I$ (of her fist) when she clenches$_T$ her fist.[15]

---

[15] Perhaps Nora's causal contribution includes the clenching$_I$ of *her* fist, when the clenching$_I$ is a non-deviant effect of her desires. But this relies on the notion of deviance,

4.2

In the last paragraph, I assumed that a person acts when she tries to clench$_T$ her fist, even if her fist does not clench$_I$. More generally, a person acts when she tries to Φ, even if she does not Φ. Trying to Φ is doing *something*, even if it is not Φ-ing. Still, there is something special about sentences like

(34) Nora tried to lift the rock.

The verb 'try' takes a propositional complement, and the relevant proposition is not a Patient. Let us say that 'to lift the rock' specifies the *Content* of the trying. Then on a straightforward application of the event analysis, the logical form of (34) is

(34a) $\exists$e[Agent(e, Nora) & Trying(e) & Content(e, to lift the rock)].

Given my proposal about the relation of Agents to actions, (34a) is true iff

(34*) $\exists$e{$\exists$a[grounds(a, e) & action(a, Nora)] & Trying(e) & Content(e, to lift the rock)}.

But 'try' is not in the relevant class of verbs with 'melt', 'move', 'clench', 'contract', etc. Indeed, there is no pressure to say that a trying must be grounded by some action that is a proper part of the trying. Intuitively, (34) does not say that Nora's action stands in some causal relation to another event (perhaps specified by an intransitive verb). Rather, (34) reports a feature of the trying itself; it says that an event *with a certain content property* occurred.[16] Moreover, if tryings are grounded by (but not identical with) actions, what *are* these hidden grounders of tryings? We can avoid this question, by saying that Nora's trying *is* her action: if (34) is true, $\exists$e{$\exists$a[grounds(a, e) & action(a, Nora) & a=e] &Trying(e) & Content(e, to lift the rock)}; although this is not the logical form of (34). In this sense,

and it requires either a bias in favour of the peripheral, or the claim that some (basic) actions are complex events. If one allows talk of non-basic actions, one can treat the clenching$_I$ of Nora's fist as part of her causal contribution, like the motion of a rock after it leaves her hand. But then the question will be whether peripheral bodily motions ever count as basic actions, or whether basic actions are more robustly internal.

[16] The embedded clause in (34) has an unvoiced subject, which is linked to the matrix subject: Nora$_i$ tried [e$_i$ to lift the rock]. So the subject of the propositional content is Nora. One might require that an action ground *some* event other than itself, since it is hard to see how mere tryings would be points at which persons contribute to the causal order. But perhaps a recently paralysed person can try to move$_T$ his arm, even if he cannot produce any effect (in his arm or muscles); cf. McGinn (1982). In any case, I do not insist that all tryings are actions. One can say that only tryings with a causal *future* are actions, or that this is a constraint on genuine tryings. And saying that Nora is the Agent of her tryings does not ascribe strange powers to Nora; for Nora's reasons cause the trying. (I return to this point in Sect. 5.)

in action descriptions can 'ground out' in the actions themselves.
(1 ne$_E$ trying is the$_A$ trying.) One might have worried that pushing actions
inside the head would lead to some kind of vicious regress. But one can say
that the grounders of complex events like liftings (pullings, shootings, etc.)
just *are* events that satisfy the sortal 'try'; and there are such events, given
the truth of sentences like (34) and the event analysis.

This fits well with the internalist conception of action that motivates
identificationist claims. What a person tries to do is within her control, if
anything is. Nature must cooperate if attempts are to be successful. But a
person normally has it in her power to *try*. More importantly, (34) can be
true, even if Nora lifts the rock. As O'Shaughnessy (1973, 1980) and
Hornsby (1980) have argued, it may be *pragmatically inappropriate* to say
that someone tried to Φ when she succeeded in Φ-ing; and 'Φ-ing' may be
conceptually prior to 'trying to Φ', much as 'seeing an X' is conceptually
prior to 'seeming to see an X'. (Following Sellars (1956) and Smart (1959),
we can characterize this last notion in terms of being in a condition internally like the condition of seeing an X. When one sees an X, the event
of seeming to see an X can be the event of seeing an X; similarly, when
things go as planned, we can identify tryings with doings.) But it does not
follow that a person who successfully Φs *did not* try to Φ. On the contrary,
it would be bizarre to deny that someone tried to Φ on the grounds that they
succeeded. One can say of a person who lifts a rock, 'I knew she would try
to lift the rock, but I did not think she could lift it.' That is, after the fact,
one will characterize such a person as one who tried *and* succeeded.

If Nora successfully tried to lift the rock, then:

> ∃e{∃a[grounds(a, e) & action(a, Nora)] & Trying(e) &
> Content(e, to lift the rock)}, and
> ∃e{∃a[grounds(a, e) & action(a, Nora)] & Lifting(e) &
> Patient(e, the rock)}.

It would be gratuitous to say that the action that grounds the trying does
not also ground the lifting. Nora did not do two separate things—try to
lift the rock, and lift the rock. Rather, she performed one action that can
be described (without reference to its effects) as a trying, or as (the ground
of) a lifting. And we have reason to identify the trying with the action that
grounds the trying. So we have reason to identify the trying with the action
that grounds the lifting. That is,

> ∃e{∃a[grounds(a, e) & action(a, Nora) & Trying(a) &
> Content(a, to lift the rock)] & Lifting(e) & Patient(e, the rock)},

although this is not the logical form of 'Nora successfully tried to lift the
rock'. Similarly, if Nora successfully tried to move$_T$ her finger, Nora's
action *is* the event of her trying to move$_T$ her finger.

In general, if N successfully tried to Φ, I would identify N's a<
Φ-ing with N's trying to Φ (see O'Shaughnessy 1973, 1980; ‹
Armstrong 1971). This is not to deny that one can try to Φ by Ψ-ing. Nora
might try to impress Nick by lifting the rock. In this case, one might identify the trying (to impress Nick) with the lifting, which is a complex event
grounded by an action. But my claim is that paradigmatic actions are tryings, not that every trying is an action. And the lifting is still grounded by
a trying that is not grounded by a distinct action. Nonetheless, one might
allow that actions are tryings, yet insist that a person's action of moving$_T$
her finger just is the motion of her finger. For one might identify *successful* tryings (to move$_T$ one's body) with bodily motions, or complex events
that terminate in bodily motions, while perhaps allowing that unsuccessful tryings are inner events.[17]

I cannot prove that the class of tryings is not disjoint in this way. But if
the simpler view is available, one begins to suspect that behaviouristic/
verificationistic scruples are behind the insistence that many actions be
bodily motions. Moreover, such disjointness would be at odds with generalizations like: if N intends to Φ when C obtains, and comes to believe that
C obtains, N will try to Φ (*ceteris paribus*). For if Nora intended to lift the
rock at noon, and did so, then on the view being considered: her
action/trying is a bodily motion; so the generalization above often relates
intendings to bodily motions. But this seems wrong. If Nora was not
strong enough to lift the rock, this would tell us nothing about her *intentional* profile. One can say that Nora's action would have been an inner
event had she failed to lift the rock; but this concedes that bodily motions
are not what matters to the intentional generalization.[18]

Let me summarize the last few pages. To say that Nora moved$_T$ part of
her body is already to describe an action by reference to its effects. If Nora
tries to contract$_T$ her muscles and succeeds, her action is her trying, which

---

[17] O'Shaughnessy (1980) would say that a successful trying to move$_T$ one's finger
'encompasses' the finger motion. I think his view can be expressed in my terminology, by
saying that such a trying is a complex event that terminates in the motion of one's finger.
But, other things being equal, I think considerations of simplicity favour identifying actions
with causes of limb motions. O'Shaughnessy also provides valuable discussion of our epistemic relation to our bodily motions; though I think one can capture the relation between
actions and the bodily motions to which we bear the relevant epistemic relation, by saying
that actions ground complex events that terminate in such bodily motions.

[18] And recall that I am operating with a quasi-technical notion of 'action', used to track
the (intentional) causal contributions of persons. My goal is not to describe our ordinary
language practice with respect to 'act' or 'try'. Having mentioned intentions, let me note
that I have focused on actions that require no *planning*. Nora can move$_T$ her finger without
forming an intention and executing a plan. A full treatment of the relations among actions,
tryings, and bodily motions would get beyond this massive simplification. Davis (1979:
22–3) offers the plausible suggestion that many tryings—like trying to carry on a conversation—are processes that involve 'monitoring' a series of subactions. See also Bratman
(1987).

causes the contracting$_I$ of her muscles. If she tries to clench$_T$ her fist, but her fist is held open, then the action/trying occurs without causing a clenching$_I$. Actions like mental calculations (standing still, etc.) pose no special difficulties. For when Nora tries to do a division and succeeds, her action can be her trying; though success does not involve a peripheral bodily motion. And recall Smith, who spilled his drink through nervousness. Smith's beliefs and desires fail to *rationalize* his behaviour, I suggest, because his thoughts did not cause his bodily motion *by causing an action/trying*.

4.3

My argument has been that our best semantics of action sentences, in conjunction with strong intuitions about actions (and bolstered by reasons for not identifying actions with bodily motions), has the consequence that actions are causes of bodily motions. More specifically, (paradigmatic) actions are tryings. Still, the claim that actions are inner events can seem wrong. So let me address some objections.

One might rebel at the very idea that actions are in the head. But I see nothing unintuitive in the suggestion that a person's action—*her* contribution to the causal order, prior to events brought about with the help of nature—is a mental event causally upstream of any bodily motion. Indeed, I think pretheoretic intuitions favour this conception of actions. (Philosophers who know the failings of traditional volitional theories may distrust the idea that actions are in the head; but distrust is not counterevidence.) One might think that my view is rooted in a hopelessly dualistic view of persons. But that is a different objection, and one I aim to address in the rest of this book.

It is also important that one not automatically saddle appeals to tryings with the difficulties faced by traditional appeals to volitions. In particular, while I can agree that acting requires an inner act of will, one can will that Φ (try to Φ) without willing that one will that Φ (trying to try to Φ). My claim is not that actions precede tryings. Since every event grounds itself, every action is *grounded by* an action. But it does not follow that actions are *initiated by* actions. If Nora tried to lift the rock, there was an act of willing in Nora; but this act just was the event of Nora's trying to lift the rock. Perhaps there are rare cases in which a person tries to try. But it is no part of my view that whenever a person tries to Φ, she tries to try to Φ (see O'Shaughnessy 1973; Hornsby 1980). One wants to hear more about what tryings are. But note that there must be such events, given the event analysis and true instances of 'N tried to Φ'.

I have focused on cases in which a person successfully tries to do something. Clearly, though, one can do something without trying to do it. To borrow Davidson's example, if Nora flips the light switch, she may alert the burglar *unintentionally*. Nora's action of alerting the burglar is not a trying to alert the burglar. But Nora's action can be a trying. It can be a trying to flip the switch. So I am not saying that anyone who Φ'd tried to Φ. If a person tries to Ψ, her trying may have an effect in virtue of which she is correctly described as having Φ'd, even if she never tried to Φ. (Correspondingly, while 'x grounded y' is an extensional context, 'Φ' is an opaque position in 'Her trying to Φ grounded y.')

I do not say that *all* actions are tryings. Nora may act without trying when she 'mindlessly' drums her fingers, or 'instinctively' ducks under a low doorway. Nora may act when she *decides* (or *forms the intention*) to change jobs; yet I doubt that she tries to decide (or tries to intend). If Nora does not vote yes, she may act without her 'negative' action being one of her tryings. But such actions require special treatment on any view. My claim is only that paradigmatic—i.e. clearly intentional—actions are try- ings; though I return to a suggestion about how to deal with some of the special cases just mentioned.

One might object that we cannot see tryings, though we can see many actions. (And we do see bodily motions.) This is probably the root of much resistance to the idea that actions are inner events. But I think we can see— or at least make reliable, non-inferential judgements about the occurrence of—inner events. I return to this point, and the visibility of causes in general, in Chapter 7. But even if tryings are invisible, because they do not occur at the body's periphery (or visible surface), this is not incompatible with the truth of perceptual reports concerning actions. In Section 1, I endorsed the following analysis of 'Nora heard Fido bark': ∃e∃f[Hear(e, Nora, f) & Bark(f, Fido)]. Similarly, suppose the unelaborated logical form of (35) is (35a), with the relevant portion of thematic structure represented in (35b):

(35) Todd saw Booth pull the trigger

(35a) ∃d∃e[See(d, Todd, e) & Pull(e, Booth, the trigger)]

(35b) ∃d∃e[See(d, Todd, e) & Pulling(e) & Agent(e, Booth) & Patient(e, the trigger)].

If (35) is true, Todd saw the pulling, the complex 'e-position' event. But it does not follow that Todd saw the action that grounds the pulling; though in my view, she may well have seen Booth's action. If Todd saw Booth pull the trigger, Todd saw *what Booth did*; what Booth did was *pull the trigger*; and we can use 'the pulling of the trigger' as a means of referring to Booth's action/trying. But the truth of (35) does not entail that Todd saw a trying. And there is no good reason for denying that we can see complex events like pullings, even if such events are grounded by invisible tryings. For we speak of seeing plants, even though they have parts that are below ground. So my account is compatible with the truth of (35).

One would like some explanation of why it is so *tempting* to identify actions with bodily motions. So let me conclude this section by noting that if we confuse features of event *descriptions* with features of the events described, it can seem that bodily motions are more basic than any other candidates for actions. Modifying Hornsby's (1980) proposals to fit my terminology, let us say that a description Δ of action a is more C-basic than another description Δ^* of a, if the event (grounded by a) that satisfies the matrix event sortal in Δ is a proper part of the event (grounded by a) that satisfies the matrix event sortal in Δ^*. Then 'Booth's$_A$ pulling of the trigger' is more C-basic than 'Booth's$_A$ shooting of Lincoln'. The pulling is a proper part of the shooting, which has parts that occur after the trigger has gone back. In order of *causation*, the end of the pulling is more basic than the end of the shooting. If we forget about contracting$_T$ our muscles, and moving$_T$ our fingers with pencils, it is easy to think that no action descriptions are more C-basic than those that describe (peripheral) bodily motions.

Let us also say that a description Δ of some action performed by person x is more B-basic than another description Δ^*, if 'x Δ^*-d *by* Δ-ing' is true, and 'x Δ-d *by* Δ^*-ing' is false. Booth killed Lincoln by pulling the trigger; he didn't pull the trigger by killing Lincoln. So 'Booth's$_A$ squeezing of his finger' is more B-basic than 'Booth's$_A$ pulling of the trigger'. Booth pulled the trigger by squeezing his finger, yet he did not squeeze his finger by contracting$_T$ his finger muscles. So 'Booth's$_A$ contracting$_T$ of his finger muscles' is *not* more B-basic than 'Booth's$_A$ squeezing of his finger', although the first event description is more C-basic. This also makes bodily motions seem special. We typically do not move$_T$ our bodies *by* doing anything else; we just move$_T$ our bodies. So an action description that involves reference to a bodily motion will often be more B-basic than other descriptions of the same action.

One might hope to use this intuition in showing that actions are bodily motions. But I think the 'by'-locution invites confusion of the causal order with the order of an actor's *intentions*; so I would not put too much weight on intuitions about sentences of the form 'x Δ^*-d by Δ-ing' (cf. Bennett 1988). One can kill Louis by decapitating him. Arguably, the decapitating *is* the killing. Yet one cannot decapitate Louis by killing him. Similarly, Nora can move her hand by raising it, without raising her hand by moving it. If actions are bodily motions, the raising and the moving are each identical with some one bodily motion. So especially if one says that actions are bodily motions, one must grant that the 'by'-relation can be asymmetric, even given two descriptions of a single event; and hence, the truth of 'x Δ^*-d by Δ-ing' is sensitive to more than the mind-independent relations that hold between the events described. So the falsity of 'Booth squeezed$_T$ his finger by contracting$_T$ his muscles' hardly shows that Booth did not contract$_T$ his muscles, or that the motion of his finger was not caused by Booth's action.[19]

As Hornsby notes, we can say that description Δ of action *a* is more T-basic than description Δ* if in virtue of *a*'s occurrence (and its effects), x intentionally Δ'd* by Δ-ing. In order of *teleology*, 'the$_A$ decapitating of Louis' is more basic than 'the$_A$ killing of Louis'. Typically, there will be no Δ such that a person intentionally moves$_T$ her fingers by Δ-ing. So in this sense, we often bear a special relation to our finger motions. But this does not show that finger motions are among the actions of persons.

Of course, one can *define* 'action' so as to include (i) bodily motions caused by tryings, or (ii) complex events, grounded by tryings, that terminate in bodily motions. But given that actions include tryings, and that tryings cause bodily motions, we need not say that actions include (i) or (ii). And there is reason not to say this. It makes the semantics of action sentences unnecessarily complex, by failing to treat verbs like 'move', 'raise', and 'contract' on a par with 'melt'. Our language strongly suggests that actions typically cause bodily motions; and this (independently motivated) thesis is defensible.

5. Being an Agent without Trying

Having based so much on the event analysis, I must address some loose ends in my version of it.

5.1

On the event analysis, as developed here, the logical form of (36) is (36a), decomposed as (36b):

(36) The rock broke$_T$ the window

(36a) $\exists e[\text{Agent}(e, \text{the rock}) \& \text{Breaking}_T(e) \& \text{Patient}(e, \text{the window})]$

(36b) $\exists e\{\text{Agent}(e, \text{the rock}) \& \exists f[\text{Terminates-in}(e, f) \& \text{Breaking}_I(f) \& \text{Patient}(f, \text{the window})]\}$.

Assuming that the logical form of (37) is (37a),

(37) The window broke$_I$

(37a) $\exists f[\text{Breaking}_I(f) \& \text{Patient}(f, \text{the window})]$,

---

[19] I am not sure whether 'Nora contracted$_T$ her muscles by clenching$_T$ her fist' is ever true. (Her action of contracting$_T$ can cause the clenching$_I$, while the 'by'-sentence is false.) But if this sentence can be true, the 'by'-locution would seem to be *primarily* about intentional (not causal) order.

we have an explanation of why (36) entails (37). But this analysis raises two related questions.

We can imagine situations, or at least understand stories, in which rocks break$_T$ windows by hurling themselves up from the ground. But (36) can be true in mundane scenarios where the rock does not *act*. The rock may simply move$_I$ (due to a strong wind) along a path that passes through the window, which breaks$_I$. Yet how can something be an Agent without acting? This is ruled out by the schema: Agent(e, N) iff ∃a[action(a, N) & grounds(a, e)]. Moreover, my account has been based on the idea that verbs like 'move$_T$' are true of complex events grounded by actions. So even if 'Agent' is defined so that a rock can be an Agent of *some* events, how can a non-actor be the Agent of a breaking$_T$? How can there be a *breaking$_T$* of y, on my view, if no action grounds a complex event that terminates in a breaking$_I$ of y? Yet without a breaking$_T$ of the window, (36a) is false, whether or not rocks can be Agents.

So the questions raised by (36) cannot be avoided just by saying that its logical form is

(36Θ)　∃e[Θ(e, the rock) & Breaking$_T$(e) & Patient(e, the window)],

where Θ is some thematic role with no implication of agency. Similar questions arise with respect to

(38)　Nora broke$_T$ the window

as used in contexts where no *action* of Nora's caused the breaking$_I$ of the window. Suppose Nora was holding a stick near the window when a loud noise startled her.[20] Perhaps (38) is semantically ambiguous, having readings that correspond to (36a) and (36Θ). But there is no independent reason for thinking that (38) is lexically or syntactically ambiguous. And if logical forms are more finely grained than syntactic structures, the mapping from syntax to logical form is non-trivial. An account would be owed of when 'Nora' in (38) is associated with 'Agent', and when it is associated with some other thematic role. Moreover, Baker (1988, 1997) offers considerable empirical support for the Uniformity of Thematic Assignment Hypothesis (UTAH), according to which noun phrases with the same grammatical role have the same thematic role. So I want to broaden my initial proposal about what it is to be an Agent.

---

[20] Such cases differ from those in which an action has unintended effects. If Nora swings a bat, forgetting about the window behind her, the breaking$_T$ is a complex event grounded by her action. See Feinberg 1965 on the 'accordion effect'. This effect is at best strained in cases like (36). If the breaking$_I$ of the window woke the baby, it seems odd to say that the rock woke the baby.

5.2

Recall that a breaking$_T$ is an event that terminates in a breaking$_I$. Since every event terminates itself, every breaking$_I$ is a breaking$_T$. So not every breaking$_T$ is grounded by an action. Earlier, this may have seemed like a mere technical point. But now, its importance should be clear. Setting aside the question of whether rocks can be Agents (for the moment), there is no puzzle about the truth of

(36a) $\exists e[Agent(e, the rock) \& Breaking_T(e) \& Patient(e, the window)]$

given that there was a breaking$_I$ of the window. If there is a breaking$_I$, it *follows* that there is a breaking$_T$.

This can seem like cheating, since I stressed that actors are Agents of complex events. If

(27) Nora melted$_T$ the chocolate with her lens

is true, the melting$_T$ (i.e. the event that was With-her-lens) was a complex event distinct from any melting$_I$. But if (27) is true, there is a melting$_I$ of the chocolate, and this melting$_I$ is also a melting$_T$, although this second melting$_T$ was not With-her-lens, for reasons discussed in Section 3.4 above. With respect to (36), though, the only breaking$_T$ is the breaking$_I$. If (36) is true, then

$\exists e\{Agent(e, the rock) \&$
$\exists f[(e=f) \& Breaking_I(f) \& Patient(f, the window)]\}.$

But the semantic decomposition of (36a) is

(36b) $\exists e\{Agent(e, the rock) \&$
$\exists f[Terminates-in(e,f) \& Breaking_I(f) \& Patient(f, the window)]\}.$

The fact that every breaking$_I$ is a breaking$_T$ also suggests an answer to our other question: how can a rock be the *Agent* of a breaking$_T$? We must say that a rock can be the Agent of a breaking$_I$. Suppose there are indeed two importantly different kinds of breakings$_T$: simple ones (i.e. breakings$_I$) and complex ones (i.e. events that begin with an action and end with a breaking$_I$). Then perhaps there are two importantly different ways of being the Agent of a breaking$_T$. To be the Agent of a complex breaking$_T$ is to perform the action that grounds it. But a simple breaking$_T$ is not grounded by any action. So let the Agent of such an event be its *salient initiator*. And in general, let us say that the Agent of an event is its salient initiator, where performing an action that grounds a complex event is the paradigmatic case of initiating an event.

This is a version of Dowty's (1979) proposal that 'Agent' is a prototype notion. On Dowty's view, which Baker (1997) endorses, an Agent is the most actor-like event participant in an event. So if Nora acts, she is an Agent. But an event that includes no action can still have an Agent if some event participant (say, a moving rock) is enough like an actor. Similarly, if a breaking$_T$ is complex, its Agent is the actor whose action grounds the breaking$_T$; but if the breaking$_T$ is a simple breaking$_I$, its Agent is the event participant most like an actor, i.e. the salient initiator of the breaking$_I$. The idea is that something can be like an actor, by participating in a cause of an indicated effect; and the rock participates in an event (its motion) that causes the breaking$_I$ of the window. (On this view, the rock's breaking$_T$ the window is the window's breaking$_I$. But if one finds this consequence intolerable, one could say that the rock is the Agent of some other event intimately related to the breaking$_I$ of the window.)

I have not said what *makes* something the Agent of an event not grounded by an action. But given UTAH, the notion of 'Agent' must be understood in a relaxed fashion. So my thesis about what it is to be an Agent must be restated as: Agent$_P$(e, X) iff $\exists$a[action(a, X) & grounds(a, e)], where the subscript indicates that the notion of *prototypical* Agency is being characterized.[21] These remarks are sketchy. But they still shed some light on cases that otherwise seem puzzling. If a rock can be the Agent of a breaking$_I$, it is not hard to see how a kettle can be the Agent of a whistling. So the logical forms of (39–40) can be as indicated:

(39)   The kettle whistled
(39a) $\exists$e[Whistling(e) & Agent(e, the kettle)]
(40)   Nora whistled
(40a) $\exists$e[Whistling(e) & Agent(e, Nora)].

In each case, the grammatical subject (the kettle/Nora) is the salient initiator of the whistling. But while Nora performs an action that grounds a complex event culminating with some air passing through Nora's mouth, the kettle performs no action. Still, the kettle is like Nora: a change in the kettle causes a sound when steam passes through the relevant aperture. In this sense, the kettle is more like Nora than the rock, whose motion is not internally generated. So one can draw distinctions among non-acting Agents. Indeed, one might take the kettle's whistling to be a complex event

---

[21] One wants to hear more about non-prototypical Agency. But we face an analogue of the Euthyphro problem: is a participant Π in event e represented as the grammatical subject of a true sentence about e, because Π is the salient initiator of e; or is Π the salient initiator of e, because Π is represented as the grammatical subject (of a true sentence about e, and) UTAH governs the mapping from grammatical to thematic roles? I have nothing useful to say on this score, though my hunch is that neither 'because'-claim will be satisfactory. Let me also stress that while I think UTAH is compatible with the sentences discussed here, my claim is not that relaxing the notion of 'Agent' avoids every objection to UTAH (see Pesetsky 1995; Baker 1997; Pietroski forthcoming *b*).

grounded by a (non-intentional) change in the kettle, and terminating in the resulting sound. If there is such an event, one might define a notion 'action*' that includes both tryings and the grounders of events like the kettle's whistling.[22]

Reflection on kettles may shed light on cases in which a person 'instinctively' ducks or 'mindlessly' drums her fingers. Earlier, I described these as non-paradigmatic actions, and set them aside as special cases. But if a notion of 'action*' can include the whistling of a kettle, or the walking$_I$ of a dog walked$_T$, duckings and drummings may be actions*. At any rate, one can begin to see how Nora could be the Agent of such events without there being any trying that is her action of ducking or drumming. And a person can be the Agent of her tryings, even though a person's relation to her tryings differs from her relation to the complex events of which she is the Agent. Nora initiates the lifting of a rock in virtue of performing an action distinct from (though a part of) the lifting; Nora *tries* to lift the rock. But Nora does not initiate her trying in virtue of performing an action distinct from the trying. Nora is the Agent of her tryings, simply because they are hers; Nora's tryings stem from *her* reasons. Initially, it may have seemed odd to say that Nora is the Agent of complex events grounded by tryings and the tryings themselves. But if there is more than one way to be a salient initiator, we should expect a certain diversity amongst the events of which a person is the Agent.

5.3

One might think this manœuvring trivializes UTAH. Instead of saying that 'X broke$_T$ the window' has different logical forms, depending on which thematic role is associated with the subject, I have said that there are many ways to be an Agent. Perhaps this a kind of ambiguity; for there are important differences between rocks, kettles, and paradigmatic actors. But thinkers can notice differences not marked by the language itself. We know that rocks are not actors, but I don't think we know this simply by virtue of knowing a natural language. Correspondingly, I doubt that 'Nora broke$_T$ the window' and 'The rock broke$_T$ the window' have different *entailments* with respect to who or what acted. (Again, we can understand stories in which rocks act; and Nora can break$_T$ the window without acting.)

---

[22] I do not say that kettle-whistlings *are* complex events. It is hard to find semantic/spatio-temporal arguments as persuasive as those that apply to pullings and shootings. But *perhaps* the rock's breaking$_T$ the window is a complex event grounded by an action*. If the rock broke$_T$ the window with considerable force, the breaking$_T$ was with considerable force; and one *might* deny that the breaking$_I$ also has this property. These considerations also bear on inferences like 'Nora walked$_T$ the dog, so The dog walked$_I$' and 'The explosion broke$_T$ the window, so the window broke$_I$'; see Pietroski (1998*a*: 106–7).

Moreover, it is not arbitrary to classify rocks that break$_T$ windows with persons who successfully try to break$_T$ windows. In each case, the window breaks$_I$ because of an event intimately related to the relevant subject. So returning to an earlier issue, it seems that the logical form of 'Booth shot Lincoln' is (1b), with (1*) reflecting the further claim that Booth is a paradigmatic Agent:

(1b) ∃e[Agent(e, Booth) & Shooting(e) & Patient(e, Lincoln)]

(1*) ∃e{∃a[action(a, Booth) & grounds(a, e] & Shooting(e) &Patient(e, Lincoln)}.

In this sense, the ambiguity of action descriptions is not purely semantic. But often, we know that we are speaking of paradigmatic Agents; and many event sortals, including 'shoot' and 'kill', may apply only to events grounded in actions. Moreover, the main point is that we can use event descriptions like 'Booth's shooting of Lincoln' in referring to a complex event (the$_E$ shooting), or the action/trying that grounds it. And the action that grounded Booth's shooting of Lincoln *caused* the motion of Booth's trigger-finger.

2

Fregean Innocence

In the last chapter, I approached questions about actions via the semantics of action sentences, and concluded that (paradigmatic) actions are tryings—inner events that have contents. This raises the question of what contents are. My discussion begins with the semantics of 'N believes that P'. This strategy is familiar, since contents are commonly taken to be the referents of 'that'-clauses. I adopt a Fregean view of such clauses. In Chapter 3, I turn to constructions of the form 'the fact that P explains the fact that Q' and '*c* caused *e*', where events *c* and *e* are the truth-makers for sentences 'P' and 'Q'. For my plan is to combine the event analysis and a Fregean account of propositional attitude ascriptions, as part of a larger view about intentional explanation and mental causation. But first, we need a defensible Fregean semantics of propositional attitude ascriptions.

According to Frege (1892), every meaningful linguistic expression has a semantic value (*Bedeutung*) and a sense (*Sinn*). In particular, the semantic value of a sentence is its truth-value; the semantic value of a referring term is its referent; the sense of an expression is a way of thinking about (or a way of presenting) its semantic value; and the semantic value of 'that P' is the sense of 'P'. This yields an attractive treatment of so-called opaque contexts. But considerations of compositionality led Frege to say that terms inside 'that'-clauses do not have their usual semantic values: in 'Booth believed that Lincoln was a tyrant', the semantic value of 'Lincoln' is said to be a sense—a *way of thinking about* Lincoln, not Lincoln himself. This claim turns out to be problematic. But one can maintain the essential aspects of Frege's view, while holding that the semantic value of 'Lincoln' is always Lincoln, by assigning a semantic value to the complementizer 'that'. My specific proposal avoids many criticisms of Fregean theories, once we are clear about what compositionality does not entail.

1. Sinn *and Shifty Values*

Frege's interest in logic led him to express his famous puzzle mainly as a question about identity statements: if 'a = b' is true, how can it differ in meaning from 'a = a'? But here it will be useful to begin with a closely related puzzle concerning the compositionality of propositional attitude ascriptions.

Following Frege, Davidson (1965, 1967c) and others have argued (usually by adverting to our capacity to understand arbitrarily many novel sentences) for the following compositionality thesis:

> every meaningful expression of a natural language **L** has a semantic value, such that the truth conditions of any declarative sentence Σ of **L** can be determined (perhaps relative to a context) as a function of Σ's logical form and the semantic values of Σ's constituents,

where for these purposes, the logical form of a sentence Σ is to be understood as the (semantically significant) way in which the (semantically primitive) constituents of Σ are arranged in Σ.[1] Given this, it seems that natural languages must also satisfy the following substitutivity thesis:

> if a sentence $\Sigma 2$ is the result of replacing some expression in sentence $\Sigma 1$ with an expression having the same semantic value, then $\Sigma 1$ and $\Sigma 2$ have the same truth conditions.

If the truth conditions of a sentence are determined (given its logical form) by the semantic values of its constituents, it seems that substituting expressions with the same semantic value must preserve truth. For reasons discussed below, I assume that co-referential terms have the same semantic value. But, apparently, substituting co-referential terms can affect the truth conditions of sentences like

(1) Nora believes that Fido barked.

Suppose that every night, Nora hears her neighbour's dog bark, followed by the neighbour yelling 'Fido, be quiet!' Every morning, Nora sees (but never hears) a certain dog in the park. The person walking this dog often says, 'Rex, I am so glad you never bark.' Nora thus comes to believe that Fido barks, and that Rex does not. Indeed, she wishes that Fido were more like Rex, the quiet dog from the park. Of course, Fido is *very* like Rex. Unbeknownst to Nora, the morning dog is the evening dog (as

---

[1] In this sense, the logical form of a natural language sentence Σ is a syntactic property of Σ. It is standard practice in philosophy to say that the logical form of Σ is some sentence σ of a formal language, where σ makes explicit what follows from Σ (and what Σ follows from). I take this practice (which I followed in Ch. 1) to be justified, insofar as the relevant formal language sentences make explicit the semantic contributions of the relevant modes of combination employed in natural languages. But while the relation between natural language syntax and logical form deserves extended discussion (see e.g. n. 10 in Ch. 1), I think we can set these issues aside for present purposes.

in Schiffer's (1992) example). Fido's owner hired a dog-walker, who is better with animals than names. So 'Fido' and 'Rex' are presumably co-referential. But intuitively, (1) is true, while

(2) Nora believes that Rex barked

is false. In short, compositionality seems to imply substitutivity, which appears to be false.

Many reponses to this puzzle, including Frege's, retain the idea that substitution of co-referential terms (even inside 'that'-clauses) always preserves truth. I think this is a mistake. Compositionality does not imply substitutivity. Once we are clear about *why* this is so, there is little reason for the manœuvring required, in order to deny that (1–2) present a counter-example to the substitutivity principle above.[2] But before defending this view, let me be clear about which aspects of Frege's view I accept.

1.2

I endorse the following Fregean thesis:

> (FT$_1$) A sentence of the form 'N believes that P' is true (relative to context C) iff N believes the thought expressed by 'P' (relative to C)

where the thought expressed by a sentence Σ is the sense of Σ, which is determined by the senses of Σ's constituents, given Σ's logical form. (Later, I suggest that a thought *is* the relevant organization of subsentential senses.) On this view, (1) is true iff Nora believes the thought expressed by

(3) Fido barked.

Similarly, (2) is true iff Nora believes the thought expressed by

(4) Rex barked.

Co-referring names differ in sense if they are associated with different ways of thinking about the same thing, e.g. thinking about something as the evening dog, versus thinking about it as the morning dog. So (3) and (4) can express distinct thoughts, each of which is partly determined by a particular way of thinking about a certain dog. So if Nora can believe exactly one of these thoughts, it follows from (FT$_1$) that (1) and (2) have

---

[2] I consider various attempts to preserve substitutivity below. Schiffer (1992) considers denying compositionality. But methodologically, I see no alternative to assuming that natural languages are compositional. So far, this attitude has been productive. And the alternative is to replace the puzzle described in the text with another: how do we understand sentences of the form 'N believes that P'; and why does the meaning of 'N believes/ hopes/etc. that P' seem to depend on the meanings of its parts?

different truth conditions. And it is independently plausible that 'Fido' and 'Rex' differ in a way that matters to the thoughts expressed by sentences in which these names appear. Intuitively, 'Fido is Rex' expresses a non-trivial thought that differs from the trivial thought expressed by 'Fido is Fido'; one can use the former claim to convey that two ways of thinking about something are ways of thinking about the same thing.

So far, this is a plausible diagnosis of the phenomenon: (1) and (2) have different truth conditions, because (3) and (4) express different thoughts; and the difference between these thoughts is grounded in the different ways that a subject might think about a certain dog. Of course, one wants to hear more about senses and their individuation. Frege tells us that 'P' and 'Q' express distinct thoughts if a thinker could (without irrationality) believe that P yet not believe that Q. In the appendix, I try to say something a bit more substantive. But for now, we can work with an intuitive suggestion that Evans (1982) develops: whenever one thinks of something, one thinks of it in some way or other; different thinkers often think about the same thing in a same way; and a thinker can think about one thing in different ways (without realizing that she is thinking about a single thing in different ways).

While (FT$_1$) is attractive, though, it is not obviously compatible with other Fregean theses:

—each semantically significant expression is associated (perhaps relative to a context C) with some value, an entity that Frege called the expression's *Bedeutung*;

—the *Bedeutung* of a matrix sentence (a sentence not embedded in another) is its truth-value;

—the *Bedeutung* of any complex expression is determined, given its logical form, by the *Bedeutungen* of the expression's constituents.

Earlier, I translated '*Bedeutung*' as 'semantic value'; one might also use 'valuation'. But henceforth I simply use '*Bedeutung*' as a technical term characterized by the claims above, all of which I endorse.

As Evans (1982: 8) says, it is 'natural to think of each significant expression as having . . . a *semantic power*'. Frege proposes that an expression's semantic power is its power to affect the truth of sentences in which the expression appears. This is what it means to say that the *Bedeutung* of a matrix sentence is its truth-value. As Dummett (1973) says, Frege also uses the name–bearer relation as the prototype for the expression–*Bedeutung* relation. But Frege is not merely stipulating (or taking it to be intuitively obvious) that co-referential names have the same semantic power. His characterization of semantic power was theoretically fruitful. And if the *Bedeutung* of a matrix sentence is its truth-value, there is an independent reason for saying that names for the same object share a *Bedeutung*.

Inferences like

(3) Fido barked; therefore, (4) Rex barked

preserve truth. This would be mysterious if co-referential names had different semantic powers. But if co-referential expressions share a *Bedeutung*, compositionality explains why substituting such expressions typically preserves truth. For just this reason, though, it is hard to see how

(1) Nora believes that Fido barked

can ever differ in truth-value from

(2) Nora believes that Rex barked.

If 'Fido' and 'Rex' share a *Bedeutung* in (1) and (2), compositionality is in tension with the intuition that the inference from (1) to (2) is not truth-preserving. The tension becomes an outright paradox, given two apparently innocuous claims: (1) and (2) have the same logical form; and with the possible exception of 'Fido'/'Rex', each word in (1) has the *Bedeutung* of the corresponding word in (2). Frege concludes that 'Fido' and 'Rex' have the same *Bedeutung* in (3) and (4), but not in (1) and (2).

If 'Fido' and 'Rex' share a *Bedeutung* in (3-4), but not in (1-2), then a name must shift its *Bedeutung* in 'that'-clauses. Frege thus holds that an expression's *Bedeutung* depends on the context of use, and not just in the way that the referent of an indexical like 'me' depends on the context. An expression's syntactic position—in particular, whether or not it appears in a 'that'-clause—is said to be part of the expression's context of use.[3] So the *Bedeutung* of 'Fido' in (1) can differ from the *Bedeutung* of 'Fido' in (3), holding the extralinguistic context fixed; similarly for 'Rex' in (2) and (4).

This abandons what Davidson (1968) calls semantic innocence: the idea that an expression has the same semantic power across syntactic contexts. An innocent theory would always assign the same *Bedeutung* to names for the same dog. But it can seem that Fregeans *must* abandon innocence. Given

(FT₁) A sentence of the form 'N believes that P' is true (relative to context C) iff N believes the thought expressed by 'P' (relative to C),

the truth conditional contribution of an embedded sentence—i.e. its power to affect the truth of matrix sentences—resides in the thought expressed by the embedded sentence. Frege thus takes the *Bedeutung* of an embedded sentence to be its customary sense. On his view,

---

[3] Being in a 'that'-clause, not in the scope of certain verbs, seems to be what matters. Consider: 'The key point at the trial was that —— barked'.

(FT$_2$) 'N believes that P' is true (relative to context C) iff N believes
the *Bedeutung* of 'P' (relative to C, which will be a context in
which 'P' appears in a 'that'-clause).

This preserves compositionality: the *Bedeutung* of 'that P' is the (shifted)
Bedeutung of 'P'. And it coheres with Frege's construal of epistemic relations as relations to the senses of sentences. In

(1) Nora believes that Fido barked

the *Bedeutung* of 'Fido barked' is a sense, viz. the thought expressed by

(3) Fido barked.

But this violates semantic innocence, since the *Bedeutung* of (3) is a truth-
value.

Moreover, the *Bedeutung* of a complex expression is always determined,
given its logical form, by the *Bedeutungen* of its constituents. So the
Bedeutung of 'Fido' in (1) must partly determine the thought expressed by
(3), making the sense of 'Fido' in (3) the obvious candidate for the
Bedeutung of 'Fido' in (1). Similarly, the *Bedeutung* of 'Rex' in

(2) Nora believes that Rex barked

is said to be the sense (and not the *Bedeutung*) of 'Rex' in

(4) Rex barked.

The sense of 'Rex' in (4) differs from the sense of 'Fido' in (3). So replacing
'Fido' in (1) with 'Rex' is not a case of substituting words with the same
Bedeutung. Relativizing *Bedeutungen* to syntactic context thus lets Frege
preserve his semantic principles, by letting him preserve substitutivity in
the face of examples like (1–2).[4] Nonetheless, I reject (FT$_2$) and
substitutivity, in favour of semantic innocence. For the price of *Bedeutung*-
shifting is high.

1.3

A familiar worry concerns the interpretation of pronouns linked to
embedded terms. In

(5) Nora believes that Fido$_i$ barked, and he$_i$ did bark

---

[4] In a (logically proper) substitutional language that eschews *Bedeutung*-shifting, one
might render (1) and (2) as 'Believes{Nora, that(f*, b*)}' and 'Believes{Nora, that(r*,
b*)}'; where 'f*', 'r*' and 'b*' stand for the senses of 'Fido', 'Rex', and 'barked'—and 'that'
represents a function from (subsentential) senses to thoughts. No *single* term of such a language translates all uses of 'Fido' (see Burge 1979*b*).

the second conjunct is true, just when a certain dog barked. So if the *Bedeutung* of 'Fido$_i$' is a sense, one cannot simply identify the *Bedeutung* of 'he$_i$' with the *Bedeutung* of the co-indexed name. Similarly, Frege cannot allow that 'Nora' shares its *Bedeutung* with 'she' in

(6) Nora$_i$ believes that she$_i$ saw Rex.

Perhaps one can formulate more complicated rules that capture the relevant generalizations concerning the interpretation of pronouns, even given the possibility of *Bedeutung*-shifting. But the need for such complications can at least motivate a preference for semantic innocence.

Bedeutung-shifting also seems to require shifts in the semantic role of logical form. Suppose the only relevant aspect of logical form for 'Fido barked' is noun–verb concatenation. The *Bedeutung* of a matrix sentence is a truth-value. So ordinarily, the semantic contribution of matrix noun–verb concatenation is a function from the customary *Bedeutungen* of nouns and verbs to truth-values. Suppose that in

(1) Nora believes that Fido barked

the *Bedeutung* of 'Fido' is a thought. Then in (1), the *Bedeutung* of 'Fido barked' is a thought, and the contribution of concatenating 'Fido' and 'barked' is a function from senses of words to thoughts. Moreover, it is prima facie plausible that (a use of) 'Fido' is semantically associated with both a dog and some way of thinking about that dog. But there is little support for the claim that noun–verb concatenation is associated with two functions—one for ordinary contexts, another inside 'that'-clauses.[5]

These objections are magnified if the *Bedeutung* of 'Fido' in

(7) Olga believes that Nora believes that Fido barked

is a way of thinking about the *Bedeutung* of 'Fido' in (1). There is no independent reason to say that a name is associated with a way of thinking about a way of thinking about its bearer. And in the scope of *two*

---

[5] See Burge (1979*b*) for discussion. Note that given the event analysis, the *Bedeutung* of 'N-V' is not the value of the function that is the *Bedeutung* of 'V' given the *Bedeutung* of 'N' as argument. If 'bark' is true of events, or ways of thinking about events, talk of functions comes in precisely when we specify the semantic contribution of logical form. Higginbotham (1986) shows how to generalize Frege's strategy of syntactic relativization, so that the *Bedeutung* of expression E relative to its smallest sentential clause can differ from the *Bedeutung* of E relative to its matrix sentence. He argues that some non-opaque constructions (e.g. 'Every boy$_i$ fails unless he$_i$ studies') require such relativization anyway. But this is tendentious. Higginbotham also grants that his manœuvre weakens the traditional (more computationally tractable) notion of compositionality, and that such weakening should be exploited only when necessary. My point is that Fregeans need not resort to such weakening to account for opacity.

complementizers, the contribution of noun–verb concatenation would have to be a function from ways of thinking about ways of thinking about things (like dogs and barkers) to ways of thinking about thoughts. The worry iterates, given sentences like

> (8) Pat believes that Olga believes that Nora believes that Fido barked.

Of course, one can introduce 'Gottlob' as a name for the usual sense of 'Fido'. Then

> (9) Gottlob is a way of thinking about Fido

is true; and the sense of 'Gottlob' will be a way of thinking about a way of thinking about Fido. Let 'Bertrand' be a name for the sense of 'Gottlob' in (9), and so on (see Church 1951). But Gottlob and Bertrand can each exist without ever being a *Bedeutung* of 'Fido'. And there is no independent motivation for saying that Bertrand is a secondary (or indirect) sense of 'Fido'.

So if one appeals to *Bedeutung*-shifting, there is pressure to say that *Bedeutungen* (and the semantic contributions of logical form) shift only once: in the scope of one or more complementizers, an expression's *Bedeutung* is its sense; an expression never takes a way of thinking about its sense as its *Bedeutung* (see Dummett 1973: 268–9; Parsons 1981). But this has an unhappy consequence. Fregeans have no reason to deny—and Frege did not deny—that distinct terms of a language can have the same sense. (If 'snow' and the German word 'schnee' can share a sense, why not two words of English?) For illustration, suppose 'lawyer' and 'attorney' are such terms. Then (10–11) express the same thought:

> (10) Lawyers lie.   (11) Attorneys lie.

So on a Fregean view, (12–13) are true in the same circumstances, as are (14–15):

> (12) Nora believes that lawyers lie.
> (13) Nora believes that attorneys lie.
> (14) Nora believes that lawyers lie, if Nora believes that lawyers lie.
> (15) Nora believes that attorneys lie, if Nora believes that lawyers lie.

I take this result to be acceptable, although I will deny that (12–13) express the same thought. But intuitively, the following iterations (inspired by Mates (1950)) can differ in truth-value:

> (16) Olga never doubted that [Nora believes that lawyers lie if Nora believes that lawyers lie].

(17) Olga never doubted that [Nora believes that attorneys lie if Nora believes that lawyers lie].[6]

Yet if *Bedeutungen* shift only once: the sense of 'lawyers' in (10) is the *Bedeutung* of 'lawyers' in (16); and the sense of 'attorneys' in (11) is the *Bedeutung* of 'attorneys' in (17); so 'attorneys' in (17) has the same *Bedeutung* as 'lawyers' in (16); hence (16–17) cannot differ in truth-value.

It is tempting to bite this bullet, saying (with Soames (1987*b*)) that contrary intuitions reflect the fact that (16–17) differ in pragmatic appropriateness. But it is hard to see how Fregeans can say this, yet insist (*pace* Soames (1987*a*)) that 'Nora believes that Fido barked' can differ in truth-value from 'Nora believes that Rex barked.' Why not say these sentences differ only pragmatically? (I return to this question in Section 4.) So there is pressure on Fregeans to say that (17) can be false while (16) is true. And if distinct terms are never substitutable *salva veritate* in contexts like (16–17), one wants to know why this is so. In short, no amount of *Bedeutung*-shifting yields a satisfactory account of (16–17).

2. *Substitutivity and Context Sensitivity*

From this perspective, the task is to capture the initially attractive Fregean thesis

(FT₁) 'N believes that P' is true iff N believes the thought expressed by 'P'

without *Bedeutung*-shifting. And to reject *Bedeutung*-shifting is to reject

(FT₂) 'N believes that P' is true iff N believes the *Bedeutung* of 'P'.

Frege endorsed (FT₂), because he accepted substitutivity. But even setting propositional attitude ascriptions aside, there are reasons for thinking that natural languages violate substitutivity (without violating compositionality). This suggests a way of preserving (FT₁) without (FT₂).

---

[6] The intuition is less sharp with 'believes' as the matrix verb. But compare 'said', 'realized', 'argued', 'wondered (whether)', 'is certain', etc. It is tempting to say that (12–13) can differ in truth-value, even if (10–11) share a sense: if in *Nora's* idiolect, 'lawyers' and 'attorneys' differ in sense, she might assent to (10) yet dissent from (11). But if *we* associate the same sense with 'lawyers' and 'attorneys', (12–13) have the same truth conditions in *our* language: we ascribe the same thought to Nora with either sentence. If Nora interprets (11) differently from us, her dissent from (11) hardly shows that (13) is false.

2.1

Quine (1953*b*) draws our attention to apparent failures of substitutivity like

> (18) Slim is so-called because he is thin.
> (19) Jim is so-called because he is thin.

Even if 'Jim' has the same *Bedeutung* as 'Slim', (19) can be false while (18) is true (see also Cartwright 1971). But this is no violation of compositionality if 'so-' has a *Bedeutung*, and the *Bedeutung* of 'so-' in each case depends on the phonetic (or orthographic) properties of the matrix subject. Or consider

> (20) Slim is called that when he visits his family (but not when he is at work).
> (21) Jim is called that when he visits his family (but not when he is at work).

In general, the effect of a term on the truth of its matrix sentence need not be wholly determined by the term's *Bedeutung*. For a term T can affect the truth of its matrix sentence in two ways: directly, by virtue of the fact that T has a certain *Bedeutung*; and indirectly, by virtue of the fact that the *Bedeutung* of another term in the sentence depends on features (besides the *Bedeutung*) of T. But the *Bedeutung* of a complex expression (relative to context C) can still be a function of the *Bedeutungen* of its constituents (relative to C), given the expression's logical form. Forbes (1990) speaks of 'logophors' to capture the idea of terms that have indirect semantic effects; see also Crimmins (1992).[7]

As I noted above, Frege takes the semantic power of an expression to be its power to affect the truth of matrix sentences in which the expression appears. But (18–21) suggest that if effects on truth include an expression's indirect effects—i.e. the effects on truth an expression has because it affects the *Bedeutung* of another expression—then terms with the same *Bedeutung* will not always have the same semantic power. On the other

---

[7] One might argue that (18–21) do not violate substitutivity. If (18) is used in a context where 'so-' is associated with a demonstration of 'Slim', one might insist on evaluating (19) relative to a context where 'so-' is associated with the very same act of demonstration. (The *Bedeutung* of 'so-' need not depend on a term in its own sentence. Consider: 'Slim is a nice guy. He is so-called because he is thin.') But on my view, 'that' is a kind of indexical whose *Bedeutung* is always established by the sentence it introduces. So I think 'that'-clauses are genuine counter-examples to substitutivity. In any case, (18–21) are counter-examples to the following principle: E1 (as uttered in context C1) and E2 (as uttered in a context C2 like C1, except that E2 was uttered instead of E1) have the same *Bedeutung* if they differ only in that some term T appears in E1 where T* appears in E2, and T* has (in C2) the same *Bedeutung* as T (in C1).

hand, if we understand semantic power as the power to affect truth-values directly, then substituting terms with the same semantic power will not always preserve truth. Either way, Frege's notion of substitutivity is violated.

Sentences like (18–21) bear an obvious affinity to examples involving quotation, like

(22) He is called 'Slim'   (24) Nora said, 'Slim is thin'
(23) He is called 'Jim'   (25) Nora said, 'Jim is thin'.

Replacing 'Slim' with 'Jim' can clearly fail to preserve truth. I return to this point. But for now consider an analogy to indirect discourse reports:

(26) Fido barked. Nora said so.
(27) Rex barked. Nora said so.

Suppose that in each case, the *Bedeutung* of 'so' is the sense of the first sentence. Then replacing 'Fido' with a co-referential term that differs in sense will affect the *Bedeutung* of 'so'. This will not affect the truth of the first sentence, but it might well affect the truth of the second. Or to mirror Davidson's (1968) analogy to parataxis, consider the demonstrative 'that' in

(28) Fido barked. Nora said that.
(29) Rex barked. Nora said that.

If the *Bedeutung* of 'that' is the sense of the previous sentence, it will differ in each case.

No single sentence in (26–9) is such that replacing co-referential terms in *it* affects *its* truth-value. So one might try to handle all apparent failures of substitutivity with paratactic analyses, given which, the substitution does not occur in a sentence that includes the term whose *Bedeutung* is affected by the substitution. I will not argue against this strategy here. (In Section 2.3, I mention one problem; Seymour (1994) and Stainton (1998) review others.) Such drastic hypotheses about the logical forms of (1–2, 18–25) are unneeded. If the *Bedeutung* of one term can depend on features of another, substitutivity can *fail* even given compositionality. Prima facie, 'that' is a complementizer (not a demonstrative) in

(30) Nora said that Fido barked.
(1) Nora believes that Fido barked,

where 'Fido' is a constituent of the sentence whose subject is 'Nora'. And Fregeans can retain this *syntactic* innocence while saying that the *Bedeutung* of a complementizer is a thought.

2.2

Let me introduce a simple hypothesis that will need modification, but which illustrates my central claim that Fregeans can usefully exploit the gap between compositionality and substitutivity. Suppose the *Bedeutung* of the complementizer 'that' in (1) is the sense of its embedded sentence. Then the *Bedeutung* of 'that' in (1) will be the thought expressed by

(3) Fido barked.

Similarly, the *Bedeutung* of 'that' in

(2) Nora believes that Rex barked

will be the thought expressed by

(4) Rex barked.

If the *Bedeutung* of 'that P' (relative to context C) is the *Bedeutung* of 'that' (relative to C), the *Bedeutungen* of 'that Fido barked' and 'that Rex barked' are, respectively, the senses of (3) and (4).

On this view, 'that'-clauses serve as devices for referring to thoughts. So (1) and (2) have different truth conditions, given that 'N believes that P' is true just when N believes the *Bedeutung* of 'that P'. The main idea is simple: replacing 'Fido' in (1) with a co-referential term that differs in sense affects the *Bedeutung* of 'that'; and such replacement can affect the truth of the matrix sentence without affecting the truth of the embedded sentence. This view preserves

(FT$_1$) 'N believes that P' is true iff N believes the thought expressed by 'P'.

But it rejects the thesis that leads to *Bedeutung*-shifting, namely,

(FT$_2$) 'N believes that P' is true iff N believes the *Bedeutung* of 'P'.

For the *Bedeutung* of 'that P' is the *Bedeutung* of 'that' (not the *Bedeutung* of 'P'), and the *Bedeutung* of 'that' is the sense (not the *Bedeutung*) of 'P'. The *Bedeutung* of a sentence is a truth-value, even when embedded. So embedded names need not have senses as *Bedeutungen*. Sentences (1) and (2) can differ in truth-value, while 'Fido' and 'Rex' co-refer, since terms can have indirect effects on the truth of matrix sentences. The effect of 'P' on the truth of 'N believes that P' depends on the sense of 'P'; but if 'P' has an indirect effect on the truth of its matrix sentence, the *Bedeutung* of 'P' need not be its sense.

Assigning *Bedeutungen* to complementizers can seem odd. But on Frege's own view, complementizers have a semantic power: they affect the *Bedeutungen* of embedded terms (and the semantic contribution of embedded syntax). And it should be no surprise if the *Bedeutung* of a complementizer phrase depends on the *Bedeutung* of its complementizer. One might worry about letting a syntactically primitive term take the sense of a sentence as its *Bedeutung*. But recall

(9) Gottlob is a way of thinking about Fido

in which 'Gottlob' is a name for the sense of a word. Now consider:

(31) The sense of 'Fido barked' is a fine thought, and Nora believes it.

Given that there *are* Fregean thoughts, the sense of 'Fido barked' can be the *Bedeutung* of the syntactically primitive term 'it' in (31). And the present proposal is that a complementizer functions semantically as an indexical, in that its *Bedeutung* is a contextually determined sense.

Since there is no *Bedeutung*-shifting, one can adopt the simple view that in

(5) Nora believes that Fido$_i$ barked, and he$_i$ did bark

the *Bedeutung* of 'he$_i$' just is the *Bedeutung* of 'Fido$_i$', which is the dog Fido; and similarly for other examples involving the interpretation of pronouns. The treatment of

(7) Olga believes that Nora believes that Fido barked

is straightforward. The *Bedeutung* of the matrix 'that'-clause is the *Bedeutung* of the matrix complementizer. And the *Bedeutung* of the matrix complementizer in (7) is the sense of

(1) Nora believes that Fido barked.

So (7) is true iff Olga believes the sense of (1). The *Bedeutung* of 'that' in (1) is the sense of

(2) Fido barked.

And the sense of 'Fido' partly determines the sense of (2). The *sense* of 'that' in (1) is thus a way of thinking about a thought partly determined by the sense of 'Fido'. So the sense of (1), which is the *Bedeutung* of the matrix complementizer in (7), is partly determined by a way of thinking about the sense of 'Fido'. But 'Fido' has a single sense, and 'Fido' never takes a sense as its *Bedeutung*. The iterated ascription (7) provides distinct terms—viz. the matrix and embedded complementizers—that take as *Bedeutungen* the senses of (1) and (2), respectively.

Turning to Mates-sentences, if (10–11) share a sense, (12–13) share their truth conditions.

(10) Lawyers lie   (12) Nora believes that lawyers lie
(11) Attorneys lie   (13) Nora believes that attorneys lie.

On the present proposal, the *Bedeutung* of a complementizer is the thought expressed by the embedded sentence. That is, one refers to a thought by using a complementizer. So in (12–13), 'that' has the same *Bedeutung*. And the *Bedeutung* of each embedded complementizer in

(16) Olga never doubted that [Nora believes that lawyers lie if Nora believes that lawyers lie].

(17) Olga never doubted that [Nora believes that attorneys lie if Nora believes that lawyers lie].

is the shared sense of (10–11). But if the *sense* of the second occurrence of 'that' in (16) differs from the *sense* of the second occurrence of 'that' in (17), (16–17) have different truth conditions.

   On a Fregean view, whenever one refers to something, one thinks about it in some way. Intuitively, if one refers to a thought Θ by using a complementizer, one thinks about Θ *as the thought expressed by* the relevant embedded sentence. The complementizer in 'that lawyers lie' thus presents a certain thought *as* the thought expressed by 'lawyers lie'; the complementizer in 'that attorneys lie' presents the same thought *as* the sense of 'attorneys lie'. If these are different ways of presenting the same thought, the second occurrences of 'that' in (16) and (17) differ in sense, in which case the bracketed expressions differ in sense. If the bracketed expressions differ in sense, the matrix complementizers in (16) and (17) have different *Bedeutungen*. So (16) can be true while (17) is false. Olga may have been unsure about whether the thought expressed by the bracketed expression in (17) is true, without ever doubting that the thought expressed by bracketed expression in (16) is true.

2.3

It is crucial to this view that an expression whose *Bedeutung* depends on the context can have different senses in different contexts. So as Burge (1986, 1990) notes, an expression's sense must be distinguished from its conventional meaning—or character, to use Kaplan's (1989) term. The character of the demonstrative 'that' is given by some rule like: 'That is Φ' is true, relative to context C, just when the object demonstrated in C satisfies 'is Φ'. Such a rule determines a context insensitive mapping from contexts to *Bedeutungen*; so the character of the demonstrative will remain the same across contexts. But two uses of

(32) That is a lawyer

can express different senses, even if the *Bedeutung* of the demonstrative is the same each time. Suppose Nora accepts (32) as uttered in a courtroom, with the speaker pointing at the back of a (well-dressed) man who has approached the bench; but Nora later dissents from (32) as uttered outside the courtroom, with the speaker pointing to the same (now ill-dressed) member of the bar. The corresponding uses of

(33) Nora believes that that is a lawyer

differ in truth-value, on a Fregean view, because the demonstrative has different senses on the two occasions of use. Taking this to be a legitimate Fregean position, I see no reason to deny that in

(12) Nora believes that lawyers lie.
(13) Nora believes that attorneys lie.

the complementizers differ in sense, while sharing a *Bedeutung*. So (12–13) express different thoughts. In this respect, (12–13) is like the pair 'Fido barked'/'Rex barked': for Fregeans, sentences can express different thoughts yet be true in the same circumstances.

Still, things are not ideal. Let Θ be the thought expressed by 'lawyers lie' and by 'attorneys lie'. On the present view, Θ is the *Bedeutung* of each embedded complementizer in

(16) Olga never doubted that [Nora believes that lawyers lie if Nora believes that lawyers lie].
(17) Olga never doubted that [Nora believes that attorneys lie if Nora believes that lawyers lie].

The account of why (17) can be false, while (16) is true, trades on the claim that thinking of Θ *as* the sense of 'lawyers lie' differs from thinking of Θ *as* the sense of 'attorneys lie'. But one wants to know why (and how) the first way of thinking about Θ differs from the second, and why this matters (if 'lawyers' and 'attorneys' share a sense). And one wants a semantic theory to *show* why distinct terms are never substitutable *salva veritate* in contexts like (16–17).

Moreover, while a demonstrative can be used to refer to another expression in the sentence or to some thought, these are just manifestations of the fact that a demonstrative can be used to refer to anything in the context at hand. But the 'that' of a 'that'-clause cannot be used to refer to just anything. The present account accommodates this, by effectively treating complementizers as indexicals (or 'dedicated' demonstratives): they must refer to the senses of their embedded sentences. But the disanalogy between complementizers and demonstratives is deeper. Consider

(34) Every lawyer$_i$ believes that he$_i$ lies.

Paratactic theorists deny that the variable 'he$_i$' is a constituent of a sentence that includes 'Every lawyer$_i$', making it hard to see how the former can be bound by the latter.[8] The present account fares better. Allowing for counter-examples to substitutivity (in natural languages) preserves semantic innocence *and* the claim that embedded terms are parts of the same sentence as matrix subjects. But there is still no single sense of 'he$_i$ lies' for the complementizer 'that' in (34) to take as its *Bedeutung*.

3. A Role for Linguistic Forms

Instead of taking the *Bedeutung* of 'that' in 'that P' to be the sense of 'P', suppose the *Bedeutung* of 'that' is the sentence 'P' itself. And suppose the *Bedeutung* of 'that P' is the sense of the (sentence that is the) *Bedeutung* of 'that'. On this view, 'that P' still serves as a device for referring to the sense of 'P'; and this result is still achieved without *Bedeutung*-shifting. Before showing how appeal to sentences helps, though, let me say how sentences are to be individuated for these purposes.

3.1

Intuitively, 'lawyers lie' and 'attorneys lie' are different sentences, because they *sound* different. Utterances that sound the same can also be utterances of distinct sentences. The sound of 'small dogs and cats' can be paired with two syntactic structures: [[small dogs] and [cats]], or [small [dogs and cats]]. So the sound of 'Nora hates small dogs and cats' is associated with two different sentences. The sound of 'bank' is associated with several words: 'bank$_1$', 'bank$_2$', etc. So the sound of 'Nora went to the bank' is also homophonous; and similarly for 'The doctor lost her patients/patience.'

This says nothing about the interpretation of sentences. And one might identify the *Bedeutung* of 'that' in 'that P' with the sentence 'P', where sentences are individuated non-semantically. The *Bedeutung* of a complementizer would then be a purely formal object—a structuring of lexical elements; and the *Bedeutung* of 'that P' (relative to context C) would be specified as *the sense associated* (relative to C) with the non-semantically

---

[8] Or consider 'Every lawyer$_i$ explained why she$_i$ defended Smith without preparation', which has a reading where 'without preparation' modifies the explaining. So on a paratactic theory, constituents of the same sentence as 'explained' can appear after expressions that are not constituents of that sentence. And note: 'N explained that P' differs in meaning from 'N explained that', where 'that' is used to demonstrate (the thought expressed by) 'p'; see Pietroski (forthcoming *b*) for discussion.

individuated sentence 'P'. This may be acceptable. But it seems to make context do all the work, suggesting that a 'that'-clause acquires its *Bedeutung* in the manner of a demonstrative (as opposed to a syntactically structured clause). Fregeans can avoid this appearance, and make it clear why the *Bedeutung* of 'that P' is the very sense expressed by 'P', by taking the *Bedeutung* of a complementizer to be the *interpreted linguistic form* of its (sentential) complement. This will be a purely formal object coupled with an interpretation of it; where the Fregean interpretation of a linguistic form (relative to context C) is its sense (relative to C). If the sense of an embedded sentence is part of what individuates the *Bedeutung* of its complementizer, then complementizers will have different *Bedeutungen* whenever their embedded sentences differ in sense.

Let me make this suggestion more precise, by taking a linguistic form to be a phrase marker whose terminal nodes are lexical items. A phrase marker is a suitably labelled *tree*: a partial ordering of points, such that the resulting structure has a unique root; where each point—i.e. each node of the tree—is labelled as a token of some syntactic type in accordance with a correct theory of syntax for the language in question (see Higginbotham 1986). At least for present purposes, a lexical item is an n-tuple of features, including a phonetic form (or perhaps a feature that corresponds to a phonetic form) and a point labelled as a terminal phrase-marker node. How much information is lexicalized is an empirical question. But verbs have subcategorization features relevant to the shape of phrase markers, e.g. 'barked' takes a single noun–phrase argument as its subject, while 'likes' takes noun-phrases as subject and object. Ignoring many syntactic details that are not relevant here, the linguistic forms of 'Fido barked' and 'Rex barked' can thus be represented as shown in Figure 2.1.

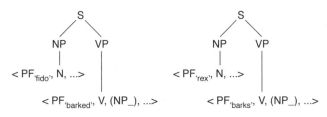

FIG. 2.1

We obtain a Fregean interpretation of a linguistic form, by replacing each terminal node with the sense of that lexical item, and each non-terminal node with the sense of that expression (which will be determined by the senses of its constituents, given its logical form). The result is the sense of a sentence, perhaps relative to a context of use. For 'Fido barked' and 'Rex barked', we get

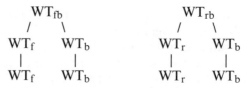

Here the various nodes are *ways of thinking about*: the common truth-value of the two sentences, the dog Fido/Rex, and the barkings. Thus $WT_{fb} \neq WT_{rb}$, because $WT_f \neq WT_r$.[9]

On the view I am urging, the *Bedeutung* of 'that' in

(1) Nora believes that Fido barked

is the interpreted linguistic form of 'Fido barked'. An interpreted linguistic form is the pairing of a linguistic form with a sense. So the *Bedeutung* of 'that' in (1) is the ordered pair shown in Figure 2.2. And the *Bedeutung* of 'that Fido barked' is the second element of this pair (not the entire interpreted linguistic form). This captures an attractive idea: a 'that'-clause abstracts away from many linguistic features of the embedded sentence, leaving the sense expressed. Thus, a German 'that'-clause ('daß'-clause) can share a *Bedeutung* with an English 'that'-clause. Similarly, the *Bedeutung* of 'that' in

FIG. 2.2

(2) Nora believes that Rex barked

is the interpreted linguistic form of 'Rex barked', which is the ordered pair shown in Figure 2.3. The second element of this pair is the *Bedeutung* of 'that Rex barked', which differs from the *Bedeutung* of 'that Fido barked'. But 'Fido' and 'Rex' share a *Bedeutung*, even in 'that'-clauses. Substitutivity fails, because replacing 'Fido' with 'Rex' affects the *Bedeutung* of 'that', and hence the 'that'-clause.

---

[9] I assume that x satisfies 'barked' iff x is an event of barking. (I continue to ignore tense for simplicity.) The sense of 'Fido barked' is thus a *Fido-as-Agent-of-a-barking* way of thinking about a truth-value. I develop this idea (of senses as eventish ways of thinking about truth-values) in Ch. 3. For now, it can be regarded as a way of stating an implication of the Fregean claim that the sense of any expression is a way of thinking about its *Bedeutung* (given that the *Bedeutung* of a sentence is its truth-value). Other theorists (e.g. Larson and Ludlow 1993) have appealed to pairings of linguistic forms with interpretations obtained by replacing nodes with *Bedeutungen*. I discuss this alternative in Sect. 4 below.

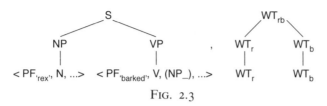

FIG. 2.3

3.2

The proposal of Section 2 has been altered in just one respect: the *Bedeutung* of a complementizer includes specifically linguistic features (in addition to the sense) of the embedded sentence. Often, this will make no difference. But the added complexity pays off.

It will be useful to use so-called quote-names as devices for referring to the relevant interpreted linguistic forms. I suggest below that this convention offers a plausible semantics of quotation. But for now, let me stipulate that 'Fido barked' is an ordered pair, whose first element is a linguistic form and whose second element is a Fregean sense. If Θ is the sense of 'Fido barked', then Θ is the second element of the ordered pair that *is* 'Fido barked'. If 'lawyers lie' and 'attorneys lie' share a sense, then these ordered pairs share a second element. If two uses of 'That is a lawyer' differ in sense, then relative to context C_1, 'That is a lawyer' is $<LF, \Theta_1>$, where LF is a linguistic form; but relative to context C_2, 'That is a lawyer' is $<LF, \Theta_2>$, where $\Theta_1 \neq \Theta_2$.

Recall that the proposal of Section 2 left one wondering why 'that P' and 'that Q' always differ in *sense*, whenever the embedded sentences differ in any respect. This was relevant to why

(16) Olga never doubted that [Nora believes *that* lawyers lie if Nora believes that lawyers lie]

(17) Olga never doubted that [Nora believes *that* attorneys lie if Nora believes that lawyers lie]

have different truth conditions. If (17) can be false while (16) is true, the bracketed expressions must differ in sense; so given the compositionality of sense, the italicized complementizers must differ in sense. Appeal to interpreted linguistic forms lets one give a semantic theory that shows why introducing 'attorneys lie' as opposed to 'lawyers lie' affects the sense of 'that'.

While 'lawyers lie' and 'attorneys lie' share a sense, they differ in linguistic form; they have different lexical features. Let x and y be the linguistic forms of (i.e. the first elements of) 'lawyers lie' and 'attorneys lie', respectively; let $ is their shared sense. Thinking about $ as the sense paired with x differs from thinking about $ as the sense paired with y.

Moreover, the italicized complementizers in (16–17) have different *Bedeutungen* : <x, $> and <y, $>, respectively. If the italicized term in (16) has a different *Bedeutung* from the corresponding term in (17), these terms must also have different senses. For I assume that sense determines *Bedeutung*, at least relative to a context.[10]

The difference between (16) and (17) is thus due to the differing contexts in which the italicized complementizer is used: it introduces 'lawyers lie' in (16), and 'attorneys lie' in (17). (The proposal has always been that the sense and the *Bedeutung* of a complementizer depend on the context of use.) In general, 'that P' will differ in sense from 'that Q' relative to context C, just when 'P' and 'Q' are distinct interpreted linguistic forms relative to C. For if 'P' is distinct from 'Q', then the *Bedeutung* of 'that' in 'that P' differs from the *Bedeutung* of 'that' in 'that Q'—and hence, the two complementizers must also differ in sense. For this reason, 'N believes that P' can differ in sense from 'N believes that Q', even if 'P' and 'Q' share a sense. In particular,

(12) Nora believes that lawyers lie
(13) Nora believes that attorneys lie

differ in sense, as do the bracketed expressions in (16–17). Thus, the matrix 'that'-clauses in (16–17) have different *Bedeutungen*. For the *Bedeutung* of 'that P' is the sense of 'P'.

This bears on whether the inference from (12) to (13) is valid. If the *Bedeutung* of a complementizer were simply the sense of its embedded sentence, such an inference would be like 'Nora saw that, so Nora saw that', where the *Bedeutungen* of the demonstratives are (perhaps known to be) the same. But the current proposal suggests a different analogy, since the complementizers in (12–13) have different *Bedeutungen*: 'Nora saw his$_i$ mother, so Nora saw his$_j$ mother' where the *Bedeutung* of 'his' is different in each case, but the mothers are (perhaps known to be) the same. In (12–13), the same sense is associated with distinct linguistic forms. By analogy, the same mother might be associated with two individuals; the referents of 'his' might be brothers. But 'Nora met his$_i$ mother, so Nora met his$_j$ mother' does not strike me as a valid inference, even it is known that he$_i$ is his$_j$ brother though in some sense the inference preserves truth. (I return to issues of validity in Section 4.)

The current proposal also yields an attractive treatment of quantified constructions like

---

[10] That is, the sense–*Bedeutung* relation is a many-to-one. Like Evans (1982), I take senses to be partly individuated by their *Bedeutungen*. (I do not identify senses with verificationist rules for establishing *Bedeutungen*.) If β is the *Bedeutung* of E, then to give E's sense is to say how some subject thinks of β; and two subjects think about β in the same way, only if they both think about β.

(34) Every lawyer$_i$ believes that he$_i$ lies.

Fregeans will say (34) is true, just when each lawyer i believes a thought whose predicative component is the sense of 'lies' and whose other component is a way of thinking about i. But there is no specific way that each lawyer must think of himself; (34) can be true in a scenario where only some lawyers think of themselves in a distinctly first-personal way. So let the Fregean interpretation of the variable 'he$_i$' be a function **F** that maps each possible assignment i onto a class of ways of thinking about i. That is, let the sense of 'he$_i$' map each lawyer onto a class of ways of thinking about that lawyer. Given the sense of 'lies', **F** determines a function **G** that maps possible assignments to i onto classes of thoughts:

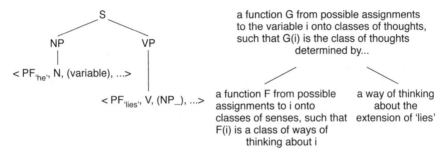

FIG. 2.4

The *Bedeutung* of 'that P' is the interpretation of 'P'. So given a value for i, 'that he$_i$ lies' will be true of *various* thoughts composed of the sense of 'lies' and a way of thinking about i. And we can say that x satisfies 'believes that P' iff x believes at least one of these thoughts. When the embedded sentence contains no variable, the *Bedeutung* of 'that P' will be a single thought. But (34) is true just when each lawyer i believes a thought composed of the sense of 'lies' and some way of thinking about i.[11]

Appealing to interpreted linguistic forms also suggests a way of unifying the semantics of propositional attitude ascriptions and quotational constructions, which also exhibit failures of substitutivity. I will just briefly mention the main idea, developed in a little more detail elsewhere (Pietroski 1996, 1998*b*): quote-marks are a kind of complementizer and

---

[11] Letting 'e' range over events and states (see Ch. 3), 'N believes that P' is true iff: $\exists e\{\text{Agent}(e, N) \& \text{Believing}(e) \& \exists y[\text{Content}(e, y) \& y \in Bedeutung(\text{'that P'})]\}$. Forbes's (1987) treatment of other quantified constructions is designed to accommodate *Bedeutung*-shifting. But it can be adapted to the present account. See also Forbes (1990). If one finds the proposed truth conditions for (34) too liberal, one can impose restrictions on the relevant functions. See Pietroski and Hornstein (MS) for discussion of so-called *de re* readings of propositional attitude ascriptions.

the *Bedeutung* of " 'P' " is 'P' itself. I assumed that the underlying structure of 'N believes that . . .' is: [s N [vp believes [cp that [s . . .]]]]. So suppose that, similarly, the underlying structure of (35–6) is roughly as indicated in (35Q–6Q):

> (35) Nora said, 'Fido barked'
> (35Q) [s Nora [vp said [cp quote [s Fido barked]]]]
> (36) Nora said, 'Rex barked'
> (36Q) [s Nora [vp said [cp quote [s Rex barked]]]].

If the *Bedeutung* of (the complementizer) 'quote' is the interpreted linguistic form of the sentence it introduces, and the *Bedeutung* of (the complementizer phrase) 'quote P' is the *Bedeutung* of 'quote', then 'quote P' is a device for referring to 'P', while 'that P' is as a device for referring to the sense of 'P'. This captures the idea that 'quote'-clauses do not abstract away from lexical features of embedded terms; the *Bedeutungen* of the quote-clauses in (35–6) are, respectively, 'Fido barked' and 'Rex barked'. Again, if the *Bedeutung* of a complementizer depends on features (other than the *Bedeutungen*) of the words in its scope, then substituting 'Rex' for 'Fido' in (35) can affect the *Bedeutung* of the complementizer. So (35) can be true while (36) is false, without violating semantic innocence.[12]

3.3

Let me conclude this section by addressing some potential objections. One might think true belief ascriptions are rare if ascribers and ascribees must

---

[12] Many languages use overt complementizers in both indirect and direct discourse reports. Consider an example from Korean (complementizers italicized, case markers ignored), provided by Kwang-Soup Kim:

John-um Bob-i chemchay-*lako*	John-um Bob-i chemchay-ya-*laka*
malhayssta	malhayssta
John said that Bob is a genius	John said, 'Bob is a genius'.

The essays in Coulmas (1986) provide similar data from a wide variety of languages. Perhaps there is also a *formal* version of quotation, where the *Bedeutung* of the 'quote'-clause is the relevant *uninterpreted* linguistic form. But I think 'Nora yelled, 'Fire!'' would typically be false if Nora's exclamation meant what 'Help' means, even if it had the formal features of 'Fire' (cf. Cappelen and Lepore 1998*a*, *b*; see Pietroski 1998*b* for a reply). Note that the indirect complementizer 'that' must be followed by a sentence, however, while any part of speech can be quoted. Moreover, terms embedded in direct discourse reports must often be understood as though uttered by somone other than the reporter (cf. 'Nora said that I am tall' and 'Nora said, "I am tall" '). And Munro (1982) also offers evidence suggesting that direct discourse reports are less transitive, and more adverbial, than indirect reports. Perhaps (35) is true iff Nora was the Agent of a saying done in a 'Fido barked' manner, where a saying is done in a 'Fido barked' manner if it is done by using 'Fido barked'.

think of things in the *same* way. But we often use loose standards for what counts as the same. Suppose

(37) Nora's dog is the same size as Olga's dog

counts as true in most contexts. Still, when precise measurements matter, (37) may count as false. Similar considerations will be relevant to whether Nora and a belief ascriber count as thinking about Fido in the *same* way. Moreover, someone who often thinks of x in a way that is unavailable to others may be able to think of x in ways that are available to others. (Consider the many ways in which one thinks of oneself, one's spouse, one's job, etc.) And one can believe a thought partly constituted by a way of thinking about x, even if one does not ordinarily think of x in that way. Let B(W1) be a thought composed of the sense of 'barked' and Nora's usual way of thinking about Fido. Suppose Nora believes B(W1), but also B(W2), where W2 is some reporter's usual way of thinking about Fido. (Perhaps W1 is unavailable to the reporter.) In this situation, the reporter's utterance of 'Nora believes that Fido barked' is still true. If only for this reason, I do not identify the sense a thinker associates with term T as the thinker's 'total conception' of T's *Bedeutung*. (If such identification is required by verificationist construals of senses, so much the worse for these construals.) But in any case, it seems clear that a thinker can think of x in various ways, holding her total conception of x constant.[13]

Another worry concerns ascriptions like 'Nora believes Fido barked', where 'that' is absent. The obvious response is that an unvoiced complementizer is present at logical form. This is tendentious when the embedded verb is untensed, as in 'Sam believes Fido to be a barker.' But given Chomsky's (1995) treatment of such constructions, the verb phrase is

---

[13] See Frege (1918). I treat Kripke's (1979) related puzzle separately, in Sect. 4 below; but since he often trades on the Cicero/Tully example, let me note here that there may be various explanations of cases in which 'Cicero is F' and 'Tully is F' express different thoughts. We can think of famous people *as the bearers* of famous names. Moreover, the context of ascription may let an ascriber associate different senses with 'Cicero' and 'Tully'; for the context will include the way(s) in which the ascribee is thinking about Cicero. And as Burge (1986) notes, a sense need not enable a thinker to distinguish a *Bedeutung* from all other entities *in abstraction from the context*. See Owens (1995) for discussion of related points. If the reporter is to *convey* which thought is being ascribed to Nora, the *listener* must be able to figure out (in the context) how the reporter is thinking of Fido; though often practical demands of communciation may be satisfied by conveying that Nora believes some thought constituted by the sense of 'barked' and *some* way of thinking about Fido. In particular, experts must take care not to ascribe overly sophisticated thoughts to others. Chemists may think of water in ways unavailable to non-chemists. But non-chemists presumably think about water in many ways available to chemists; see Sect. 2.3 above and Sect. 4.2 below. One might introduce a context-sensitive relation $\Re$ of *suitable similarity* between senses: 'N believes that P' is true just when N believes* a sense that bears $\Re$ to the sense of 'P', where 'believe*' is a technical term. But (following Segal 1989; Larson and Ludlow 1993), I would prefer to avoid this manœuvre.

plausibly analysed as: $[_{VP} [_V \ldots] [_{CP} [_C \varnothing] [_S \ldots]]]$; where '$\varnothing$' is unpronounced. And this proposal can be extended to 'Nora wants/tried to raise her hand': $[_{NP} Nora_i [_{VP} [_V \text{wants/tried}] [_{CP} [_C \varnothing] [_S e_i \text{ to raise her hand}]]]]$; where e_i is an unpronounced subject.[14]

Finally, I do not deny that arguments like the following are valid:

(P1)   it is true that Fido barked, and (P2) Fido is Rex; so (C) it is true that Rex barked.

Sometimes, substitutions of co-referential terms inside 'that'-clauses preserves truth. But this does not show that 'that Fido barked' and 'that Rex barked' have the same *Bedeutung* in the scope of 'it is true'.

For consider schema-T: it is true that p iff p. Given schema-T and (P1) above, it follows that

(3)   Fido barked.

Given (3) and (P2) above, it follows that

(4)   Rex barked.

The conclusion (C) follows, given (4) and schema-T. In Fregean terms: 'it is true that Fido barked' is true, just when the thought expressed by (3) is true; and if this thought is true, then a second thought like it *except that it involves a different way of thinking about the same dog* is also true.

4. Still a Role for Senses

In this final section, I compare my treatment of attitude ascriptions with two others. Developing proposals of Harman (1972), Higginbotham

---

[14] This is not to say that every complementizer has the same semantic effect; perhaps some (unvoiced) complementizers do not induce opacity. Nor do I deny that untensed embedded verbs introduce complications (Ormazabal (1995) for a review of syntactic facts that a semantics for 'want' and 'try' must accommodate). The overt subject 'Fido' may have to raise (to a case-marking position); and depending on how antecedents are related to traces, this may affect the truth conditions of the matrix clause. (But the data are not crystal clear: at least for some speakers, opacity intuitions wobble with respect to embedded subjects of untensed verbs.) A potentially related point is that co-referential substitution for 'Nick' preserves truth in 'Nora saw Nick laden with groceries', but not in 'Nora considered Nick a clever guy.' An event analysis treatment of perceptual verbs, as in Ch. 1, would explain the former fact; and to explain the latter, I would look for a hidden complementizer that introduces the (small clause) complement of 'consider'. Constructions like 'In her view, Fido is a menace' may be parasitic on others ('Her view is that Fido is a menace'). Or perhaps the relevant underlying (small clause) stucture is: $[_{SC} [_{CP} [_C \varnothing] [_S \text{Fido is a menace}]]$ in her view]; where this construction is true iff her view includes the thought expressed by the embedded sentence.

(1986, 1991), and Segal (1989), Larson and Ludlow (1993) offer a detailed semantics of 'that'-clauses based on appeals to the forms and interpretations of embedded sentences. But on their view, interpretations are composed of *Bedeutungen* (not senses). So a Fregean who appeals to linguistic forms and senses owes some reason for not adopting the more parsimonius account. Fregeans must also respond to those who eschew senses in favour of treating opacity as a pragmatic phenomenon. In later chapters, I appeal to senses in saying how explanation is related to causation and in saying what it is to have intentional states. If the resulting account is attractive, that is further reason to posit senses. Moreover, on the assumption that there are ways of thinking about things (and linguistic forms), Fregean thoughts are not *additional* theoretical entities. But my aim here is just to show that appealing to senses remains attractive within semantic theory.

4.1

Some theorists would claim that sentences like

    (1) Nora believes that Fido barked
    (2) Nora believes that Rex barked

must have the same truth conditions if 'Fido' and 'Rex' are names for the same dog. So let me say why I reject this view, even though it has been resourcefully defended.

    Salmon (1986) and Soames (1987*a*, 1987*b*, 1995) hold that pairs like (1–2) do not violate substitutivity. For they take the *Bedeutung* of 'that P' to be the Russellian proposition expressed by 'P': an abstract object composed of the *Bedeutungen* of the primitive expressions in 'P'. For these purposes, let the *Bedeutung* of an embedded verb be a property, and make the simplifying assumption that noun–verb concatenation is the only aspect of syntax relevant to the embedded sentences in (1–2). If **B** is the property of barking, and '∧|–|' stands for Fido/Rex, then according to Salmon and Soames the *Bedeutung* of 'that Fido barked' is the ordered pair < ∧|–|, **B** >; and this abstract object is also the *Bedeutung* of 'that Rex barked'. (The crucial claim is that 'Fido' and 'Rex' make the *same* contribution to the *Bedeutung* of 'that —— barked'.) Given compositionality, and assuming that the logical forms of (1–2) are as they appear to be, it follows that (1–2) have the same truth conditions.

    Theoretically, this is an attractive view. But the intuition that (1–2) have different truth conditions—that the inference from (1) to (2) is *not* licensed, even given that Fido is Rex—is as strong a linguistic intuition as one finds. So declaring that speakers are wrong about this is risky business: one wonders what intuitions can be trusted. Salmon and Soames have urged, however, that our intuitions about such cases reflect something other than truth-conditional differences. Salmon posits a ternary relation BEL that holds among thinkers, (Russellian) propositions, and modes of presenting propositions. The idea is that (1–2) suggest different modes, m1 and m2, of presenting $< \wedge\mdash, \mathbf{B} >$; it is possible that [BEL(Nora, $< \wedge\mdash$, $\mathbf{B} >$, m1) & ¬BEL(Nora, $< \wedge\mdash$, $\mathbf{B} >$, m2)]; and we slip from recognizing this possibility into saying that (1) can be true while (2) is false. But this concedes much to Fregeans, and one can avoid the additional complexity (and attribution of error to speakers). On my view, the *Bedeutung* of 'that' just is the mode of presentation Salmon appeals to anyway. So let me focus on Soames's more radical suggestion that our intuitions about (1–2) stem from a pragmatic constraint: it would be *misleading* to use (2), if Nora would assent to 'Fido barks' but dissent from 'Rex barks'.

Prima facie, the evidence is against this proposal. Consider:

> (38) Nick is certain that coriander is coriander
> (39) Nick is certain that coriander is cilantro.

Suppose Nick returns from the store saying, 'They had no coriander, but they had this', while handing over the cilantro. Then (38) seems trivial; but (39) seems clearly *false*, not just misleading. Similarly for

> (40) Nick knows a priori that [he thinks of coriander, when he thinks of coriander]
> (41) Nick knows a priori that [he thinks of coriander, when he thinks of cilantro].

Or replace 'knows a priori' with 'introspectively recognizes' (see Owens 1995). Moreover, suppose Nick learns that coriander is cilantro, and then becomes convinced (in a philosophy class) that: whenever he entertains the thought that coriander smells nice, he entertains the thought that cilantro smells nice. On Soames's view, Nick becomes convinced that: whenever he entertains the thought that coriander smells nice, he entertains the thought that coriander smells nice. But Nick doesn't *become* convinced of that.

If one holds that compositionality entails substitutivity, apart from quotational constructions, bullet-biting will seem unavoidable. But as I noted in Section 2, there are many counter-examples to substitutivity. There I focused on closed sentences, whereas direct reference theorists often focus on sentences with variables. But if a term *t* makes an indirect contribution to the truth of its matrix sentence S (i.e. if the *Bedeutung* of another expression in S depends on features of *t* other than its *Bedeutung*), and O is the result of replacing *t* in S with the variable x, then O is *not* satisfied (*à la* Tarski) by the sequence that assigns to x the semantic value of *t*. Consider

(42) If the first name in this sentence rhymes with the second, then Jim is taller than Tim

(43) If the first name in this sentence rhymes with the second, then x is taller than Tim.

Replacing 'Jim' with the co-referential 'James' in (42) does not preserve truth. And correspondingly, one cannot evaluate (43) by assigning *people* to the variable. For in (42), the contribution of 'Jim' is not exhausted by its *Bedeutung* (Jim/James); in (42), 'Jim' also serves to provide the phonetic form that figures in determining the proposition expressed by (42).[15] Similarly, to assume that one can evaluate

(44) x is Rex, and Nora believes it

by assigning objects like Fido to the variable is to *assume* that 'Fido' makes no indirect contribution to

(45) Fido is Rex, and Nora believes it.

Given this assumption, Nora believes that Fido is Rex if she believes that Fido is Fido; and the contribution of 'Fido' (to the *Bedeutung* of 'that —— barks') is its direct contribution to truth (i.e. its *Beduetung*). But this is no *argument* against Fregeans. The same point applies (*pace* Salmon 1986) to

(46) Nora believes that x barked
(1) Nora believes that Fido barked.

One is not entitled to assume that (46) is evaluable relative to assignments of dogs to x if it is plausible that in (1) 'Fido' makes an indirect contribution to the truth conditions of its matrix sentence. Correspondingly, Soames (1995) notes that

---

[15] Other examples abound. According to the OED, 'mot' (rhymes with 'dot') is a synonym for 'word'. Hence, substituting synonyms can fail to preserve truth: the third word/mot in this sentence rhymes with the second. Soames's own view guarantees counterexamples to substitutivity: if Fido is Fido/Rex, this conditional's antecedent has the pragmatic force of a tautology. Given that words have features besides their *Bedeutungen*, and that one can use expressions to refer to other expressions in the same sentence, one must be prepared for counter-examples to substitutivity. But *any* diagnosis of the relevant intuitions will trade on the first of these claims, and the second is a brute fact. Soames (1987: 104) effectively defines compositionality in terms of substitutivity (but in a footnote he allows that substitutivity can fail). And his remarks suggest that he might take the position mentioned in n. 7 above.) Perhaps it will be said that all such examples are quotational, in a broad sense of quotation that can apply to words that are used (and not mentioned). But propositional attitude ascriptions are arguably quotational in such a broad sense. So setting quotational constructions *aside* would be to evade the real issue. Moreover, since 'Fido' appears to be a lexical element in 'Nora said, "Fido barked" ', one owes an explanation for the apparent compositionality of such constructions where substitutivity clearly fails; see Davidson 1979.

(47) Fido is such that Nora believes that he barks
(48) Rex is such that Nora believes that he barks

can both be true. I grant that the *Bedeutung* of 'he' in (47–8) is the dog
Fido/Rex. But it does not follow that the semantic contribution of the pro-
noun is exhausted by its *Bedeutung*. In (47) the sense of 'he' is the sense of
'Fido'; in (48) the sense of 'he' is the sense of 'Rex'. The *Bedeutung* of 'that
P' is the sense of 'P'. So substituting 'Rex' for 'Fido' can affect the
Bedeutung of the 'that'-clause. Absent an argument against this Fregean
theory, we have no reason to abandon our strong pretheoretic intuitions
about (1–2).

4.2

For just these reasons, one might grant that the *Bedeutung* of a 'that'-
clause must be at least as finely grained as the embedded linguistic expression. But one might think that this renders appeal to senses otiose.
According to Larson and Ludlow (1993)—henceforth, L&L—

(1) Nora believes that Fido barked

is true iff Nora believes (what they call) the interpreted *logical* form of

(2) Fido barked.

I prefer to speak of interpreted *linguistic* forms, since I want to say that
(2) and

(4) Rex barked.

have the same logical form. For L&L, an expression's logical form includes
its lexical features. (So substitutions typically affect logical form.) But one
can bypass this terminological dispute, and speak of LFs, where by
hypothesis (2) and (4) have different LFs. The important point is that for
L&L, the interpretation of a logical/linguistic form is a tree whose terminal nodes are the *Bedeutungen* of the lexical items, and whose non-
terminal nodes are the *Bedeutungen* of the relevant complex expressions.
So for L&L, the interpretation of (2) and (4) is:

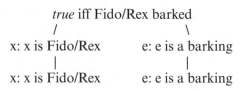

The nodes of this (coarse-grained) interpretation are a dog, the barkings,
and a truth-value. (L&L do not explicitly appeal to the event analysis, but
nothing hangs on this.)

An interpreted LF is a pairing of the relevant LF with its interpretation. L&L take the *Bedeutung* of 'that P' (relative to context C) to be the interpreted LF corresponding to 'P' (relative to C).[16] So on this view, the *Bedeutung* of 'that Fido barked' is as depicted in Figure 2.5. And (1) is true, just when Nora believes this (abstract) object—i.e. just when the extension of 'believes' includes <Nora, y>, where y is the interpreted LF above. The *Bedeutung* of 'that Rex barked' is said to be the following pairing of a distinct LF with the same interpretation (see Figure 2.6). By letting the *Bedeutung* of 'that P' depend on lexical features of 'P', L&L can assign different *Bedeutungen* to 'that Fido barked' and 'that Rex barked' *without* appealing to senses.

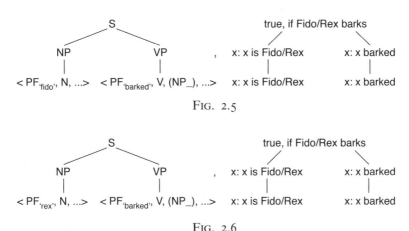

FIG. 2.5

FIG. 2.6

So (1) and

(2) Nora believes that Rex barked

can differ in truth-value. In general, 'N believes that P' and 'N believes that Q' will differ in truth-value, just when 'P' and 'Q' have different LFs *or* different (coarse-grained) interpretations.

This is an attractive account, but its simplicity has costs. If a monolingual German believes that Fido barked, he believes an interpreted LF with *English* lexical content. L&L reply that one *believes* the interpreted LF

---

[16] L&L do not assign *Bedeutungen* to complementizers. Correspondingly (and *pace* their n. 5), their theory is not one in which the semantic value of every expression is a function of the semantic values of its *immediate* constituents. On their view, the *Bedeutung* of [cp [c that] [s . . .]] is a function of: the LF of [s . . .] and the *Bedeutungen* of [s . . .] and all its constituents. Perhaps this is the strongest notion of compositionality that natural languages satisfy. But one could modify L&L's theory to let the *Bedeutung* of [c that], be the (coarse-grained) ILF corresponding to [s . . .].

corresponding to 'P' if one has a belief that is correctly reported with 'P', where what counts as a correct report is a pragmatic matter. But even if this is acceptable, it gives up the idea that phonetically distinct 'that'-clauses can co-refer. And Fregeans will say that if Nora can use 'Fido barked' to correctly report Hans's belief, she and Hans share a way of thinking about Fido.[17]

More importantly, there seem to be cases where L&L do not individuate the *Bedeutungen* of 'that'-clauses finely enough. Focusing on examples like (1) and (3) can make senses appear unnecessary: since the embedded sentences differ formally, why say that they *also* differ in interpretation? But in other cases, the embedded expressions do not seem to differ with respect to their LFs or their *Bedeutungen*. Suppose Nora assents to

(49) That is a lawyer

relative to context C1, but not relative to C2—even though the referent of 'That' is the same in each context. (In C1, the speaker points to the back of someone approaching the bench; in C2, the speaker points to the front of someone in a toolshed building a bench.) Then plausibly,

(50) Nora believes that that is a lawyer

is true relative to C1, and false relative to C2. Fregeans can say that the sense of a demonstrative depends on the context. But on L&L's view, if the demonstrative has the same *Bedeutung* in both contexts, (50) has the same truth conditions in both contexts. L&L thus deny that the *Bedeutung* of a demonstrative is simply its intuitive referent. Instead, they take the *Bedeutung* of a demonstrative to be a pairing of the object demonstrated with an act of demonstration.

Relative to C1, the *Bedeutung* of 'That' in (49–50) is said to be $<x, a1>$, where x is the lawyer in question and a1 is the speaker's act of demonstration in C1; relative to C2, the *Bedeutung* of 'That' in (49–50) is $<x, a2>$, where a2 is the distinct act of demonstration in C2. In either context, though, the truth of (49) depends solely on whether x is a lawyer. That is, the differing acts of demonstration can affect the truth of (50), but not (49). This seems to concede the Fregean point: relative to each context, a demonstrative is associated with a (demonstrative) way of thinking about its referent; and this is relevant to the truth of matrix sentences, when the demonstrative is embedded in a 'that'-clause. As L&L note, Burge (1974) offers independent reasons for appealing to acts of demonstration in stat-

---

[17] On my proposal, the sense of the embedded complementizer in 'Hans believes that Nora believes that Fido barked' is a way of thinking about the pairing of a sense Θ and an English LF. But the ascriber can think of this interpreted LF in a way available to Hans—namely, as the pairing of Θ and a suitable LF of the language of ascription (see Sect. 3.2, and especially n. 13, above.)

ing the truth conditions of constructions like (50); and *perhaps* the best way to incorporate such appeals, independently of attitude ascriptions, is by taking the *Bedeutungen* of all demonstratives to be ordered pairs. But it not clear that L&L's manœuvre is both motivated and non-Fregean.

4.3

Cases inspired by Kripke (1979) allow one to make the much same point with proper names. Suppose Nick is Nora's neighbour, who Nora sometimes sees in the hallway. Nick is wealthy, but usually appears otherwise: he dresses shabbily, lives in a one-room apartment, etc. Thus,

(51) Nora believes that Nick is poor

is true in many contexts. Once at a party, though, Nora met a prosperous man called 'Nick', who resembled her neighbour. Of course, Nick was Nick; but he never let on, and Nora never suspected. Nora believed that this man was not poor. So at least in some contexts,

(52) Nora does not believe that Nick is poor.

Before turning to L&L's response to such cases, note that Fregeans can hold—and as Burge (1986) notes, Frege held—that the sense of a name can *differ* across contexts, much like the sense of a demonstrative. The sense of 'Nick' in a context where (51) is true might well differ from the sense of 'Nick' in a context where (52) is true. From a Fregean perspective, an asserter of (51) might be thinking of Nick in the way Nora usually thinks of her neighbour; while an asserter of (52) might be thinking of Nick in the (distinct way) Nora sometimes thinks of that party attender. Someone who knows what Nora does not can still think of Nick in different ways—just as we can still think of Venus in different ways, after learning that Hesperus is Phosphorous. And from a Fregean perspective, propositional attitude ascribers try to (and sometimes do) think of *Bedeutungen* in the same way as ascribees; but this sometimes requires ascribers to adjust how they think of *Bedeutungen*. (For the same reason, 'Nick is Nick' need not be a triviality; in this context, it is not.)

For Fregeans, then, (51–2) no more present a contradiction than do

(53) Nora believes that that is a lawyer
(54) Nora does not believe that that is a lawyer.

Each ascription is true in one context. The demonstrative has the same *Bedeutung* in both contexts. But in no context are both (53) and (44) true. Relative to each context C, the sense of the demonstrative is such that only one of these belief ascriptions is true; and similarly, *mutatis mutandis*, for

(51–2). Given coarse-grained interpretations of embedded sentences, however, 'Nick is poor' has the *same* interpretation relative to each context—
assuming that the *Bedeutung* of a name is its bearer. L&L do not deny this.
Instead, they say that 'Nick' is ambiguous, and that the homophonic
names share a *Bedeutung*.

I grant that in *Nora's* idiolect, 'Nick' is ambiguous. Suppose Nora
thinks her neighbor is shy, but not witty; while she thinks the man from the
party is witty, but not shy. Then Nora will see a possibility of equivocation
in the following argument: Nick is shy, and Nick is witty; so Nick is shy
and witty. But my intuition is that this inference is valid. (Unlike: banks
are damp, and banks are secure; so banks are damp and secure.) So I think
that 'Nick' is unambiguous in my idiolect. And (51–2) are sentences of *my*
language—or better, *our* currently shared language. Thus, it is not clear
that the ambiguity resides where it must, if coarse-grained interpretations
and linguistic forms are to do the work of senses.

A possible response is that we can add names to our lexicon when
ascribing attitudes. We introduce 'Nick$_1$' and 'Nick$_2$' to say what Nora
believes. So perhaps it *seems* that the inference above avoids any equivocation, since we introduce the names on the understanding that: Nick$_1$ =
Nick = Nick$_2$. On this view, (51–2) are ambiguous. Their true readings
are:

> (51a) Nora believes that Nick$_1$ is poor.
> (52b) Nora does not believe that Nick$_2$ is poor.

Here the embedded sentences have different LFs; so Nora can believe
exactly one of them. Perhaps this is as plausible as saying that ascribers
can associate a single lexical item ('Nick') with different senses in different
contexts. But on L&L's view, one expects no *sound* reading of the following inference:

> Nick is shy, and Nora believes it.
> <u>Nick is witty, and Nora believes it</u>.
> Nick is shy and witty.

On L&L's view, Nora believes the interpreted LFs 'Nick$_1$ is shy' and
'Nick$_2$ is witty'; and one would expect the referent of 'it' in each premiss
to be the interpreted LF of the first conjunct. So if the second conjunct of
each premiss is true, there is equivocation on 'Nick', and the argument is
invalid. My intuition, though, is that the argument can be sound. Fregeans
can explain this: the same lexical item 'Nick' appears throughout, but with
different senses in the two premisses. This preserves formal validity—
assuming that predicate conjunction is valid in natural languages—while

making it possible for 'it' to refer to distinct senses in each case.[18] L&L might allow that the argument has a sound reading, by saying that *in certain circumstances* arguments involving equivocation can still be valid. (Perhaps when names are introduced on the understanding that they co-refer, one can speak of 'implied premises' without obliterating the distinction between valid arguments and arguments that someone takes to be truth-preserving.) But Fregeans avoid the need for this manœuvre. And if the argument above can be sound, L&L's account conflicts with an intuition that I want to keep: 'Nick$_1$ is poor, so Nick$_2$ is poor' *fails* to be valid, as does 'Fido barked, so Rex barked.'[19]

4.4

If L&L face difficulties only with respect to attitude ascriptions involving homophonic terms with the same *Bedeutungen*, one might think their account is doing well. But the question is whether we need Fregean senses as the interpretations of embedded sentences, or whether we can make do with coarse-grained interpretations (given LFs). If the former, considerations of effective communication would still lead one to expect that sentences expressing different Fregean thoughts will typically have different LFs. So it hardly tells against Fregeans if most attitude ascriptions that differ in truth-value also involve embedded sentences with different LFs. To decide whether 'Fido barked' and 'Rex barked' have different interpretations, we must consider sentences like 'That is a lawyer' and 'Nick is poor.' For it is here that

---

[18] This is, in several respects, an unFregean thing to say. If the sense of 'Nick' differs in the premises, one can (without irrationality) endorse the thoughts expressed by the premises yet not endorse the thought expressed by the conclusion. For Frege, validity is (not primarily a relation between sentences, but) a relation between thoughts that we aim to represent in a logically perspicuous language. The fact that names can have different senses in different contexts shows that natural languages are not logically perfect. But we can speak of 'Nora walked' following from 'Nora walked slowly', even if 'Nora' is associated with different ways of thinking about Nora; and similarly for examples involving predicate conjunction. So long as the same lexical item appears throughout, the model-theoretic notion of validity applies: any interpretation of the primitive elements that would make the premises true would also make the conclusion true (holding fixed the semantic contributions of logical particles). See Pietroski (forthcoming *a*).

[19] That said, questions about validity (and the relation between syntax and truth-preservingness) are subtle; see Etchemendy (1990); Hanson (1997). The methodological problem is that the following tasks are inseparable: getting clear about the notion of validity relevant to natural language semantics; saying how an agent's beliefs are related to the number of lexical items in her idiolect; and providing a theory of attitude ascriptions that yields an adequate treatment of Kripke-cases and Mates-sentences. I have also ignored a potential complication: the propositional objects of thought may be diverse. Perhaps many attitude ascriptions relate persons to senses, while *some* ascriptions relate thinkers (and/or quasi-thinkers) to more coarsely grained entities sets (like sets of possible worlds). Dwyer and Pietroski (1996) offer one reason for taking this possibility seriously with respect to the explanation of our linguistic abilities.

the costs of eschewing senses will be visible. Of necessity, then, we must focus on examples of this sort. (Not surprisingly, these are also the cases where questions about validity become hardest.)

The basic attractions of Frege's view have never been in doubt, however. The question has been whether objections can be addressed. In reply, I have granted that Fregeans cannot make do with senses alone. In my view, Mates-sentences show that senses are not fine-grained enough to do all the needed work. Semanticists also need linguistic forms. (The opacity of quotation points in the same direction.) But we still have reason for appealing to senses, even once we have appealed to linguistic forms. And importantly, the virtue of innocence is not in tension with a tendency towards *Sinn*. The essential aspects of Frege's theory do not require *Bedeutung*-shifting; so the (high) costs of such shifting can be avoided. One must allow for the context-sensitivity of senses, but this is not implausible. Moreover, as we shall see in later chapters, appealing to senses also proves useful outside semantics.

3

From Explanation to Causation

Thus far, I have defended versions of Davidson's event analysis and Frege's approach to propositional attitude ascriptions. In this chapter, I combine these proposals, and offer a thesis about how causation is related to explanation: event C caused event E if a true thought about C (in a sense of 'about' to be characterized) explains a true thought about E, where true thoughts—the senses of true sentences—are facts. After motivating this thesis, I use it to sketch an account of how some events could have non-neural mental causes. This sketch is filled out in later chapters. But here, my goal is to connect appeals to events and senses in a way that draws attention to a certain conception of causation.

1. Explainers and Causes

Like many others, I think causation is primarily a relation between events, while explanation is primarily a relation between facts. But I do not say that *only* events can be causes (or effects). Perhaps other entities, like states or facts, can be relata of causal relations (see Mellor 1995). Similarly, perhaps facts are not the only relata of explanatory relations. Speakers certainly use 'cause' and 'explain' in a hodgepodge of ways. And it is not my aim to characterize the extension of these terms. For present purposes, I only need relatively modest claims: we have a concept of causation that is a concept of a relation between events, which are individuated non-intentionally; and we have a concept of explanation that is a concept of a relation between facts, which are individuated intentionally. I will be defending a sufficient condition for event causation, not a necessary condition on the truth of 'x caused y'; and I will be concerned only with a particular species of explanation, viz. explanations relating facts that are about particular events. Still, even the modest claims are not trivial. So they warrant some discussion.

1.1

Suppose, recalling the example from Chapter 2, that Nora hears a dog called 'Fido' barking every night. Nora also sees (but never hears) a dog called 'Rex' in the park every morning. Nora comes to believe that Fido barks, and that Rex does not. But in fact, Fido is Rex. Eventually, Nora learns that Fido barks whenever he sees Garfield, a cat who passes by every night: there's something about Garfield that Fido just doesn't like. One night, Nora and Nick hear Fido bark. Nick asks why Fido barked. Nora answers, by saying (correctly) that Fido saw Garfield. Let us assume that in this scenario:

(1) the fact that Fido saw Garfield explains the fact that Fido barked.

By hypothesis, Fido is Rex. But while (1) is true, (2–3) seem false:

(2) the fact that Rex saw Garfield explains the fact that Fido barked
(3) the fact that Fido saw Garfield explains the fact that Rex barked.

One thing explains another, if the former renders the latter (more) comprehensible. Intuitively, the facts referred to in (2–3) are not so related.[1] This suggests that explanation is a relation whose relata are individuated in part by *how thinking subjects think of* things. And a Fregean semantics supports this view, given a plausible premiss: if P, then the *Bedeutung* of 'that P' is the fact that P. The *Bedeutung* of 'that P' is the thought expressed by 'P'; so if this thought is true, the *Bedeutung* of 'that P' is the true thought that P. (Compare: if Chris is a woman, the *Bedeutung* of 'Chris' is the woman Chris.) I see no good reason for distinguishing the fact that P from the true thought that P. (The woman Chris is the female person Chris.) So following Frege, I identify facts with true thoughts. On this view, the fact that Fido saw Garfield differs from the fact that Rex saw Garfield, and the fact that Fido barked differs from the fact that Rex barked. So (1) does not entail (2) or (3), for the same reason that (4) does not entail (5):

(4) Nora believes that Fido barked
(5) Nora believes that Rex barked.

The embedded sentences express different thoughts/facts, since 'Fido' and 'Rex' differ in sense.

I return to concerns about individuating facts intentionally. But first, let me recognize that (1–3) are not the only uses of the verb 'explain'. Consider:

(6) The fact that Fido saw Garfield explains why Fido barked
(7) Nora explained why Fido barked.

---

[1] Explanation is context-sensitive; and my claim is only that (1–2) differ in truth-value, relative to at least some contexts. Perhaps (1–2) can both be true relative to some contexts where 'Fido' and 'Rex' still differ in sense. An asserter of (2) might be in the process of informing Nora that Fido is Rex; or suppose the asserter thought that scientists had (somehow) linked Rex's visual system to Fido's vocal apparatus.

In these sentences, the direct objects are 'why'-clauses, as in:

> (8) Nora knows why Fido barked
> (9) Nick asked why Fido barked.

But 'why' and 'that' differ. A thinker can know *that* Q, yet not know *why* Q. Moreover, (7) is like (9), in reporting something Nora did. And like (8), (6) reports a certain state of affairs, though not the mental state of any particular thinking subject. This does not affect my main point, since in (6–9), substituting 'Rex' for the co-referential 'Fido' still affects the truth conditions of the matrix sentences. So (6–9) provide no reason for doubting that (1) is true iff a certain intentionally individuated entity explains another. Indeed, (1) and (6) seem to have the same truth conditions. Nonetheless, this variation in the use of 'explain' calls for some comment.

1.2

Like 'that'-clauses, 'why'-clauses are complementizer phrases. But as I noted in my brief discussion of 'quote'-clauses, complementizer phrases need not be true of *thoughts*. Intuitively, 'why'-clauses are true of *questions*, which differ from thoughts: the former have right and wrong answers, not truth conditions.[2] Still, the question of why Fido barked is closely related to the thought that Fido barked: the latter is a presupposition of the former. In general, if ¬Q, the question of why Q has no right answer. And I assume that to explain why Q is to explain *the factual presupposition of* the question that is the *Bedeutung* of 'why Q'. In this sense, 'why Q' and 'the fact that Q' are interchangeable as direct objects of 'explain': x explains why Q, just when x explains the fact that Q.[3]

---

[2] In terms of the Ch. 2 framework, one can say that 'why' is a special kind of complementizer whose *Bedeutung* just is the 'why'-question corresponding to the relevant embedded sentence. Note that if (9) is true, Nick asked a certain question, viz. the question of why Fido barked; and if Nora asked every question that Nick asked, then given (9), it follows that Nora asked why Fido barked. Similarly, just as Othello was plagued by the thought that Desdemona loved Cassio (hence, that Desdemona loved Cassio is a thought which plagued Othello), one can be plagued by the question of why Desdemona loved Cassio (hence, why Desdemona loved Cassio is a question) (see Higginbotham 1993). Pesetsky (1982) discusses the role of prepositions in 'the question *of* why Q' and 'wondered *about* whether Q'. I assume that 'whether'-questions and 'why'-questions differ, in that only the former have yes/no answers.

[3] Perhaps the syntax of 'explains why Fido barked' is: [VP explains [DP Ø [CP why Fido barked]]], where this means something like 'explains *the factual presupposition of* (the question) why Q'. Similarly, perhaps a subject knows why Fido barked, just when she knows *an answer to* the question of why Fido barked (see Higginbotham 1993; Pietroski forthcoming *b*). If there is a non-factive use of 'explain', given which x can explain why Q when 'Q' is false, then I am restricting attention to explanations of truths.

The other feature of 'explain' is more significant for our present concerns. A fact can be explained by another fact, as reported in (1), or by a person. Consider (7) or

(10) Nora explained the fact that Fido barked.

Indeed, the event analysis applies most naturally to (10). If (10) is true, Nora engaged in a certain tutorial *activity*; she was the Agent of an event. Yet intuitively, (1) does not have any *episode* as its truth-maker. Rather, it seems that (1) is true, because a certain fact has a certain explanatory *feature*: the fact that Fido saw Garfield has the property of rendering comprehensible the fact that Fido barked. Correspondingly, it seems that 'explain' can appear in a *stative* or an *eventive* form. (Compare: 'the river provides a source of water'; and 'Nora provided a source of water.') Some such distinction is needed in any case, given the ancient observation that many verbs are sortals for enduring traits of objects, while other verbs are sortals for changes that objects initiate or undergo (see Taylor 1985; Lombard 1986).

Stative verbs often appear with continuous tense, as in 'Nora like*s* Nick.' And even with past tense, the suggestion is that the subject bore a trait that endured for some time: compare 'liked' with 'kissed'. I return (in Section 1.5) to the relation between events and states. But for now, let me simply note that semanticists can encode an event–state distinction, by marking the relevant metalanguage sortals: $Shooting_\varepsilon$, $Asking_\varepsilon$, etc.; $Liking_\sigma$, $Believing_\sigma$, etc. Assuming that states have Subjects, as opposed to Agents, the logical form of 'Nora likes Nick' is: $\exists e[Subject(e, Nora)\ \&\ Liking_\sigma(e)\ \&\ Theme(e, Nick)]$. And the logical form of (4) is

(4a) $\exists e[Subject(e, Nora)\ \&\ Believing_\sigma(e)\ \&\ Content(e, that\ Fido\ barked)]$.

I also assume that complementizer phrases specify Contents, while noun (or determiner) phrases like 'Nick' and 'the dog' specify Themes when they appear as direct objects of transitive stative verbs.[4]

---

[4] If the mapping from grammatical to thematic categories is uniform (see Ch. 1, Sect. 5), either Subjects are non-paradigmatic Agents, or stative verbs differ syntactically from eventive verbs. I think the latter option is plausible; see Pietroski (forthcoming *a*). It would also be unsurprising if 'that'-clauses specified a distinctive thematic role (see n. 3 above). And note that the eventive form of 'explain' can take a 'that'-clause: when Nick asked why Fido barked, Nora explained that Fido saw Garfield. I think the syntax is as it appears: [vp explained [cp that Fido saw Garfield]], which is true of explainings whose Content is that Fido saw Garfield. But the Theme of Nora's explaining—the explanandum—is the (contextually specifed) proposition that Fido barked. So I think we can explain the difference between 'explained that Fido barked' and 'explained the fact that Fido barked' in thematic terms. But given 'Nora believes that', states with Contents may be representable as having Themes (see Pietroski forthcoming *b*).

One can still maintain that the relevant domain of quantification includes only events, by holding that states are special cases of events. But I prefer to say that we quantify over events *and* states. Dowty (1977) suggests 'eventuality' as a term of art to cover the various event*ish* things quantified over—including processes—if these are distinct from events (see Steward 1997). And following Parsons (1990), we can say that events (the ε-type eventualities) *culminate* at a particular time, while states (the σ-type eventualities) *hold* through time. Given this 'eventuality analysis', the logical forms of (1) and (10) are:

(1a) ∃e[Subject(e, the fact that Fido saw Garfield) & Explaining$_\sigma$(e) & Theme(e, the fact that Fido barked)]

(10a) ∃e[Agent(e, Nora) & Explaining$_\varepsilon$(e) & Theme(e, the fact that Fido barked)].

The truth-maker for (1a) is a state; the truth-maker for (10a) is an event; and 'e' ranges over eventualities.

The Fregean point remains. With respect to (4a), the existence of a believing whose Content is *that Fido barked* does not entail the existence of a believing whose Content is *that Rex barked*, even if Fido is Rex. With respect to (1a), the existence of an explaining$_\sigma$ whose Theme is *the fact that Fido barked* does not entail the existence of an explaining$_\sigma$ whose Theme is *the fact that Rex barked*. Let F1 be the fact that Fido saw Garfield; let F2 be the fact that Fido barked; and let F3 be the fact that Rex barked. There can be a state of explaining$_\sigma$ whose Subject is F1 and whose Theme is F2, without there being a state of explaining$_\sigma$ whose Subject is F1 and whose Theme is F3. For F2 differs from F3, in a way that matters to comprehensibility. Similarly, there can be an explaining$_\varepsilon$ whose Agent is Nora and whose Theme is F2, without there being an explaining$_\varepsilon$ whose Agent is Nora and whose Theme is F3.

At least until Chapter 7, I take no stand on whether the eventive or stative use of 'explain' is somehow primary. Bromberger (1962) and Matthews (1983) note that Θ1 explains$_\sigma$ Θ2 (relative to context C), only if (in C) a 'tutor' could explain$_\varepsilon$ Θ2 to a 'pupil' by citing Θ1. That is, one fact explains$_\sigma$ another only if it is possible to explain$_\varepsilon$ the latter fact by citing the former. But similarly, one can explain$_\varepsilon$ Θ2 by citing Θ1 only if Θ1 explains$_\sigma$ Θ2. If the facts do not stand in an explanatory relation, independent of tutorial activities, then one cannot explain$_\varepsilon$ Θ2 (as opposed to merely telling a story about why Θ2 obtains) by citing Θ1. In any case, issues about primacy need not detain us at this point. For now, the important claim is that facts are among the relata of the explanation relation, where facts are individuated intentionally. Correspondingly, claims like

(1) The fact that Fido saw Garfield explains the fact that Fido barked

are often true. And henceforth, I focus on explanation as a relation
between facts, as reported in (1).

1.3

One can use 'fact', so that the fact that Fx is the fact that Gy if the following conditions obtain: x is y, where 'x' and 'y' are names; and the property
of being F is the property of being G, where properties are individuated
non-intentionally. I have no objection to the coarsely grained abstract
objects one appeals to by using 'fact' this way. But I prefer to call them
'situations' or 'states of affairs'. If the fact that P is the referent of 'that P'
(given that 'P' is true), and the referent of 'that P' is a thought, then facts
are (true) thoughts. Moreover, facts stand in *logical and confirmational*
relations, and this is relevant to comprehensibility. Nora does not *and
should not* infer that Rex barked from her belief that Fido barked. Nora
fails to know that Rex barked, but not because she failed to draw a good
inference: that Fido barked does not logically entail (or even confirm) that
Rex barked. Every fact logically entails itself. So there are two distinct
facts here. Similarly, explaining why Fido barked is one thing, explaining
why Rex barked is another.[5]

On any Fregean view, thoughts are abstract entities that do not exist in
spacetime. So if facts are true thoughts, facts are *abstracta*; and if explanation holds between facts, explanation holds between entities that do not
exist in space-time. I endorse these consequences. But let me stress that
Fregeans need not divorce the realm of thought from the spatio-temporal
realm in a way that renders the former (and our access to it) utterly mysterious. As we just saw, there is an important connection between one fact
explaining$_\sigma$ another and someone explaining$_\varepsilon$ a fact; and the activity of
explaining$_\varepsilon$ occurs in space-time. Moreover, the rest of this chapter
emphasizes the connection between explanation and causal relations
between spatio-temporal particulars (events). And it is potentially misleading to say that thinking subjects have beliefs *in virtue of* being cognitively related to Fregean thoughts—as though the senses of sentences were
like dogs, only harder to perceive. It is much better, in my view, to say that
subjects are cognitively related to thoughts in part by virtue of thinking
about particular things in certain ways.

Frege may have viewed the matter differently. But if one wants to
account for belief as a relation *to* something, I would express the Fregean

---

[5] If one insists that facts follow from other facts *only relative to certain representations of
them*, one can replace 'fact' with 'fact*', where fact*s are individuated intentionally, perhaps because fact*s are ordered pairs of (coarse-grained) facts and ways of thinking about
them.

point this way: Nora believes that Fido barked partly by virtue of bearing a certain relation to Fido—viz. the relation of *thinking about in an evening-dog way*. If Nora believes that Fido barked, she bears some relation to the sense of 'Fido barked'; but similarly, anyone who sees two dogs bears some relation to the number two. Nora may be more intimately related to senses than numbers, since she thinks about Fido in a way W, such that the sense of 'Fido barks' is partly determined by W. But the crucial aspect of Frege's view is not that believing is a relation between thinking subjects and intentional entities. Rather, this is how a Fregean semanticist expresses the idea that states of believing are individuated in terms of how subjects think about things, not just the things themselves. Similar remarks apply to events of asserting, explaining, etc.

Thus, I would not say that 'Nora explained$_\varepsilon$ the fact that Fido barked' is true *in virtue of* Nora's being suitably related to the sense of 'Fido barked'. Nora is suitably related to that sense. But this is not an invitation to investigate the nature of Nora's relation to an abstract object; it is a reflection of how we count explainings$_\varepsilon$. And even if 'the fact that P explains$_\sigma$ the fact that Q' does not itself involve reference to events, it involves reference to senses where senses can and do partly individuate intentionally characterized events like explainings$_\varepsilon$ and tryings. (I return to these issues in Chapter 7.)

1.4

One can count facts in a Fregean way, yet grant that Fido's barking is the same *event* as Rex's barking. Events, unlike facts, are spatio-temporal entities. And there are not two distinct barkings in the same place at the same time, just as there are not two distinct dogs in the same place at the same time. For simplicity, let 'X's seeing Y' be short for 'the event of X's coming to see Y'. Then Fido's seeing Garfield *is* Rex's seeing Garfield. Let '*c*' be a name for this event; let '*e*' be a name for Fido's barking. If *c* caused *e*, then: Fido's seeing Garfield caused Fido's barking; Fido's seeing Garfield caused Rex's barking; Rex's seeing Garfield caused Fido's barking; and Rex's seeing Garfield caused Rex's barking. We rarely honour unimportant events with names. But if someone refers to *e* as Fido's barking, they use the name 'Fido'. And the following inferences are intuitively compelling, where 'A', 'B', 'C', and 'D' are names for objects participating in events: A's Φ-ing caused B's Ψ-ing, A = C, and B = D; so C's Φ-ing caused D's Ψ-ing. In my view, this inference is valid, as is the corresponding inference employing names for events: *c* caused *e*, *c*=*d*, and *e*=*f*, so *d* caused *f*.

In this respect, 'caused' is like 'preceded'. Suppose that *c* preceded *e*, and *c* was the F, and *e* was the G. Then the F preceded *e*, *c* preceded the

G, and the F preceded the G. If Fido's seeing Garfield was the first sighting of Garfield that night, and Fido's barking was the disturbance that
woke Nora, then the first sighting of Garfield that night preceded the disturbance that woke Nora. In general, if one asserts of two events that the
first preceded the second, one is saying that a certain binary relation holds
between two particulars that are individuated without regard to how they
are described (or thought about).

I endorse the parallel claim about causation, though one might be wary
here. Even if the sighting of Garfield caused the disturbance, perhaps other
examples provide reason for thinking that causal claims are description-
sensitive after all. Suppose Fido's barking caused Nora's complaint, but
unbeknownst to Nora, the barking was the event that made her rich.
Fido's wealthy owner felt guilty about the noise; so he put a large sum of
money in Nora's mailbox. Given this scenario, one might hesitate over

(11) The event that made Nora rich caused Nora's complaint.

But I think the hesitation is due to two related facts: (11) would be
implausible if asserted out of the blue; and we often fail to distinguish
singular causal claims from causal explanations (see Davidson 1967*b*;
Strawson 1985). The fact that Nora complained is not explained by the
occurrence of the event that made Nora rich. And causal claims will seem
implausible if we see no explanatory connection between facts concerning
the events in question. So examples like (11) do not provide good reason
for denying the following claim: if one asserts of two events that the first
caused the second, one is saying that a certain binary relation holds
between two particulars that are individuated without regard to how they
are described (or thought about). Another kind of example is worth mentioning, though.

Suppose Nora complained, because Fido barked *loudly*: if he hadn't
barked loudly, Nora would not have awakened, and so would not have
complained. Then one might think that

(12) Fido's barking loudly caused Nora's complaint
(13) Fido's barking caused Nora's complaint

differ in truth-value. A potential source of confusion here is that 'Fido's
barking loudly' (cf. 'Fido's loud barking') is easily heard as a device for
referring to the fact that Fido barked loudly. But if we treat the gerund
phrase as an event description, Fido's barking loudly just *is* Fido's bark-
ing. For his barking loudly was a barking (in place *p* at time *t*); his bark-
ing was a barking (in *p* at *t*); and there were not two barkings (in *p* at *t*). So
if (12) is true while (13) is false, different descriptions of an event—'Fido's
barking loudly' *vs.* 'Fido's barking'—can affect the truth of causal claims
involving those descriptions. This might lead one to say that 'the F caused

the G' is true relative to context C iff the quadruple $<x, d_1, y, d_2>$ satisfies 'caused', where 'd_1' and 'd_2' are contextually determined descriptions of (or ways of thinking about) events x and y, which are respectively the F and the G.[6]

I cannot prove that this response to examples like (12–13) is mistaken. But it strikes me as an unnecessary use of elaborate semantic machinery. In *explaining* why Nora complained, one will appeal to the fact that Fido barked loudly, which is distinct from the fact that Fido barked. (The former fact does not follow from the latter.) So in many contexts, (12) is more pragmatically appropriate than (13). And it is easy to get confused: one supposes, tentatively, that (13) is inappropriate because it is false; one sees that *if* (12) and (13) have different truth conditions, Fido's barking loudly is distinct from Fido's barking; and *barking loudly* is a different property from *barking*, which suggests that perhaps there are two different events here. Given the argument above, Fido's barking loudly is Fido's barking; yet the idea that (13) is false remains, suggesting that the truth of causal claims is description-sensitive.[7]

If one is still nagged by the thought that causal claims *ought* to be sensitive to how events are described, this may stem from the correct thought that causal claims involve modality. One needn't adopt any particular theory to think that causation has *something* to do with laws of nature, or that 'C caused E' is closely related to 'if C had not occurred, then E would not have occurred'. And for many modal relations R, the inference 'R(the Φ, the Ω) & (the Φ = the Ψ), so R(the Ψ, the Ω)' is invalid. (Let R be the relation: *precedes in all possible worlds where Socrates is born alive and Plato is taught by someone*. In all the relevant worlds, the birth of Socrates precedes the death of Socrates; and in fact the birth of Socrates was the birth of Plato's teacher. But there are possible worlds where Socrates dies shortly after birth, and Plato is taught by someone born after the infant death of

---

[6] Alternatively, perhaps 'the F caused the G' is true relative to context C iff the pair $<\Gamma_1, \Gamma_2>$ satisfies 'caused', where Γ_1 and Γ_2 are contextually determined facts about x and y. In the simplest case, the relevant descriptions/facts would be those suggested by the linguistic forms of 'F' and 'G'. Note that if Fido's barking loudly is an event distinct from Fido's barking, every loud barking (by x) has to be associated with a barking (by x), to account for the entailment 'Fido barked loudly, so Fido barked.'

[7] Similarly, I think the event of Nora's painting the wall scarlet can be the event of Nora's painting the wall; Nora's painting the wall a shade of red; etc. Kim (1976) suggests a strategy for denying event identities of this sort. He is inclined to say that the following *causal* claim can be true: the collapse was caused, not by the bolt's giving way, but the bolt's giving way so suddenly. Kim tentatively concludes that the bolt's giving way and the bolt's giving way so suddenly are 'different events, though one is "included" in the other' (ibid. 42). Kim says that his proliferation of events is 'not in itself serious', since the word 'event' is not a typical count noun (ibid. 46). But my concern is not about the mere number of events. It is that there are not two barkings (givings-way) in the same place at the same time, just as there are not two dogs (bolts) in the same place at the same time.

Socrates.) As Davidson (1970) notes, however, a causal claim can be backed by a law without being backed by a law stated in the same terms as the causal claim. More generally, a cause can bear a modal relation R to an effect, without there being any way of determining R from a given pair of descriptions that are true of the cause and effect.

1.5

In the course of distinguishing explainers (facts) from causes (events), I also distinguished events from states. But as I noted on the first page of the Introduction, events cause other events against a background of states; and as I emphasize in Section 3, background conditions matter, even if the focus is on event causation. So let me end this section with a brief digression on this point, before turning to the relation between events and facts.

Suppose Nora went to the airport at 4 p.m., because she believed that Nick's plane was due at 5 p.m., wanted to be at the airport when the plane was due, and believed that it takes an hour to get to the airport. This explanation presupposes that, at 4, Nora believed it was 4. The story is presumably that at 4, Nora *came to believe* it was 4 (perhaps she had set an alarm), and this mental event caused her airport-directed behaviour. But Nora's coming to believe it was 4 had this effect, only because Nora had certain background intentional states, including a desire to be at the airport by 5. Similarly, suppose that (at 1) Nora came to believe the plane was due at 5, because she got a phone call, and so came to desire that she be at the airport by 5. The coming to believe caused the coming to desire, only given background intentional states, like a desire to meet Nick. But given those states, Nora's coming to believe that Nick would arrive at 5 caused the formation of a desire that was part of the background against which Nora's coming to believe (at 4) that it was 4 caused her airport-directed behaviour. (In Dretske's (1988) terms, mental events are triggering causes of bodily motions, while mental states are structuring causes; and event dualists deny that mental events are neural-triggering causes.)

Thus, focusing on event causation does not ignore the causal role of states. On the contrary, states are such that events cause other events against a background of them. I am not wedded to any particular conception of states. (They are what we quantify over when we use sentences that include state sortals.) But intuitively, causes have the effects they do, because objects have the properties they do. So perhaps states should be construed in terms of properties. On this view, to say that x is in a state of Φ-ing is to say that x has the property expressed by 'Φ' or a variant on 'Φ' that preserves grammaticality. Nora is in a state of liking Nick (or believing that P), just when Nora has the property of *liking Nick* (or *believing that P*). Some philosophers stress this gloss of state-talk, in response to what they regard as illicit reification of mental states.[8] But one can still draw analogies between mental states and states of machines with certain input/output profiles. For an attractive idea is that genuine properties (as opposed to Cambridge properties, like *being 7 miles from King's College or Harvard Square*) are those that matter to how objects behave in various circumstances. As Shoemaker (1984) argues, the notion of a property may itself be a causal notion. And this fits well with the independently attractive idea that at least many mental events are changes of mental states (see n. 1 of the Introduction).

I mention this conception of event–state relations, not because I insist on it, but because one might worry that (if correct) it turns the thesis that mental events are neural events into the less plausible thesis that mental properties are neural properties. Suppose that Nick comes to believe that he can have salmon or chicken. And suppose this mental event is a change of mental state in Nick. For reasons discussed in Chapter 5, event dualists will deny that Nick's mental event is some change of biochemical state in Nick.[9] But I will *not* argue as follows: mental properties are distinct from biochemical properties; so changes of mental properties are distinct from changes of biochemical properties; so mental events are distinct from biochemical events.

I return to these issues in Chapter 6. But by way of contrast, consider Kim's (1976, 1993) view that an event is a complex entity with three constituents: an object, a (genuine) property, and a time. The event $[x, N, t]$ is said to exist (occur) iff object x has property X at time t; and $[x, N, t]$ is said to be identical with the event $[y, M, t^*]$ iff $x = y$, $N = M$, and $t = t^*$.

---

[8] It is tempting to say that someone in a state of believing that P *has as a part* some entity σ, such that σ is suitably related to the proposition that P. But Rudder-Baker (1995) suggests that being in a state of believing that P is more like being in a state of emergency; and a system in a state of emergency is not in that state by virtue of having as a part some entity with the right property. One might say that a person in a state of panic (believing that P) is in that state by virtue of having a nervous system with the property *disposes the containing system to be panicky* (*disposes the containing system to be believes-that-P-ish*). But such claims, which verge on vapidity, appeal to *global* features of nervous systems. And as Robinson (1990) argues, this threatens the idea of intentional states as *localized* brain parts that interact to produce behaviour. See also Steward's (1997) criticism of appeal to 'token states'.

[9] Or fusion of such changes. Not all mental events are acquisitions of enduring mental states. A fleeting recollection or daytime reverie may have no lasting effects; and if Nick decides to have the salmon, his decision may cause (but not be) the formation of an intention to order the salmon. Similarly, if Nick raises his arm to get the waiter's attention, then I would say that Nick's action/trying is a mental event, but his action is not the acquisition of a mental state. Still, when Nick plumps for the salmon, and tries to call the waiter, Nick seems to be the subject of changes. (And perhaps whenever x is the subject of a change C, we should count C as a change in some state of x.) But whether or not these mental events are changes of state, event dualists deny that decidings and tryings are biochemical changes in Nick.

This conception of events excludes the possibility that a given event (say, Nick's coming to believe that he had certain options) is identical with a change of some (neural) property N *and also* identical with a change of some distinct (mental) property M.[10] Event dualists will agree that changes in neural properties are not changes in mental properties. But I would not try to establish this conclusion by assuming Kim's fine-grained conception of events.

My reasons for rejecting neuralism are compatible with a coarse-grained conception, according to which a single event can be a change in distinct properties. But I have no brief for coarse-grained conceptions. Like Kim, I have doubts about the stability of views that combine property dualism with event monism. And if event dualism is defensible, that undercuts one argument for a coarse-grained conception (viz. mental properties are not neural properties, yet mental events are neural events). Still, one should not argue for or against neuralism by presupposing a view about how to count events if only because it is *very* hard to say whether a single event can be a change in two genuine properties.

One cannot stipulate that x has property Δ iff x has Φ or Ψ, and then argue as follows: $\Delta \neq \Phi$, since they have different extensions, but a change in Φ will be identical with a change in Δ. The response will be that Δ (or Φ) is not a genuine property. Similarly, while the property *being near an earthquake* differs from the property *being near a catastrophe*, the latter might be identified with a disjunction of genuine properties related by human interests. Higher-order properties—i.e. properties an object has because it has another property that satisfies some condition—raise further issues. (Though Kim argues that such properties are also disjunctions of genuine properties; see Chapter 6.) But to repeat, my denial of neuralism is not a matter of denying that mental properties are not biochemical properties—say, because mental properties are higher order—and then insisting on a fine-grained conception of events.

Since I have stressed that events can satisfy multiple descriptions, let me also note (as Kim does) that this does not favour either conception of events. A certain eruption of Vesuvius was the cause of Pompeii's destruction. Suppose it was also the worst thing that happened to the residents of Pompeii, the most famous eruption of all time, etc. This does not touch the

---

[10] Kim plays down the event–state distinction. For him, the road's leading to Rome is as much an event as Caesar's walking along the road; similarly for Nora's being a winner at noon and Nora's crossing the finish-line at noon. But perhaps *changes* are Kim-events whose constitutive property is expressed by certain natural language verbs (see Taylor 1985). Let us set aside events that involve no objects, and objects that exemplify the same property twice (as when Bob hits the wall with each hand, at time *t*). And for these purposes, assume that the relevant mental and biochemical properties can be instantiated by the same individual; cf. Chs 5 and 6, where I also discuss Kim's further view that mental properties instantiated by human thinkers are not distinct from biochemical properties.

question of how finely grained an entity that eruption was. The event has simply been described as *the x such that Φx*, for several instances of 'Φ', which ranges over predicates satisfied by events. If '*c*' is a name for the eruption in question, and '*e*' is a name for the destruction of Pompeii, *c* is the cause of *e*. But this tells us nothing about whether *c* is a change in two or more distinct properties. (Similar remarks apply to actions; see Chapter 1.)

2. *Thoughts about Events*

Even if causation holds between events, while explanation holds between facts, Fido's barking (in place *p* at time *t*) is importantly related to the fact that Fido barked (in *p* at *t*). Correspondingly, the truth of

(1) The fact that Fido saw Garfield explains why Fido barked

is importantly related to the truth of

(14) Fido's seeing Garfield caused Fido's barking.

I think we can go some way towards spelling out these connections, by viewing at least some Fregean thoughts as ways of thinking about events.

2.1

Let us ignore issues of tense and thematic decomposition for present purposes. Then

(15) Fido barked at *t*

is true iff $\exists e[\text{Bark}(e, \text{Fido})\ \&\ \text{At}(e, t)]$. Assume that *t* is specified so that there is exactly one event *e*, such that *e* is a barking by Fido at time *t*. Then the Fregean thought expressed by (15) is true by virtue of *e*'s occurrence. Let us say that a *singular event thought* is the sense of a sentence S, such that for some condition Φ exactly one event satisfies Φ; and it follows from the event analysis that S is true iff $\exists e\Phi e$. (By definition, then, all singular event thoughts are true.) The sense of (15) is a singular event thought. And if an event is describable at all, it is presumably the truth-maker for many singular event thoughts.

On a Fregean view, senses are ways of thinking about *Bedeutungen*. The *Bedeutung* of a sentence is its truth-value. So Fregean thoughts are ways of thinking about truth-values. But a singular event thought can also be regarded as a way of thinking about a certain event. Indeed, it seems that the sense of (15) is about The True, *because* this thought is about an actual it. This is not to say that a sentence expressing a singular event thought is a name for some event. On the event analysis, 'Fido barked' is an existentially quantified claim. So even if Fido barked only once, and 'Fido barked' thus has a unique truth-making event e, 'Fido barked' is true in possible situations where e does not occur but some other barking by Fido does occur. (By analogy if Nick is the only yeller, the thought expressed by 'Someone yelled' is intuitively about Nick. But 'Someone' is not a name for Nick; it could have been that someone yelled while Nick stayed quiet.) Nonetheless, we can say that the sense of (15) is a way of thinking about the event of Fido's barking at t. If Θ is the sense of (15), then given that (15) is true, Θ is a fact; and since Θ is a way of thinking about e, some facts are ways of thinking about events. The sense of

(16) Rex barked at t

is also a fact. It is a fact is distinct from Θ. But the sense of (16) is also a way of thinking about e.

It can seem strange to say that facts are *ways of thinking about* things—truth-values or events. But this mode of speech can be paraphrased. Senses are abstract objects to which different thinkers can be related. In this respect, senses are objective. Fregean thoughts are not *episodes* of thinking. Thoughts serve to classify episodes of thinking as tokens of intentional types. Thoughts thus reflect how we individuate mental events (and states). To say that singular event thoughts are ways of thinking about events is to say that they are individuated in terms of how subjects think about events (and not just in terms of the events and their participants). And to say that one singular event thought explains another is to say that the relation of explanation holds between ways of thinking about events. (If explanation is a relation among facts and potential tutors/pupils, we still individuate potential episodes of explaining in part by reference to ways of thinking about events.)

Fregeans can also grant that our capacity to think about particular events (and truth-values) is not independent of our capacity to think about mundane objects. On the view offered in Chapter 2, a thought is composed of primitive senses. Nora presumably thinks the thought that Fido barked, by thinking about Fido in the evening dog way; thinking about the barkings in the right way; and arranging these ways of thinking (about a dog and certain events) in a semantically significant way, so that the arrangment of primitive senses is true iff $\exists e[\text{Bark}(e, \text{Fido})]$.[11] The truth of this thought depends on whether an event of a certain type occurs. If such an event occurs, Nora's thought is true, and so her thought is a fact.

---

[11] Davies (1991) thus argues that Fregeans are committed to something like the language of thought hypothesis (see the appendix for further discussion).

So it is unmysterious that singular event thoughts can be about events in this sense.

2.2

Now consider

(17) Fido saw Garfield at t^-

where t^- is a time just prior to t. Let c be the truth-maker for (17); and let e be the truth-maker for

(18) Fido barked at t.

The senses of (17) and (18), which are singular event thoughts about c and e, satisfy 'the fact that Fido saw Garfield at t^-' and 'the fact that Fido barked at t'. So

(19) The fact that Fido saw Garfield (at t^-) explains the fact that Fido barked (at t)

is true iff the sense of (17) explains the sense of (18). Hence, (19) is true iff a certain way of thinking about c explains a certain way of thinking about e. This is intuitively plausible. For if (19) is true, subjects can think about Fido's seeing Garfield and Fido's subsequent barking in ways that render the (occurrence of the) latter event comprehensible given the former; and if the fact about the seeing explains the fact about the barking, then (19) is true.

This suggests a sufficient condition for (event) causation stated in terms of explanation:

event C caused event E, if there are singular event thoughts $\Theta 1$ and $\Theta 2$, such that $\Theta 1$ is about C, $\Theta 2$ is about E, and $\Theta 1$ explains $\Theta 2$.

Some qualification is needed, however. Events C and E must be distinct. The fact that the mean molecular energy is rising (in region r at time t) may explain why the heat is rising (in r at t); but since the increase in energy *is* the rise in heat, the explanation does not license a singular *causal* claim. Similarly, if C constitutes (but is not identical with) E, a fact about C might explain a fact about E, without C causing E. Perhaps there are other cases in which a thought about one event explains a thought about another event, absent a causal relation between the events. But I have been unable to think of any. Bear in mind that only *singular event* thoughts are in question. Explanatory relations between other facts—e.g. facts expressed by lawlike sentences, facts about the capacities of objects, or mathematical facts—are irrelevant.[12] Still, to avoid the risk of

---

[12] Hanson (1958) suggests that causation be understood in terms of explanation; cf. Kim (1981, 1988a, 1994). Owens (1992) offers interesting discussion and a similar but more

counter-example, maybe I should say that C caused E if a singular event thought about C explains *in an appropriate way* a singular event thought about E. I will soon offer a sufficient condition for explanation (leaving it open how many forms of explanation license singular causal claims); and one can read this as a proposed sufficient condition for *appropriate* explanation. So if necessary, one can mentally replace 'explains' with the technical term 'A-explains', which is short for 'explains in the fashion specified by the proposed sufficient condition for explanation'.

Quite apart from such niceties, one might worry that a sufficient condition for causation stated in terms of explanation will be uninteresting (and/or viciously circular). When contraposed, the claim above yields a necessary condition on explanation: a singular event thought about C explains a singular event thought about E, only if C caused E. This is another reason for offering a sufficient condition for explanation. But at least for now, I am not trying to advance a substantive thesis about causation. My present aim is just to offer a thesis that captures the point I have been stressing: at least often, causation holds spatio-temporal particulars that are individuated without regard to ways of thinking about things, while explanation holds between ways of thinking about spatio-temporal particulars. Initially, it can seem surprising that a relation between Fregean senses is intimately connected with a relation between mind-independent entities. This can make it seem puzzling that explanation is intimately connected with causation. But if the proposed sufficient condition is correct, there is nothing surprising here.[13]

Let Θ_1 be the fact that Fido saw Garfield at t^-, and let Θ_2 be the fact that Fido barked at t. By hypothesis, the former fact explains the latter. So the sufficient condition above tells us that Fido's seeing Garfield at t^- caused Fido's barking at t. Any thought about Fido's seeing Garfield is a thought about Rex's seeing Garfield. Similarly, any thought about Fido's barking is a thought about Rex's barking. So if the fact that Fido saw Garfield (at t^-) explains why Fido barked (at t), then the proposed sufficient condition for causation licenses the following singular causal claims:

detailed view of how causation is related to explanation. Child (1994) also favours the idea that explanations of *why an event occurred* are always causal; see also Steward 1997. Counter-examples to the thesis in the text would be cases of the form: the fact that $\exists eFe$ explains the fact that $\exists eGe$; there is exactly one F-ish event and exactly one G-ish event; the F-ish event is distinct from the G-ish event; and the F-ish event did not cause the G-ish event. Among cases where the first two conditions are clearly met, it seems that the third *or* fourth condition is met (but not both). And let me stress that I am offering a *sufficient* condition for event causation, with the aim of shedding light on mental causation. There may be other sufficient conditions (say, in terms of probability-raising); and there are puzzles (especially in the philosophy of science) that my sufficient condition does not speak to.

[13] In Ch. 7, I discuss Strawson's (1985) distinction between *natural* and *intentional* relations, and the (resistable) temptation to think of causation as the *primary* relation (with explanations being presentations of causal relations to thinking subjects).

Rex's seeing Garfield caused Fido's barking; Fido's seeing Garfield caused Rex's barking; and Rex's seeing Garfield caused Rex's barking. If event C is event C*, then any way of thinking about C is a way of thinking about C*. So if a singular event thought Θ_1 explains another singular event thought Θ_2, then the events that Θ_1 and Θ_2 are about stand in the relation of cause to effect, no matter how those events are described or thought about.

Thus, one can state a sufficient condition for causation in terms of explanation, without causation being an intentional relation. The idea is that you get causation if you extentionalize explanation. (Child (1994) urges a similar view.) And extensionalization can be valuable. For often, one wants to talk about the events that facts are about. When one fact renders another comprehensible, one often wants to speak of the events *in virtue of which the facts obtain*, in order to talk about how these events are related *independently of how we think about them*. And *linking* explanations often requires two descriptions of a single event. Let Θ_3 be the singular event thought that Fido barked loudly (at *t*); let Θ_4 be the singular event thought that Nora complained (at t^+, a time shortly after *t*); and suppose Θ_3 explains Θ_4. Fido's barking loudly (at *t*) *is* Fido's barking (at *t*); so Θ_3 is a way of thinking about Fido's barking. But

(20) The fact that Fido barked explains the fact that Nora complained

can be false. Similarly, the fact that Fido saw Garfield explains the fact that Fido barked. But

(21) The fact that Fido saw Garfield explains the fact that Nora complained

can be false. Explanation is notoriously intransitive. Even more obviously

(22) The fact that Rex saw Garfield explains the fact that Nora complained

can be false. Nonetheless, Rex's seeing Garfield caused Nora's complaint; for Rex's seeing Garfield caused Fido's (loud) barking, which caused Nora's complaint.

2.3

At this point, let us look at Figure 3.1. Singular event thoughts (represented by ovals) are about events (represented by solid squares). The indicated relations of explanation and entailment hold between the thoughts; causal relations hold, left to right, between the events. And the transitivity of causation is easily accommodated.

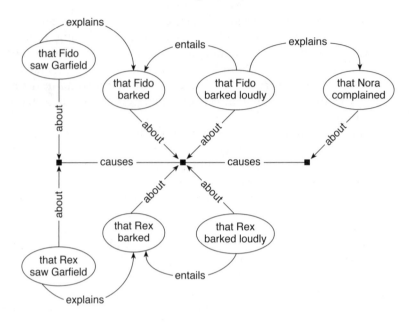

FIG. 3.1

C caused E if there is an ordered n-tuple of events $<D_1, D_2, \ldots, D_n>$, such that $C = D_1$, $E = D_n$, *and* for each i (i < n) there are singular event-thoughts Θ and Θ^*, such that Θ is about D_i, Θ^* is about D_{i+1}, and Θ explains Θ^*.

Let D_1, D_2, and D_3 be (respectively) Fido's seeing Garfield, Fido's barking, and Nora's complaint. The fact that Fido saw Garfield explains the fact that Fido barked; the former fact is about D_1, the latter is about D_2. The fact that Fido barked loudly, another fact about D_2, explains the fact that Nora complained; and this last fact is about D_3. So it follows, given the condition above, that D_1 caused D_3. Hence, Rex's seeing Garfield caused Nora's complaint. (In Chapter 7, I also argue for the converse thesis: if C caused E, then a singular event-thought about C explains a singular event thought about E.)

Connecting different explanations requires that events be related in a way that is independent of any particular way of thinking about the events. But this does not preclude a sufficient condition for causation formulated in terms of an intentional relation. And it can be useful, I suggest, to think of causation as the transitive closure of the extensionalization of explanations involving singular event thoughts. I often reduce this mouthful by saying that causation is the extensionalization of explanation; but the restriction to singular event thoughts is always intended, and transitivity is assumed (unless otherwise noted). The idea is that a causal chain of events is what remains if you take a series of singular event thoughts each of which explains the next, and ignore the *ways* in which the events are presented in thought (focusing on the events themselves). In one sense, this is a mundane claim about how causation and explanation—or perhaps our concepts of causation and explanation—are related. But accounting for (the possibility of) mental causation may be largely a matter of getting clear about the implications of this mundane claim.

3. A Possible Account of Mental Causation

In the rest of this chapter, I offer a sketch of how the work done so far might be applied to the causes and effects of actions. (In the next three chapters, I fill out this sketch.) I have drawn attention to a sufficient condition for causation in terms of explanation, because I plan to combine it with a sufficient condition for explanation in terms of covering laws. In my view there are laws linking mental events (via actions) to bodily motions; citing these laws lets us see how mental events can satisfy a sufficient condition for being causes of bodily motions, whether or not mental events are neural events; and this lets us see how non-neural mental events could be causes of bodily motions.

3.1

For purposes of illustration, pretend that

(23) if a dog sees a cat at t, it barks at t^+

is a law where t^+ is a time shortly after t. A traditional rendering of (23) would be:

(24) $\forall x \forall y \forall t[Dx \ \& \ Cy \ \& \ Sxyt \Rightarrow Bxt^+]$,

where '$\Rightarrow$' is the appropriate connective for expressing nomic relations. A more faithful event analysis rendering of (23), without thematic elaboration, would be:

(25) $\forall x \forall y \forall e \forall t\{Dog(x) \ \& \ Cat(y) \ \& \ See(e, x, y) \ \& \ At(e, t) \Rightarrow \exists f[Bark(f, x) \ \& \ At(f, t^+)]\}$.

This makes reference to events—causes and effects—explicit. But for simplicity, assume (24) and the following initial conditions: Fido is a dog (Df); Garfield is a cat (Cg); and Fido saw Garfield at t (Sfg$t$). It follows that Fido barked at t^+ (Bft^+). But it does not follow that Rex barked at t^+ (Brt^+), unless one adds that Rex is a dog (Dr) or that Rex is Fido (r = f). So the opacity of explanation is mirrored by what can(not) be derived from a certain body of claims that includes a relevant generalization. Indeed, following Hempel (1965) and others, one might hope to defend (a restricted variation on) the following sufficient condition for explanation:

> if **B** is a body of true claims consisting of a law *L* and an instance of each initial condition of *L*, and F is an instance of the consequent of *L*, and the inference from **B** to F is valid, then **B** explains F.

One could go on to say that if **B** explains F, and F is a singular event thought, and **B*** is the only singular event thought represented in **B**, then **B*** explains F. This yields a sufficient condition for causation, given that C caused E if a singular event thought about C explains a singular event thought about E.

Unfortunately, this sufficient condition is all but useless, because of a trade-off between truth and derivability. Given (24), and the statement of initial conditions 'Df & Cg & Sfg$t$', one can derive a statement of the explanandum 'Bft^+'. But (24) is false: dogs don't always bark when they see cats. It is tempting to think that a more elaborate law, which mentions certain types of dogs and cats, will be true:

(26) $\forall x \forall y \forall t [Dx \ \& \ \Phi x \ \& \ Cy \ \& \ \Psi y \ \& \ Sxyt \Rightarrow Bxt^+]$,

where 'Φ' and 'Ψ' are conditions yet to be specified. But even if a Φ-ish dog is apt to bark at Ψ-ish cats, *many* things can keep such a dog from barking. The dog might be drugged or muzzled; it might die when it sees the cat; etc. This makes the task of specifying 'Φ' at least daunting. Of course, this is just a toy example. But for reasons discussed in Chapter 4, most (and perhaps all) explanatory laws seem to face counter-instances. So instead of viewing laws as strict exceptionless generalizations—the form illustrated by (24–6)—I view laws as generalizations that hold *ceteris paribus*; and I will offer a proposal about what it is for a law to hold *ceteris paribus*. Here, let me just mention two constraints that an account of non-strict laws must respect if it is to be of any help in providing a sufficient condition for explanation.

First, an account of *ceteris paribus* (cp) laws must help us understand the relation between explanation and instantiating (non-strict) laws. Suppose we replace (24) with the following:

(27) $cp\{\forall x \forall y \forall t [Dx \ \& \ Cy \ \& \ Sxyt \Rightarrow Bxt^+]\}$,

where (27) is logically compatible with at least some instances of (Dx & Cy & Sxyt & ¬Bxt$^+$). If one insulates laws from easy falsification in this way, then one cannot also *derive* statements of explananda (like 'Bft^+') from laws and statements of initial conditions (like 'Dx & Cy & Sxy$t$'). If there can be cat-sightings by dogs who fail to bark, then by hypothesis, the inference from cat-sightings to dog-barkings is not valid. But how can an invalid inference provide an explanation of anything? Moreover, it seems that a positive instance of a non-strict law can fail to be an explanatory instance. Suppose that Fido saw Garfield, but Fido was under the influence of a drug that would have kept him from barking if only Nora had not stepped on Fido's tail. The initial conditions of (27) are satisfied: Df & Cg & Sfg$t$. And because Nora stepped on Fido's tail, the consequent of (27) is also satisfied: Bft*. But it seems wrong to cite (27) in explaining why Fido barked, since seeing Garfield was irrelevant to the barking.

Second, an account of cp laws must preserve the much discussed asymmetry of explanation. Consider the ideal pendulum law (where P is the period, L the length, and g the gravitational constant):

(28) $P = 2\pi \sqrt{(L/g)}$.

Given (28) and a claim about the length of a pendulum, one can derive a claim about its period. Similarly, given (28) and a claim about the period of a pendulum, one can derive a claim about its length. But intuitively, length explains period, and not vice versa.[14] Given my focus on singular event thoughts, I will be concerned only with laws that relate *events*, like changes in length and changes in period. So the relevant constraint is that an account of cp laws should license the first *but not the second* of the following generalizations:

cp{if the length of a pendulum changes,
its period changes in accordance with (28)}
cp{if the period of a pendulum changes,
its length changes in accordance with (28)}.

I will offer an account of cp laws that has just this feature.

3.2

By the end of Chapter 4, I hope to have made it plausible that C caused E if a singular event thought about C is suitably related by a (non-strict) law to a singular event thought about E. In Chapters 5 and 6, I apply this sufficient condition for causation to cases of mental causation.

Suppose Nora is at an auction, and comes to believe that she will buy a certain painting if she raises her arm. (Nora believes that she will bid $100 by raising her arm, and that no one will outbid her.) Nora wants to buy

---

[14] Such cases are often presented as counter-examples to covering-law models of explanation. But this is unwarranted, as I argue in Ch. 4, Sect. 4.

ιne painting. So she raises her arm. Let M be the event of Nora's acquiring her conditional belief; then M is a mental cause of Nora's action. On
the view defended in Chapter 1, Nora's action is a trying that caused the
rising of her arm. Let T be the trying, and let B be the relevant bodily
motion. Then we can represent the causal sequence of events as follows:

$$\ldots \to M \to T \to B.$$

(I ignore muscle contractions, which introduce further complications,
until the end of Chapter 7.) Bodily motions with mental causes have
neural causes. And my strategy will be to accommodate this fact, without
saying that mental events are neural events, by defending the following
picture:

$$\ldots \to M \to T \quad \searrow$$
$$\qquad\qquad\qquad\qquad B$$
$$\ldots \to N_{k-2} \to N_{k-1} \to N_k \quad \nearrow$$

Initially, this can seem absurd: how can a bodily motion be caused by
neural events *and* distinct mental events? But thinking of causation as the
extensionalization of explanation makes this less mysterious. Suppose we
interpret the arrow, so that $C \to E$ iff relative to some ways of thinking
about C and E, the occurrence of the former event explains the occurrence
of the latter event. It is not absurd that the occurrence of a mental event
can explain the occurrence of another event, even if mental events are not
neural events. And perhaps a plausible sufficient condition for explanation
will help us see how a mental event can be a non-neural cause. Of course,
I need to deliver the goods.

   Unsurprisingly, my view is that intentional explanations can relate singular event-thoughts in a way that licenses singular causal claims. Saying
just this, however, is unlikely to help anyone see how mental events can be
non-neural causes. For it is easy to think that our notion of causation
(together with facts about how human bodies work) make the following
view unavoidable: our mental events are causes—and hence, intentional
explanation is causal explanation—only if our mental events are neural
events. So I want a sufficient condition for explanation that helps to show
how this view can be avoided. I want a plausible condition of the form
'Θ_1 explains Θ_2, if . . . Θ_1 . . . Θ_2 . . .' that meets several desiderata: if M is
a mental cause of a trying T, some pair of singular event thoughts about
M and T satisfy the condition; and similarly if T is a cause of some bodily
motion B; the condition is substantive, in that (instead of saying merely
that facts about mental events and their effects stand in an explanatory
relation) it focuses on a feature common to intentional explanations and
other causal explanations; and for this reason, the condition helps us see
how there can be non-neural mental causes.

At this level of abstraction, my strategy can be pursued in different ways. (This is a good thing, since it is unlikely that my particular proposal is correct in detail.) But I think a promising idea is that one can formulate a suitable sufficient condition for explanation in terms of *ceteris paribus* laws. When a person tries to do something because she acquired a conditional belief, an intentional explanation of her action may well involve the practical syllogism: if N wants Ψ to be the case, and comes to believe that doing Φ will make Ψ the case, then N will try to Φ. (Describing this generalization as *the* practical syllogism is a massive simplification, to which I return.) But for the moment, the relevant point is just that an action/trying can be rendered comprehensible, at least in part, by locating it in a rationalizing pattern. In this sense, I take (at least some) intentional explanations to involve covering laws. The relevant laws are ineliminably hedged. That is, they hold only *ceteris paribus*. But this is not a reason for denying that there are genuine laws couched in intentional terms. As I argue in Chapter 4, many of our best scientific explanations advert to hedged laws; explanation requires *idealization*.

If there are *ceteris paribus* (cp) laws couched in intentional terms, perhaps this will help account for the causal status of intentional explanations. (See Section 3 of the introduction, and the brief discussion of Fodor's (1989) view.) At least for now, grant that the practical syllogism can be formulated as a true cp law of the form: if a certain initial condition obtains (N wants Ψ to be the case), and an event of type T1 occurs (N comes to believe that Φ-ing will make Ψ the case), then an event of type T2 will occur (N will try to Φ). Intuitively, Nora tried to raise her arm, because she came to have a certain belief. So as a first pass that will need qualification, suppose that a singular event thought Θ1 explains another singular event thought Θ2 if Θ1 is an instance of the fact that an event of type T1 occurred; Θ2 is an instance of the fact that an event of type T2 occurred; and it is a law that cp[if a T1-event occurs, a T2-event occurs]—or cp[if C, then (if a T1-event occurs, a T2-event occurs)], where 'C' is a statement of some initial condition that actually obtains. And for now, just assume that a singular event thought about a trying can explain a singular event thought about a bodily motion, in that these (trying-motion) event pairs are also covered by cp laws.

In its simplest form, the idea is that C caused E if (a singular event thought about) C explains (a singular event thought about) E; and reasons can explain tryings, which can explain bodiiy motions, via cp laws. Given the assumptions of the last paragraph, and taking causation to be the extensionalization of explanation, it follows that the event of Nora's acquiring her conditional belief caused her action (of trying to raise her arm), which in turn caused the rising of her arm. It does not follow that the mental events in this causal chain are *neural* causes of the arm-rising.

But one might think this will follow, given further considerations. Perhaps bodily motions would be (objectionably) overdetermined, unless every mental event is a neural event. In Chapter 6, I argue that this is not so. And in Chapter 7, I speak to a cluster of concerns associated with the mind-independence of causal relations, as part of showing that my proposed sufficient condition for explanation satisfies the desiderata mentioned above.

3.3

Let me conclude this chapter, by returning to a complication earlier set aside. When I speak of the practical syllogism, I am referring to a *class* of generalizations couched in intentional terms. The generalization mentioned above, which relates the acquisition of conditional beliefs to tryings (given suitable desires), is just one example. A similar generalization relates the acquisition of desires to tryings (given suitable conditional beliefs). But these simple examples apply only when time-sensitive reasoning and *planning* are not at issue. Often (and perhaps typically), when a person who wants Ψ to be the case comes to believe that Φ-ing will make Ψ the case, Φ-ing is not something she can do there and then. On Monday, Nora may come to believe that she can buy the painting, if she *bids $100 at the auction on Wednesday*. But this is not something Nora will try to do, upon acquiring her belief. What will happen on Monday, other things being equal, is that Nora will *form an intention* to make her bid at the auction on Wednesday. And forming this intention will have further effects, given Nora's other beliefs and desires. For example, she may form the intention to leave her house at noon on Wednesday, in order to attend the auction; and given this intention, the acquisition of a suitable belief about the time (on Wednesday) will cause Nora's action of leaving her house, other things being equal.

Of course, Nora's action of leaving her house may itself be a structured action that involves finding her keys, locking the door, etc. But I have nothing useful to say about the role intentions play in structuring complex actions and updating a broader *plan* (see Bratman (1987) for discussion). I simply assume that some generalizations like the following are true, where t^+ is a time shortly after t: if (at t) N wants Ψ to be the case, and (at t) N comes to believe that Φ-ing *when condition C obtains* will make Ψ the case, then (at t^+) N will intend to Φ when C obtains; and if (at t) N intends to Φ when C obtains, and (at t) N comes to believe that C obtains, then (at t^+) N will try to Φ.

One might grant that there are intentional generalizations that connect the acquisition of beliefs and desires (perhaps via intentions) to tryings, yet be more dubious that there are psycho*physical* laws of the sort proposed. In sketching my account of mental causation, I assumed that there are laws that cover event pairs of the form <T, B>, where B is a bodily motion caused by the trying T. Proper defence of this claim will require the Chapter 4 account of cp laws. But let me motivate the claim, and speak to some obvious sources of scepticism, by emphasizing points from earlier discussions.

The simplest putative law that would cover tryings and their effects is 'cp[if N tries to Φ, N Φs]'. Alas, this is implausible. The world is not arranged so that, as a matter of law, our tryings are successful. If Nora *tries but fails* to lift a heavy rock (solve a problem, make a million dollars), this need not be a case of other things failing to be equal. You can't always get what you want, not even if you try real hard, not even *ceteris paribus*. Restricting 'Φ' to bodily movements helps, since effects *external* to persons are ignored, but the problem remains. It may be that cp[if Nora tries to jump, she jumps]. It is not true, however, that cp[if Nora tries to jump 100 feet, she jumps 100 feet]. Similarly, a backflip is a bodily movement. But it doesn't follow that, cp, I can do one. So perhaps we should restrict 'Φ' to bodily movements, and say 'cp[if a person who *can* Φ tries to Φ, then she Φs]'. I think this is on the right track, though the relevant sense of 'can' is not obvious. An athlete who jumps 27 feet may have tried to do so. Yet it seems wrong to insist that *cetera* are not *paria* on any other occasions when the athlete tries but fails to jump 27 feet, though in one sense of 'can', he can make such a jump. And even if he could jump 27 feet *today*, it does not follow that cp, he will jump that far upon trying (see Thalberg 1972).

Still, persons without disabilities *can* move their bodies in many ways. And for many instances of 'Φ', it is plausible that cp[if a (human) person tries to Φ, she Φs]. Consider 'move her hand', 'raise her arm', 'stand up', etc. Many such instances will include verbs of the sort discussed in Chapter 1—verbs that take a transitive and an intransitive form, with the transitive being satisfied by complex events that culminate in bodily motions that satisfy the intransitive. (As we shall see in Chapter 7, this relation between cp laws and the causative verbs is hardly accidental, but neither does it lead to vicious circularity.) In Chapter 4, I take the mark of a cp law to be that apparent failures of the law call for (and can be given) explanations of a special sort. Intuitively, no explanation is called for if Nora tries but fails to jump 100 feet; while special explanation is called for if Nora tries but fails to raise her arm. As the long-jump example suggests, the mere *possibility* of moving one's body in manner *m* does not ensure that cp[if one tries to move one's body in manner *m*, one does so]. A real cp law requires something more. One might speak of having a *capacity* to move one's body in manner *m*; where explanation is required, if a capacity to Φ is exercised and not manifested in a Φ-ing (see Chapter 4, n. 13).

Strictly speaking, instances of 'cp[if a person tries to move her hand, she moves her hand]' are not cause–effect pairs. Given the argument of

Chapter 1, the trying *grounds* (rather than causes) the moving$_T$, which is a complex event. In this particular case, reformulating the law is easy: cp[if a person tries to move$_T$ her hand, her hand moves$_I$].[15] But unless all action verbs are causatives, this strategy does not generalize. And in any case, 'cp[if a person tries to pull a rope, she pulls it]' is unlikely to be true. The (already taut) rope might be attached to a heavy object, and I would not want to insist that other things fail to be equal in such a case. But normally, persons might well have the capacity to *pull on* a rope. That is, perhaps cp[if a person tries to pull a rope, she pulls on the rope], where an event of pulling-on is a bodily motion relevantly like a motion that would occur if one successfully pulled the rope, abstracting away from whether or not the rope moved.

More generally, the idea would be to specify bodily motions as events that *would* be parts of certain complex events (that fall under familiar sortals) *were* certain external conditions favourable. Just as we can speak of those events like events of seeing an apple, abstracting away from whether or not there really was an apple, so we can speak of those events like pullings of ropes abstracting away from whether or not the rope really moved. So for many instances of 'Φ', there may well be a bodily motion type Ψ (perhaps specified in terms of familiar sortals, but abstracting away from whether or not external conditions are favourable), such that cp[if N tried to Φ, then there is a bodily motion of type Ψ]; or, alternatively, cp[if N tried to Φ, N's body moves$_I$ in a Ψ-ish manner]. This may sound contrived. But we do not have many sortals for bodily motions, apart from the intransitive sortals that figure in causative entailments. Our predominant method for referring to bodily motions is by referring to them *as* the motions caused by certain mental events. So in saying that bodily motions with mental causes also have neural causes, we may already be committed to describing such bodily motions along the lines suggested.

I will assume, therefore, that the complications just surveyed do not present insuperable difficulties for the following idea: a fair number of familiar action sortals correspond to psychophysical cp laws that relate tryings to bodily motions. And for now, the crucial point is that my proposal applies to a given event pair if these events are covered by *some* cp law. So I need not endorse the extremely general and implausible claim, 'cp[if a person tries to Φ, she Φs]'.

In this context, let me stress once again the distinction between causation and explanation. Suppose Nora tries to raise her hand, and as a result, her hand rises. Her hand rises some distance, say 17¼ inches. But it

---

[15] One might also modify the sufficient condition for explanation, and allow cp laws to cover *either* cause/effect *or* grounder/complex-event pairs. For perhaps a law covering the event pair <T, B*>, where T grounds the complex event B* which culminates in B, also covers <T, B>.

does not follow that Nora tried to raise her hand 17¼ inches. Indeed, there may be no *intentional* explanation for why Nora's hand rose 17¼ inches. Nonetheless, the event of her hand rising was the event of her hand rising 17¼ inches. The trying caused the rising. So Nora's trying to raise her hand caused the event of her hand rising 17¼ inches. And I need not say that cp[if Nora tries to raise her hand 17¼ inches, she does so]. The occurrence of her trying explains the occurrence of the rising, *relative to at least one* way of thinking about the rising. In the terminology recently introduced, the fact that Nora's hand rose (at time t), and the fact that her hand rose 17¼ inches (at t) are distinct singular event thoughts about the same event. And there can be an intentional explanation of the former fact, absent an intentional explanation of the latter. Correspondingly, I can say that a trying T caused a bodily motion B, so long as there is *some* way of thinking about B, such that the occurrence of T explains the occurrence of B relative to that way of thinking about B.

Note also that nothing in Chapter 1 conflicts with the following truism: a person often tries to do one thing *by* doing something else. Nora may try to get the painting by raising her arm. Her action is her trying to raise her arm. If we like, we can also describe Nora's action as her trying to get the painting. And if Nora is successful, she gets the painting because she raised her hand. But I need not posit the putative law, 'cp[if Nora tries to get x, she gets x]'. The task is to explain why Nora's arm rose and, for this purpose, her action is best described as a trying to raise her arm. Of course, one may acquire the capacity to move one's body in a sophisticated way. It may come to be true, for some Φ, that cp[if Nick tries to Φ, he Φs]. And if a person practises Φ-ing (by Ψ-ing), he may eventually acquire the capacity to Φ (without trying to Ψ). Nick may be able to bang out an F♯-minor scale on the piano, but only by thinking through each step: hit the F♯, then the G♯, then the A, and so on; Nick tries to play the scale by trying, for each of the eight keys, to hit it (and by trying to produce these actions in sequence). By contrast, a skilled pianist will simply try to play the scale; and other things equal, he will manifest a capacity to do so. That is, cp, a pianist will move his fingers in an F♯-minor-scale way, where the action of moving his fingers in this way *is* the pianist's trying to play the scale (successfully, as it happens). Correlatively, the pianist does not play the scale by doing anything else. Indeed, it is a familiar point that *trying* to carry out the steps can botch a practised performance.

Finally, by way of showing how these points interact, let me offer some speculative remarks about the athlete who successfully tries to jump 27 feet. (My aim is not to capture all the complexities of such mind–body interactions, but to illustrate how event dualists can avoid positing implausible instances of 'cp, a person who tries to Φ will Φ'.) Precisely because the jumper's accomplishment is close to the wall of physical

Causing Actions

possibility, it seems wrong to say that cp[if he tries to jump 27 feet, he does so]. A person does not have a *capacity* to perform at this level, just because he once jumped that far. But world-class jumpers differ from the rest of us, and not just by virtue of having bodies that make longer jumps physically possible for them. Training and 'mental toughness' let good athletes regularly come close to the limits of what is physically possible for them. To put it somewhat paradoxically, most of us cannot jump as far as we can jump. Lack of technique, and lack of a capacity to push oneself to the limit, keep our performances well short of the (still meagre) results we might otherwise achieve. But perhaps: cp[if a practised jumper tries to jump as far as he can (in circumstance C), then he jumps about as far as he can (in C)]. And our athlete might jump 27 feet, on a given occasion, by trying to jump as far as he can. There may be no intentional explanation of why he jumped 27 feet. But there will be an intentional explanation of why he jumped about as far as he could—viz. he tried to do so (and has the capacity to do so). And his jumping 27 feet can *be* the event of his jumping as far as he could (on that occasion).

I hope this is enough to make the proposed sufficient condition for causation (in terms of explanation) seem worth exploring. Before saying more about the intentional, however, I need to make the sufficient condition for explanation (in tems of cp laws) at least plausible. And here, a potential stumbling block presents itself immediately. How can a true law have exceptions? Without an answer to this question, accounting for mental causation in terms of cp laws is to explain the puzzling in terms of the obscure. With an answer, I contend, one can defend a (restricted) covering-law account of explanation that in turn provides a plausible sufficient condition for (event) causation.

4

Other Things Being Equal

Appeal to *ceteris paribus* clauses is at once ubiquitous and dubious. It is nearly impossible to provide unhedged empirical generalizations that are both true and theoretically interesting. For the world is a complex place. When we study it, and try to formulate the laws that govern its operation, we always focus on certain factors while ignoring others. This practice of abstraction, or *idealization*, is essential to understanding. But it guarantees a loss of descriptive adequacy in our theoretical generalizations, making appeal to *ceteris paribus* (cp) clauses unavoidable. Still, suspicion of cp clauses is easily bred.

An honest generalization, one might think, is a bold conjecture that wears its falsification conditions on its sleeve: when someone claims that all Fs are Gs, her claim is false if some F is not G. From this perspective, a cp clause turns an honest generalization into something disreputable—an allegedly falsifiable claim that is somehow compatible with counter-examples. Faced with an F that is not G, one retreats to the claim that all Fs are Gs, *other things being equal*. This invites the thought that generalizations modified by a cp clause (and thus insulated from easy falsification) are vacuous. Put most starkly, one might charge that 'cp, all Fs are Gs' says merely that all Fs are Gs, except for those Fs that are not Gs.

I view this as a puzzle of the type described in the Introduction: we have strong reason to think that many laws hold only cp, yet it is hard to see how cp clauses can relax generalizations without trivializing them. So I devote much of this chapter to providing a sufficient condition for non-vacuity. With this proposal in place, I return to the sufficient condition for explanation offered at the end of Chapter 3, and argue that it is *not* open to objections that plague traditional covering-law models.

1. The Need for Idealization[1]

We look to science for good explanations. One important form of scientific explanation involves citing laws from which the explanandum can be

---

[1] As noted in the preface, the first three sections of this chapter are (with some modification) from Pietroski and Rey (1995). But I am solely responsible for Sect. 4.

derived.[2] To take a familiar example: with the aid of certain assumptions or statements of boundary conditions, the ideal gas law explains why the pressure of a gas sample rises, given an increase in its temperature (holding the volume constant). Laws have traditionally been schematized as generalizations of the form '$\forall x[Fxt \Rightarrow \exists y(Gyt + \varepsilon)]$', where 'F' and 'G' are (perhaps complex) kind predicates of the science in question, t is a time, ε is an interval, and '$\Rightarrow$' is the appropriate connective for nomic conditionals. I often abbreviate such schemata by omitting time references, or by writing '$F \Rightarrow G$', intending the quantificational structure noted above.[3]

The key feature here is the universal quantifier. Laws say that, *whenever* some initial condition obtains, some other condition obtains. On the traditional view, a single instance of ($F \& \neg G$) shows that '$F \Rightarrow G$' is false. At least in the special sciences, however, one often hypothesizes that $F \Rightarrow G$, knowing full well that instances of ($F \& \neg G$) are easy to find. Philosophers of mind have been especially interested in the prevalence of apparent exceptions to generalizations couched in overtly intentional terms. But it is a familiar point that the ideal gas law is only rarely satisfied by actual gas samples. Similar 'counter-examples' plague generalizations in geology, economics, non-intentional psychology, etc. This is, I contend, an inescapable feature of generalizing with the aim of explaining in a complex world. So the task is to show how laws can be explanatory in the face of counter-instances.

I. I

Any example of an alleged cp law will be open to debate. But it is worth exploring one in a little detail. Following Sober (1984), I think there are laws of evolutionary biology. In particular, consider what might be called Darwin's Conditional. If within a population, (1) organisms possessing a property P are better able to survive and reproduce than organisms possessing an alternative property P*, and (2) P and P* are heritable, then (3) the proportion of organisms having P will increase. Given some Mendelian genetics, (2) can be glossed as: P and P* are controlled by gene complexes g and $g*$, respectively. So if (1) and (2) obtain, the proportion of organisms in the population having g will increase. Evolution is com-

---

[2] There are other forms of explanation; see e.g. Cummins (1983). And while appeal to cp clauses may not be restricted to explanations that invoke laws, I focus here on nomic subsumption.

[3] Such schemata are simplifications. Further conditions might be relevant to the statement of any given law. In particular, it might be stipulated that other relations hold between x and y: identity (if the temperature in a volume of gas rises, the pressure exerted by *it* rises), locality (y is in x's light cone), etc. For simplicity, I set such conditions aside, in the hope that (with reasonable supplementation) what is said in the text will apply to laws with slightly different quantificational structures.

monly characterized as a change in gene frequencies in a population. Thus, one can also formulate the law as follows: if (1) and (2), there will be evolution in favour of the gene complex that controls P.

As Sober (1984) quickly points out, though, 'a *ceteris paribus* clause needs to be added here: heritable variation in fitness will result in evolution only on the assumption that no counteracting forces cancel its effects (ibid. 27–8)'. Evolutionary theory itself tells us why Darwin's Conditional is an idealization, not a generalization that is automatically falsified if (1) and (2) ever obtain without the corresponding evolution. If certain organisms have a gene g_1 that controls a useful phenotypic property P, and the competitor of g_1 at its locus controls a selectively inert trait, then one would expect the proportion of organisms having g_1 (and P) to increase in the population. But this will not always happen. When a gene is replicated, nearby genes are sometimes copied as well. This is one of several ways in which genes controlling distinct phenotypic traits can be linked. Suppose now that g_1 is linked to another gene g_2, which controls a very deleterious trait Q, and the competitor of g_2 at its locus is selectively inert. Then the proportion of organisms in the population having g_1 may decrease. (I say 'may', since g_1 might be linked to gene g_3, which controls a very useful trait.)

Genetic drift, the biological analogue of sampling error in statistics, would be another source of counter-example to an unhedged principle of natural selection. If ten balls are drawn from a box containing fifty red and fifty blue balls, there is a chance that more than five (and perhaps all ten) of the balls drawn will be red. Similarly, the distribution of genes that come to reside in zygotes may differ from the distribution of genes in the sexually reproducing population at large. For each zygote will be composed of one gamete from each parent, each gamete having only one of the pair of parental genes for each locus. So even if organisms with gene g are somewhat better able to survive and reproduce than organisms with a competitor gene g^*, the net result may be evolution in favour of g^* if the drift is strong enough. Another factor is the rate of mutation: if g mutates more often than g^*, selective pressure in favour of g may be nullified by mutation (or by a combination of mutation and drift). Or organisms with gene g may happen to be struck by lightning more often than organisms with the competing gene g^*.

It is tempting to reply, by building conditions like 'genes are not linked and do not mutate' into the antecedent of the unhedged generalization. But this would have a perverse consequence: Darwin's Conditional would apply (non-vacuously) only when all the relevant genes are unlinked and do not mutate. Gene linkage is, however, pervasive in complex organisms; and mutation is a source of the phenotypic variation on which the very process of selection operates. Similarly, requiring that drift and natural disasters affect the distribution of competing traits *equally* would restrict application of Darwin's Conditional to the vanishingly few actual scenarios where non-selective forces have the very *same* effect on relevant subpopulations (in our example, those organisms with g and those with g^*).[4]

Another temptation is to treat all cp laws as merely probabilistic—i.e. as having the form: $(\forall x)\{Fxt \Rightarrow$ with probability $n[\exists y(Gyt+\varepsilon)]\}$, for some n. Some biological factors do have a statistical character. But as we shall see, this is not the case for every source of apparent exceptions to cp laws. More importantly, treating cp laws as probabilistic laws misses a crucial aspect of the puzzle about cp laws. In many cases, ideal circumstances are not merely rare, they are *nomologically impossible*. It would seem to be (biologically) impossible for there to be no gene mutation or linkage. Or returning to an earlier example, one source of counter-example to a strict version of the ideal gas law is the inelasticity of containers; and containers *cannot* be perfectly elastic. Similarly, markets cannot be totally free of outside forces. Correlatively, I claim, the need for cp laws stems from the need to idealize in a complex world, not the need to describe a chancy one.

It may be that, as a matter of genuine probabilistic law, some radioactive particle has a 50 per cent chance of decaying in a specified time. But we do not think the same is true of containers—i.e. that there is some stable objective chance of containers in general being negligibly inelastic. Similarly, a free-fall law idealizes away from friction and wind, without there being any particular chance (say 27 per cent) that the law will describe a falling body's motion correctly. Moreover, even if one could speak of the objective chance that an arbitrary falling body will accelerate towards earth at a rate of 32ft/sec.², a free-fall law does not *function* as a merely probabilistic claim. Given a falling body that does not accelerate at 32ft/sec.², we do not just say: that's the way it goes sometimes. As I emphasize below, each apparent failure of the law *calls for explanation* in a way that improbable instances of a probabilistic law do not (cf. an unlucky dice run, or a group of particles most of which do not decay in their half-life).

A final temptation is to deny that special sciences state laws (see Schiffer 1987, 1991). But by itself, this response won't do. For (*pace* Schiffer) when

---

[4] One can also trivialize Darwin's Conditional by restricting it to cases in which factors other than fitness have 'negligible' effects on evolution, where this just *means* that non-selective factors do not result in counter-examples. Following Sober (1984: 31–7), I take the following conditional to be another cp law: if the organisms in generation G of a diploid population produce haploid gametes, then the distribution of genotypes in the next generation will be the Hardy–Weinberg function of the distribution of genotypes in G. This generalization idealizes away from *all* evolutionary forces, including natural selection; cf. the claim that a body in motion (at rest) stays in motion (at rest). While such laws face *many* abNormal instances, they can still help explain phenomena (e.g. the distribution of traits in a controlled population of fruit flies, or the motion of bodies in space).

the biologically fittest increase their percentage share in a population, we often explain this fact by citing Darwin's Conditional. Similarly, we often cite Boyle's equations when the pressure of a gas rises upon being heated; we cite supply/demand curves when the cost of a product increases following a decrease in supply, etc. So if one denies that the special sciences state laws, one must either: (i) explain away the illusion that explanations like those just mentioned advert to laws—explaining, moreover, how the special sciences can provide good explanations without having any laws to advert to; or (ii) deny the immensely plausible claim that the special sciences sometimes provide good explanations. Either way, there is a serious cost.[5]

I.2

One might think that this problem arises *only* for special sciences, and not for the basic (or, for some, the *real*) science of physics. But Cartwright (1983, 1989) has argued that, on their most plausible interpretations, many familiar statements of physical law are themselves far from exceptionless. Cartwright's conclusions are highly controversial, and my aim is not to defend them. Nor will I provide a detailed assessment of her examples. My aim is to offer a response to a certain *kind* of example, without denying that our best sciences often state true laws that figure in good explanations.

Newton's law of gravity ($F = Gmm^*/d^2$) tells us that the force exerted by one object on another varies directly as the products of their masses and inversely as the square of the distance between them. (Like Cartwright, let us ignore relativistic considerations, which are tangential to her point.) Together with a law relating force to mass and acceleration ($F = ma$), the law of gravity yields claims about the motion of bodies. Indeed, it is *via* such claims that we test and confirm the law. But by themselves, these equations and initial values for the variables will not always lead to correct claims about the motions of the relevant bodies. Describing the motions of charged bodies requires Coulomb's Law ($F = kqq^*/d^2$); and for small charged bodies, the relatively weak gravitational effect is swamped by the

---

[5] Hempel (1988) makes similar remarks, though he recognizes the need for an alternative account of special sciences. Schiffer (1987: 287, n. 10) complains that 'Other things being equal' clauses are simply fudges when it is unclear what the 'other things' are, or what it would be for them to be 'equal'. But as we shall see, cp clauses are needed precisely when it is *not* clear what the other things are. So we need an account that shows why such clauses are not 'simply fudges'. Schiffer also says that cp clauses are a kind of ellipsis; for he understands 'cp($F \Rightarrow G$)' as '(F & . . .) $\Rightarrow G$'. He thus concludes that a cp-modified lawlike sentence expresses no proposition. But on my account, 'cp($F \Rightarrow G$)' is not elliptical; and it expresses the (perfectly fine) proposition that cp($F \Rightarrow G$).

electromagnetic effect.[6] Similarly, the motion of small charged objects may not be described by Coulomb's Law: if there is a large dense mass in the vicinity, gravitational effects are non-negligible.

Cartwright concludes that statements of the fundamental laws are not even approximate truths. In the absence of a unified field theory that explains *how* gravitation and electromagnetism interact, Cartwright (like Joseph 1980) denies that the real laws of physics are composition principles. And for various methodological reasons, she rejects Creary's (1981) claim that fundamental laws describe entities (forces) that *cause* the motions of bodies. Instead, Cartwright offers an account of explanation that does not require approximately true laws, but rather distinguishes among false lawlike sentences (e.g. $F = Gmm^*/d^2$ *vs.* $F = Gm^2/dm^*$), some of which express commitments to what she calls 'capacities'.

For reasons discussed in Section 3 below, Cartwright also rejects the idea that laws contain implicit cp clauses. On this view (which is compatible with saying that physical laws describe forces and/or certain effects of objects on the surrounding space-time), bodies obey the law of gravity and Coulomb's law, cp. But *cetera* aren't *paria* with respect to the former law when the bodies are charged, or with respect to the latter law when the relevant particles are affected by a nearby mass. Similarly, the cp condition may be violated when advantageous genes are linked to deleterious genes, when a rise in supply is concomitant with a rise in demand, etc. (And I will suggest that most of Cartwright's view is compatible with appeals to cp laws, once unsatisfactory conceptions of cp laws are set aside.)

1.3

Let a *strict* law be one that contains no cp clause, even implicitly (cf. Davidson 1970, 1974). I claim that not all laws are strict. But I do not say that no laws are strict. Consider the claim that all humans are mortal. More interestingly, physical processes seem to conserve mass/energy without exception; though at various times, apparent counter-examples to conservation principles were dealt with by postulating new sources of mass/energy that had previously been ignored. Perhaps a future quantum theory of gravity will also provide an example of a strict law, though it is not obvious that a unification of gravity with the other fundamental forces will take the form a strict law governing certain tiny particles. In any case, current science hardly justifies the view that explanatory laws must be

---

[6] Joseph (1980), Hempel (1988), and Laymon (1985, 1989) make similar observations. I assume that such equations can be treated as abbreviations of cumbersome law statements, along the lines of:

$$(x)(y)(m)(m^*)(d)\{(x \text{ has mass } m \ \& \ y \text{ has mass } m^* \ \& \ d = \text{the distance between x and y}) \Rightarrow (\exists F)(F = \text{the force between x and y} \ \& \ F = Gmm^*/d^2)\}.$$

strict. On the contrary, the question is whether any explanatory laws are strict.

One might insist, however, that laws be *exceptionless*. And in order to avoid terminological disputes, let me grant this point. If there are exceptions to

(1) cp[$(\forall x)(Fx \Rightarrow \exists y Gy)$],

then *a fortiori* (1) is not a law. But what counts as an exception depends on the right theory of cp laws. For example, an initally plausible (if ultimately mistaken) gloss of (1) is

(2) $C \Rightarrow (\forall x)(Fx \Rightarrow \exists y Gy)$,

where C is some condition yet to be specified, but which is specifiable in finite and non-circular terms. (I return to this gloss of cp clauses in Section 3.1 below.) On this view, exceptions to (2) would be instances of [C & Fx & $\neg(\exists y)Gy$]. But when C is *false*, instances of

(3) Fx & $\neg\exists y Gy$

will not be exceptions to (2). So if (1) is glossed as (2), then (1) could be preserved in the face of at least some instances of (3). Similarly for other possible glosses of (1). In general, let me stipulate that conditions are Normal with respect to (1), when and only when there are no instances of (3). Then (1) says that Normally, $(\forall x)(Fx \Rightarrow \exists y Gy)$; and instances of (3) will be abNormal instances of (1). If this were all that could be said about Normalcy, then cp laws would indeed be open to the charge of vacuity raised above. So the task is to find a characterization of Normalcy that avoids this charge.

My goal is *not*, however, to provide a philosophical analysis of cp laws (or 'cp laws'). It is to show that such laws can be—and, indeed, probably need to be—perfectly respectable parts of a scientific theory. In particular, cp laws are not open to the charge of vacuity that allowing apparent exceptions seems to invite. Thus, I will not be providing a necessary and sufficient condition for being an acceptable cp law *tout court*, but only a sufficient condition for being a non-vacuous cp law. This will also render my proposal compatible with a variety of views about laws and explanation. I do, however, take for granted that *some* notion of scientific explanation is legitimate—and similarly for talk of facts explaining other facts. My claim is not that explanations (as opposed to laws, or causal capacities) and facts (as opposed to objects, events, properties, or propositions) are somehow *basic*. But I think the notion of explanation is, at least pretheoretically, clearer than that of cp law. So one can use the notion of explanation to help resolve the puzzles surrounding cp laws.

In the next section, I sketch and motivate a view of cp laws based on the idea that apparent exceptions to true nomic generalizations are to be explained as the result of interference. Briefly and metaphorically, cp-clauses are promissory notes written on the banks of other theories: a cp clause says that apparent exceptions to its generalization can be explained by citing factors that are (in a sense characterized below) independent of the apparent counter-example.[7] In Section 3, I distinguish this view from two other initially attractive alternatives. Finally, in Section 4, I argue that familiar objections to covering-law models of explanation do not apply to subsumption under cp laws, and that this removes at least one source of concern about my proposed sufficient condition for explanation.

2. *Abstracting away from Interference*

I suggested a cheque-cashing metaphor for cp clauses: such clauses represent a promise that all abNormal instances of a putative law can be explained away. If the promise cannot be kept, the cheque was no good. A more traditional metaphor is that a cp law holds in a *closed* system—one considered in abstraction from various factors actually at work. Such a systematization is non-vacuous only to the extent that deviations from its constitutive regularities can be explained by citing the confounding factors. The idea is that 'cp(F $\Rightarrow$ G)' is a true law only if its apparent exceptions are merely apparent, in that all instances of (F & ¬G) can be explained away by citing interference—factors one has idealized away from in stating the generalization. (Hart and Honoré (1959) suggest a similar gloss of *ceteris paribus* conditions, as does Wiggins (1973).)

Endorsing the *ceteris paribus* gas law '$P = nrT/V$' (where r is a constant, and n is the number of moles of a gas sample with pressure P, temperature, and volume V) commits one to saying that deviations from predicted values can be explained by citing factors ignored when one takes only the pressure, temperature, and volume of the gas into account. But we know that there are several such factors, including the electrical attraction between molecules, the fact that molecules take up space, and the inelasticity of containers. (I return to this example in more detail below.) Similarly, Darwin's Conditional commits one to saying that when herit-

---

[7] While it is often useful to speak of explaining something by citing a fact*or*, I assume that such talk can be glossed in terms of citing the presence of some such factor Φ—i.e. by citing *the fact that* Φ is present (and operative). If we take factors to be (causally relevant) properties, the instantiation of a factor is independent of any way of thinking about it; but the fact *that Φ is instantiated* is a Fregean thought partly constituted by a certain way of thinking about Φ (or its extension).

able variation in fitness does not lead to evolution in favour of the fittest, this can be explained by citing factors ignored when one focuses solely on natural selection and its effects on evolution. But again, we know that many non-selective factors (some of which fall within the province of biology) bear on evolution.

2.1

The requirement that factors be *independent* is intended to exclude alleged factors whose only explanatory role is to save a proposed cp law. For example, suppose Smith holds that people with red hair have telekinetic powers, and thus advances the following generalization: cp{if X has red hair, and X concentrates on a (fairly light, nearby) object O, and X 'wills' O to move, then O moves}. Suppose that Smith also appeals to ectoplas-mic interference to explain why, in experiments designed to test this gen-eralization, the spoons stay put. If the only evidence for this alleged interfering factor is the repeated failure of the putative telekinesis law, then appeal to ectoplasmic interference would seem to be a thinly disguised way of tautologizing the putative law (in effect, replacing the cp-clause with 'unless not', as discussed above). So a natural requirement is that the inter-ference cited do explanatory work *other than* merely accounting for abNormal instances of the (putative) law in question.

That is, the cited interference has to explain the apparent counter-example to the cp law, *and* something else. Unsurprisingly, it is not easy to spell out this idea in detail. For instance, a factor will not count as inde-pendent if it explains only logical (or analytic) consequences of an abNormal instance: explaining *why Q or R* is not relevantly different from explaining *why Q*. Similarly, an alleged factor must explain more than mere causal consequences of an abNormal instance. Suppose the experi-mental apparatus was arranged so that a red light would flash if the spoons remained motionless throughout the trial. Then explaining why the red light flashed, or why observers scoffed at Smith, is not relevantly different from explaining the abNormal instance of Smith's putative law. If the presence of ectoplasm explains the flashing, or the scoffing, it is only by more directly explaining why the telekinesis failed. As a (surely imper-fect) attempt to capture this intuition, let me stipulate that an interferer to a cp law explains an abNormal instance of that law only if the interferer is independent of the law's abNormal instances, where independence requires that the interferer explain something that is not a logical/ana-lytic/causal consequence of the abNormal instance in question.

An interferer can be a positive factor or the absence of such a factor. Apparent failures of Darwin's Conditional might be explained by a meteor strike or by the sudden absence of oxygen, since both phenomena would explain many other concomitant facts. Even appeals to ectoplasmic interference would be substantive *if* they explained something besides failures of the putative telekinesis law—say, the relevant subjects' correlated bouts of depression (provided that these were not fully explainable in some other way).[8] The putative telekinesis law might still be false, but it would not be *vacuous*—or at least not vacuous by virtue of the fact that some of its abNormal instances were explained by appeal to ectoplasm. Citing the further phenomena also explained by appeals to ectoplasm would amount to citing the 'independent evidence' that is intuitively needed to avoid *ad hocery*.

On this view, a chemist holding that $cp(P = nrT/V)$, is committed to the following: if a gas sample is such that $P \neq nrT/V$, independent factors (e.g. electrical attraction) explain why $P \neq nrT/V$ with respect to that gas sample. These independent factors count as interference, or *noise*, with respect to the cp law in question. For when scientists state cp laws, they ignore various aspects of the complex phenomena under investigation. So abNormal instances are to be expected. But such instances must be explicable by citing the factors ignored, else the putative cp law is either vacuous or false.[9] In stating cp laws, scientists try to focus on particular factors (e.g. pressure or natural selection) and thereby carve complex phenomena (e.g. the evolution of gases or populations) in a theoretically important way. If a putative law is such that its abNormal instances can be explained by citing independent factors, the original cut was a good one. If there are inexplicable abNormal instances, the putative cp law is either vacuous or false.

Since the present aim is to provide a sufficient condition for non-vacuity, let me offer an explicit proposal (whose clauses I go on to elucidate) based on the preceding discussion:

'cp[$\forall x(Fx \Rightarrow \exists yGy)$]' is non-vacuous *if*
  (i) 'F' and 'G' are otherwise nomological; and
  (ii) $\forall x(Fx \Rightarrow$ *either* $\exists yGy$ *or* there is an interferer INT such that INT explains why $\neg\exists yGy$ (despite Fx); and
  (iii) *either* some instance of F explains some instance of G, *or* some instance of F in conjunction with an interferer INT explains some fact from which it follows that $\neg\exists yGy$.

---

[8] Of course, the other phenomenon must be *real*. Ectoplasmic forces cannot explain clairvoyance if there is no such thing. And one tries to adjudicate disputes about which phenomena are real, by looking for untendentious data. (In Chs 6 and 7, I take up issues surrounding explanatory exclusion, which bear on the question of when a phenomenon has been sufficiently explained.)

[9] One might reject 'cp[$P = nrT/V$]', claiming that spatial extension is not a *factor* that explains abNormal instances (cf. van der Waal's equation, discussed below). I take a liberal attitude about explanatory factors. But my proposal can be conjoined with an attitude that permits fewer cp laws.

An 'otherwise nomological' property is one that plays whatever special role lawlike properties need to play in explanation generally, *apart from considerations of cp laws*. The point of clause (i) is simply to forestall putative counter-examples that show merely that familiar problems of projectability and inductive scepticism apply to cp laws.[10] Clause (ii) is the heart of the proposal. It says that if initial conditions obtain, then either the consequent of the main generalization is satisfied, or there is an independently explanatory factor at work. As we shall see (in Section 2.2), abNormal instances may be explained by the interferer alone, or by the interferer *in conjunction with the law in question*. But either way, there must be an explanation for why the consequent of the cp law failed to obtain, given that the antecedent did obtain. Clause (iii) imposes the further demand that the putative cp law *actually do* some explanatory work, though (as we shall see) this demand must be formulated disjunctively, since a sharply quantitative law can do explanatory work absent any instances of (F and G). *Perhaps* some capacities are never manifested, and some laws explain nothing actual. But if so, such laws would face charges of vacuity that I do not pretend to answer. My aim is to show how cp laws that *do* figure in explanations can be nonvacuous.

Again, the substantive part of the proposal is the requirement that all abNormal instances be explained by citing (independent) interfering factors. If an abNormal instance is not explicable in this sense, the apparent counter-example to the putative law is a genuine. Thus, cp laws are far from tautologous on this account. While I explicitly allow for abNormal instances, each such instance carries an explanatory commitment. But crucially, the details of that commitment need not be *spelt out*: there is an *existential quantification over* interfering factors, not a citation of the factors themselves.

This point is connected with the independence requirement on interfering factors. Earlier, I discussed appeals to ectoplasmic interference as a way of saving a putative cp law of telekinesis. But consider the more interesting postulation of Neptune, which was hypothesized to save celestial mechanics after the (apparently anomalous) orbit of Uranus was seen to be in conflict with the theory. While the hypothesis turned out to be right, one might worry that such *post hoc* manœuvring leads to theories that are irrefutable. But this is a passing appearance. Putting aside general sceptical worries about providing evidence for anything, it will be possible (at

---

[10] For present purposes, I remain neutral about what nomologicality consists in. The proposal is, I believe, compatible with: Goodman (1979) style theories of entrenchment; Armstrong (1978) and Tooley (1987) style accounts of relations among universals; Ramsey (1928) and Lewis (1973) style approaches, based on counterfactual-supporting generalizations that balance various epistemic virtues; and Cartwright (1989) style appeals to underlying capacities of objects that satisfy the law's antecedent.

least in principle) to collect evidence *independent of the particular theory being saved* for the alleged interfering factor. This is precisely what happened in the case of Neptune. Once it was hypothesized, ample independent observations were made, and the existence of the planet was established. The existence of Neptune explained (*inter alia*) optical phenomena that were independent of the facts (about Uranus' orbit) that seemed to be at odds with Newtonian theory.

When this process fails, and efforts to confirm postulated sources of interference fail, it becomes reasonable to doubt hypotheses so defended. The Vulcan hypothesis is a case in point. The perihelion of Mercury provided an abNormal instance for Newtonian mechanics. Scientists tried to explain away the anomaly by postulating another planet, Vulcan, between Mercury and the Sun. But there was no such planet. Or at least there was (and is) no further known phenomenon that the presence of Vulcan would explain. Unless current physical theory is badly mistaken, there is no independent factor that explains the relevant abNormal instances of Newtonian mechanics. (So Newton's laws are false, even as cp laws, although they remain useful for many purposes.)

Note that, just as the truth of a cp law depends on there *being* independent factors that explain its abNormal instances, so the warranted assertability of a cp law depends on the *available evidence* for such interfering factors. Thus, we might not be in a position at a given time (or perhaps ever) to know if a putative explanation of some abNormal instance is correct. It is justifiable practice not to waste resources checking out every recherché hypothesis about distant planets exerting odd forces. But some recherché hypotheses turn out to be true. (And what counts as recherché will depend on our confidence in the putative law. Consider the postulation of neutrinos, by Pauli and Fermi, to account for the loss of energy in beta decay; while it took twenty-five years to confirm the hypothesis experimentally, the search was sustained by confidence in the conservation of energy.) Confirming explanations of abNormal instances will typically require further investigation that we may or may not be able to carry out. As we know from other contexts, there is no hard-and-fast decision procedure for when to reject a theory. Appeal to cp laws does not change this. For it is hard to be certain that a putative explanation of some Abnormal instance would not be confirmed if only we looked a bit harder.

2.2

I said above that an interferer can explain an abNormal instance *in conjunction with* the cp law in question. In discussing this important point, let me distinguish two kinds of abNormal instance—the catastrophic, and the mundane. In catastrophic cases, interfering factors have their effect in a fashion that completely stifles the normal effects of the law's antecedent condition. For example, if certain sheep come to have increased immunity to some sheep disease, then *ceteris paribus* there will be corresponding changes in the sheep population. But a nuclear war, or a similar cataclysmic event, could render the effect of natural selection completely irrelevant. A cp law of intentional psychology might face an abNormal instance because the relevant agent suffered a seizure, or a blow to the head. In such cases, one can explain (often, easily) why the consequent condition of the cp law does *not* obtain, even given the cp law and relevant initial conditions. When abNormal instances are catastrophic, the interfering factor is obvious. But the cp law provides no positive explanation of what *does* happen.

The more interesting cases involve mundane abNormal instances. Here, the fact that apparently falsifies a cp law is partly explained by that very law. A trivial example will illustrate the basic point. Other things being equal, an object will move in the direction it is pushed. This generalization is not falsified if a ball pushed north moves slightly east of north, in the presence of a breeze from the west. Moreover, the generalization can help explain why the ball moved as it did, even though the ball's motion constitutes an abNormal instance of the generalization. Correspondingly, citing the wind doesn't explain the actual motion, except against the background of a generalization for which the wind counts as interference. But given the cp law, citing the wind may explain why the ball moved slightly east of north. A less trivial example is the orbit of Uranus, which deviated from original predictions based on Newton's laws and known initial conditions. Neptune was hypothesized to explain *deviations from* the expected (roughly elliptical) orbit; by itself, Neptune hardly explains why Uranus orbits the Sun as it does. And Neptune could do the explanatory work required of it, only because there were generalizations against the background of which Neptune counted as an (independent) interfering factor.

A cp law cannot *wholly* explain a fact that presents an abNormal instance of the law. But the cp law may *partially* explain such a fact. If phenomena are typically complex, and cp laws ignore some relevant factors, one should *expect* cp laws to provide only partial explanations of actual phenomena. Anyone who (with Mill) thinks that laws describe 'real causes', and that explanation works by citing the composition of causes, should be comfortable with this claim. But even if scientific practice does not commit us to the composition of causes, it does commit us to partial explanations of phenomena. This commitment is perfectly reasonable if the complexity of the world precludes explaining most phenomena all at once, and the prevalence of cp laws reflects the world's complexity.

This notion of a partial explanation is unmysterious. For cp laws partially explain phenomena by whittling down *what* needs explaining.

Suppose the question is: why did the ball move five degrees east of north? One can make significant progress towards providing a full answer by noting that the ball was pushed north, and that *ceteris paribus*, an object moves in the direction it was pushed. These facts do not constitute a complete explanation. We wanted to know why the ball moved *five degrees east of north*, not why it moved *north ± five degrees*. Moreover, citing the relevant facts constitutes a correct partial explanation, only if the promised explanations for abNormal instances can be provided. But having cited the cp law and intitial conditions, what needs explaining is not that the ball moved five degrees east of north, *as opposed to all the other things it might have done* (moved south, stayed still, exploded, quacked like a duck, etc.). Rather, what needs explaining is that the ball moved five degrees east of north, *as opposed to due north*. This transformation of the explanatory task is a part—and perhaps the most important part—of explaining why the ball moved as it did. One can, I suggest, render a fact F* partially comprehensible by showing that a contrary (but related) fact F was to be expected on the basis of a cp law and certain known facts, and then explaining why *F* as opposed to F* was the case because of certain *other* facts not intially accounted for. The value of this two stage process is that there may be no laws that allow one to show directly why F* was to be expected.[11]

A consequence of this account is that some *Normal* instances of a cp law may call for special explanation. Other things equal, interfering factors don't appear in Normal cases. But sometimes they do. Suppose that a particular body fell *n* feet in exactly the time predicted by the free-fall law ($a = 32\text{ft./sec.}^2$), even though the body was affected by substantial friction. Friction could have explained why the body took slightly longer to fall the same distance, which suggests that either (i) there is still further interference that cancels out the effect of friction—perhaps the object was propelled towards the earth, and so not in free fall after all, or (ii) there is an inexplicable possible abNormal instance of the free-fall law—viz. the instance that would have occurred had one controlled for friction. (As I note below, one must be careful with such counterfactual reasoning; but often it is perfectly legitimate. In the case described, confidence in the cp law would lead one to look for further interference.) Thus, abNormal instances *and Normal instances in the presence of what would count as interference* call for explanation. But in the latter case, the explanation takes the

---

[11] I discuss other examples in Sect. 4, where I respect the distinction between explanation and expectability more scrupulously. See Bromberger (1966) and van Fraasen (1980) for discussion of related points concerning 'Why Questions'. I am also sympathetic to Laymon's (1985, 1989) proposal that an idealized generalization is *confirmed* if (other things being equal) its predictions become increasingly more accurate, as increasingly more possible sources of interference are accounted for.

form of citing further interference that cancels out the first. I return to this important point.

2.3

A natural question that arises with regard to cp laws is how much to include in their antecedents. For every cp law that quantifies over some interfering factor INT, there might be another cp law identical to the first, except that its antecedent explicitly mentions the *absence* of INT. That is, if INT is an independent factor that can explain abNormal instances of

(4) $cp[(\forall x)(Fx \Rightarrow \exists y Gy)]$

there might be a corresponding law of the form:

(4*) $cp[(\forall x)(\{\neg INT \& Fx\} \Rightarrow \exists y Gy)]$.

Call [¬INT] an *enabling condition* for (4). And call any putative law L of the form (4) an *interferable*, where corresponding instances of (4*) are *L-enablers* relative to some interferable, L. A more ambitious version of (4*) would also offer some positive account of INT's effects.

For example, consider the ideal gas law ($P = nrT/V$) in the following conditional form:

(L₀) $cp[\forall g \forall n \forall x \forall y \forall z \{M(g,n) \& T(g,x) \& V(g,y) \Rightarrow \exists z[P(g,z) \& z = nrx/y]\}]$,

where 'M(g,n)' means that n is the number of moles of gas sample g; 'T(g,x)' means that x is the temperature of g; similarly for 'V(g,y)' and 'P(g,z)'. In stating this simple idealization—the pressure of a gas (in a container) is a function of its temperature and volume—we abstract away from certain facts that bear on pressure, which is determined by the number of times gas molecules strike the container. In particular, gas molecules occupy space; they are not point masses. So the space in the container available for molecular motion is less than the volume of the container; and reducing the 'free volume' tends to increase the number of strikes on the container. On the other hand, while temperature (i.e. the energy) of a gas is the main determinant of pressure (holding the volume fixed), there are other factors at work that tend to reduce the number of molecule strikes on the container—thus complicating the relation of temperature to pressure. Gas molecules exert attractive forces on one another, and they sometimes collide, resulting in a loss of kinetic energy.

The more complex van der Waal's equation, which (by and large) accounts for these facts, is as follows: $P = nrT/(V - nb) - an^2/V^2$; where a and b are further constants characteristic of the gas (e.g. hydrogen or oxygen) in question. Roughly speaking, '$V - nb$' represents the free volume, and '$-an^2/V^2$' corrects for the loss of pressure due to molecular attraction and collision. Let '$R_V(g,b)$' mean that b is the 'volume reduction' constant for the gas of which g is a sample; let '$R_P(g,a)$' mean that a is the 'pressure reduction' constant for the gas of which g is a sample. Then we can express van der Waal's equation as:

(L$_1$) cp[$\forall g \forall n \forall x \forall y \forall z \forall a \forall b\{$M(g,n) & T(g,x) & V(g,y) & R$_P$(g,a) & R$_V$(g,b) $\Rightarrow \exists$z[P(g,z) & z = nrx/(y$-$nb) $-$ an^2/y^2]$\}$].

The law (L$_1$) adds the clause '$R_P(g,a)$ & $R_V(g,b)$' to the antecedent of (L$_0$), thus refining the idealization: the pressure of a gas is a function of its temperature, its volume, and certain other factors (like molecule size and attractive forces) that vary from gas to gas. The conditional L$_0$ can be derived from (L$_0$) as a limiting case, where a and b equal 0. And as an illustration of interferences cancelling out, it is worth noting that (L$_0$) and (L$_1$) yield the same results when (Vna $-$ PV^2b $-$ abn^2) = 0; for example, when just over a mole of argon gas is placed in a half-litre container at about one atmosphere. In such cases, the reduction of free volume is effectively balanced by an independent reduction in pressure.

While (L$_1$) is an (L$_0$)-enabler, (L$_1$) is also an interferable cp law, since (L$_1$) still abstracts from the elasticity of containers. (It also goes awry at extreme temperatures and pressures.) But stating L-enablers can be a perspicuous way of capturing certain positive conditions required to have a Normal instance of an interferable. This can deepen our understanding of interfering factors appealed to in the course of explaining abNormal instances of interferables. It does not follow, however, that interferables must be replacable by L-enablers until *all possible* interfering conditions are made explicit.

This is the traditional demand (mentioned at the end of Section 1) that cp clauses be replaced by an explicit list of the *cetera* and when they are *paria*. As we will shall soon see, there is reason for doubting that this requirement can ever be met in the case of most macro-sciences; and it may not be met in the micro-sciences either. In any case, I don't see why such a requirement should be imposed: a generalization that fails to mention relevant factors can still be non-trivial, informative, and—depending on the other criteria for nomologicality—expressive of a genuine law. I offer no recipe for when one should treat a condition as interfering with a law, as opposed to mentioning its absence in a related law. But I see no reason for not regarding both the interferable and the L-enabler as potentially equally legitimate cp laws, though perhaps *other* explanatory concerns can be invoked for preferring one to the other. (Perhaps one of the laws will 'carve nature closer to its joints', more plausibly advert to genuine capacities, exhibit better conditions for human control, or mesh better with other laws.) Again, my goal is to defend cp laws against charges of vacuity, not to present a full account of explanatory adequacy.

2.4

Such permissiveness might seem to provide a *reductio* of this approach. Every true claim of the form 'the Φ caused the Ψ' presents a candidate interferable: 'cp(all Φs lead to Ψs)' might quantify over conditions that prevent Φs from bringing about Ψs. If Fido's first bark of the day caused Nora's favourite event of the day, perhaps cp(Fido's firsts lead to Nora's favourites), and *cetera* have been *paria* only once. But it is important to distinguish vacuity from falsity; and I need not say that every true singular causal claim corresponds to a cp law formulated in the same terms if only because I offered a sufficient condition for non-vacuity (not a sufficient condition for truth). Consider the sometimes legitimate observation that tossing a certain coin caused it to come up heads. The proposed account of cp-laws does not itself exclude 'cp(if that coin is tossed, it comes up heads)'. Yet while it would be nice to rule out such putative laws, my main concern is to distinguish genuine cp laws from vacuities like the alleged telekinesis law; and the putative coin-toss law may be false rather than vacuous. Someone might reply that this renders my proposal uninteresting. But I think this would overlook the likely complexity of any account of laws.[12] And the proposal is offered in response to a certain puzzle—how can a hedged law be non-vacuous—not as a complete philosophy of science. Moreover, there is an important connection between examples like the putative coin-toss law and the explanatory commitments induced (on my view) by abNormal instances of a cp law.

Recall that Normal instances of a putative cp law call for explanation if they occur in the presence of interfering factors. If a body affected by friction accelerates at a rate of *exactly* 32 ft/sec.[2], an explanation is owed. Confidence in the free-fall law will lead us to look for a *further* source of interference that, in this case, cancelled out the friction. In general, if someone says that a factor INT explains an abNormal instance of a cp law L on one occasion, she is committed to saying that INT is always a *potential* interferer with respect to L; so Normal instances of L in the presence of INT will call for explanation—perhaps the presence of a further factor

---

[12] The more *biased* the coin, the more plausible the putative cp law. If p[heads/tossing] $= 99/100$, perhaps cp(Tossing $\Rightarrow$ Heads). And even if p[heads/tossing c] $= 1/2$, the issue seems to be (not vacuity, but) the *interrelationships* of competing putative cp laws—and/or the underlying metaphysics of explanation. In any case, there may be more laws than traditionally supposed. Recipes and algorithms may reflect chains of 'local' cp laws, like 'cp(if an IBM computer is running WordPerfect, then F5 brings up the print menu)'. Psychology may traffic in many such laws. So one might not want to exclude all the candidate cp laws suggested by worries about stray singular causal claims.

INT* that interfered with INT. If there is some such factor, well and good. But this induces still another commitment: abNormal instances of L are not yet explained by INT if INT* is also present, though perhaps there is a *third* factor INT** that either cancels out INT* or itself explains the abNormal instance of L. And so on. Once one starts appealing to interfering factors, explanatory commitments proliferate. (In writing a cheque to the effect that L is interfered with by INT, one commits oneself to writing another cheque if a Normal instance of L occurs in the presence of INT, etc. And we can often do an experiment to test whether a cheque will bounce.)

Thus, the putative coin-toss law will be plausible only if the explanations for its abNormal instances can be *sustained*, in the sense that *all* the explanatory commitments it generates can plausibly be met. Given a toss that comes up tails, an explanation is owed. If the defender of the putative law cites an unusual wind, then a toss that comes up tails *in the presence of the same kind of wind* calls for explanation (by citing another independent interfering factor that cancelled out the unusual wind), etc. Similarly, for each interfering factor cited to explain a tails-event. This is a severe constraint on laws.[13]

There is, however, a complication that will prove relevant. Sometimes, 'cp(F $\Rightarrow$ G)' can be true, even given an instance of (F & G) in the presence of uncancelled interference. For while Normal instances in the presence of interference call for explanation, the explanation does not have to take the form of citing a further *cancelling* factor. It may be that G obtains *fortuitously*, in the presence of what would otherwise be a standard abNormal instance. Suppose the organisms that survive an earthquake, or some other catastrophic source of interference to Darwin's Conditional, happen

---

[13] Taking up an idea of Dupré (1984), Cartwright (1983) says that causes have 'contextual unanimity' when they change the probability of the effect given the cause 'in the same direction in every homogeneous background'; contextual unanimity is missing if 'the probability of the effect sometimes goes up with the presence of the cause, and sometimes goes down' (ibid. 143). Cartwright goes on to argue that such a conception of causation presupposes 'the conceptual framework of capacities': if Cs ever actually cause Es (by virtue of being Cs), Cs must have the capacity to cause Es; and 'that capacity is something they can be expected to carry with them from situation to situation' (ibid. 145). Thus, cp laws may well be correlated with underlying capacities that explain contextual unanimity. But Cartwright (1989) does not *require* contextual unanimity for causation; it is enough for her that whenever a cause *fails* to raise the probability of its effect, there be an *explanation for why it doesn't*. (See Pietroski (1995) for discussion of the increasingly complex debate about unanimity, including Dupré's (1993) criticisms of Cartwright; the relation between appeals to cp laws and probability-raising approaches to causation; and the need for laws that are idealized *and* probabilized.) In the text, I ignore the possibility that a factor INT might interfere with a law only N% of the time. But in appealing to a stochastic interferer to law L, one would commit oneself to saying that Normal instances of L in the presence of INT call for independent explanation N% of the time (1 − N% of cases being marked down to chance). Such claims can be just as (im)plausible as deterministic claims.

to be the fittest. In such a case, natural selection does not explain the survival of the fittest; the interference renders Darwin's Conditional irrelevant to the explanation of its consequent condition. (This is so, even if it is not entirely coincidental that the fittest survived: perhaps adaptationists saved the fittest members of each species.)

Thus, an instance of (F&G) in the presence of an interfering factor INT actually carries a disjunctive commitment: either there is a further factor INT* that cancels INT; or G obtains fortuituously—i.e. for reasons independent of the cp law, which really was interfered with by INT. So if all instances of (F&G) count as Normal instances of 'cp(F → G)', one must allow that not every instance of (F&G) is an *explanatory* instance of the law. Alternatively, one can restrict the notion of a Normal instance, so that instances of (F&G) *in the presence of uncancelled interference* are neither Normal nor abNormal instances of 'cp(F → G)'. I prefer the latter option, since such instances neither falsify nor confirm the law. But however we speak, treating a given instance of (F&G) as fortuitous will itself carry commitments for other relevantly similar cases. And commitments of any kind add up.

3. Contrasts with Other Views

Cartwright (1983) and Joseph (1980) are instructively critical of cp laws *if* such laws are understood in certain (tempting) ways. Comparison with these alternatives will help clarify my own.

3.1

A natural idea, mentioned above, is that lawlike sentences of the form

(1) $cp[(\forall x)(Fx \Rightarrow \exists y Gy)]$

are true iff there is some finite statement of enabling conditions C, such that

(2) $C \Rightarrow (\forall x)(Fx \Rightarrow \exists y Gy)$

is a strict law. In the terminology of Section 2: every interferable law L is to be replaced by an L-enabler, until the quantification over interferences is needless, because every (nomologically possible) intereferer has been explicitly mentioned. Various critics of cp laws (e.g. Cartwright 1983; Schiffer 1987) have assumed that if there are cp laws, this is how such laws are to be construed.

I will not argue in detail against this 'spell-out' view. Suffice it to note that for (2) to be a law, on this account, 'C' must cover all possible abNormal instances of (1), and the number of things that can go awry with special science generalizations seems potentially endless. Think of all the possible circumstances in which a decrease in supply might not result in an increase in price: simultaneous decrease in demand, nuclear war, a drug in the air that temporarily makes entrepreneurs generous, etc. Or think of all the scenarios in which fitter organism types don't become more prevalent in a population. I don't think one can *prove* that the spell-out view is false. But the chances seem dim that any finite statement of hedging conditions will cover all the possible interferences. And a defender of the spell-out view owes plausible examples of special science generalizations in which the relevant condition C has been (at least approximately) spelled out. Moreover, it is at least logically possible that the actual world is *infinitely* rich in sources of interference. The observable universe may be a small stability in a massive complexity. So it is conceivable that no finite antecedent would cover even the actual abNormal instances of (1). My proposal leaves this possibility open; for again, the idea is that one quantifies over abNormal instances, saying that each can be explained by *some* interfering factor.[14]

Another serious problem (noted by Cartwright) is that the spell-out view fails to explain how cp laws can figure in explanations when other things are *not* equal. The spell-out view flows naturally from the claim that all laws are strict, and that explanation by nomic subsumption takes the form of deduction from strict laws. But if C is false, (2) will be useless in a deduction. Given an instance of (Fx & ¬Gy), we can conclude that C is false. But this very fact seems to render (2) explanatorily inert if we want to cite the connection between F and G in partially explaining what did happen—even though the actual situation was non-ideal (see also Laymon 1985, 1989). Moreover, as Cartwright (1983: 112) observes: when we try to write down the 'more correct' equations, we get a longer and longer list of complicated laws of different forms, and not the handful of simple equations that are presumably a hope of physical theory. She concludes that laws which explain by composition of causes fail to satisfy a facticity requirement. If laws are to explain how phenomena are brought about, they cannot state the facts (ibid. 73).

A less radical conclusion is that it can be a fact that $cp(F \Rightarrow G)$; and as we have seen, this fact can be explanatory whether or not interfering factors are at work. It is worth emphasizing, however, that I agree with

---

[14] There may be *one* true instance of (2) *if* the following counts as an instance of C: there are no independent factors that can explain abNormal instances of (1). For reasons discussed in the next section, the antecedent of such a law might never be satisfied (in any nomologically possible world). Moreover, this hardly preserves the spirit of the view that real laws are strict: instead of specifying particular source(s) of interference, possible factors are quantified over.

Cartwright (1983) in important respects. Explanations need not—and if current science is any indication, they typically do not—invoke strict regularities. (Indeed, the spell-out view seems to be motivated by the very philosophical picture of laws that Cartwright rejects.) Cartwright argues that the focus of scientific inquiry should not be upon laws, but upon what she calls 'capacities' or 'tendencies to cause or bring about something' (ibid. 226). My proposal is compatible with appeal to capacities. And as should be clear by now, I fully agree with what might be called Cartwright's *localist* concerns: explanation of specific phenomena can proceed in ignorance of indefinite (and indefinitely many) sources of potential interference with the regularities cited in the explanation. Many of those regularities may rightly be thought of as capacities. But it is hard to see how there could be a capacity of the sort Cartwright appeals to (a 'tendency to cause or bring about something') without it being true that, *ceteris paribus*, when certain initial conditions are satisfied, such and such will result.

3.2

On the spell-out view, cp laws are stand-ins for indicative conditionals whose antecedents may go unsatisfied. Joseph (1980) considers, but ultimately rejects, another initially attractive view—a '*ceteris absentibus*' reading of cp clauses. A ball pushed north moves north, cp. If a force from the west is exerted on the ball as well, the ball may in fact move north-west. But intuitively, were it not for the westerly force, the ball would have moved north. In general, the cp law appears to be intimately linked to the following subjunctive conditional: were there no other factors, the ball pushed north would have moved north. (If there are interfering factors, this is a counterfactual; if not, it is a semifactual.) So one might try to state the truth conditions of cp laws in terms of the nearest possible world where any interfering factors actually present are absent.

In particular, Joseph (1980) considers the possibility that the laws of physics, while false without a cp modifier, are true if stated in the following form: were all other factors absent, then given certain initial conditions, certain resultant conditions would obtain (ibid. 777). The actual force exerted between two bodies may not be given by the law of gravity. But if gravity had been the only effect on masses m and m*, and had any other bodies exerting gravitational force on m and m* been absent, perhaps the force exerted between the bodies would have been equal to Gmm^*/d^2. And perhaps in general, 'cp($F \Rightarrow G$)' is true iff were all other factors absent, then given F, G would have been the case.

Speaking of factors being *absent* may be acceptable in physics, but it is less satisfactory in other domains. The price of widgets may fail to rise following a reduction in supply, because demand for widgets also declined. Yet economists will not want to cash out the relevant cp law in terms of what would happen to price in the absence of demand. Similarly, memory limitations and other limitations of finite capacity are relevant to various psychological generalizations. One would expect such limitations to be handled by appeal to cp clauses; and these generalizations do not purport to say what would happen if agents had *no* memory. But perhaps laws can be true in virtue of what would happen if memory posed no limitations. The general spirit of *ceteris absentibus* readings is that 'cp(F $\Rightarrow$ G)' is true iff had other factors which did interfere not interfered, then given F, G would have been the case.

On this view, cp laws do not merely make indicative conditional claims that are satisfied vacuously when *cetera* are not *paria*; they make counterfactual claims about actual objects. But this strength of the proposal is also its weakness. Consider what the law of gravity says about protons and electrons on such a *ceteris absentibus* reading. We wanted to say that the law of gravity holds, other things being equal, and that other things aren't equal when protons and electrons are the bodies in question (since these bodies also have charge). But what counterfactuals shall we consider here? It seems absurd—indeed, it borders on the unintelligible—to say that *had* protons and electrons lacked charge, the force exerted between them *would have been* equal to Gmm*/d². Joseph rejected the *ceteris absentibus* proposal for essentially this reason, and I concur. It is a matter of physical law that protons and electrons have charge; arguably, having charge is *constitutive* of being those particles. We have no clear idea of what it would be to be a proton or electron without charge, much less how such particles would behave. And it seems perverse to gloss laws in terms of what would happen in such bizarre circumstances. At a minimum, proposals that don't account for the nomic in terms of the nomologically and/or constitutively impossible should be preferred to those that do, other things equal.

Such examples are easily multiplied. The ideal gas law would have to be understood in terms of what would happen if molecules took up no space and failed to be subsumed by Coulomb's law. Or consider a particularly striking case from astrophysics: Dicke, Peebles *et al.* (1965) famously argued that a temperature in excess of (10^{10}) °K in the very early stages of the universe would be detectable now in the form of microwave (black-body) radiation. On this basis, they predicted that at a certain wavelength, measurements of radiation would reveal temperatures slightly higher (by about 3°K) than the temperature that would be expected on the basis of known sources of radiation. Independently, but reported along with Dicke, Peebles *et al.*, Penzias and Wilson (1965) discovered—but had been unable to explain—just such a discrepancy in their measurements of radiation at the relevant wavelength. The experiments have been confirmed, spectacularly, across a range of wavelengths. And it has become a tenet of modern cosmology that our local region of the universe is awash in low-level radiation that is essentially residue from the Big Bang.

With this is mind, consider the various lawlike sentences that (together with statements of initial conditions) led Penzias and Wilson to expect a temperature slightly *lower* than the temperature they found. Taken in isolation or in combination, these sentences could hold only cp. Indeed, Penzias and Wilson considered and then ruled out several possible sources of interference—from radiation generated by their own antenna, to the possible effects of pigeon droppings. But a *ceteris absentibus* reading of the relevant cp clauses would be unassessable, since one of the sources of interference would be the Big Bang itself. A cp law concerning the amount of radiation in our local region of the universe is *not* to be understood as a claim about how much radiation there would be if the Big Bang had not occurred. One can sensibly speculate about what would have been the case absent pigeons, but not absent the Big Bang. (In addition to its unique place in our history, the Big Bang was responsible for such fundamental facts as the values of the universal constants.) At any rate, there is no reason to think that citation of Big Bang radiation as a source of interference *depends* upon such speculations.[15]

In short, there is no need to spell out cp clauses as extra antecedents to the generalizations they modify. Nor do cp laws have to be glossed as counterfactual claims about what would happen in the absence of interfering factors. It is enough to existentially quantify over independent interferences in the manner described above. A cp law carries sundry explanatory commitments. But the law itself can be non-vacuous without making each of its commitments explicit.

4. Explaining with Idealized Covering Laws

In Chapter 3, I suggested the following as (a first pass at) a sufficient condition for explanation: Θ_1 explains Θ_2 if Θ_1 and Θ_2 are singular event thoughts that instantiate a cp law (perhaps relative to certain initial conditions). In the terminology developed here, the fact that Fa explains why

---

[15] I think Kripke (1982) too quickly rejects dispositional responses to his plus/quus puzzle, because he glosses cp laws in this implausible way (see Pietroski and Rey (1995: 106–8), for elaboration). In certain contexts, one might say 'if not for the Big Bang, there would be less local radiation', intending to hold fixed everything that the Big Bang has done for us *except* its contribution to local radiation. But then one's assertion will *not* be a judgement about how things would have gone without the Big Bang; it will be a judgement about how things are, treating background radiation as an interfering factor for generalizations to which one is independently committed.

Gb if (Fa & Gb) is a Normal instance of 'cp(Fx $\Rightarrow$ Gy)'. Let me conclude this chapter by applying the discussion of cp laws to this sufficient condition. For I want to show that it is *not* open to familiar objections that plague traditional covering-law accounts of explanation.

4.1

A familiar view is that a body of facts ($F_1 \ldots F_n$) explains a particular fact G if 'G' can be derived from relevant sentences ('F_1' ... 'F_n'), all of which are true and at least one of which is an empirical law that figures essentially in the derivation. In the simplest case, the explanans would consist of a law and a statement of initial conditions, while the explanandum would state that the consequent condition obtained, for example, '$\forall x(\Psi x \to \exists y \Phi y)$ & Ψa, hence $\exists y \Phi y$'. (And if '$\exists y \Phi y$' is true because Φb, it is usually held that explaining why $\exists y \Phi y$ explains why Φb.) If my remarks about the need for idealization are correct, this sufficient condition for explanation is all but useless: if most explanations are not based on strict laws, the covering-law model applies to few if any explanations. A more common criticism, though, has been that the covering-law model faces counter-examples.

Suppose that at 1.00, my barometer rose, as did my neighbour's barometer. And suppose that

> (5) if a barometer B rises (at time t), and B* is a barometer near B, then B* rises (at t).

Then on a covering-law model, we could explain why my neighbour's barometer rose, by citing (5) and the fact that my barometer rose. But what *explains* why my neighbour's barometer rose is the relation between his barometer and atmospheric pressure, not the relation between his barometer and mine. Such examples have suggested to many that subsumption under law is not sufficient for explanation.

Let me emphasize, however, that a *counter-example* to the covering-law model requires a derivation from a true law. Derivations from false lawlike sentences are irrelevant. And read as a strict law, (5) is false. It is easy to create situations in which one barometer rises, but a nearby barometer does not: just put an appropriate hole in one of the barometers. Nor is there any true, strict variant on (5) that will license the derivation required for a counter-example to the covering-law model. This should come as no surprise; for there is no reason to think there *are* any (non-vacuous) strict laws about barometers. But avoiding counter-examples at the cost of vacuity is pyrrhic. (Hempel (1988) makes this point, and discusses the need to modify the traditional covering-law model.)

Moreover, there was a general moral behind the cases offered in response to covering-law models: the *direction* of explanation may differ from the direction of a sound derivation; and one might expect this point to survive a shift from strict to cp laws. I return to the *asymmetry* of explanation. But for now, note that

>   (6) cp{if a barometer B rises (at time *t*), and B* is a barometer near B, then B* rises (at *t*)}

is also false. Suppose that Smith applies a source of (non-atmospheric) pressure to the relevant mechanism in his barometer on a fair day, while his neighbour's barometer operates in the usual way. Then (6) will face an abNormal instance: Smith's barometer will rise, while a nearby barometer remains steady. This abNormal instance will not be explicable in the sense relevant to saving cp laws. For the fact that Smith applied the pressure will not explain why (6), a generalization about *barometers*, faces an abNormal instance. The fact that Smith applied the pressure will not explain why his neighbour's barometer failed to rise (given that Smith's barometer rose).[16]

Intuitively, the law at work here relates atmospheric pressure to barometers. And one might try to avoid abNormal instances of (6), by restricting attention to possible situations in which atmospheric pressure is rising. Building such a condition into the antecedent of (6) would, however, make reference to barometer B otiose; and a plausible condition on laws is that their antecedents not be otiose. So I see no prospects for a variant of (6) that will provide a counter-example to the claim that Normal instances of a cp law stand in an explanatory relation. Counter-examples must be based on true laws.

4.2

Consider another much discussed example. The period P of a pendulum is given by

>   (7) $P = 2\pi \sqrt{(L/g)}$,

where L is the pendulum's length, and *g* is the gravitational constant. At least in this form, the 'pendulum law' does not distinguish between deductions like the following:

---

[16] Claiming that a given abNormal instance is explained by (say) a certain kind of wind will induce further (implausible) explanatory commitments of the sort discussed in Sect. 2.4 above. It bears emphasis that 'cp(if F then G)' and 'cp(if F then K)' can be true, while 'cp(if G then K)' is false. To see this, it will usually suffice to consider cases in which G-events occur in the *absence* of an F-event, and the causes of the G-events are not causes of K-events. Some of these cases are likely to present inexplicable Abnormal instances of 'cp(if G then K)'. There may be (rare) cases in which G-events will occur *only if* F-events occur. But I suspect they will involve special features exploitable by covering-law theorists.

$$P = 2\pi\sqrt{(L/g)}$$
$$\underline{L = 2 \text{ ft.}}$$
$$P = 2\pi\sqrt{(2/g)} = 1.57 \text{ secs.}$$

$$P = 2\pi\sqrt{(L/g)}$$
$$\underline{P = 1.57}$$
$$L = g(1.57/2\pi)^2 = 2 \text{ ft.}$$

But only the first deduction tracks the direction of explanation: period depends on length, not vice versa. Moreover, as Cummins (1983) notes, neither deduction has a statement of an *effect* as its conclusion. Both deductions represent acceptable problem solutions for one of the variables in (7). But neither deduction (as it stands) is even a candidate for a causal explanation of some event.

One can, however, interpret (7) as part of what Cummins calls a *transition theory*—a theory that aims to explain certain changes of state in objects of the theory's domain. The idea is that an equation like (7) captures a fundamental relation between its variables. But if (7) is to be used in the explanation of particular *events*, or as a recipe for providing explanations of events of certain types, then (7) must be understood as implying that a certain relation holds between *changes* of period and *changes* of length. And I claim only that subsumption under a *transition* law suffices for explanation. (Correspondingly, the sufficient condition for explanation applies only to singular *event* thoughts.) The issue of asymmetry remains, however. Given (7), one can formulate *two* putative transition laws: given a change of length (from u to v), there is a change in period (of $2\pi[\sqrt{(v/g)} - \sqrt{(u/g)}]$); or given a change of period (from u to v), there is a change in length (of $gv^2/4\pi^2 - gu^2/4\pi^2$).

In this sense, (7) does not tell us which putative transition law to use in a deduction. Like many others, Cummins takes this to show that subsumption under a transition law is explanatory only if the law says that events of one type *cause* events of another type. He compares the following deductions:

A change of u to v in L causes a change of $2\pi(\sqrt{(v/g)} - \sqrt{(u/g)})$ in P; L increased from 1 to 2 ft.	A change of u to v in P causes a change of $gv^2/4\pi^2 - gu^2/4\pi^2$ in L; P increased from 1.11 to 1.57 sec.
P increased from 1.11 to 1.57 sec.	L increased from 1 to 2 ft.

Only the first deduction appeals to a *true* transition law, assuming (as we do) that changes in length cause changes in period, but not vice versa. On this view, nomic subsumption can distinguish explanatory claims from mere singular causal claims. In saying that an event pair <C, E> is covered by a law, however, one *presupposes* that C caused E. For many purposes, such a presupposition will be acceptable. But for my purposes, it is not. While my aim is not to reduce causation to explanation, I do hope to shed light on our concept of causation, by appealing to a notion of explanation that is understood in terms of nomic subsumption. And one should expect no thanks for telling someone that C causes E if C is a T1-event, and E is a T2-event, and it is a law that T1-events cause T2-events. Even if this sufficient condition is true, its application will not help resolve any puzzles.

This raises the worry, to which I return in Chapter 7, that *any* attempt to gloss causation in terms of explanation will be at best unhelpful. Cummins (1983) gives voice to a familiar view, when he says 'the decision to represent changes in length in the "cause" slot rather than the "effect" slot *is motivated solely by a prior conviction* that changes in length cause changes in period' (ibid., my emphasis). But while I agree with much of what Cummins says about explanation, I think he moves too quickly at this point. One can accommodate the asymmetry of explanation in another way if one takes the need for idealization seriously (instead of treating it as a complication to be ignored in accounts of explanation).

Consider, once again, the two putative transition laws corresponding to (7): if there is a change of length (from u to v), there is a change in period (of $2\pi[\sqrt{(v/g)} - \sqrt{(u/g)}]$; or if there is a change of period (from u to v), there is a change in length (of $gv^2/4\pi^2 - gu^2/4\pi^2$). Read as *strict* laws, both generalizations are false. One can shorten the length of a pendulum without shortening its period, by introducing a source of drag at the same time. Similarly, one can shorten the period of a pendulum affected by drag without shortening its length, by eliminating some of the drag.[17] I think these (relatively boring) points are relevant to the issue of asymmetry, once we get clear about a potential source of confusion—namely, the symmetry of *equations*.

At least before talk of transition laws is introduced, a plausible reading of

(7) $P = 2\pi\sqrt{(L/g)}$

is that the period of a pendulum is 2π times the square root of its length divided by g. If (7) is true, so is

(8) $L = g(P/2\pi)^2$,

which says that the length of a pendulum is g times the square of its period divided by 2π. A pendulum affected by a source of drag provides a counter-example to *both* of these (unqualified) claims. This makes it tempting to think that one can ignore the need for idealization, in considering the asymmetry of explanation. And if (*per impossible*) gravity were

---

[17] One might want to focus on *ideal* pendulums—those affected *only* by the earth's gravity. But what sort of object could swing from a fixed point, yet be utterly unaffected by friction (cf. the discussion of *ceteris absentibus* conditions)? And even setting this concern aside, the question remains: how can a law restricted to ideal conditions figure in explanations of actual events, when conditions are non-ideal?

the only factor affecting a pendulum, apart from its length, then a change in length would always be accompanied by a corresponding change in period for, by hypothesis, there would be no countervailing factors. Similarly, if length were the *only* factor other than gravity affecting period, then a change in period would always be accompanied by a corresponding change in length. (This assumes that the length of a pendulum would affect the period, even if factors like friction had no effect on period, and that there are no uncaused changes in period.)

This can make it seem that any transition laws corresponding to (7) and (8) will be on a par. But the symmetry of (7) and (8) *as equations* does not show that *cp modified transition laws* based on (7) and (8) will be equally plausible. This will depend on the right treatment of cp laws, which need not be read in a *ceteris absentibus* fashion. So consider the two candidate transition laws with cp modifiers, where such modifiers are understood, as discussed above, as quantifying over abNormal instances: (i) if there is a change in L (from u to v), then *either* there is a change in P (of $2\pi[(\sqrt{(v/g)} - \sqrt{(u/g)}])$ *or* there is an interfering factor explanation for why the change in P did not occur given the change in L; (ii) if there is a change in P (from u to v), then *either* there is a change in L (of $gv^2/4\pi^2 - gu^2/4\pi^2$) *or* there is an interfering factor explanation for why the change in L did not occur given the change in P.

I think that (i) is plausible, but (ii) is not. Imagine a case like that of Smith and his barometer. If Smith changes the period of his pendulum by introducing a new source of drag, leaving the length unchanged, then (ii) will face an abNormal instance. And this abNormal instance will *not* be explicable by citing interfering factors. The new source of drag may explain many things, but not why the length of Smith's pendulum *failed to decrease*. So if (ii) covers instances of period-change/length-change, that is not a source of concern. There is no reason to think (ii) is a law. The asymmetry of explanation is accommodated, because if 'cp(F → G)' is a law, every instance of (F & ¬G) is explicable as the result of independent interference; but 'cp(G → F)' need not be a law, since some instances of (G & ¬F) may not be explicable as the result of independent interference.

In this context, let me also note that a generalization like 'cp(if blue-eyed humans successfully mate, their offspring will be blue-eyed)' can fail to be a cp law on my account, even if blue-eyed matings typically produce blue-eyed offspring—at least if *being blue-eyed* is construed as a phenotypic property (cf. Segal and Sober 1991). For it is at least possible, if only because of cosmetic surgery, to have blue eyes without having zygotes of the relevant genotype. So at least some (nomologically possible) matings of 'superficially blue-eyed' humans will be Abnormal instances of the putative cp law, even though conditions with respect to mating and growth of offspring are free of any interfering factors. Thus, one could say (with

Fodor 1989) that properties projected by cp laws are causally relevant, without saying that *being blue-eyed* is causally relevant with respect to producing blue-eyed offspring.

4.3

To summarize: if we focus on transition laws, recognizing that such laws are idealizations, we will see an asymmetry in the truth of putative cp laws that parallels the asymmetry of explanation. Given a change in the pendulum's length, one can (by citing interfering factors) explain away the cases where the period does not change as predicted; but given a change in period, one cannot always explain why the period does not change as predicted. So only one of the putative cp laws is plausible; and the other is not a source of embarrassment for my proposed sufficient condition for explanation. Other familiar examples, like flagpoles and their shadows, exhibit the same pattern.

For reasons I have stressed, it is very unlikely that the period of a pendulum will be exactly $2\pi\sqrt{(L/g)}$. So the true pendulum law will not *wholly* explain many (if any) actual periods. But it will *partially* explain them. And a false generalization like 'cp(if the period changes . . . the length changes . . .)' cannot even partially explain changes in length. Given qualitative laws, Normal instances are easier to find. Evolution often does favour traits that increase fitness.[18] Or recall the generalization discussed briefly at the end of Chapter 3: cp[if N wants Ψ to be the case, and comes to believe that Φ-ing will make Ψ the case, N will try to Φ]. Agents often do try to satisfy their desires. In the remaining chapters, I explore the implications of this point. But let me end this chapter with a caveat.

In Section 2, I noted that an explanation is owed, given a Normal instance of a cp law in the presence of interference. Often, such explanation will take the form of citing a second interfering factor that cancels out the first. But one can maintain 'cp[$\forall$x(Fx $\Rightarrow$ $\exists$yGy)]', even given an instance of (Fx & Gy) in the presence of uncancelled interference. For the instance of Gy may be *fortuitous*. The fact that $\exists$yGy may have nothing to do with the fact that Fx; the effects associated (other things equal) with F may have been blocked, perhaps catastrophically. To recall the earlier example, the fitter organisms might just happen to be those that survive the earthquake. So my proposed sufficient condition for explanation is not purely formal, in this sense: if there is uncancelled interference, (Fx & Gy) is not an explanatory instance of 'cp[$\forall$x(Fx $\Rightarrow$ $\exists$yGy)]'.

---

[18] A principle aimed at capturing the *precise* effect of selection on evolution would, like the pendulum law, face abNormal instances. Drift and other non-selective forces would interfere with a sharp quantitative version of Darwin's Conditional (cf. the Hardy–Weinberg law, mentioned in n. 4).

As I said above, my preferred way of expressing this point is to say that not every instance of (Fx & Gy) is a Normal instance of 'cp[∀x(Fx ⇒ ∃yGy)]'. Correspondingly, the law does not cover every instance of (Fx & Gy) in a relevant sense of 'cover'. This can make it seem that I have, after all, built the notion of causation into the notion of a covering-law explanation. But I am not just *stipulating* that (Fx & Gy) is fortuitous—and hence, not an explanatory instance of the law—if something other than Fx is causally responsible for Gy. I am characterizing fortuitous instances, and thus restricting the notion of a Normal instance, via the notion of interference already appealed to: (Fx & Gy) is a fortuitous instance of 'cp[∀x(Fx ⇒ ∃yGy)]' if there is an uncancelled interfering factor. The intuition is that (Fx & Gy) is not a Normal instance of a law if there is interference that could have explained why the law faced an abNormal instance. Normal instances are not defined as causal instances. But given the possibility of uncancelled interference, a *formal* instance of a law may fail to be an explanatory instance.

On the proposed view, it is *true* that (Fx & Gy) is a Normal instance of the transition law 'cp[∀x(Fx ⇒ ∃yGy)]' only if the relevant events stand in an appropriate causal relation. But this should come as no surprise. For the proposal is that when one singular event thought explains another, the relevant events are related as cause to effect. And trivially, a sufficient condition for X stated in terms of Y can be recast as necessary condition on Y stated in terms of X. (This does not, I assume, establish that every sufficient condition is doomed to vicious circularity.) Moreover, insofar as my account of cp laws appeals to causation, it does so via the notion of an interfering factor. Causation is brought in, one might say, to handle *deviance from* the Normal pattern. But at least where laws are qualitative, many cases will fit the Normal pattern. And while *ceteris absentibus* readings of cp laws are not adequate, there can be cases in which an instance of a cp law occurs in the absence of any (uncancelled) interfering factors that would render the instance unexplanatory. Still, one might worry that my account of *ceteris paribus* laws presupposes too much about causation, for the account to shed any appreciable light on how (non-neural) mental events could be causes. I devote much of Chapter 7 to this concern. But here, my aim has just been to show how cp laws can be non-vacuous, and to show that the resulting conception of cp laws respects the asymmetry of explanation.

5

Personal Dualism

Let me begin with a quick review. Actions are tryings, which cause bodily motions. Tryings, like other intentionally characterized events, have Fregean contents. Event C caused event E if a singular event thought about C explains a singular event thought about E. A singular event thought is the Fregean sense of a sentence, such that for some condition Δ satisfied by exactly one event, it follows from the Davidsonian event analysis that the sentence is true iff $\exists e \Delta e$. One singular event thought explains another if: the first thought is an instance of the fact that an event of type T_1 occurred; the second thought is an instance of the fact that an event of type T_2 occurred; it is a (transition) law that $cp[T_1 \rightarrow T_2]$—or alternatively, it is a law that $cp[\mathbf{IC} \rightarrow (T_1 \rightarrow T_2)]$, where **IC** is an initial condition that actually obtains; and the relevant instance of this law is Normal (i.e. not fortuitous), in that there is no uncancelled interference. To a first approximation, it is a *ceteris paribus* law that a person will try to Φ, if she wants Ψ to be the case and comes to believe that Φ-ing will make Ψ the case.[1] And I assume that when a person moves her body, the occurrence of her action/trying explains the relevant motion of her body, in that the trying and the motion constitute a Normal instance of a suitable cp law.

With this in mind, consider Nora's behaviour at the auction: she raised her arm, after coming to believe that raising her arm would make it the case that she buys a certain painting. If she wanted to buy the painting, and there were no uncancelled interfering factors, then the fact that Nora acquired her (conditional) belief explains why she tried to raise her hand; so the event of Nora's acquiring her belief caused the trying. Similarly, the trying caused the rising of Nora's arm. The causal sequence of events is:

mental cause of action $\rightarrow$ action $\rightarrow$ peripheral bodily motion
(acquisition of Nora's belief) (her trying) (the rising of Nora's hand)

Nora's bodily motion has mental causes. And I just sketched an account of how this is possible, without presupposing that Nora's mental events are neural events. (For simplicity, I ignore muscle contractions until Chapter 7.) Thus, my proposed sufficient condition for (mental) causation

---

[1] See Ch. 3 (Sect. 3.3) for a second approximation with reference to intentions.

allows for the view gestured at below, according to which bodily motions have neural causes *and distinct* mental causes

$$\text{mental causes of action} \searrow$$

$$\text{bodily motion}$$

$$\text{neural causes of bodily motion} \nearrow$$

My aim in this chapter is to motivate this conception of mental causation, and to undermine some initial sources of resistance to it. I distinguish the proposed version of event dualism from Cartesian dualism, but in a way that respects many of the reasons for finding Descartes' view attractive.

1. Cartesian Intuitions without Cartesian Interaction

Let M be the acquisition of Nora's belief (that raising her arm would make it the case that she buys the painting). And assume that we can isolate an external stimulus S—say, an utterance by the auctioneer—that caused M, given Nora's background states of belief. For present purposes, it does not matter whether or not S caused M via some inference. Perhaps S initiated a chain of rationally connected mental events:

$$S \rightarrow ME_1 \rightarrow \ldots \rightarrow ME_n \rightarrow M.$$

But the intervening mental events do not matter here. Let T and B, respectively, be the relevant trying and bodily motion. Then we can represent the causal chain as follows, with intentional causes in bold:

$$S \rightarrow \mathbf{M} \rightarrow \mathbf{T} \rightarrow B.$$

Event B will have neural causes; and S will affect various parts of Nora's brain, like those devoted to audition and language processing. Any account of mental causation must accommodate such facts in a plausible fashion. So a non-neuralist account must show how S can have neural effects, and how B can have neural causes, while distinguishing these neural events from **M** and **T**.

1.1

According to Descartes, a *single* causal chain can include mental *and* neural events, because mental events lie *between* neural events.[2] Applied to

---

[2] Let a causal chain be an ordered n-tuple of events $\langle e_1, e_2, \ldots, e_n \rangle$ such that for each e_k, $k < n$, e_k is a cause of e_{k+1}, where e_k may or may not be a *proximal* cause of e_{k+1}, in that there is no e_{k*} such that e_k causes e_{k*} which causes e_{k+1}. What causes what will depend on

our example, the auctioneer's utterance causes certain changes in Nora's brain, which caused certain mental events, which caused other neural events that finally caused a motion of Nora's body. The basic Cartesian picture is simple:

$$S \to N_1 \to \ldots N_k \to \mathbf{M} \to \mathbf{T} \to N_p \to \ldots \to N_z \to B.$$

A stimulus initiates a chain of neural events, the last of which (N_k) has a mental effect ($\mathbf{M}$) that causes a trying ($\mathbf{T}$) that causes some neural event (N_p), which initiates another chain of biochemical events culminating with the bodily motion (B). Descartes does not speak of actions as tryings. But a Cartesian might well appeal to tryings, in cashing out the following idea: in order to move her body in a certain manner, a person produces an act of will that affects her brain in the way needed to get her body moving in that manner. (This is not to say that tryings *should* be understood as exercises of a Cartesian mind; see O'Shaughnessy 1973.) The basic Cartesian picture is simplified, since each event could have several *partial* causes, as when we together push a rock that neither of us could move alone. So a more realistic diagram might have multiple arrows converging on each event, which is in turn a partial cause of several events on different causal chains. But the simple picture will do for our purposes.

The idea that mental events occur between neural events taps into an alluring picture (famously criticized by Ryle 1949): a mind operates, and receives information from, a machine. Limb motions are typically caused by the machine, and events on the machine's periphery—i.e. the effects of sensory transduction—are relevant to the production of mental states. Suppose an evil demon destroyed all the apples, but affected Nora's sensory systems in an apple-ish way. Nora would still *come to believe* that there was an apple before her, and she would still move her body accordingly. For this and other reasons, Cartesians are led to say that minds and brains interact. Imagine a line of dominoes: some black ones, then some red ones, then more black ones. Toppling the first domino (providing the stimulus) initiates a sequence of events ending with the toppling of the last domino (the bodily motion). The causes of this last event include the toppling of every other domino, given that causation is transitive.

The domino analogy is, however, imperfect. On a Cartesian view, the chains from S to N_k and from N_p to B are *mechanical*, while chains involving mental events are not. Mental events are said to be *influenced*, not

relevant background states, and in isolating event C as a cause of event E, we take certain background conditions for granted. This practice may be interest relative in that, given other interests, we could have isolated event G (which is neither a cause nor an effect of C) as a cause of E, taking other conditions for granted—including, perhaps, the occurrence of C. We might say that a fire was caused by dropping a match, the wind, the dry conditions, etc. (see van Fraasen (1980), Bromberger (1966), Hart and Honoré (1959)). But this does not affect the issues at stake here.

determined, by the external stimulus and subsequent neural events. Causation involving mental events is *not* to be understood in terms of a mechanical model.[3] But the difference between determination and influence, mechanical versus non-mechanical causation, is not pellucid. While there were (and are) reasons for drawing some such distinction—as Chomsky (1966) emphasizes—Descartes' associated view of substances made mental causation puzzling for other reasons. Moreover, Descartes' conception of the mechanical proved inadequate, even for the physical world. So I prefer to speak of impersonal versus rationalizing causes: most causes are not intentional; only certain causes are someone's reasons for action. Regardless of terminology, though, instances of causation involving mental events seem different from other instances of causation.

This intuition, which the domino analogy obscures, is connected to our view that our actions are in some sense *free*. Indeed, being a locus of freedom is arguably a constitutive feature of persons; one denies that I am a person if one denies that my actions (*my* contributions to the causal order) are properly characterized in terms of freedom. It does not follow that actions are uncaused. On the contrary, my actions are mine (and free as opposed to random), because they lie within my control; that is why *I* am responsible for them. And my actions lie within my control, at least in part because they are caused by my reasons—events that are changes in *me*. McDowell (1994) nicely combines Sellarsian and Kantian metaphors here, by saying that the space of reasons is the realm of freedom. But whatever our choice of metaphors, the causation of an action by mental events seems importantly unlike the causation of a billiard ball's motion by the motion of some other ball. Causation in the presence of freedom, which requires reasons, is special. (This will be a repeated theme. Cf. Kant 1956.)

Nonetheless, Descartes' conception of mental causation is untenable. Even if it is stripped of soul-stuff, and the mechanistic physics that is no longer plausible, the Cartesian picture requires that actions be accompanied by anomalies. According to Descartes, a neural event at the edge of the pineal gland causes a subsequent neural event (that causes a rationally appropriate bodily motion) only by causing a mental event. Recall the diagram:

$$S \to N_1 \to \ldots N_k \to \mathbf{M} \to \mathbf{T} \to N_p \to \ldots \to N_z \to B.$$

---

[3] On this model, chains of the N_p-to-B type account for reflexes; a bodily motion need not have a mental event in its aetiology. (As Fodor (1983) notes, *some* mental events are also reflex-like. If observation conditions are good, and a red apple is before you, it will seem that something red is before you. See also McDowell's (1994) discussion of the *passivity* of experience.) And chains of the S-to-N_k type help Cartesians explain one kind of error: N_k will be misleading if it occurs because one of its neural causes c was produced by something other than the usual cause of c; for the mind will infer from the sensation caused by N_k to the usual cause of N_k, which will be the usual cause of c.

The occurrence of N_k *and then* N_p should be inexplicable from the impersonal point of view: a free will bridges the gap; a person's mental events lie *between* these neural events. But there is no reason to think, and ample reason to deny, that the impersonal order exhibits such causal/explanatory gaps.

Cartesians need not say that the pineal gland is the site of mind–brain interactions, or that there is a single site. But we have not discovered any locus of neural anomaly, and a host of familiar puzzles attend the supposition that such loci exist. Does N_p begin after N_k ends? (If so, what happens in the brain during the interim? If not, why do mental processes seem to take time?) Do N_k and N_p occur in physically contiguous regions of space? (If so, why deny that the former is a proximal cause of the latter? If not, how is such non-local causation between neural events possible?) And so on. If bodily motion B has mental causes, Cartesians *deny* that there is a corporeal causal chain from some stimulus to B, where such a causal chain is corporeal if every event in the chain has a biochemical event (or the stimulus) as a proximal cause. This denial leads to trouble. So let me grant that when a person moves her body, the bodily motion lies at the end of a corporeal chain that begins with some event external to the person. Some dualists might grant this, by saying that events can have both mental and neural events as *partial* causes. But I cannot believe that biochemical events produce certain bodily effects only with help from the mental—even if biochemistry is not a 'closed' system, in that quantum effects can intrude. So I want to defend a thoroughly non-Cartesian kind of event dualism.

1.2

Consider the following picture of mental causation, in which two distinct causal chains (one of which is corporeal) connect the stimulus S to some bodily motion B:[4]

$$
\begin{array}{ccc}
 & M \to T & \\
 \nearrow & & \searrow \\
S & & B \\
 \searrow & & \nearrow \\
 & N_1 \to \ldots \to N_z &
\end{array}
$$

In Chapter 6, I address the concerns about overdetermination that must be faced on such a view. But let me say at once that I do *not* take the

---

[4] Saying what it is for chains to be distinct, in the relevant sense, is non-trivial. One difficulty concerns chains like $<e_1, e_3, e_5>$ and $<e_1, e_2, e_4, e_5>$ if $<e_1, e_2, e_3, e_4, e_5>$ is also a chain. But let a *maximal* causal chain be one such that each non-terminal event is a proximal cause of the next event in the chain. I assume that C_1 and C_2 are distinct chains if C_1 is (or can be expanded into) a maximal causal chain that fails to include some event in C_2; and I assume that there is a maximal corporeal chain from S to B.

bodily effects of tryings to be like the toppling of a domino knocked over by two distinct dominoes. My claim is not that a person houses two independent but coordinated causal processes—one in the mind, one in the brain—like a room in which two hammers strike a bell at the same time. Rather, there are two ways of explaining bodily motions by citing and describing inner causes. When a person moves her body, her bodily motions can be seen as effects of events that rationalize her actions; and a person's bodily motions can be seen as effects of neural events. But it does not follow that the rationalizing causes are a subset of the neural causes. Given the right background views about causation and explanation, I claim, one can say that the two styles of explanation here are ontologically *incommensurate*: they cite causes that lack the common metaphysical basis required if each rationalizing cause is to be identified with some impersonal cause.

Eventually, the simple picture above will have to be modified. Given the arguments of Chapter 1, we need to see how tryings can be causes of *the muscle contractions that cause* bodily motions. Moreover, stress effects and placebo effects suggest that mental events can have corporeal effects apart from bodily motions. And perhaps mental events can be caused by direct stimulation of a person's brain. But such possibilities can be accommodated *if* the basic picture can be defended against various objections. It is easy, though, to think that such effort is unmotivated.

Neuralists can (as in Fodor 1983) restrict mental events to a 'central processor' flanked by sensory and motor systems, thus offering a monistic variant on Descartes' picture:

$$S \rightarrow N_1 \rightarrow \ldots N_k \rightarrow N_\alpha/M \rightarrow N_\omega/T \rightarrow N_p \rightarrow \ldots \rightarrow N_z \rightarrow B.$$

On this view, a corporeal chain connects S to B, but some neural events are not mere neural events; some neural events *are* tryings and their mental causes. This way of distinguishing mental and non-mental causes requires no spatio-temporal gaps, no strange causal processes, and no metaphysical distinctions among events. It also avoids the need for any special account of how B can have mental *and* neural causes. So given the availability of such a view, why bother with any form of event dualism?

The reason is that neuralism faces its own difficulties. Some of the specific objections will not emerge until later. But it is worth stressing that neuralism is a general thesis—every (human) mental event is a token of a certain type—none of whose instances have been confirmed. No one endorses neuralism on *inductive* grounds. On the contrary, we lack even the roughest idea of how to complete sentences like 'When Nora came to believe that Fido barked, her mental event was . . .' in the language of neuroscience. So it is hardly irrational to explore alternatives to neuralism. Certain abstract (metaphysical) considerations about causation can make it difficult to see alternatives. But this is not a licence to ignore competing considerations about persons and reasons.

Neuralism also makes it hard to see why the domino analogy is at all *in*adequate. Indeed, neuralism invites one to press the analogy in a way that intensifies worries about epiphenomenalism: in a chain of dominoes, some may have red spots; so some topplings may be red-spotted-domino top-plings; but each *toppling* is just like every other. Such comparisons raise questions about whether mental properties can have any interesting causal status, if mental events are describable in non-mental terms (see Drestke 1981; Heil and Mele 1993 for discussion). Moreover, such comparisons conflict with the thought that instances of mental causation differ impor-tantly from impersonal instances of causation. Suppose Nora comes to believe that Fido barked because she heard the barking, and coming to have this belief causes Nora's action of shutting the window. Intuitively, this is *not* just like other causal chains. In particular, it seems importantly unlike what happens when sound waves cause certain events in Nora's auditory system, which cause certain events in her central nervous system, which cause the motions of Nora's arms and legs. For *the person Nora*—the individual who acted for reasons—seems to get lost in this latter causal chain. In my view, this intuition can motivate alternatives to neuralism, even if it does not (yet) support a convincing anti-neuralist argument. (We will need to see how instances of mental causation can be special, yet still be instances of *causation*; but this is the topic of Chapter 7.)

1.3

It is worth dwelling a bit on the idea that persons get 'lost' when we focus on neural causes of bodily motions. Nagel (1986: 38) speaks of the 'grad-ual erosion of what we do by the subtraction of what happens'. As we learn more about ourselves as potential objects for impersonal explana-tion, the 'area of genuine agency' (and legitimate moral judgement) seems to 'shrink under scrutiny to an extensionless point' (ibid. 35). For as I stressed in Chapter 1, our conception of action—what a *person* does, what *she* contributes to history—seems to exclude anything that merely hap-pens due to nature. If Nora throws a rock, the rock's motion is not her action; it is something that happens in nature (in part because Nora acted). Changes in Nora can also be mere happenings. If Nora gets hit by a thrown rock, and is bruised as a result, it would be a bad joke to say that the discolouring of her skin is one of *Nora's* contributions to history (on the grounds that it is her skin); and similarly, it seems, for any biochemical changes that occur inside Nora (see also Taylor 1963).

Nagel fleshes out the idea that actions are not mere happenings by tapping into the intuition that some events cannot be specified without bringing onto the scene a person, an individual with a subjective point of view. (It would not be surprising if questions about mental causation connected up with questions about how to square subjective and objective points of view.) The falling of a brick is a mere happening. So is the bruising of my skin, or the beating of my heart; while one can talk about these events via reference to me, bringing a thinking subject into the discussion is not necessary. One could, without loss, talk about my heart or my skin via reference to a certain body. Thoughts and deeds, however, seem different. A strong Cartesian intuition is that one cannot talk about my mental events and actions while leaving *me* out of it. Actions are done for reasons, which cannot be separated from *persons* and their perspectives. One might say that reference to mental events requires reference to persons as persons. This is not to deny that actions and their mental causes are events, things that happen. It is to say that these events are special because they are changes in persons, where 'in' reflects not just the idea that mental changes are causes *inside* persons, but also the more basic idea that persons are the *subjects of* mental events. (I return to the sense in which mental events are spatially inner.) Crucially, mental events do not happen *to* persons. It is part of our self-conception that our actions and reasons are not things that befall us. But if our mental events cannot be described without bringing a thinking subject onto the scene, while neural events *can* be described in some such impersonal manner, we need an alternative to neuralism.[5]

Of course, it can be hard to maintain our self-conception, given what we know from an objective point of view. As Nagel (1986: 38) says, it seems that 'everything we do belongs to a world we have not created'; for if we subtract from the world everything that merely happens, nothing remains. If one could wander through a person's body—entering through the sensory systems, and passing out through the motor system—one would never observe anything (like a self) that could not be described impersonally. This prompts the thought that mental events *must* be describable in non-intentional terms. And this thought is reinforced if one sees Cartesian dualism as the only alternative to neuralism.

Another route to this thought is by way of Sellars' (1963) contrast between the manifest and scientific images (of man-in-the-world): in the former image, persons and reasons (which are manifest to us without scientific theories) render various aspects of the world comprehensible; in the latter image, phenomena are explained by positing impersonal theoretical

---

[5] One can refer to the bravest action of the week, and this action can be Nora's. But Nora has not been left out of the picture. For we are referring to her action *as* an action— a product of the reasons/perspective of some person, who turns out to be Nora. One can also think of mental events as changes in intentionally characterized states; for such changes are changes in persons.

entities and laws governing them. For reasons elaborated in Chapter 7, the success of our scientific perspective on the world can make it seem that we must repudiate the manifest image if it cannot be reconstructed from within the scientific image. Or to use more recent terminology, it can seem that we must choose between eliminativism and naturalism with respect to rationalizing causes, where naturalism is understood (not as the mundane claim that nature includes minded individuals, but) as a philosophical thesis about the possibility (and urgency) of carrying out the reconstruction project. For most of us, eliminativism is not a serious option. And neuralism is arguably a *sine qua non* of reconstructing manifest image particulars out of materials visible from a scientific perspective, at least if reasons are to be preserved as causes. (I have been influenced by McDowell (1994) here and in what follows; see also Hornsby (1993), who cites Nagel approvingly.)

This may explain part of neuralism's attraction. But one does not solve the puzzle of mental causation, by noting that it is hard to see any non-eliminativist alternative to neuralism. (When faced with a choice between two options, the job of philosophy is often to find a third.) Neuralism preserves the idea that bodily motions have *inner* causes. But we need to ask whether neuralism really lets one see how *mental* causation is possible. For if the neuralist is right, one can talk about events that have intentional descriptions without bringing persons—and their reasons and perspectives—onto the scene. The neuralist can allow that there is value in talking about certain events in intentional terms, and that talking about thoughts and deeds in impersonal terms is to give up talking about them *as* thoughts and deeds. But given neuralism, my mental events (including my tryings) are biochemical events; and it is hard to see how such events can be *mine* in the sense that my mental events are mine. The worry remains that genuine agency has been eliminated, while certain impersonal events have simply been *labelled* ours as a sop to our self-conception. Perhaps this worry is, in the end, misguided. But it is reasonable to wonder whether neuralists preserve mental causation, or replace it with an ersatz substitute.

One might reply that an action/trying is mine if it is a neural event of the right sort caused (in the right way) by other neural events of the right sort, and these neural events are mine, where saying what it is for a neural event to be mine is no harder than saying what it is for an arm to be mine. But such remarks are unsatisfying, and not just because the right sorts and ways await specification. The sense in which a person's neural events are his seems too much like the sense in which a person's heartbeats are his, and not enough like the sense in which his reasons and actions are his.[6]

---

[6] Some individuals can control their heart rate to a certain degree. But this does not make their heartbeats *theirs* in the relevant sense. In any case, processes of biofeedback are unlikely to explain how all of my mental events can be neural events that are *mine*.

1.4

On the other hand, the proposed alternative picture

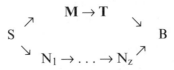

lets us say that mental events *are* distinctive. We can say that mental events, unlike neural events (heartbeats and bruisings), belong to the space of reasons/freedom. And if persons are the subjects of mental events, we can view our actions as *our* contributions to the causal order. On this view, intentionally characterized events cannot be characterized from an impersonal point of view; one cannot talk about thoughts and deeds in any terms that leave persons out of the picture. Nonetheless, persons act without creating anomalies. For every bodily motion lies at the end of a corporeal (impersonal) chain of events. Again, the idea is that one can use both intentional and non-intentional language to cite and describe causes of a person's bodily motions. But in doing so, one is not talking about the same causes in different ways. In describing what happens inside persons *in a distinctively personal way*, one is speaking about events that cannot be described in impersonal terms. (Hornsby (1986) offers a similar picture.)

At bottom, this is my real reason for exploring event dualism: it lets one say, in a way that neuralism does not, that our thoughts and deeds are *ours*. That said, it is not hard to sympathize with those who would deny that persons (and causation in the presence of freedom) are special in the way I have suggested. The neuralist will say that *if* my actions are free, then certain neural events (and their bodily effects) are free in the same sense. I have suggested that this is to invite eliminativism; for I think our conception of ourselves as persons requires that our actions/tryings be free (and the products of reasons) in a way that neural events are not. The dialectic, however, is subtle. If the causal contributions of persons are describable in impersonal terms, then contrary intuitions about freedom and reasons are misleading; and if we want to avoid false views, we will have to modify our self-conception appropriately. But if one can defend a version of event dualism, according to which actions and their mental causes are distinct from any events describable in impersonal terms, it will be question-begging for neuralists to argue as follows: our intuitions provide no motivation for event dualism, since those intuitions presuppose a mistaken conception of ourselves.

One might think it equally question-begging to suppose that anti-neuralist intuitions are coherent. Haven't we learned that, at least where nebulous notions like freedom are concerned, our self-conception is untrustworthy? At the risk of sounding retrograde, I suggest that taking such an attitude towards our self-conception should be the philosophical option of last resort. In an intellectual climate where it is easy to regard the impersonal point of view as the sole arbiter of what there (really) is, we should work at *recovering* some of our Cartesian intuitions. Our view of ourselves as persons is potentially confusing but, in my view, it is not indefensible. Our Cartesian intuitions have inherited a bad rap—a kind of guilt by association with a particular theory (Cartesian dualism) whose failings we recognize. So instead of jettisoning our intuitions, we can look for another way of reconciling them with our impersonal view of the world that includes us. If possible, our account of mental causation should be based on a view of causation that lets us see how some caused events can still be free, and our account of mental events should be such that actions are among the caused-but-free events.

Of course, it is not easy to square freedom with causation. Kant, who described the problem for us so vividly, was led to identify the loci of freedom with transcendental egos: beings that do not exist, along with causes and effects, in space and time. But appeal to noumenal and empirical selves results in a dualism no better than Descartes'. Our freedom is still purchased at the cost of making us the sort of beings that cannot exercise their freedom to act as a form of genuine causality. Still, I share Kant's desire for a view that preserves the intuitive connection between reasons and freedom, *even though* reasons are causes. (And *pace* Davidson (1970), I do not think the absence of strict psychological laws preserves my freedom, if each of my mental events is covered by some impersonal law.)[7] The difficulty of doing justice to our intuitions can indeed tempt us into

---

[7] One might worry that freedom is *incompatible* with laws, even cp laws. If Nora wants Ψ to be the case, and believes that Φ-ing will make Ψ the case, she can still refrain from trying to Φ. So how can the practical syllogism be a law? The answer, I think, is fairly simple: Nora is free to refrain from trying to Φ (and thus create an Abnormal instance of the law); but *ceteris paribus*, she will try to Φ. If Nora doesn't try to Φ, other things are not equal; some interfering factor—say, another desire (perhaps even an existential desire to rebel against reason)—explains why Nora didn't act in the expected (rationalizable) fashion. And this doesn't trivialize the cp law; see Ch. 4. This in turn raises concerns about akrasia. How can the practical syllogism be a law if a person can fail to act on her strongest desire, due to weakness of will? Suppose Nora really wants the painting, she really believes that she can get the painting by raising her arm, and she has no mental states that explain why she didn't raise her arm; Nora just couldn't bring herself to act at the crucial moment, and not because she decided at the last minute to save the money. Such cases present difficulties for any view of intentional explanation, and not just those that appeal to mentalistic laws. But there are two available strategies for dealing with such cases: treat the onset of akrasia as an arational interfering factor (something like a seizure); or restrict the application of the practical syllogism, by adding an initial condition that specifies (hopefully, in some non-circular way) that the agent is not in an akratic state, i.e. that the agent is in a state of responsiveness to judgement. Either way, the idea will be to capture the intuition that it is not Normal for a person to be akratic.

'obscure and panicky metaphysics', as Strawson (1962) noted in a related context. But it does not follow that our intuitions are defective, for they need not be a source of obscurity or panic.

2. Unified Persons

In Section 1, I made the familiar point that Cartesians are committed to the existence of certain gaps in the impersonal causal order, and that (unless we are badly mistaken) there are no such gaps for mental events to fill. A related point is that Cartesians view persons as unions of minds with bodies. And this thesis is problematic, for reasons that Strawson (1958) discusses. Reviewing the argument will help distinguish my version of event dualism from Descartes'. It will also clarify a claim I have made on several occasions: rationalizing explanations of actions cite person-internal causes that cannot be described in impersonal terms. It is tempting to think that an intentional description of what happens inside a person must be a description of events describable without bringing a person onto the scene. But one can resist this temptation while also rejecting the Cartesian conception of persons.

2.1

Thus far, I have ignored a question that can motivate Cartesian dualism: how is it possible that some things have mental properties *and* corporeal properties, given that these properties are so different? Even setting consciousness aside, one might want to know how something can have both non-intentional features (like *weighing 75 kg*, or *having a brain*) and intentional features (like *believing that Desdemona loved Cassio* and *wanting to get revenge*). As Strawson (1958: 331) puts it, 'among the things we ascribe to ourselves are things of a kind we ascribe to material bodies to which we would not dream of ascribing others of the things we ascribe to ourselves.'

There is nothing troubling in the mere fact that individuals with properties of one sort also have properties of another sort. But this can be troubling with respect to intentional and non-intentional properties. For in the first-person case, the way in which one ascribes intentional properties seems *very* different from the way in which one ascribes non-intentional properties. There is a sense of 'look' in which I have to look, in order to know what I weigh, while I typically know what I believe without looking. And this epistemic distinction is apt to be conjoined with a seductive idea: very different ways of knowing things reflect different types of things known. In particular, Cartesians hold that mental and non-mental properties are so different that no single entity can be the bearer of both kinds of properties. On this view, persons are composite entities, though composites of a special sort:

Nature also teaches me . . . that I am not merely present in my body as a sailor is present in a ship, but that I am very closely joined, and as it were, intermingled with it, so that I and the body form a unit. (Descartes 1642: 192)

Descartes uses terms like 'person' ('man', 'I') ambiguously. Sometimes, his intended referent is a mind; sometimes, it is a mind-body unity. But focus on this claim: a person is a mind that is closely united with a body, where the person has the properties had by each of the substances that make up the union. An ambiguity remains, though, if persons do not *have* their mental and corporeal properties in the same sense. Say that an individual has$_1$ the properties suited to it, and has$_2$ the properties had$_1$ by anything with which it is united. If person Π is mind M, in union with body β, then Π has$_2$ the properties had$_1$ by β; while Π, being a thinking thing, has$_1$ the mental properties had$_1$ by M.[8] It is implausible, however, to deny that persons have corporeal properties in the same sense that bodies have such properties. Yet on the Cartesian view, persons have$_2$ properties like *being six feet tall* only by virtue of being united with bodies that have$_1$ such properties; the person Nick (as opposed to Nick's body) cannot be six feet tall in the same way as a bookshelf. This makes it surprising that we ascribe corporeal properties to persons at all: why say 'I am six feet tall', instead of 'My body is six feet tall'?

More importantly, while we can locate other bodies by looking, Descartes' view makes it unclear how we even begin to locate other minds. The worry is not merely that we may lack evidence for distinguishing automata from bodies united with minds. The deeper point is that Cartesians make a mystery of the fact that we ascribe mentality to others, and thereby make a mystery of the fact that we ascribe mentality to ourselves. As Strawson (1958, 1959) notes, ascribing mental properties *to an individual* makes sense only if one can ascribe such properties to more than one individual; in ascribing mental traits *to someone*, even myself, I ascribe traits to one person as opposed to others. And I can ascribe mentality to others only if I can identify other thinkers. In this sense, being able to identify other minds is a precondition of being able to ascribe mental properties to oneself. But on the standard Cartesian view, I locate other minds by noting that *my* body bears some complex causal relation **R** to *me* (my

---

[8] A Cartesian might treat 'person' as a sortal term for unions, with 'have$_2$' defined accordingly: if Π is the union of M with β, then Π has$_2$ the properties had$_1$ by β, and Π has$_2$ the properties had$_1$ by M. But this view suffers from at least as many problems as the position discussed in the text.

mind), and then inferring that another body bears **R** to another mind. Even if some such inference is warranted, how am I to start by noting that some body bears **R** to *me*?

That is, for Cartesians, a precondition of my identifying other thinkers is that I notice a certain relation between my body and my mind; and this seems to get things backwards. I cannot notice any relation between a body β and *my* thoughts, as opposed to a relation between β and thought in general, unless I have already located myself as a subject of thoughts. But if I have located myself as a subject of thoughts—thus distinguishing *I think that P* from the weaker *there is a thinking that P*—I must already be able to locate thinkers besides myself. Again, ascriptions of thoughts *to me* make sense only if it makes sense to ascribe thoughts to individuals besides me. Otherwise, there could be no point in ascribing certain mental properties to *me* (or in describing certain mental states as *mine*).

This leaves the Cartesian in a deeply unsatisfying position. He owes an account of how one thinker can ascribe thoughts to others. It seems that the account must take the form of an inference by analogy. (I somehow infer that other bodies bear to other minds the same complex causal relation that my body bears to my mind.) But such an explanation of how one ascribes thoughts to others will presuppose that one can locate oneself as a subject of thoughts. And being able to locate oneself as a thinker presupposes the very ability that the Cartesian is supposed to be explaining. So it seems that the Cartesian view is structurally incapable of explaining how one can ascribe thoughts to others, and hence structurally incapable of explaining how one can meet an important precondition of being able to ascribe thoughts to oneself. In this sense, the Cartesian makes a mystery of all mental ascriptions—ascriptions to oneself, and ascriptions to others. This is a good reason for abandoning Cartesian dualism. Metaphysical views should help resolve puzzles; they should not render puzzles intractable.

2.2

So the question remains: how can something have mental *and* corporeal properties? Cartesians reject a presupposition of this question, denying that one thing has$_1$ both kinds of properties, in favour of substance dualism. But perhaps nothing has$_1$ corporeal properties, or perhaps nothing has$_1$ mental properties. The former (idealist) position is no longer taken seriously. So the latter position can seem to be all that is left. For not only might one fail to see other options, one might think that ordinary ascriptions of mental properties presuppose Cartesian dualism. After all, there is *something* odd about there being such different ways of (correctly) ascribing mental properties to ourselves and others. And it is tempting to diagnose this oddness as the result of our attachment to the mistaken picture of mentality that Descartes made explicit.

Strawson thus considers the suggestion that only bodies have properties, and that bodies have mental properties in a sense distinct from the ordinary sense in which they have corporeal properties. On this view, Nick's body has$_1$ the property of being six feet tall, just like his bookshelf; but Nick has$_3$ mental properties, where 'has$_3$' expresses a kind of causal dependence. Return to the intuition that, for each person, some body bears a special causal relation **R** to that person's mind. To speak of this relation is to summarize a cluster of facts about the dependence of a normal person's mental properties on various features of the person's body. There is a body β such that if the eyelids of β are closed, I see nothing; what I see at any moment depends, in part, on how the eyes of β are oriented; and which fields of vision are possible for me, at any moment, depends on where β is located (see Strawson 1959). Such facts are important. They motivate even the Cartesian to speak of a particular body as *his*. And one might try to exploit such facts by saying that a body has$_3$ the mental properties that depend on it.

On this view, nothing has$_1$ mental traits. To suppose otherwise, by positing Cartesian egos (or by saying that bodies have$_1$ mental traits), is to be duped by a linguistic illusion fostered by the Cartesian picture. I will not discuss this strange position in any detail. But this is where one is led *if* one starts with the assumption that a person is a compound of two kinds of thing—a subject of mental attributes, and a subject of corporeal attributes.

Many questions arise when we think this way. But, in particular, when we ask ourselves how we come to frame, to get a use for, the concept of this compound of two subjects, the picture—if we are honest and careful—is apt to change from the picture of two subjects to one subject and one non-subject. (Strawson 1958: 340)

Unsurprisingly, this 'no-ownership' view of mentality does not do justice to how we think of persons. For example, we can say *whose* thoughts (or mental properties) depend on a given body. If the body is mine, *my* thoughts depend on it; if the body is Smith's, *Smith's* thoughts depend on it, etc. These claims are not tautologous. One can imagine cases in which my thoughts depend, for a while, on the sensory organs of a body other than mine. At first glance, the no-ownership theorist can make similar claims. If the body is me, who has$_3$ my mental properties, then my mental properties depend on it; and so on. But on this view, to speak of *my* mental properties is to speak of properties that causally depend on body β; and if asked which properties these are, it is no answer to say, 'the ones that depend on β'. So if the no-ownership view is right, we cannot assert what we appear to assert.[9] This strongly suggests that persons have$_1$ mental properties; such properties are not merely had$_3$ by—i.e. they are not merely causally dependent on—certain bodies. So I follow Strawson in rejecting the trouble-making idea that persons are compounds of more basic things. (For similar reasons, I also reject the trouble-making idea that persons are Kantian transcendental egos; see Strawson 1966.) This does not yet answer any questions. But it puts us in the right frame of mind for addressing questions we can answer.

Strawson summarizes his point by saying that the concept of a person is primitive. It is 'the concept of a type of entity', such that both mental predicates and corporeal predicates 'are equally applicable to a single individual of that single type'; and this type is *not* a 'secondary kind' that can be understood in terms of its relation to two primary kinds (1958: 340, 343). Of necessity, anything that has intentional properties has non-intentional properties, in an unambiguous sense of 'has'. Persons have minds and bodies. But this is just the truism that persons have mental and bodily traits. It is *not* that persons are unions of minds with bodies. One can speak of Smith's mind and Smith's body. But this is to speak of Smith, abstracting away from either his corporeal or mental features.

Such remarks are non-trivial. But they will seem unhelpful if the question is *how* persons can have both mental and corporeal traits. Instead of answering this question, Strawson suggests that its point lies elsewhere. One can ask 'what is it in the natural facts that makes it intelligible that we have' the concept of a person (1958: 348). And some hard questions about first person authority must be addressed if persons correctly ascribe mental properties without ambiguity to themselves and others.[10] But to repeat,

---

[9] The no-ownership theorist aims to ensure that whatever depends on body β *could have depended* on another body β*, so that mental ascriptions will be contingently true (see Schlick (1949), and Moore's (1955) representation of Wittgenstein). But *analysing* 'my mental traits depend on my body' as 'the traits that depend on B depend on B' renders the former claim non-contingent.

[10] If persons are *essentially* thinking things, there will also be (morally loaded) questions about how to describe certain individuals that lack the capacity for normal adult thought. Presumably, I existed on the day of my birth; and if I am now essentially a person, it is hard to see how I could exist at any time *t* without being a person. But if human beings are persons at birth (or earlier), it can seem that the concept of a person is not very demanding in terms of the thinking capacities required. Perhaps this is reason to deny that persons are essentially persons. Or perhaps, given our nature as biological beings who develop, we should say that: any individual that will become a thinking thing is already a person; if two individuals have the same capacities, and one is a person, then both are persons; so there are persons who will never develop and manifest the thinking capacities of adult persons; but for just this reason the (non-disjunctive) concept of a person allows for core and peripheral cases; so the mere fact that an individual is a person may carry less moral significance than one might think, although it may not be *mere* speciesism to say that being a member of *Homo sapiens* (a species whose mature members are thinking things) carries some moral significance. (Note that this line of thought is based on modal considerations, *not* the idea

Strawson offers an argument for facing these questions: ascribing mental traits to anything requires that one be able to ascribe such traits to things that are not oneself (but are of the same logical type as oneself); being able to ascribe mental traits to others requires that one be able to identify other potential bearers of mental traits (each of whom is of the same relevant type as oneself, given that one self-ascribes mental traits); and one can identify other potential bearers of mental traits, only if those individuals (like oneself) also have corporeal traits (ibid. 342).

2.3

Asking how persons can have both minds and bodies is important, even if (as posed) this question can only be answered by noting that our concept of a person is primitive. For questions about mental causation are questions about persons. And framing these questions in Strawsonian terms makes it clear that denying neuralism is *not* tantamount to adopting Cartesian dualism. One can deny that the mental causes of a bodily motion B are certain neural causes of B, without saying that persons are composite entities, or that mental events are alterations in a soul united with a body. For one can regard the different ways of explaining why B occurred (not as different ways of thinking about the same causes of B, but) as explanations that cite different kinds of person-internal causes. This goes beyond Strawson's own claims. But in my view, a person is neither a body that turns out to be a thinker, nor a thinking substance that turns out to have a body.

A person is an individual of a special sort, a single thing with a dual nature. It is in the nature of persons to have both intentional and corporeal properties. Since persons have a rational nature, it is no surprise that many bodily motions have rationalizing causes; and if a bodily motion has any internal cause, it has an impersonal internal cause, since persons have a corporeal nature. In this sense, I endorse a 'dual-aspect' view. But let me stress that we are talking about aspects of *persons*, which need not be identified with bodies. In asking whether or not mental events are neural events, we are not asking (at least not in the first instance) whether or not certain *bodily* changes are describable in neuroscientific terms. To assume that mental changes are bodily changes is already to go a long way towards accepting neuralism. For Nora's body will undergo various changes when Nora comes to believe that Fido barked; and on the usual understanding of 'body', it is untendentious that bodily changes are describable in impersonal terms. The question is whether some of these changes are also mental. (If it is stipulated that mental events are bodily

that non-adults are persons because they have a certain kind of future.) I am indebted to Susan Dwyer for discussion on this point.

events, then one cannot assume that all bodily events have impersonal descriptions.)

The alternative suggestion is not that Nora is a mind, but rather that Nora is an individual who undergoes bodily changes *and* changes that cannot be described in impersonal (or 'topic-neutral') terms. Perhaps this non-Cartesian form of dualism is wrong, and the rationalizing causes of our bodily motions just are biochemical causes of those motions. But the neuralist thesis does not follow from the mere fact that thinkers have a corporeal nature. When we explain someone's action in rationalizing terms, we treat her *as* a person, i.e. as an individual of a rather special sort. And this may involve the ascription of causes that cannot be described without bringing a thinking subject onto the scene. (Again, this possibility is not idle, given the considerations about reasons and freedom alluded to above.)

It is crucial, in this regard, to distinguish theses about persons from theses about mental events: persons, unlike events, think; and mental events, unlike persons, have propositional contents. If Nora comes to believe that Fido barked, then Nora comes to have the (person-level) intentional property *believes that Fido barks*. If any individual *i* has this property, then *i* has various non-intentional properties. Indeed, one can view Strawson as providing an argument for an identity thesis that Descartes rejected: the bearer of a person's intentional properties just *is* the bearer of that person's corporeal properties. Event dualists can and should endorse this claim. The dispute with neuralists concerns subpersonal entities. When Nora comes to believe that Fido barked, she comes to be in a state whose content is *that Fido barked*.[11] Our question is whether such mental changes are biochemical. Strawson's claims do not settle this question in favour of neuralism. On the contrary, they allow for a coherent formulation of event dualism. But for now, the point is simply that event dualists can and should adopt Strawson's (anti-Cartesian) identity thesis.

2.4

I have stressed that a person is something with a corporeal nature. This raises the question of how a Strawsonian person is related to her body (see Schaffer 1968). The simplest suggestion would be that a person is identical with her body: persons have rational natures, and some bodies have rational natures. (Our *concept* of a person may be primitive, even if in fact that concept applies to bodies.) On this view, my body has mental states in

---

[11] Recall that 'N believes that P' is true iff $\exists e[\text{Subject}(e, N) \& \text{Believing}_\sigma(e) \& \text{Content}(e, \text{that } P)]$, where 'e' ranges over events and states, and 'σ' indicates that 'believe' is a stative verb. In the appendix, I return to the fact that mental events have contents, and I contend that this tells against neuralism.

the same sense that *I* have mental states; indeed, a certain body is the *subject* of those events that are mental changes in me. This is logically compatible with the rejection of neuralism. For perhaps when a (human) body B undergoes mental changes, these mental events are distinct from any neural changes in B. But my version of event dualism goes hand-in-hand with denying that persons are their bodies.

In my view, persons are ontologically fundamental particulars, and not merely in the sense that persons are not Cartesian unions. Persons, along with their reasons and actions, occupy a fundamental position in the explanatory scheme of rationalizing explanations (the Sellarsian manifest image). Persons are not 'macro objects' in an explanatory scheme (the Sellarsian scientific image) where physics is basic and every event can be described in the language of some impersonal science. In this sense, intentional psychology is not one among many 'special sciences', even though persons are *composed* of quarks and such. Anyone who endorses such a view is likely to endorse some of the traditional arguments, sketched below, for not identifying persons with bodies. But I mention these arguments mainly to indicate my view of persons, not because I regard them as compelling in their own right, i.e. absent a defence of some dualistic alternative to a person–body thesis.

I am a reasoner, a thinker, the subject of a rational perspective on the world; but my body is not. And when I die, *I* will cease to exist; yet my body will continue to exist, albeit in a different state. My body can endure certain changes in my body, like the cessation of heartbeats, that I cannot endure. For when certain of my bodily functions cease, the subject of my rational perspective will cease to be. So I am not my body. Correlatively, my body can exist independently of me. While I actually exist (at the present time t), I might have been killed in an accident yesterday. In that case, I would not have existed (at t), but my body would have existed (in an alternative state at t). So I am not my body. (Note that a Cartesian would say that persons—i.e. souls—can survive their bodies.) Persons may well supervene on bodies in the following sense: for every (human) person Π there is a body β, such that for many possible states of β—in particular, states of being alive with certain sorts of brain activity—Π exists in every possible world in which β is in one of those states. But Π can still have properties that β lacks.[12]

---

[12] Does Π fail to exist in every possible world where β is not in one of these states? I am not sure; but a negative answer would not threaten person/body supervenience. (Perhaps I could survive gradual replacement of all my body parts with prosthetic devices, while at some point my body ceases to exist.) I return to questions about supervenience in Ch. 6. More importantly, one cannot evade the argument against person–body identity, by saying that Π is β *so long as β is in one of the relevant states.* For β will continue to be β, while Π will not, even when β ceases to be in any of the relevant states. It is tempting to introduce a new entity, β-in-S, where S is the disjunction of states such that Π exists in every possible

One might worry that this proliferates entities in a dangerous way. For if Π weighs 75 kg, so does β, yet Π and β can each be located on a chair that will hold only 100 kg. But in distinguishing Π from β, one is not denying that β is Π's body, or that many of Π's properties are determined by β and its properties. Consider a familiar analogy. One might distinguish a bronze statue from a lump of bronze that occupies the same region of space (at some time *t*), on the grounds that the statue has distinctive persistence conditions and/or modal properties; and this metaphysical view need not have the unpalatable consequence that pedestals are 'over-occupied'. Two particulars *of different sorts* can be in the same place at the same time (see Wiggins 1980). If x is a bronze statue, x does not 'compete for space' with the lump of bronze that constitutes x. And one need not say that a statue takes up space only by virtue of being initimately related to something *else* that takes up space. Statues simply are the sorts of things that take up space, though many properties of a statue—including its spatial properties—are determined by properties of the matter from which the statue is composed. (See Hornsby (1985) and Pietroski (1994) for discussion of parallels to event overdetermination. See also Section 3 of the Introduction.)

Correspondingly, one might distinguish a person from his body, while still recognizing that persons have corporeal traits in the same way that mere bodies have such traits. Saying that Nick weighs 75 kg is not a mere *façon de parler*, which would be better expressed by saying that he weighs$_2$ 75 kg; Nick does not have (or have$_2$) a certain weight by virtue of being united with, or otherwise intimately related to, something else that weighs (or weighs$_1$) 75 kg. Rather, Nick is a person; and our concept of a person is a concept of something with a corporeal nature—the *sort* of thing that has a weight. Many properties of a person, including his weight, are determined by properties of the matter from which the person is composed. So unsurprisingly, Nick has the weight that his body has.

Having offered this analogy, let me stress: my claim is *not* that the relation of a person to his body is just like the relation of a bronze statue to the lump of bronze out of which the statue is formed. Temporal and modal arguments may apply in both cases. But statues are not reasoners with perspectives; their distinctive identity conditions presumably rely on the intentions of their makers and observers. And at least for me, the intuition that persons are individuals *of a special sort* is rooted in the idea that persons (unlike bodies) are subjects of a rational perspective on the world.

world where β is in S, and β-in-S ceases to exist when β ceases to be in one of the relevant states. But note that β-in-S is not an individual in the usual sense (i.e. a bearer of properties), but an *individual-in-a-state*. So it is not clear that β-in-S could be the bearer of a person's corporeal properties. Moreover, β-in-S is specified by reference to the person Π, since S is specified in terms of Π's existence. So appeal to β-in-S does not avoid appeal to Π.

One way of conveying this idea is by noting that when we die, we are *gone*, while our bodies are merely changed; and had we died, we would have been gone, while our bodies would have remained. But these arguments are devices for getting at an intuition about persons that does not apply to statues. And at least for me, this intuition survives sophisticated responses to the Leibniz Law arguments. For even if these arguments are somehow question-begging, they still give voice to the idea that thinking subjects are distinctive—indeed, distinctively fragile—entities.[13] The statue analogy also serves to remind us of a familiar metaphysical view that is available to non-Cartesian dualists: objects of different *sorts* can occupy the same space (have the same weight, etc.) without over-occupying the space (straining the chairs, etc.); for the material properties of any object will be determined by properties of its matter.

Of course, one might reject the intuition that underlies the Leibniz Law arguments as applied to persons and bodies, thereby avoiding the conclusion that persons are individuals of a special *sort*. Perhaps the idea of assigning special metaphysical status to persons must give way to the idea that (while our *concept* of a person may be special) persons are fusions of molecules, or four-dimensional fusions of molecules-at-an-instant, or five-dimensional 'modal fusions' of space-time worms at the actual and counterfactual worlds.[14] Or perhaps persons can be identified with other

[13] Is a rabbit an individual distinct from its body? Talk of rabbits being 'gone' when they die strikes me as overly anthropomorphic. But I take no stand here on which (if any) non-human animals are persons. Perhaps the notion *subject of experience* can be extended to live rabbits if they (like human reasoners) have a perspective that makes it appropriate to say that when relevant bodily functions cease, a certain individual ceases to exist, even while the body remains. But mere consciousness, whatever that is, may not be sufficient (or necessary) for having a perspective in the sense that is relevant here—at least not if consciousness is understood in terms of qualitative states like pains, with no assumption that the bearer of such states is a *reasoning subject of* such states. (See McDowell's (1994) discussion of, and his own variation on, Evans' (1982) view that animals lacking states with conceptualized content are not subjects of experience in the way that persons are.) If we conclude that persons are ontologically special entities, there may be less reason to resist a similar conclusion about other animals. But for reasons discussed in the text, one cannot establish conclusions about persons by reflecting on rabbits and/or statues.

[14] See e.g. Heller (1984, 1990) and Lewis (1971, 1986); cf. Thomson (1980). As I have already indicated, my intuitions are with those who think that two distinct objects (of different sorts) can occupy the same space at the same time. But I will not try to defend this view here, though my hope is that a defence of event dualism will undermine part of the motivation for denying that we endure (as opposed to perdure) through time; cf. Lewis. It may be worth recalling, though, a familiar line of thought which suggests that even four dimensions may not be enough for those who wish to reject the 'endurantist' intuitions underlying the Leibniz Law arguments mentioned in the text. Suppose that Toonces *nearly* lost her tail; and let F be a fusion of Toonces-time-slices that occupies the same region of space-time as Toonces. Let α be the actual world, and let w be a world where Toonces exists tailless. Arguably, F does not exist at w, and so Toonces ≠ F. (And if F exists altered at w, consider Groonces: Toonces until *t,* and Toonces' tailless body thereafter. Groonces is not

entities characterized so as to accommodate the allegedly distinctive properties of persons, thereby blocking any inference to the Cartesian conclusion: persons are entities of a kind K, such that no impersonal entity is of
kind K (and so K is 'over and above' the kinds of things that can be found
in the Sellarsian scientific image). I cannot prove that no such metaphysics
of persons is correct. And for those who regard ontological parsimony as
sufficient reason to overthrow our conception of ourselves, nothing short
of proof is likely to suffice. But in my view, mere ontological parsimony is
an overrated virtue. (If we are willing to be sufficiently revisionary, we can
adopt *very* simple views, like 'all is water'.) I see no good reason for abandoning the idea that persons are things of a special sort, apart from the
absence of a viable alternative to neuralism. Given the failure of Cartesian
dualism, this is a serious gap to fill. But Strawson at least provides the
resources needed to begin.

3. Locating Mental Events

On my view, persons and their mental events are spatio-temporal particulars. At any given moment, I occupy a certain region of space; and every
change in me occurs (somewhere) within the region of space occupied by
me. Few contemporary philosophers would challenge these anti-Cartesian
claims. But one might wonder if anti-neuralists are *entitled* to make such
claims. In this section, I address a series of such concerns, by way of further clarifying and motivating my kind of dualism.

3.1

I have spoken of mental events both as changes that persons undergo, and
as events that occur inside persons.[15] But one might think this is a confusion, stemming from two interpretations of the claim that mental events are
changes *in* persons. Moreover, one might think that dualists must reject the
idea that mental events are inner causes of bodily motions. For if we look

a cat at α, at least not after *t*, since there cannot be two cats in the same place at the same
time. Arguably, Toonces would not have been something that is not a cat; so at w, Toonces
is not Groonces, even though Toonces and Groonces occupy the same region of space-
time.) Moreover, even if one says that (so-called) continuants have modal parts, this helps
avoid the idea that continuants like persons are ontologically special, only if one can make
sense of appeal to modality *independently* of appeal to continuants and their modal properties; and as I note in Ch. 6, I am sceptical (see Wiggins 1980; Hornsby 1985).

[15] If I am a Cartesian mind, my mental events do *not* occur inside me, though my
mental events may be proximal causes of events that occur inside a body to which I bear a
special causal relation.

inside human heads, we can see—or at least detect, by means of devices not unlike telescopes and microscopes—biochemical activity of various sorts. Yet if dualists are correct, one cannot open Nora's head and (on the basis of what is thereby laid open to view) witness the acquisition of her belief that Fido barked. Dualists cannot allow that such events are detectable by methods that do not require bringing a thinking subject onto the scene: we can see actions/tryings, at least sometimes; but we do not see them by opening heads or using brain scanners. By contrast, neuralists can and should say that mental events are detectable via impersonal methods, although such events need not be recognized *as* mental. Now perhaps some philosophers would be happy to reject the idea that our mental events occur within us. And if 'inner' is defined so that inner events must be detectable by impersonal methods, then I cannot say that mental events are inner causes. But this would be an unfortunate stipulation. For a familiar cluster of facts supports the intuitive claim that mental events do occur within us; and these facts are compatible with my kind of dualism.

Unlike Descartes, I think mental events have spatial location. At a minimum, my mental events occur within the region occupied by me, and as a Strawsonian person, I have extension. Indeed, I occupy the very region of space occupied by my body. This is a fairly weak claim. A person's mental events occur where he is. But many bodily motions have mental causes, and these causes are not (like events in our environment) external to us. So there is pressure to endorse a slightly stronger claim. For each mental event M that has some bodily effect, M occurs in the spatial region occupied by some *part* of the body that fails to include the part of the body where the effect of M occurred. If the bodily effects of mental events include muscle contractions and other subdermal events—like changes in blood pressure, or changes in adrenalin levels—the importance of this point is compounded; and similarly, if mental events can be caused by bodily events, like changes at the sensory peripheries. Some parts of the body also seem to be irrelevant to mentality. My spleen can be removed without affecting my ability to think or act. So it seems safe to say that my mental events occur within the spatial region defined by my body minus my spleen. If each mental event occurs in some subpart of the region occupied by the relevant person, then at least to this extent mental events occur within persons.

One can say that mental causes are inner causes, in this sense, without saying that events are highly localized events that have no global character. Suppose, no doubt oversimplistically, that Nora's central nervous system occupies the smallest subregion of her body, such that the event of Nora's coming to believe that Fido barked occurred in that subregion. And suppose that, simultaneously with acquiring this belief, Nora came to desire a pizza. (She had been thinking about dinner when the dog barked.)

For all I have said, Nora's central nervous system may occupy the smallest subregion of her body, such that the event of Nora's coming to desire a pizza occurred in that subregion. Distinct mental events *need* not have distinct spatial properties if something can simultaneously undergo two distinct global changes of state. As an analogy, imagine a malleable lump of stuff that changes in shape, perhaps in response to external stimuli, as follows: from cubical to spherical, then conical, and back to cubical. We can also imagine that the lump simultaneously changes colour: from red, to blue, then yellow, and back to red.

Of course, the morphing lump is an imperfect analogy for persons undergoing mental changes, especially if mental events are not 'surface' changes. And one might think the analogy is improved, in a way that favours neuralism, if we imagine a larger system of which the morphing lump is a part. Why not say that Nora's mental events are changes of which her central nervous system is the subject? Sometimes, a person undergoes a change that can be identified with a change in some part of the person. An event of going blind can *be* some change (perhaps brought on by disease) in a person's visual system; and this change is presumably describable in non-intentional terms, even if it cannot be described *as* a change in some person without bringing a person onto the scene. A change of the same type in the visual system of a congenitally blind person would not be an event of going blind. But given the right context, a change in X's visual system can be the event of X's going blind.

It is tempting to extend this thought: losing a practical ability, like the ability to touch-type, is relevantly like going blind; and acquiring a practical ability is also an inner event (or process) that can be described in impersonal terms. Perhaps a person who acquires such an ability comes to be in a state, such that because he is in that state, certain perceptual stimuli are apt to cause bodily motions (like the motions of fingers that occur in the course of typing). And perhaps acquiring a belief is an event of the same sort, only more complex. But it is not clear that acquiring a skill is relevantly like losing a skill—say, through trauma or lack of practice. For one typically *tries* to do various things in the course of acquiring a skill, even if the goal is to achieve a state by virtue of which desired results are achieved without trying. More importantly, in a debate between neuralists and event dualists, it would be question-begging to assume that there is no crucial difference between (i) cases in which a perceptual stimulus causes some bodily motion without an intervening action/trying, and (ii) cases in which a person acts (freely) in response to a perceptual stimulus, thereby moving her body in some appropriate way. This defensive claim does not show that a person's mental events are not changes in her nervous system. But granting that mental events are inner events is not tantamount to endorsing neuralism.

3.2

I said above that mental events occur within persons, since each mental event occurs in some subregion of the region occupied by the relevant person. One would like to know how far this line of thought can be pushed. Given a mental event e, what is the *smallest* subpart S of the body, such that e occurred in the region occupied by S? Following Hornsby (1981, 1997), I think there is considerable indeterminacy here, and that this tells against identifying mental events with biochemical events. The former apparently differ from the latter with respect to the *vagueness* of their boundaries; given any mental event e, it seems that every biochemical event has spatio-temporal features that can be specified more sharply than those of e. If a person tries to move her hand, and we want to say where and when the trying occurred, then it seems that we cannot do much better than in her head, just before the motion of her hand. This is not nothing, since it shows that we can locate mental events in space and time. But we can be much more precise—even if we cannot be *perfectly* precise—about the location of every biochemical event. Like Hornsby, I think this asymmetry reflects the fact that tryings are events of a sort, such that no biochemical event is of that sort; and similarly for other rationalizing causes (see also Schaffer 1968). But before comparing mental and biochemical events, let me be clear about the form of the argument under consideration.

Start with the familiar idea that there are always limits to the kinds of claims one can make, without going beyond the facts, about where and when an event occurred. If someone asks where a given tornado occurred, correct answers might include: Kansas, south-western Kansas, about a hundred miles west of Witchita, etc. If these answers are correct, then answers like the following are not: Texas, London, etc. If an event occurred (entirely) in Kansas, then it didn't occur in Texas. But not every wrong answer will involve reference to a place where the tornado was absent. Consider a square inch of land centred on the point, lying precisely on the $37°37''$ line, 98.7654321 miles to the west of a certain marker in the centre of Witchita. Even if the tornado passed over that place, it would be wrong to say that the tornado occurred there. Such an answer would confuse the right church with a specific pew. Even at a particular moment in time, a tornado covers more than a square inch of land.

Similarly, if the tornado occurred on Monday afternoon, it didn't occur on Tuesday evening. But one can specify an interval of time (say 14.35.30–14.35.31) that is too small to be the interval in which the tornado occurred, even if the tornado was present throughout that interval. There will be distinct space-time regions R, such that it is indeterminate whether (i) R encompasses the entire tornado, and/or (ii) R includes some space-time region not covered by the tornado. This does not keep us from talking about tornadoes, or saying that they have significant effects. But like (almost?) all spatio-temporal particulars, tornadoes have boundaries that are not perfectly precise. At certain scales, it is indeterminate which of two distinct sizes my neighbour's cat is. If one wants to measure a cat down to the last micron, one has to know which hairs are parts of the cat, as opposed to former parts already shed; and this is just one potential source of cat-size indeterminacy. So events like tornadoes (and wars) are hardly alone in having vague boundaries.[16] Given any particular cause, we should expect its boundaries to be vague at some scale, even though we can make determinately correct claims about its boundaries at other scales.

With this in mind, imagine a continuum of temporal intervals, with Monday afternoon and one second of that afternoon as poles; where each interval contains the next, and an interval *i* includes times when the tornado was not present only if *i* includes all the times at which the tornado was present. There will be many clear cases of intervals in which the tornado determinately occurred (in its entirety) or determinately failed to occur. But there will also be vague cases—intervals such that it is indeterminate whether the tornado occurred (entirely) within them. It may be determinate that the tornado occurred between 2 and 3, between 2.15 and 2.45, etc. And it may be determinate that the tornado lasted longer than a second, two seconds, etc. But presumably, there is no sharp boundary between the intervals in which the tornado determinately occurred and the intervals in which it determinately failed to occur. One can imagine a similar continuum of geographical regions, from Kansas to the one-inch square of Kansas, with similar room for vagueness as indicated in Figure 5.1.

---

[16] Still, the scope for indeterminacy may be greater with respect to events, since it is often unclear which vague issues matter for the spatio-temporal boundaries of events. With respect to cats, one is inclined to discount unattached hairs, and microbes on attached hairs. But it is less clear whether a tornado includes pieces of wood (or dirt) swirling around its edges. Another weather analogy: imagine a dense series of concentric spheres centred on some point within the eye of a certain hurricane (at some time *t*), such that the largest spheres contain all of planet earth, and the smallest spheres contain no point outside the eye. There will be spheres such that it is indeterminate whether they include the entire hurricane (at *t*). And this indeterminacy is compounded if we consider sequences of overlapping spheres, where each sphere delimits a region of space at some moment in time. Some sphere-sequences will definitely include the entire hurricane from start to finish; and some sphere-sequences will definitely fail to include certain (spatial and/or temporal) parts of the storm. But for some sphere-sequences, it will be indeterminate whether they are 'big enough' to encompass the entire weather event. One might be able to say that hurricane H followed a trajectory that took it within 100 miles of Miami on Monday afternoon. But claims like the following are sure to be overly precise: tropical storm H acquired hurricane strength winds at 1.37 on Sunday; the centre of the eye passed 98.7654321 miles due east of Miami at 14.34 on Monday; and H dissipated at 10.32 on Tuesday.

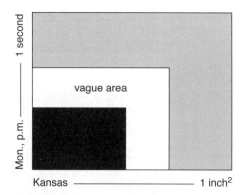

x and y axes correspond, respectively, to (decreasing) regions of space and intervals of time

Black and shaded areas represent, respectively, space-time regions in which the tornado determinately occurred and failed to occur (in its entirety)

1 second

Mon., p.m.

vague area

Kansas ———————————— 1 inch²

FIG. 5.1

This 'vagueness graph' represents a certain feature of an event's spatio-temporal boundaries—viz. the scale of precision exhibited by those boundaries.[17] And one can characterize Hornsby's argument in these terms. If event E is event F, then E and F have the same vagueness graph. But a mental event (like a trying) has a different vagueness graph than any biochemical event. So in this sense, mental events have a different grain from biochemical events.

Suppose Nora is asked to move her hand when a light flashes, and Nora wants to comply. Then the light flashing (e1) causes the event of Nora's trying to move her hand (e2), which causes the motion of her hand (e3). This imposes certain constraints on e2. For example, it does not begin before e1 or after e3. Moreover, I have followed Hornsby in saying that the trying caused the muscle contraction that caused e3; and let me grant that e2 is an effect of sensory transductions caused by e1. One can thus describe various subregions of Nora's body, and various temporal intervals characterized by reference to Nora's bodily processes, such that the trying determinately occurred there and then. But I assume that some proper parts of these regions—say, some square millimetre of Nora's brain for an interval of one millisecond—will be determinately too small to be where and when the trying occurred in its entirety. And presumably, there will be some vagueness, which can be represented as shown in Figure 5.2.

[17] Or the degree of precision that can be used in correct descriptions of those boundaries. Of course, the spatial location of a tornado changes over time; so the regions represented in the solid black area do not include the smallest regions of space-time that includes the whole tornado. But for simplicity, I ignore this dynamic feature of the example. I also ignore higher-order vagueness—it is vague where the vague area of the graph begins—which plays no role in discussion below.

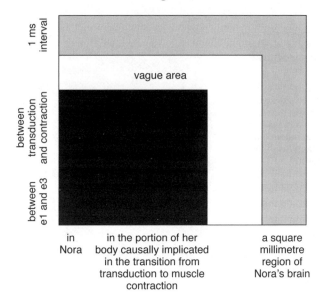

FIG. 5.2

There is, however, no independent reason for thinking that any biochemical event has boundaries that are vague in just this way. There may well be biochemical events whose spatio-temporal features *roughly* match those of the trying, especially if one allows that every fusion of biochemical events is a biochemical event. But any given biochemical event B* will (determinately) include or (determinately) not include certain synaptic firings, changes of action potential, etc. If only for these reasons, we will be able to say quite a lot about the spatio-temporal boundaries of B*. So prima facie, the vagueness graph for B* will reflect less vagueness than the graph for Nora's trying.

3.3

Appeal to vagueness graphs is, however, just a visual aid. Less picturesquely, if event E is event F, then for every spatio-temporal region $\mathfrak{R}$: E determinately occurs in $\mathfrak{R}$ iff F determinately occurs in $\mathfrak{R}$; and E determinately fails to occur in $\mathfrak{R}$ iff F determinately fails to occur in $\mathfrak{R}$. To see the import of these biconditionals, let $\mathfrak{R}1$ be a proper part of the larger region $\mathfrak{R}2$, in which both E and F determinately occur. If (all of) E determinately occurs in the smaller region $\mathfrak{R}1$, but it is not the case that (all of) F determinately occurs in $\mathfrak{R}1$, then E ≠ F; and if E determinately fails to occur in $\mathfrak{R}1$ (because part of E determinately occurs in a portion of $\mathfrak{R}2$

outside of $\Re 1$), but it is not the case that F determinately fails to occur in $\Re 1$, then E $\neq$ F.

Of course, in emphasizing this condition on event identity, one must distinguish metaphysical and epistemic claims. It may be that E determinately occurred in the smaller region R1, but we *know* only that E occurred (somewhere) in the larger region R2; and if the sense of 'E' differs from the sense of 'F', we may know that F occurred in R1, yet fail to know that E is F. The 'E'-ish way of thinking about the relevant event may be compatible with a wider range of claims about its location, as compared with the 'F'-ish way of thinking about that same event. We may know that the first lightning strike of the storm occurred within 100 yards of the barn, without knowing anything more precise about the location of that event. Nonetheless, the lightning strike can *be* an electrical discharge whose spatio-temporal boundaries can be specified more precisely. Similarly, event dualists must stay alive to the possibility that initial appearances may lead us to underestimate what can be (correctly) said about the spatio-temporal location of mental events. On the other hand, it would be question-begging for neuralists to assume that each mental event has the spatio-temporal boundaries of some biochemical event, on the grounds that each mental event *is* some biochemical event. And I see no independent reason for supposing that tryings have much sharper boundaries than initial appearances suggest.

One might appeal to the plausible claim that the trying (e2) was caused by Nora's *judging* that the light flashed, which in turn was caused by relevant events of sensory transduction. But it is not clear that this further claim helps. For the location of the judging is no more determinate than that of the trying. We can represent the two mental events as shown in Figure 5.3. And we can look for *two* biochemical events in the relevant spatio-temporal region. But there will still be many neural candidates for being (respectively) the judging and the trying. Think of all the distinct, though potentially overlapping, biochemical events that will have occurred in the relevant region. By saying that the judging must be a neural event E, which caused a neural event F that is a plausible candidate for being the trying, one might hope to constrain the candidates somewhat. But this points to another potential source of indeterminacy: where (and when) does the judging end and the trying begin?

Consider some biochemical process whose initiating event is caused by the relevant events of sensory transduction, and whose terminating event causes the relevant bodily motion. (A dualist might challenge the idea that there will always be such a process, in which one biochemical event *causes* the next, without intervening events that are chance occurrences from a biochemical perspective. But let this pass.) Think about all the possible (overlapping) ways of dividing this process into subprocesses, and all of

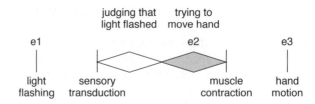

Fig. 5.3

the corresponding cause–effect pairs that one could focus on as candidates for the judging and trying. If these mental events are biochemical, there is a *correct* selection to be made from these options.

Each sodium transfer that takes place in Nora's head is part of the judging, part of the trying, or part of neither; and similarly for every other biochemical subprocess in the relevant spatio-temporal region. Since we know so little about the operation of the brain during episodes of purposive action, one can perhaps sustain hope in the following idea: for each mental cause M, there are enough constraints—given facts about the spatio-temporal properties of M, together with holistic constraints imposed by the spatio-temporal properties of other causally related events—to rule out all but one biochemical candidate for being M. But this strikes me as wishful thinking. At any rate, attending to the spatio-temporal properties of mental events hardly provides support for neuralism. On the contrary, it provides further reason for seeking an alternative (even if the anti-neuralist 'argument from vagueness' is not by itself decisive).

As Hornsby notes, one might well view the line of thought she presses as a Benacerraff-style argument. If $y \neq z$, and the choice between '$x = y$' and '$x = z$' would be arbitrary, then perhaps one should refrain from identifying x with either candidate (cf. Benacerraff 1965). If a given action/trying T is some neural event, then there is a determinate answer to the question

> (Q) Which neural event is T?

For if T is a neural event, there is a neural event N, such that: $T = N$; and for every neural event N^* distinct from N, $T \neq N^*$. So if there is no determinate answer to (Q), T is not *any* neural event. And it seems that there will be no determinate answer to (Q). There will be many distinct neural candidates for being T, and saying that T is some one of the candidates, as opposed to others, would be arbitrary. Returning to the picturesque formulation: for any trying T, there will be a range of biochemical events with roughly the same spatio-temporal properties as T, but each of these events will have a different vagueness graph than T.

One might reply that mental events are 'vague particulars' constituted by neural events, even though it is not determinate which neural events they are constituted by. But even setting aside worries about the coherence of this suggestion (cf. Evans 1978; Lewis 1988), it does not help with the metaphysics of mental causation. If each mental event is vague in a way that no neural event is—and presumably, no *neural* event is *vaguely* constituted by neural events—then each mental event is distinct from every neural event. So our central question remains: how can a bodily motion have both mental events and neural events as causes; how can a vague particular be a cause and still be the *same* cause as some less vague particular? Of course, many bodily motions have mental causes, even though mental causes evidently have different spatio-temporal properties (i.e. different vagueness graphs) from any neural causes. So *if* event dualism proves untenable, one might be driven to say that (somehow) each mental event is a neural event without being any particular neural event. But this is hardly a comfortable corner. And even if it can be occupied, one might well look for a different resting place.

Still, perhaps we can live with a little arbitrariness. It would not be surprising if the same kind of indeterminacy arises with respect to neural events and their relation to complex chemical (and quantum) events. And it would not be the end of the world if we had to engage in some arbitrary precisification, in order to preserve the idea that neural events are not causes distinct from chemical events. If this idea is worth preserving, then surely we can tolerate its consequence: given a range of chemical events that are candidates for being some neural event, the neural event is identical with one of those candidates, even if any particular identification would be arbitrary. Correlatively, one might say that each mental event is some neural event, even if it requires an arbitary decision to identify any given mental event with some particular neural event.[18] But there is an important asymmetry in the impersonal and personal cases.

It does not really matter if some neurophysiological description fails to pick out a unique event—as opposed to a certain range of events, all of which are on a par with respect to the theoretical demands of neuroscience. In general, we can tolerate a certain amount of arbitrary precisification with respect to our event descriptions, so long as arbitrary choice among the candidates for satisfying the unprecisified descriptions would not frustrate our aims in deploying the event descriptions. If our goal is to provide a theoretically interesting third-person description of (some

---

[18] And perhaps a supervaluationist approach to vagueness will preserve the thesis 'Every mental event is a neural event'; since this sentence would be true, on every precisification, even though '$\alpha = \beta$' would never be determinately true, where 'α' and 'β' are names for mental and neural events (see Fine 1975; but see also Keefe and Smith 1996).

aspect of) the world, arbitrary precisification will be acceptable, insofar as it promotes (or at least does not detract from) this goal.

Action descriptions, however, purport to be descriptions of a person's contributions to history. And it cannot be a matter of mere decision *which* event is Nora's action of raising her hand. To say otherwise—that we can simply stipulate (from a third-person perspective) which neural event is Nora's trying—is tantamount to saying that no event is *Nora's* action. Neuralists may be willing to engage in arbitrary precisification, since they are already willing to say that each mental event is describable from the impersonal perspective of the scientific image. But there is no independent plausibility in the idea that it requires an arbitrary decision to say which events are the actions of persons. Our actions are tryings; and if these events are not biochemical, we should aim to understand this fact about ourselves. A philosophy of mind should do more than delimit a certain range of biochemical events, and then simply declare that each mental event is some event in that range—but it doesn't matter which. If our task is to understand mental causation, then it matters *which* events are the distinctive contributions of persons to the causal order. This deepens the suspicion that neuralism amounts to little more than bestowing mentalistic *labels* on certain neural events, as a sop to our self-conception. So given that there will be a range of neural candidates for being Nora's trying, and given that arbitrary precisification threatens the idea that any of the candidates are the person's contribution to history, perhaps the best option is to refrain from identifying Nora's trying with *any* neural event. For the alternative is not so much a way of preserving the idea that humans act (in the face of questions about mental causation), as a capitulation to the idea that human actions are just one more species of impersonal occurrence.

6

Modal Concerns

Our concept of a person may not require that rationalizing causes have impersonal descriptions. But one might think that our concept of causation does require this. In one sense, my reply is ready: causation is the extensionalization of explanation. If a fact about event C explains (in the right way) a fact about event E, then C caused E; and given this thesis about causation, together with some claims about intentional explanation, one can adopt a non-Cartesian version of event dualism. But an obvious objection must be addressed. Given event dualism, bodily motions with mental causes are overdetermined; yet this seems wrong, especially in light of various counterfactual considerations. In this chapter, I argue that bodily motions can have neural *and* (distinct) mental causes without being objectionably overdetermined, so long as event dualists can maintain certain supervenience theses. This raises questions about the status of such theses—e.g. that the mental supervenes on the physical—and whether dualists can provide any *explanation* for these modal claims. I think dualists can provide as much explanation as required, once we are clear about what supervenience theses actually say.

1. Twice Explained, Twice Caused

Consider a paradigmatic case of overdetermination. Two assassins shoot Jones at the same time, and each shooting is a sufficient cause of his death. Or returning to an earlier analogy, imagine two lines of dominoes converging on a single domino. If the timing was just right, the toppling of the final domino would be overdetermined by two distinct topplings. Now recall the picture associated with the view of mental causation I am urging:

$$S \; \begin{matrix} \nearrow \\ \\ \searrow \end{matrix} \; \begin{matrix} \mathbf{M \to T} \\ \\ N_1 \to \ldots \to N_z \end{matrix} \; \begin{matrix} \searrow \\ \\ \nearrow \end{matrix} \; B$$

where B is a bodily motion with neural causes *and distinct* mental causes. My claim is that the mental causes (represented in bold) are members of one causal chain culminating with B, while the neural events ($N_1 \ldots N_z$) are members of a distinct causal chain culminating with the same bodily motion. This certainly looks like a case of overdetermination. And this raises a family of concerns.

First, overdetermined events like Jones's death seem rare. But given event dualism, bodily motions are regularly overdetermined. Moreover, if one asks *why* two distinct causal chains culminate with Jones's death, there seem to be only two possible answers: coincidence, e.g. the assassins were hired separately, but happened to arrive at the same time; or conspiracy, e.g. both assassins were hired by a sinister action theorist. Similarly, either the two lines of dominoes were carefully arranged so that the two penultimate dominoes would simultaneously fall onto the last domino, or there was a big coincidence. But event dualism would be unattractive if it preserved mental causation at the cost of saying that persons live in a state of continual coincidence, in which their minds and brains happen to have the same effects; and appealing to a *deus ex machina* is deeply unsatisfying. (Neuralists avoid this problem by saying that mental events 'and' neural events cause behaviour, but only in the sense that Twain 'and' Clemens wrote *Huckleberry Finn*: there is no *co*-authorship to worry about.)

In reply to the first concern, event dualists can grant that for many event *types*, only rarely is an effect overdetermined by two causes of the *same* type. Suppose that, due to the work of nefarious neurosurgeons, two distinct chains of neural events end with the rising of my hand. This sort of overdetermination seems to be rare. But to say without qualification that overdetermined events are rare is to beg the question. For event dualism *is* the position that at least some mental causes of bodily motions are tokens of a type T, such that no neural event is a token of T.[1] Moreover, it is no coincidence that mental events have effects that have neural causes. For actions and their mental causes are (among other things) typical causes of bodily motions; and given the kinds of bodies we have, it is no coincidence that our bodily motions have neural causes. Still, absent a *deus ex machina*, one might think it would be a coincidence if mental events and distinct neural events had their effects at the same *time*. Suppose I want to push a

---

[1] One can use 'overdetermination', so that it applies only to cases in which a single effect has two sufficient causes of the same (natural) type. Then *any* case of overdetermination may present serious puzzles, unless the effect can be redescribed so as to reveal the distinct effects of each cause—e.g. by describing the effects of each assassin's bullet on Jones's body (see Bunzl 1979). But given this usage, event dualists need not say that bodily effects of mental causes are overdetermined. I think it is more honest, though, to admit that event dualists are committed to a kind of overdetermination.

certain button in order to satisfy some desire. Why doesn't my finger move twice: once as the result of mental causes, and once as a pure physiological response to biochemical events in my brain.

While this 'timing problem' can make one feel queasy, I think it is the product of a bad analogy. Suppose two runners take different routes to a nearby bell, and each runner strikes the bell with a hammer when she arrives. We would expect a conspiracy of some sort if the runners always struck the bell at the same time. But we need not think of mental and neural events on analogy with the runners, who could have arrived at the common destination at different times. Again, emphasizing explanation helps make this clear. If the occurrence of event E is explained by the occurrence of event C *and* by the occurrence of event D, the occurrence of a single event can be explained in two different ways. But it is hardly mysterious that a single event occurs at the same time as itself, however its occurrence is explained. It is an interesting fact that some events, like the bodily motions of persons, can be twice explained. Or if you like, it is an interesting fact that the world accommodates a concept of something—a person—whose bodily motions can be explained in two very different ways. I don't think this is any more mysterious, though, than the fact that some events can be explained at all. (In Chapter 7, I take up the related worry that mental explanations cannot be genuinely *causal* if mental events are not neural events. But for now, my concern is overdetermination, not causal realism.)

Still, the most salient intuition about cases of overdetermination is that (barring unusual circumstances) the effect would have occurred, even if one of the actual causes had not occurred. This intuition can seem to be at odds with event dualism. For it can seem absurd to say that a person's body would have moved as it did, absent the neural causes of the bodily motion. One might reply that in *some* cases of overdetermination, the effect would not have occurred in the absence of one cause. The second gunman may have been ordered to shoot Jones only if the first assassin was also going to shoot, in which case, Jones would not have died if the first gunman had not fired. But unlike the second gunman, mental events do not somehow check to see if the relevant neurons are about to fire. So it seems that if event dualism is correct, then for any bodily motion B that has mental causes, B would have occurred even if its neural causes had not occurred. We need to see that this is not a *reductio* of event dualism.

1.2

Following Stalnaker (1969), let us analyse counterfactual conditionals in terms of possible worlds ordered by a context-sensitive similarity metric. I return to the question of what possible worlds are (Section 2.3). But for now, talk of possible worlds can be understood simply as a convenient paraphrase of talk about ways the world might have been; and I assume that there are ways the world might have been. I did not raise my right arm a moment ago, but I might have done so. An electron that struck one detector might have struck another. As we often put it, the actual world is one of many possible worlds. These possible worlds are, along various dimensions of similarity, more or less like the actual world. Let us assume that the conditional 'if event C had not occurred, then event E would not have occurred' is true (relative to context Φ) iff E does not occur in the possible world most like the actual world (along the dimension of similarity relevant in Φ) among those worlds at which C does not occur. Similarly, 'if no F-ish event had occurred, no G-ish event would have occurred' is true iff no G-ish event occurs at the world most like the actual world among those worlds at which an F-ish event occurs.

Because of the relativization to context, this theory rightly allows for the possibility that a counterfactual claim can be true relative to some contexts of use, and false relative to other contexts—holding the actual facts (apart from those germane to communicative intentions) fixed. Suppose that Nick and Nora are business partners, and that one of them must attend a certain meeting. They flip a coin, and Nick loses. On the morning of the meeting, Nick nearly misses the last train, but he gets to the meeting just fine. Given these facts,

> (1) If Nick had not attended the meeting, then Nora would have attended the meeting

can be either true or false, depending on which facts are relevant to evaluating the conditional. In a conversation about how Nick and Nora share the work, the relevant possible world is one in which the coin toss goes the other way, and Nora attends the meeting instead of Nick (who does not even try to catch the train). In a conversation about Nick's malfunctioning alarm clock, the relevant possible world is one in which Nick loses the coin toss *and* misses the train. Following standard practice, let us say that (1) is true relative to context Φ iff the Φ-nearest possible world at which Nick did not attend the meeting is a world at which Nora did attend; where a possible world w is the Φ-nearest world at which proposition P is the case iff (i) P is the case at w, and (ii) among the worlds at which P is the case, w is the most like the actual world, given the respect of similarity relevant in Φ.[2]

---

[2] For present purposes, I take this semantics of counterfactual conditionals as given. (And I assume that there can be true counterfactual claims about particular events.) But one need not assume that for any given dimension of similarity D, and any condition Φ there is a possible world *most* like the actual world, along dimension D, among the worlds where Φ is true. Following Lewis (1973), one can say that the conditional is true, so long as

Like all counterfactual claims, counterfactual claims about bodily motions (and their neural causes) are context-sensitive in this sense; and relative to the contexts in which such claims *are* true, event dualists can grant their truth. Suppose the rising of Nora's arm has a neural cause N_1 and a mental cause M_1. Now consider

> (2) If N_1 had not occurred, then the arm-rising would not have occurred

which is true relative to context Φ iff the Φ-nearest possible world at which N_1 did not occur is a world at which the arm-rising did not occur. Relative to some contexts, (2) may well be false. For given some notions of nearness, the nearest possible world at which N_1 does not occur may be a world at which some other neural event N_2 caused the arm-rising. If the arm-rising does not occur, then either M_1 does not occur, or M_1 occurs but fails to cause the arm-rising; and worlds where either of these conditions hold may be *less* similar to the actual world than some world where M_1 and N_2 are causes of the arm-rising. Put another way, it may be that if N_1 hadn't occurred, another neural event (equally capable of causing the arm-rising) would have occurred. This is not to suggest that N_2 was somehow lined up, ready to cause the arm-rising in case N_1 did not—any more than Nora was lined up, ready to attend the meeting in case Nick did not. But it is not hard to imagine that whether N_1 or N_2 occurred was effectively a chance matter, and that the difference would have been irrelevant from a large-scale perspective that includes the motions of bodies. Indeed, depending on how finely one individuates bio-chemical events, this kind of 'indifference' to biochemical details may be ubiquitous.

That said, (2) will be true relative to some contexts. But this is not yet an embarrassment for event dualists. At many possible worlds where N_1 does not occur, the actual environmental causes of N_1 do not occur either. Suppose N_1 was caused by an auctioneer's call for bids; and M_1 was Nora's coming to believe that she could purchase a certain painting by raising her arm. If N_1 fails to occur at some possible world w where the auctioneer does not call for bids, then plausibly M_1 does not occur at w either. If some such world is relevant to evaluating (2) in context Φ, then

the consequent is true at every world in the contextually relevant *sphere* of worlds (each of which is equally like the actual world) where Φ is true. One could impose constraints on similarity metrics with the effect of ensuring that, relative to all contexts, (1) is false in the scenario described. In particular, one might insist that a possible world w cannot be more similar to the actual world than some other possible world w* if w* is just like the actual world up to some time t, and w diverges from the actual world prior to t. But I see no reason to adopt such a constraint on similarity metrics, given our intuitions about cases, although we may often have a *preference* for contexts that preserve perfect matching between worlds for as long as possible (see Lewis for discussion).

dualists can grant that (2) is true relative to context Φ. But let us set aside contexts in which environmental causes of inner events are relevant. (Or put another way, let us focus on possible situations where environmental causes of the arm-rising—and hence, environmental causes of M_1, which caused the arm-rising—are held fixed.)

Event dualists can still allow for contexts relative to which

(2) If N_1 had not occurred, the arm-rising would not have occurred

is true. For one can say that relative to such contexts: if N_1 had not occurred, then (a) M_1 would not have occurred, or (b) other conditions would have differed, with the result that M_1 would not have caused the arm-rising. We know that M_1 might not have occurred, despite the presence of its actual environmental causes. If Nora's visual system had failed to operate properly, she would not have formed any perceptual belief; and if she had formed an odd background belief (e.g. that the apparent auction was really a play), she would not have judged that she really could purchase the painting. Similarly, M_1 might have occurred, while failing to have its actual effects: Nora could have chosen not to bid, even at the last minute, because she suddenly felt guilty about spending the money; or Nora might have suffered a seizure at the crucial moment. If any such world turns out to be the Φ-nearest world where N_1 failed to occur, event dualists can grant that (2) is true relative to Φ. (For related discussion, see Mellor 1995; Segal and Sober 1991.)

To extract an argument against event dualism from our intuitions about counterfactuals concerning bodily motions and their neural causes, one needs to show that there is a context Φ, such that (2) is true relative to Φ; and at the Φ-nearest possible world where N_1 does not occur, M_1 does occur in the presence of conditions that would commit the dualist to saying that the arm-rising should have occurred (even though the arm-rising did not occur). But it is hard to see how one could show this. On the other hand, one might find this Scotch Verdict unsatisfying; and one might suspect that event dualists are positing a conspiracy or coincidence, by claiming that the very possible worlds where certain biochemical events fail to occur are worlds where certain mental events fail to occur. (In the example used to motivate the context-dependency of counterfactual claims, Nick and Nora have *arranged* that one of them will attend the meeting.) Correlatively, concerns about overdetermination will not go away, until one has explicitly countenanced some sense in which mental causes are not independent of neural causes.

1.3

As I discuss below, event dualists can grant various supervenience theses. But for now, assume that (actual) mental events and neural events share a supervenience base: a class C of actual events and obtaining states—perhaps those characterizable in the language of a completed physics—such that there is no metaphysically possible world just like the actual world with respect to C, yet different from the actual world with respect to the occurrence of neural or mental events. And let me use this assumption to summarize the preceding discussion in a way that may help quell suspicion of conspiracy or coincidence.

Worlds where N_1 does not occur will be worlds that differ from the actual world with respect to C. Some of these worlds may include M_1 and the arm-rising. For supervenience does not require that M_1 occurs only in worlds just like the actual world with respect to C; and some worlds may differ from the actual world in that N_1 fails to occur, but *not* in that M_1 fails to occur. In such worlds, M_1 may well cause the arm-rising, which has some neural cause other than N_1. If such a world is the Φ-nearest world at which N_1 does not occur, then relative to context Φ (2) is false. If we focus on worlds where neither N_1 nor the arm-rising occur, and we hold external causes of the arm-rising fixed, we are (intuitively) considering worlds where the divergence from C concerns what happened in Nora's head. It is not implausible to say that in such worlds, either M_1 fails to occur, or conditions differ in ways that bear on which effects M_1 has. If M_1 fails to occur, the non-occurence of the arm-rising poses no difficulty for dualists; similarly, if M_1 occurs at worlds where Nora has mental states that would not rationalize an action of arm-raising (cf. Lepore and Loewer 1987, 1989).

If there is a problem for dualists, it lies with those worlds at which M_1 occurs; when M_1 occurs Nora's mental life is as it is in the actual world; and the arm-rising does not occur. But these are worlds at which other things are not equal with respect to some intentional *ceteris paribus* law. Either M_1 did not cause an event of Nora's trying to raise her arm, or Nora's trying did not cause her arm to rise. (Here the departures from C are correlated with abNormal instances of non-strict laws.) And if there are interfering factors that explain why Nora's arm does not rise, there is no problem for dualists. This is not a *proof* that there would have been an interfering factor if Nora's arm had not risen in the presence of M_1 (and Nora's mental life had been as it was in the actual world). On the other hand, I see no reason to suppose that this claim is false, or that dualists are not entitled to make it. And at this point in the dialectic, I am defending event dualism against objections.

One might worry that a person's reasons are not her own if at each moment her mental events are determined by (since they supervene on) her biochemical events. But I think this worry is misguided. If my mental events are distinct from any biochemical events in me—if my reasons and actions are invisible without bringing *me* onto the scene—then my mental events are mine in as strong a sense as one can reasonably demand. This point is not threatened by supervenience theses, which reflect the nature of human thinkers. (We are Strawsonian persons with corporeal natures, not Cartesian minds united with bodies.) If one insists that our reasons and actions can be ours only if our mental events do *not* supervene on our bio-chemistry, then one is effectively insisting that persons are not part of the corporeal world; and to repeat what I urged in Chapter 5, we need not suppose that our concept of a person imposes such metaphysically impossible demands on us.[3]

One might wonder, though, whether dualists really can allow that the mental depends in any sense on the non-mental. For the dualist's claim is not merely that mental events fail to be identical with neural events. The claim is that persons, along with their mental properties and events, are *primitive* in some important sense. Loci of freedom—and correlatively, the bearers of intentional properties—may exist in space and time; but on a dualist view persons and their mental events are among the fundamental spatio-temporal particulars, in a way that (at least many) 'macro' objects of the Sellarsian scientific image are not. And it is not obvious that one can consistently endorse this kind of autonomy for the Sellarsian manifest image, while also endorsing the kind of supervenience theses I have appealed to. In short, event dualists owe some account of how persons can be primitive *and* supervenient.

2. Supervenience as the Individuation of Possibility

I think the mental 'globally' supervenes on the non-mental: if $w1$ and $w2$ are possible worlds that differ in some mental respect, then $w1$ and $w2$ differ in some non-mental respect. Indeed, at least for present purposes, I grant the following: if $w1$ and $w2$ differ in any respect, then $w1$ and $w2$ differ in some physical respect, where 'physical' is to be understood in a demanding sense characterized in terms of our best physical theories (see note 1 of the Introduction). To say that $w1$ and $w2$ differ in some mental respect is not, of course, to say that possible worlds are themselves the

---

[3] I (briefly) address some related questions about our 'capacity to have done otherwise' in Sect. 4. But in saying that a person's mental events supervene on her neural events (relative to a context, which will include a time), one has not said yet anything about the relation of a person's actions/tryings to *prior* events. In traditional terms, I have thus far been concerned with the liberty of spontaneity (having one's actions be the product of one's reasons), not the liberty of indifference (having the capacity, when one acts, to have done otherwise). And while a radical libertarian might say that freedom requires the capacity to violate natural laws, my version of event dualism is designed to avoid the consequence that acting requires anomaly.

bearers of mental properties; w_1 and w_2 differ in a Φ-ish respect if w_1 contains an individual x with some Φ-ish property M, and x lacks M (or x fails to exist) at w_2. And we can say that two possible worlds differ in some respect or other only if they differ in some physical respect. If only for simplicity, let us assume that this common gloss of global supervenience is correct: no difference without a physical difference.[4]

It is not clear, however, that event dualists are entitled to endorse this modal thesis. Kim (1987, 1993) and others have posed the challenge of saying *why* the mental supervenes on the non-mental; and one might think that event dualists can offer no satisfactory account of why everything supervenes on the physical. My suggestion will be that (global) supervenience theses are best viewed as claims about the individuation of possible worlds, and that event dualists can count possibilities in the relevant way. But supervenience theses are far more commonly viewed as claims about how one family of properties *depends* on another; and I suspect that this conception of supervenience goes hand-in-hand with the idea that persons and their mental events are somehow locatable in the scientific image. So the first task is that of drawing attention to an alternative conception of supervenience.

2.1

For these purposes, it will be useful to think about supervenience in the context of some more general claims about modality, and the role played by appeal to possible worlds in thinking about modality. As noted above, I assume that there are possible worlds, where talk of possible worlds is to be understood as talk of ways the world might have been. I also assume that propositions—i.e. the Fregean senses of sentences—can be evaluated for truth at any possible world, in the usual way. A proposition P is necessarily true (false) iff P is true (false) at every possible world; P is contingent iff P is true at some but not all possible worlds. There is no possible world at which *Fido barked and Fido never barked*. Things could not have differed in *that* respect. Correspondingly, the italicized sentence expresses an impossible proposition. Similarly, the proposition that *two plus two is five* is impossible. So we can formulate and express thoughts that do not

---

[4] I can imagine being agnostic about this. Can we be sure that physically indiscernible worlds are mentally indiscernible, given the limits on measuring physical differences? Does it make sense to speak of quantum *objects* and *properties*? Could two worlds differ with respect to the structure of space-time, or the laws of nature that govern them, without differing with respect to the physical properties of fundamental particles? (see Lewis 1973, 1983*b*). But set aside any such concerns, and assume that there is a true global supervenience thesis to characterize, though I sympathize with the idea that our metaphysical assumptions should be tutored by our best physical theories. In Sect. 4, I discuss a rather different motivation for weakening the global supervenience thesis.

correspond to genuine possibilities. Indeed, we can seriously entertain such thoughts.

One would like to know which propositions are false at every possible world. But once we set aside examples from logic and mathematics, there is disagreement about where (if anywhere) language and thought take us beyond the space of genuine possibility. Opinions differ with respect to how radically the world could have differed from the way it actually is. In my view, it is a matter of necessity that thinking things have corporeal properties: there are no disembodied thinkers, and there could not have been any. Others allow for the possibility of Cartesian souls. While most of us would agree that Napoleon could not have been a rock, there will be less agreement about whether Napoleon could have had a different father (or different DNA). I could have moved my arm a moment ago. But are there possible worlds where my arm moves faster than the speed of light?

Kripke's (1980) discussion of these issues emphasizes the importance of distinguishing the space of *ways the world* might have been from the space of ways *we can conceive* the world as being, even if we regard the latter as a fallible indicator of the former. At least in this context, of distinguishing metaphysical (or genuine) possibility from mere epistemic possibility, one might view supervenience theses as claims about the space of ways the world might have been. For example, if $w1$ and $w2$ are (metaphysically) possible worlds, then $w1$ and $w2$ differ in some mental respect only if they differ in some non-mental respect. Or, put another way, suppose that $w1$ and $w2$ are alike in all non-mental respects. Then given global supervenience, $w1$ and $w2$ are alike in all mental respects; hence, $w1$ and $w2$ are alike in *all* respects; and so $w1 = w2$, on the assumption that possible worlds differ only if they differ in some respect.[5]

This is what I meant by saying that supervenience theses can be viewed as claims about the individuation of possibilities. If the mental globally supervenes on the non-mental, then *ways the world might have been* are not individuated so finely that there are *distinct but non-mentally indiscernible* ways the world could have been; and this is so, regardless of what we can conceive. Consider an analogy. If sets $S1$ and $S2$ have the same members, $S1 = S2$. Sets are not individuated so finely that there are distinct sets with the same members. Someone might *think* that $\{x: x^2 = 261/29\} \neq \{y: |7y| = 357/17\}$. But in fact, these sets have the same members, as do $\{x: x$ is Hesperus$\}$ and $\{y: y$ is Phosphorus$\}$. And given the *sort* of thing a set is, sets cannot differ without differing in their membership. If $S1$ and $S2$ have the same members, $S1 = S2$, and so $S1$ is like $S2$ in all respects. Now I do not say that possible worlds are sets. But perhaps a similar remark applies:

[5] For reasons discussed below, this assumption is plausible but not trivial. (Global supervenience can be true, even if some possible worlds differ barely—i.e. without differing with respect to any of the individuals at those worlds.)

if w_1 and w_2 are possible worlds, and w_1 is like w_2 in all non-mental respects, then w_1 *is* w_2.

Similarly, if everything globally supervenes on the physical, then *ways the world might have been* are not individuated so finely that there are *distinct but physically indiscernible* ways the world might have been: if w_1 is like w_2 in all physical respects, $w_1 = w_2$; in which case, w_1 is like w_2 in all respects. This is a substantive thesis about possibility. Cartesian dualists might well deny it, holding that the material aspect of the world could have been exactly as it actually is, while some thinking thing had at least one different thought (that had no effects in the material world). Since claims about the individuation of possibility are substantive, one cannot simply take them as given, and this is not just because of a stricture against begging questions against others. For even if we all agreed on which supervenience theses are true, we would not want to take such claims as basic (or foundational). Not only would this be epistemically unsatisfying, these very general modal claims seem like poor candidates for points at which justification comes to an end. As Kim (1993: 86) says,

If the mental globally supervenes on the physical, that cannot be a brute and unexplained fact, something we would want to adopt as a fundamental, primitive fact about the world. We would feel, I think, that there should be some explanation of it.

It may be hard to say just what this intuition—that supervenience is not a 'brute unexplained' fact—amounts to. But I share it. That said, we need to be clear about what needs explaining, and what kind of explanation is wanted.

First, while the literature typically focuses on the supervenience of mental properties, I am also concerned with objects and events. No two possible worlds differ merely in that one contains persons or mental events absent from the other; necessarily, such differences coincide with non-mental differences. If the mental supervenes on the physical, then mental properties *and their bearers* supervene on physical properties *and their bearers*, where for these purposes, persons and events count as bearers of mental properties.[6] But I assume that given

(GS) if w_1 and w_2 are physically indiscernible, w_1 and w_2 are indiscernible in all respects

one can explain the global supervenience of the mental on the physical. For it follows from (GS) that physically indiscernible worlds are

---

[6] Even though mental events are bearers of subpersonal content properties. See Kim (1988*b*) for discussion of supervenience with multiple domains. We can say that <A_2, B_2, C_2> supervenes on <A_1, B_1, C_1>, where A_1 and A_2 are families of properties had by objects of types B and C iff every complete distribution of A_1 over B_1 and C_1 entails a unique complete distribution of A_2 over B_2 and C_2.

indiscernible in all mental respects. Similarly, if 'physical' is construed so that the physical is non-mental, then the supervenience of the mental on the non-mental follows from (GS). And I think dualists can provide a satisfying account of (GS), by treating (GS) as a claim about the individuation of possible worlds.

This departs from the standard view of supervenience theses as reports of a not-quite-identity, one-way-determination relation that obtains between the mental and the non-mental (the moral and the non-moral, etc.). And this difference in perspective corresponds to a difference in the kind of explanation sought. Dualists can endorse and explain (GS) on its 'individuation' construal, by offering an account of why possible worlds satisfy the constraint described by (GS). There may be a more 'ontological' construal, given which the truth of (GS) would call for a non-dualistic explanation, though one cannot *assume* that (GS) is true on such an interpretation. I cannot prove that (GS) is true *only* on a dualist-friendly interpretation. But I hope to show that intuitions about supervenience, like intuitions about counterfactuals, do not themselves provide the basis for a good anti-dualist argument. On the contrary, insofar as we have reason to take event dualism seriously, we have reason to be suspicious of attempts to gloss supervenience theses in ways unfriendly to (non-Cartesian) dualism. It will be useful, though, to sketch the more familiar view of (GS)—and the associated strategy for explaining it.

2.2

As many authors have noted, (GS) is a fairly weak thesis. It is logically compatible with the existence of Cartesian souls, so long as no two ways the world could have been differ *only* with respect to the properties of souls. A substance dualist can say that for any way the material (portion of the) world might have been, there is a way the mental (portion of the) world might have been, such that, necessarily, had the material world been that way, the mental world would have been that way. Perhaps this is a bare truth about mind–body relations; perhaps God is responsible for its truth; or perhaps mental phenomena are epiphenomena of material phenomena. Even if such views are implausible, the mere existence of immaterial substances does not violate the rule, 'no difference without a material difference'. Similarly, (GS) does not itself ensure a plausible version of substance monism. Consider a possible world that differs physically from the actual world only in some minor respect—say, a single photon (outside our lightcone) takes a slightly different trajectory. It is logically compatible with (GS) that in such a world: rocks feel pain; I feel no pain; there is no mentality whatsoever; etc. For the requirement is merely that physically *indiscernible* worlds be indiscernible; and this is compatible with huge mental differences between worlds that differ only trivially in physical respects. Thus, (GS) is consistent with the claim that there are possible worlds at which I have a molecular duplicate whose mental life is radically different from mine—or a duplicate with no mental life at all (see Horgan 1993; Kim 1993; Stalnaker 1996).

In this sense, (GS) is a modest claim. How one reacts to this modesty will depend on what one wanted from a supervenience thesis. One would not expect a principle for individuating possibilities to tell us that faraway photons do not affect mentality in dramatic ways. (Indeed, EPR-type experiments suggest that the state of one system *can* be entangled with the state of a faraway system.) But one might have been trying to characterize a mind–body relation only *slightly* weaker than traditional type-identity theories. One wants an alternative to theories that identify mental properties with biochemical properties that are reducible to physical properties (in whatever sense properties like *being water* are, via properties like being a hydrogen atom, reducible to physical properties). For it seems that given (almost) any mental property M and reducible property P, a person could have M without having P; and Twin-Earth thought-experiments suggest that biochemically type-identical individuals can have different mental properties. Since (GS) allows for the 'multiple realizability' and 'wide individuation' of the mental, one might have hoped that (GS) would do the explanatory work of a traditional type-identity theory, while retaining the virtue of plausibility. But this hope is unsustainable.

As Kim and others have noted, identity (unlike supervenience) *explains* supervenience. If heat just *is* mean molecular motion, then two systems cannot have the same mean molecular motion yet differ in temperature. If being in pain just *is* having a brain in which C-fibres are firing, then two individuals cannot be alike with respect to whether or not their C-fibres are firing, yet differ with respect to whether or not they are in pain. Given identity theses of this sort, the (weaker) supervenience theses follow trivially. Correspondingly, identity theses provide a genuine *alternative* to substance dualism as a conception of the mental, whereas (GS) is compatible with substance dualism. Much the same point applies to 'strong' supervenience:

> (SS) Necessarily, for every individual x and every mental property M, if x has M, then there is a physical property P, such that (i) x has P, and (ii) necessarily, every y that has P also has M.[7]

---

[7] This formulation assumes (*pace* Descartes) that the bearers of mental properties are themselves the bearers of physical properties. But we could reformulate (SS) so that x could supervene on (without being identical to) some z—say, a body, or a fusion of physical particles—that is the bearer of a (presumably complex) physical property P. See n. 6 above.

While (SS) allows for the multiple realizability of mental properties, it is also compatible with the following claim: each person has an immaterial mind, but necessarily, persons are mentally type-identical if they are corporeally type-identical. If (SS) is understood as implying that a person's mental properties are determined by her *intrinsic* physical properties, (SS) may rule out the possibility of mentality depending on (unentangled) faraway photons; in which case, (SS) presumably requires that mental properties be individuated 'narrowly' (*pace* Burge (1979*a*) and others). In my view, this requirement is implausible.[8] But for the moment, the main point is that an identity thesis characterizes a (putative) sense in which the mental *depends* on the physical, while a supervenience thesis merely characterizes a relation of *determination* that calls for explanation. And dependence is at least one potential explanation of determination.

Kim illustrates this important contrast by noting that the surface area of a sphere determines its volume (and vice versa); there is a function from surface areas to volumes (and a function from volumes to surface areas) for spheres. Yet intuitively, the volume of a sphere does not depend on its surface area. Similarly, the period of an 'ideal' pendulum determines its length (and vice versa), yet length does depend on period. Given these examples, one might think that dependence can be characterized as *one-way* determination. But imagine two digital thermometers, A and B, where only A displays the temperature to the nearest tenth of a degree. The state of B is asymmetrically determined by, yet does not depend on, the state of A.[9] In this example, the determination is not exceptionless, since one of the thermometers might break. So one might claim that every *exceptionless* one-way determination relation is a dependence relation, but this is question-begging, especially given that supervenience may be the only such relation. Indeed, one can pose Kim's question in these terms. How can there be an exceptionless one-way determination relation between families of properties (objects, or events)? An adequate philosophy of mind must include an answer to this question, if the mental really does supervene on the non-mental.

[8] One can characterize a technical notion 'mental*', such that all mental* properties strongly supervene on intrinsic physical properties. And perhaps appeal to mental* properties can be motivated by reflection on the nature of (empirical) psychological explanation; see Fodor (1987, 1991*a*). But if one goes on to say that *all* mental properties are mental*, or that *all* mental events are changes in mental* properties, one owes a reply to event dualists, especially if these universal generalizations are motivated by metaphysical reflections on explanation and causation (see Burge 1993).

[9] Or suppose that B is turned on only if it is at least 32 degrees (as measured by a third thermometer): if A registers '31.9' or less, B gives no reading; if A registers '32.0' or above, B registers what A registers, rounded off to the nearest degree. A related weakness of supervenience theses is that the sum of a square's angles supervenes on the number of even primes.

One possible answer is that whenever a supervenience relation obtains between two families of properties, this is because for some relation R each property in the 'supervening' family bears R to certain properties in the 'base' family, where a supervenient property bears R to certain base properties, if *but not only if* the supervenient property is reducible to the base properties. And as Kim notes, there is at least one such relation R. Supervenient properties may be *disjunctions of* properties reducible to base properties. Consider jade. Two different minerals, jadeite and nephrite, count as jade. So the property *being jade* supervenes on the properties *being jadeite* and *being nephrite*. (Compare *being Nora or Nick*, which supervenes on *being Nora* and *being Nick*.) If w_1 and w_2 are alike with respect to all the jadeite and nephrite, w_1 and w_2 are alike with respect to all the jade: no difference in the jade, without a difference in the jadeite or nephrite. And this case of global supervenience is explained by the strong supervenience of *being jade* on *being jadeite* and *being nephrite*. One can say that *being jade* is a multiply realizable property, since it can be realized as either of two distinct properties. But *being jade* is not reducible to either of its realizing properties. Nor is it reducible to the 'heterogeneous' (non-projectible, anomic) property *being jadeite or nephrite*, on the assumption that no property can be reduced to a heterogeneous property.

As Kim notes, however, this assumption is motivated by theoretical or explanatory concerns, whereas a philosopher of mind might well be concerned with ontological reduction. And at least arguably, the property *being jade* just is the disjunction of its realizing properties. In this sense, one can be a type-identity theorist about jade, so long as one does not confuse claims about *identity* with claims about *biconditional bridge laws*. Regardless of what counts as a theoretical reduction, a property can be identical with a disjunction of properties that are reducible to physical properties. Correlatively, dualists will not be vindicated if mental properties turn out to be like the property of being jade. So as Kim notes, the mere multiple realizability of the mental does not preclude a 'disjunctive type identity' (or 'local reducibility') theory, according to which every instantiation of a mental property is the instantiation of some property that is reducible to physical properties. And if metaphysics rather than epistemology is at issue, supervenient properties can be disjunctions of many—even infinitely many—reducible properties. Indeed, Kim suggests that multiply realizable properties *are* disjunctive properties. (Thus, he can identify events with property exemplifications, while holding that each exemplification of a mental property *is* an exemplification of some realizing property; see Section 1.5 of Chapter 3.)

Similar remarks apply to the bearers of properties. If persons are fusions of physical objects, and mental events are fusions of physical events, then two possible worlds with the same physical objects and events will have the same persons and mental events. As I suggested in the introduction, any dualist worthy of the name should reject these fusion theses. But *if* every object/event is a fusion of physical objects/events, and every property is a truth-function of physical properties, then mind–body supervenience presents no mystery. The question, however, is whether this metaphysical theory is true. And crucially, *one cannot establish this form of physicalism by relying on the premiss that physical effects of mental causes are not over-determined.* Kim's own arguments rely explictly on this claim (see e.g. Kim 1989). But if the kind of dualism presented here is a viable option, then absent *independent* argument against overdetermination of the sort countenanced by event dualists, one might well prefer event dualism to a disjunctive type identity theory. For as Kim admits, his view raises the question of whether mental properties have any genuinely causal status. One is inclined to say that *being jade* turned out to be a mere Cambridge property, posited because of our mistaken tendency to co-classify importantly different things; and one might wonder whether our conception of mental events as rationalizing *causes* can survive this analogy.

2.3

My aim, however, is not to argue against Kim. And one might think that his general strategy for explaining supervenience can be developed in a less demanding way. Perhaps mental properties are realized by properties reducible to physical properties, even though the former are not disjunctions of the latter. I am sceptical that this suggestion reflects a genuine third option between Kim-style identity and non-Cartesian dualism. My kind of dualist can say that mental properties are 'realized by' physical properties, in that the former properties supervene on the latter; and similarly with respect to persons being 'composed of' physical particles. An explanation of supervenience is still owed. But it is far from clear that a more substantial account of realization can be given, without sliding back into the idea that supervenient properties are truth functions of properties reducible to physical properties.

Historically, talk of multiple realization has been linked with the idea that mental properties are functional (second-order) properties; and perhaps such properties are distinct from disjunctions of their realizing properties, because functional properties are not heterogeneous—since their instances are explanatorily unified, in a way that instances of *being jade* are not (see Antony and Levine 1997; Fodor 1998). But this departure from Kim's view may amount to a distinction without a difference if the functionalist *also* assumes that the physical effects of mental events are not overdetermined. For in that case, there seems to be no causal difference between functional properties and disjunctions of realizing properties.

Moreover, Kim's question remains: how can there be a one-way exceptionless relation between families of properties? One does not answer this question by labelling the relation 'realization'. Anyone who rejects Kim's answer owes an alternative. And I think an answer friendly to event dualism (in terms of how possible worlds are individuated) is sustainable.

Indeed, event dualism may be the proper home for the idea that the varied instantiations of mental properties are explanatorily unified (perhaps by virtue of their functional commonality). For it may be wishful thinking to suppose that mental properties can be explanatorily autonomous, without any effects of mental causes being overdetermined. In short, Kim may be right that autonomy and overdetermination go together, but wrong to dismiss the option of embracing overdetermination. But I will not try to resolve questions about the stability of 'token' physicalism. Let token physicalists say what realization is, such that realized events are not causes distinct from the physical events that realize them, and such that realized properties bear a one-way determination relation to realizing properties. I want to offer a different *kind* of explanation for global supervenience.

Following Horgan (1993), let us distinguish 'ontological' from 'conceptual' (or 'semantical') explanations of supervenience. In terms of the present discussion, Kim's account of supervenience is paradigmatically ontological; and perhaps other ontological explanations—say, in terms of a sophisticated realization relation—can be developed. By contrast, Horgan cites Hare's (1952) account of moral supervenience as an example of a proposed conceptual explanation. If the point of using evaluative terms is to teach standards (and not to ascribe properties to objects), then one would defeat the point of using evaluative terms by applying different terms to things alike in all non-evaluative respects. Or to take a more trivial example, I can define the predicate 'grood' so that two things cannot be alike in all biological respects, while only one of them is grood. One can then explain the supervenience of being grood on the biological, by noting the semantic necessity that goes along with this stipulation. Horgan uses the term 'superdupervenience' for supervenience relations that can be explained in an ontological fashion, and he suggests that good materialsts should maintain that the mental (and everything else) superdupervenes on the physical.

Without suggesting that most (or even many) interesting supervenience theses can be explained by citing constraints on the practice of using certain predicates, I do think that non-Cartesian dualists can (and should) seek a conceptual rather than ontological explanation for supervenience. In Horgan's terminology, dualists should deny that the mental superdupervenes on the physical. For the dualist's claim is that, in another important sense, persons and their mental events are ontologically *primitive*. But by granting that the mental supervenes on the physical, one grants that in an important sense, persons and their mental events are not ontologically basic.[10] I think the key to reconciling these thoughts lies in setting aside attempts to explain supervenience as a consequence of superdupervenience, and adopting the idea that supervenience theses reflect the individuation of possibility. That is, I think the way to explain

(GS)   if $w1$ and $w2$ are physically indiscernible, $w1$ and $w2$ are indiscernible in all respects,

is by seeing (GS) as a consequence of a correct view of what possible worlds are—not as a consequence of a more local supervenience thesis like (SS), which gets explained in some ontological fashion. The idea is to defend a conception of possibility, such that there are no physically indiscernible possible worlds (much as there are no sets with distinct members). Such an explanation of (GS) will not turn on any specific hypothesis about how supervenient properties are related to base properties. Rather, the explanation will turn a hypothesis about what possible worlds are. So let me now turn to this issue: what are we talking about, when we talk about ways the world might have been?

3. Arrangements of Things

In the rest of this chapter, I develop the following line of thought: possible worlds are possible arrangements of the basic objects that make up our universe; because these objects have physical natures, the space of possible arrangements of basic objects respects the constraint, 'no difference without a physical difference'; and this provides a dualist-friendly account of (GS). The underlying conception of modality is somewhat tendentious,

---

[10] Consider moral properties. Moore (1903) observed that two persons could not be alike in all non-moral respects, yet differ morally. Perhaps we know this, because of some special insight into the nature of moral properties and their relationship to non-moral properties. But it seems more likely that we take it as a constraint on acceptable moral discourse that moral differences coincide with non-moral differences. (In what sense have we *discovered*, as opposed to *insisted*, that the moral/mental supervenes on the non-moral/mental?) This raises the question of what justifies our confidence in supervenience theses. Perhaps we have a priori knowledge of relevant metaphysical facts. But even if one rejects certain 'unity of science' hypotheses—e.g. classical reductionism, or even token physicalism—one might think that good explanations are unifiable in *some* sense (see Kitcher 1981). And this may require modal connections between levels of explanation. For example, if the biological did not supervene on the non-biological, could non-biological factors (like earthquakes) *explain* Abnormal instances of biological cp laws? Would we have reason to suppose that such interfering factors would always be at least potential interferers? (See the discussion of 'catastrophic' Abnormal instances in Ch. 4.) Thus, one might argue that supervenience presupposed by appeal to cp laws in domains not reducible to physics.

but no more so than alternatives. My remarks in this regard are not novel, but it is easy to forget familiar points about modality when discussing supervenience.

3.1

Following Kripke (1980) and Stalnaker (1976), I think we should distinguish that which might have been different from the ways it might have been. *The world* might have been different; possible worlds, including *the actual world*, are ways the world might have been. While this terminology has become standard, it is potentially confusing. For on the Kripke–Stalnaker view, the actual world is *not* the world. The actual world is one (especially interesting) way the world might have been—viz. the way the world is. But the world is distinct from the way it is, much as a lump of clay is distinct from the way it is shaped. My dog is part of the world, but she is not (in this same sense) part of any way the world might have been. The world might have been different, but there is no *way the world might have been* that might have been different. Or so I claim. Thus, it may be better to speak of possible *states of the* world, where 'the world' is a synonym for 'the universe'. For while confusion might lead one to say that the world is the actual world, no such confusion would lead one to say that the universe is some possible state of the universe.[11]

Nonetheless, a nominalist might bite the bullet, and claim that the (so-called) actual state of the universe just *is* the universe—the totality of things that includes us, the dogs, the quarks and stars, etc. Having identified the world with the actual world, a certain kind of nominalist (e.g. Lewis 1973, 1986) will go on to say that there are *other* totalities of things that do not include us and our surroundings. On this view, possible worlds are things of the same sort as the universe we inhabit. So possible worlds are not abstract entities (as talk of *ways* and analogies to *shapes* might suggest); possible worlds have spatio-temporal parts, although non-actual worlds do not exist in the space-time associated with this world. Since no

---

[11] See Kripke (1980: 20). Wittgenstein's (1921) 'totality of facts, not things' is closer to what I mean by 'the actual world'; but as we will see, possible states of the universe need not satisfy all the constraints that Wittgenstein imposed on possible states of affairs (*Tatsache*). The world is the way it is but, on the natural reading of this claim, 'is' is predicational, as in 'the clay is round'. For simplicity, I speak of ways the world might *have been*. But this should be understood tenselessly to include ways the world might be (in the future), one of which will be actual (see Slote 1974). Similarly, talk of ways the world might be should be understood tenselessly to include ways the world might have been (in the past). Viewed from the first moment of time, possible worlds are happily described as ways the world might be; viewed from the last moment, possible worlds are happily described as ways the world might have been. Along the way, neither description is entirely satisfactory. But I usually opt for the latter.

individual is included in more than one universe-like totality of things, modal discourse has to be interpreted accordingly. For example, 'I might have gone to law school' is said to be true iff *some* totality includes a person *relevantly like me* who went to law school. More generally, talk of possible worlds is to be understood as talk of totalities that typically include *counterparts of* things in this world.

The main objections to this conception of modality are well known (see e.g. Lycan 1994). So I will simply mention them here. Prima facie, the central claim—that there are vastly many universe-like totalities, all of which exist outside our space and time—is grossly implausible. Even if the alleged non-actual things exist, it is hard to see how the truth of our modal claims could depend on them, or how we could know anything about them. (In this respect, Lewisian worlds are like noumenal selves.) It is far from clear that the required counterpart relation(s) can be specfied in a plausible way, especially given considerations of the sort discussed by Kripke (1980). Moreover, one of the alleged benefits of Lewisian nominalism is overrated. Instead of postulating one world and many ways it might have been, we are asked to postulate many worlds, and as Lewis rightly notes, theoretical parsimony concerns the number of entity *types*. (Other things being equal, a theory that posits fifty widgets is simpler than a theory that posits ten widgets and ten gizmos.) But the difference between positing one and two may well be important, in a way that the difference between positing two and three is not—especially when it comes to worlds, each of which has its own space-time. (It may be that in the sense relevant to parsimony, one does not *posit* any universe, until one posits two of them.) I return to a more important source of motivation for Lewis's conception of possible worlds. But for now, my primary aim is to emphasize contrasts with the (Kripke–Stalnaker) conception that I endorse: there is just one world; there are many ways it might have been; and the world is not identical with the way it is.

Still, our question remains: what *are* possible states of the universe if not Lewisian totalties? A compelling (Tractarian) thought is that possible worlds are possible arrangements of the things in the universe, where these things have natures that determine how they can be arranged. Kripke (1980: 15–20) offers the analogy of two dice. Suppose that die A has come up 1, and die B has come up 3. The mini-universe consisting of A and B has thirty-six possible states, one of which (A = 1, B = 3) is the actual state; and this space of possibility is determined by the (cubical) natures of A and B. It could have been that A came up 2 and B came up 4. Correspondingly, 'A = 2, B = 4' describes one of thirty-six possible states of the dice world, while 'A = 7, B = 8' does not. But each possible state described is not *another* pair of dice, outside the space-time in which A and B exist; and we do not evaluate counterfactual claims about A and B in terms of how matters stand with some dice *distinct from but relevantly like* the dice actually tossed.[12]

As a slightly more complex analogy, one might imagine a 'lego world', in which the objects can be connected in various ways, thereby forming structures that exhibit relations (like *larger than*) not exhibited by the unstructured pieces. Here too, the space of *ways the world might have been* is determined by the natures of the building blocks, including their capacities for combining with one another. One can also imagine successive states of the lego world, in which new structures are formed (while others decompose). So when I speak of possible *arrangements* of objects, I do not mean to suggest a static view of possible worlds. Indeed, possible worlds might well be viewed as possible world *histories* (see Slote 1974; Kripke 1980); and one can think of such histories as ways in which the objects around us could have been arranged in space, time, and perhaps other dimensions. Let me also stress that an arrangement—or a *configuration*—of objects is not a sentence or any other representation of the objects; it is a possible state of the objects, a way the totality of objects could have been arranged (given their natures). This kind of circularity would be objectionable if I wanted to reduce modal notions to something else. But this is not my project. I suspect that talk of ordinary objects is shot through with modal presuppositions, and that talk of modality is as unmysterious as talk of ordinary objects. (This is not to deny that, in certain frames of mind, talk of ordinary objects can seem puzzling. My claim is simply that talk of possibility is not *more* puzzling.)

If we say that the space of possible worlds is determined by (*inter alia*) the properties of objects in the world, then we forgo the option of reducing talk of properties to talk of individuals and possible worlds—say by identifying properties with sets of possible individuals. But the value of this option depends on whether some such reductive thesis is plausible; and *pace* Lewis (1986), I am sceptical. If anything, it might be better to view *ways the world might have been* as modal properties of the (totality of) objects in the universe (see Shoemaker 1984; Stalnaker 1984). In any case,

---

[12] We will say that there are thirty-six salient possible state *types* of this mini-universe if each die can occupy various regions of the relevant *physical* space. But in speaking of dice, we typically do not care about differences like: A = 1, A is at position p, B = 3, B is at position p*; A = 1, A is at p*, B = 3, B is at p. In any case, Kripkeans need not worry about how to determine the counterparts of A and B: this is a question, generated by a different conception of modality. Some philosophers take possible worlds to be consistent sets of propositions. But Grim (1991) argues that the required sets would be paradoxically large; and Lewis (1986) argues that a theory of modality should not reply on an appeal to consistency. Moreover, I find it hard to believe that *ways the world might have been* are sets of Fregean thoughts; and given the semantics of Ch. 2, the proposition that P is the sense of 'P'. As I discuss below, there are reasons for not countenancing worlds at which Hesperus is not Phosphorus; but the proposition that Hesperus is not Phosphorus will presumably be a member of some set that allegedly is a possible world.

it is not an a priori constraint on conceptions of modality that possible states of the universe be regarded as more basic than the properties of objects. One can, and perhaps should, embrace a less theoretically ambitious conception of modality.

Similarly, one's conception of modality need not be rooted in the project of reducing all talk of *objects* to talk of objects in some preferred class. One can say that the space of possible worlds is determined by the (properties of) objects in the world, while retaining a generous conception of object. In particular, one can allow that I am an object, as are the physical particles out of which I am composed; and in allowing this, one need not *identify* me with any fusion of particles (or particles-at-an-instant). One can allow that I am a constituent of the universe, and that one has not yet taken me into account—one has not yet included *all* of the universe's constituents—simply by including all the physical particles. And this is where supervenience theses come back into the picture.

3.2

In saying that a person is an object, distinct from any fusion of physical particles, one is not thereby saying that a person and her properties are independent of all other objects and their properties. For suppose that among the objects in the universe, there is a subclass of basic objects with the following feature: if $w1$ and $w2$ are distinct possible worlds—i.e. distinct possible arrangements of the objects in the universe—then $w1$ and $w2$ are distinct possible arrangements of the basic objects, where this space of possibility is determined by the natures of the basic objects. The familiar Tractarian idea is that there is a class of modally privileged objects, possible arrangements of which *are* the possible states of the universe. If this is correct then, in principle, each possible state of the universe can be distinguished from every other possible state without reference to any (non-basic) supervenient objects. At least many ordinary objects may not belong to the smallest class of objects, such that the space of possibility is determined by the natures of these objects. And one can grant that some objects are basic in this sense, while denying that all objects are fusions of these modally privileged objects. So even given agreement about which objects are basic, there is room for disagreement about the number—and ontological status of—supervenient objects. If persons seem not to be fusions of basic objects, then one might well adopt a generous conception of object that allows for non-basic objects, while still insisting that no two possible worlds differ without differing with respect to how the basic objects are arranged.

Of course, fusion theses can be motivated by various analogies (see Lewis 1986; Dennett 1991). Given a suitable arrangement of dots on a page, we may rightly speak of a flower that is there to be seen; but the flower is not any object distinct from a certain totality of dots, as arranged on (and against the background of) the page. But whatever the virtues of such analogies, one need not identify non-basic objects with fusions of basic objects in order to explain a 'Supervenience on the Basic' thesis:

> (SB) if w_1 and w_2 are indiscernible with respect to how the basic objects are arranged, then w_1 and w_2 are indiscernible with respect to how the objects are arranged.

For suppose that possible worlds just *are* possible arrangements of the basic objects, and so every possible world is identical with some possible arrangement of the basic objects. Then if w_1 and w_2 are indiscernible with respect to how the basic objects are arranged, $w_1 = w_2$. Given this conception of possible worlds, indiscernibility with respect to how the basic objects are arranged is indiscernibility *tout court*, and (SB) follows. Recall the analogy to sets: if S_1 and S_2 are indiscernible with respect to their members, then S_1 and S_2 are indiscernible *tout court*, since $S_1 = S_2$.

This is a kind of conceptual—or individuationist—explanation for why (SB) is true. Fusion theorists can offer a more ontological explanation. If w_1 and w_2 are indiscernible with respect to how the objects in class C are arranged, then w_1 and w_2 are indiscernible with respect to how fusions of the objects in class C are arranged; and all objects are fusions of basic objects. (I assume that 'fusion' is understood so that the first of these claims is trivial.) This explanation does not trade on the idea that $w_1 = w_2$. Nor does it presuppose a particular view of what possible worlds are. Rather, it trades on the idea that persons (and all supervenient objects) are fusions of basic objects. Perhaps this will turn out, all things considered, to be the better explanation. But if possible worlds are possible arrangements of the basic objects, then accounting for (SB) does not require any *further* explanation of the sort offered by fusion theorists. *Instead of advancing an identity thesis about the non-basic objects, one can advance an identity thesis about possible states of the universe.*

Still, even if each possible world is some possible arrangement of basic objects, this does not yet explain why the mental (and everything else) globally supervenes on the *physical*. And we wanted an explanation for

> (GS) if w_1 and w_2 are physically indiscernible, w_1 and w_2 are indiscernible in all respects.

At this point, one might ask for the evidence in favour of (GS); see note 4 above. But suppose that the basic objects are physical, i.e. that possible states of the universe are possible arrangements of the physical objects in the universe, in some demanding sense of 'physical' that does not include persons and their mental events. And consider the following individuative principle:

> (IP) if A1 and A2 are possible arrangements of the physical objects, then A1 differs from A2 only if A1 differs from A2 in some physical respect.

If possible states of the universe are possible arrangements of the physical objects in the universe, then given (IP), a possible state of the universe w1 differs from a possible state of the universe w2 only if w1 differs from w2 in some physical respect. That is, given (IP) and a certain conception of what possible worlds are, physically indiscernible possible worlds are indiscernible *tout court*. So given (IP) and this conception of possible worlds, (GS) follows.

I return to (IP) presently. But let me note that one can endorse this account of (GS) without saying that (GS) is trivial, or knowable a priori. Even if we can know a priori that there are basic objects, and that these objects have natures that delimit the space of ways the world might have been, it may not be a priori that the basic objects are all physical. (It may not be a priori that there are no immaterial souls, even if this is necessarily true.) But given that the basic objects are physical, (GS) follows from a certain claim about what possible worlds are. One might complain that a thesis about possible worlds cannot really explain (GS). I disagree. More importantly, one cannot restrict 'explain' in this way and still assume that (GS) calls for explanation. Some philosophers will object to my unrepentant talk of natures; and I would be happy to learn that such talk is inessential to the kind of explanation for supervenience theses being proposed here. But if accounting for supervenience in a dualist-friendly way requires the idea that objects have natures, I would not reject dualism on that account.

3.3

Taken out of context, (IP) might look like a substantive thesis. But I think it is almost trivially true. One might think that (IP) is false, on the grounds that some physical objects could have had a property Q, such that Q is not actually instantiated by any object; but there could have been objects with Q that were otherwise indiscernible from objects without Q. We can imagine that all and only thinking things are composed of physical particles with some such property Q. In this scenario, the difference between thinking and non-thinking things consists in some (irreducible) feature of the objects that constitute thinking things, where this feature is independent of the features that physical objects actually have. This single-substance variant on Cartesian dualism is presumably false, but one might think there are possible worlds where it is true. And if there are two physically indiscernible possible arrangements of the physical objects, only one of which contains particles with property Q, then (IP) is false.

Nonetheless, (IP) is not threatened by such reasoning. When one says that possible worlds are possible arrangements of the basic objects in the universe, talk of possible arrangements is to be understood as talk of possibility determined and constrained by the natures of these objects. (Recall Kripke's dice analogy.) I have added the claim that the basic objects are physical objects. On this view, the space of possible worlds is constrained by the nature of the physical objects in the universe as we find it. Possible worlds—ways *this* world, which includes us and other things, might have been—are possible arrangements of the physical objects that constitute this world, where the nature of these objects determine and constrain what counts as a possible arrangement of them.[13] For example, if it is in the nature of physical objects not to travel faster than (or at least not to accelerate beyond) the speed of light, then there is no possible arrangement of the physical objects in which some of those objects travel at superluminal speeds. We can, without contradiction, imagine otherwise; but this is irrelevant, given what the 'possible' in 'possible arrangement' means. The physical objects have whatever natures they have and natures impose limits, even while they make for possibility. Of course, I cannot prove that the physical objects have natures that exclude any possibility of such objects having the mind-producing property Q discussed above. But I see no reason to believe that any physical objects really could have any such property Q. Thus, I do not think that (IP) is the weak link in my defence of (GS). The more obvious objection is that my conception of modality is impoverished.

One might claim that what I call possible worlds are (at best) the physically possible worlds, and that many things are possible without being physically possible. This may be true. But it does not follow that we need more possible worlds. For a proposition—e.g. that my dog flew to Alpha Centauri and back yesterday—can be *logically* possible without describing some way the world might have been. (In this respect, my view is Kripkean and not Tractarian.) Moreover, *if* every logically possible proposition is true at some possible world, then

---

[13] Since one cannot discern the nature of physical objects a priori, a consequence of this view is that empirical considerations bear directly on what is possible. This is not the *Tractatus* view, according to which basic objects have *logical* natures (and *if* they have physical properties, which is doubtful, this does not constrain the space of genuine possibility). More on this below. But one must not adopt an overly narrow conception of how the physical constituents of the universe might have been arranged. Perhaps the laws of nature (as we now see them) would have been different, had things gone differently in the early universe. (If 'inflationary' accounts are correct—see Guth (1997)—Kripkeans may even be able to grant that there could have been more or less 'stuff' than there actually is.) And there may be distinct world histories that our *current* theories do not distinguish.

(GS) if w1 and w2 are physically indiscernible, w1 and w2 are indiscernible in all respects

is false. It is *logically* possible that the world is just as it is physically, but different in some mental respect, since it is logically possible that there are Cartesian souls. And if (GS) is false, then one can hardly complain that non-Cartesian dualists do not explain its truth. So even if my conception of possible worlds is impoverished, one needs to say which true thesis is allegedly rendered mysterious by event dualism. And I contend that any dualist-unfriendly variant on (GS) will be at least as tendentious as the proposed (dualist-friendly) account of (GS).

But before turning to defence of this last claim, let me briefly summarize the dialectic that led us here. I want to preserve some Cartesian intuitions about persons and freedom, without supposing that mental causation requires interaction between two substantially different individuals, viz. a mind and her body. So I adopted a Strawsonian conception of persons, which lets us say that a person's mental events are distinct from any (fusions of) biochemical changes in her body. Indeed, non-Cartesian event dualists can and should be thoroughly non-reductionistic; persons and their mental properties are distinct from any (fusions of) objects or (truth functions of) properties describable in non-mental terms. Proponents of this view face overdetermination objections, replies to which raise a deeper question: what *explains* the supervenience of the mental on the non-mental if not some form of reductionism? I have suggested that (GS) is best viewed as a thesis about the individuation of possible worlds. But the worry is that the required conception of possible worlds is too restrictive. My response will be that the conception of possible worlds is fine, so long as one does not insist that every notion of possibility be glossed in terms of possible worlds.

4. Species of Possibility

It is logically possible that yesterday my dog flew to Alpha Centauri and back. But it does not follow that there are possible worlds in which dogs travel faster than the speed of light. It would follow, given:

(LF) a proposition P is logically possible iff P is true at some possible world

so as long as there is no equivocation on 'possible world'. This thesis reflects a Logic First approach to the role of possible worlds in theorizing about modality. And initially, such an approach seems plausible. For one might think that appeal to possible worlds should characterize possibility in the broadest sense, and that logical possibility is the broadest sense of possibility. On the other hand, (LF) is at odds with the following Kripkean line of thought that involves no science fiction. For every x, there is no possible world at which $x \neq x$. Hesperus is Phosphorus. Hence, there is no possible world at which Hesperus is not Phosphorus (assuming that 'Hesperus' and 'Phosphorus' are rigid designators in Kripke's sense). But it is logically possible that Hesperus is not Phosphorus; a thinker could, without irrationality, hold that Hesperus is not Phosphorus. So at least one proposition P—viz. that Hesperus is not Phosphorus—is logically possible, even though there is no possible world at which P is true.

4.1

One cannot resolve this issue by stipulation. In particular, one cannot stipulate that if proposition P is possible in any sense of 'possible', then there is a possible world at which P is true—and hence that the world might have been as P says it is. For suppose I characterize a new sense of 'possible' as follows: a proposition is academically possible iff some academic has asserted it. The academically possible propositions will include propositions that are not even logically possible, and I assume that there are no logically impossible ways the world might have been. (One can use the label 'logically impossible worlds' to describe certain abstract objects— say, contradictory propositions. But this hardly shows that some ways the world might have been are impossible.)

Other examples are easily generated. If a contradiction is sufficiently complex, even a clever logician might make a mistake. So a proposition P can be seems-to-a-clever-logician possible, even if there is no possible world at which P is true. (Similarly, recalling a discussion from Chapter 2: one might be wrong about whether it really is possible for someone to doubt that Nora believes that lawyers lie iff Nora believes that attorneys lie.) Perhaps it will be said that logical possibility is a paradigm type of possibility, and that (LF) is as secure as 'I am a person'. But whatever the value of paradigm case considerations, they cannot ensure that there is only one kind of possibility. Perhaps possibility (*sans phrase*) is like jade— with logical possibility being like nephrite, and the other 'species' of possibility being captured by talk of possible worlds. That is, our label 'possible' may cover two importantly different notions, only one of which corresponds to the idea of ways the world might have been (world histories, etc.) In particular, Kripke (1963, 1980) gives us the resources for distinguishing model theory from modality; and one can say that logical possibility concerns the former, while reserving talk of possible worlds for the latter. This point is not new. But it bears emphasis in the present context.[14]

Recall that in Chapter 2 I spoke of linguistic forms: labelled orderings of lexical items (along with their phonological features). And I said that an interpreted linguistic form was the pairing of such a syntactic object with a Fregean sense. The sentence 'Fido barked' has a linguistic form Σ that (in the actual situation) is paired with a certain Fregean sense, viz. the thought that Fido barked. But this interpretation is just one of many interpretations that Σ could have supported. (Which interpretations Σ could have supported depends in part on the nature of Σ, but I assume that, at a minimum, Σ could have meant that Nora walked.)

Since Σ is an uninterpreted object, we can talk about the truth of Σ (at the actual world) relative to an interpretation: Σ is true relative to some but not all of its possible interpretations. And we can focus on possible interpretations of Σ that differ from the actual interpretation of Σ only with respect to the interpretation of non-logical lexical items.[15] Call these the possible L-interpretations of Σ. Then we can say that a proposition P is model-theoretically possible if P is the (actual) interpretation of a linguistic form Σ, such that Σ is true relative to at least one possible L-interpretation of Σ. Thus, it is model-theoretically possible that Fido is not Rex; and this is so, even though Fido is Rex. But it does not follow that there is a possible world in which Fido is not Rex. For model-theoretic possibility concerns ways of interpreting structures, not ways the world might have been; although one can speak of ways the world might have been, in which linguistic forms are interpreted differently by the speakers who use them. One can use the phrase 'possible world' to talk about possible L-interpretations of linguistic forms. But that terminological decision will not ensure that all talk of ways the world might have been is really talk about possible L-interpretations of syntactic objects.

Indeed, we have two excellent sources of motivation for distinguishing model-theoretic possibility from (what I shall call) genuine modality: our conception of ourselves as persons, and our best physical theories. I could

---

[14] See Etchemendy (1990) and Hanson (1997). And there is ample room confusion here, since it is common to talk about possible worlds in the course of providing (i) models of modal logics, and (ii) semantic theories for natural languages.

[15] That is, we can hold fixed the contributions to meaning of: (i) the semantic combinatorix, and (ii) any lexical items that express logical notions. One would like a general account of what a logical notion *is*, and which lexical items express such notions. But for present purposes, it would suffice to list the (finitely many) lexical items whose semantic contribution is held fixed, and these 'functional' items may well differ syntactically from other lexical elements of linguistic forms. See Pietroski (forthcoming *a*) for an attempt to explain some intuitions about logical possibility (beyond those having to do with overt logical connectives) in the context of Chomsky's (1995) minimalist programme for the study of natural languages.

have raised my arm a moment ago, even though I didn't, and this is not to say that a certain linguistic form ('I raised my arm a moment ago') is true relative to some interpretation. It may be model-theoretically possible that my chair raised its arm. But there is an important sense in which I, unlike my chair, could have done otherwise. There is a recurrent temptation to worry that this familiar picture—in which a person chooses one of several alternatives open to her—is just a picture: perhaps we conceive of ourselves as having options; but even when we explicitly deliberate about what to do next, there is really only one possible outcome, in any sense of 'possible' that is independent of thought and language. Laplacians feed this anxiety by suggesting that given the laws of nature, and conditions that obtained long before my birth, there was exactly one possible history of my body; hence it is false that my arm could have risen, and thus false that I could have raised my arm. (It is cold comfort to say that had things been different at the first moment in time, then perhaps I would have done otherwise if I had existed at all.) But there is no reason to think that any such form of determinism is true.

On the contrary, our best physical theories support the idea that there are many ways the world might have been. An electron detected at point A could have been detected at point B, even given the laws of nature and all the conditions that obtained before the electron passed through some slit(s). In saying this, one is not saying that a certain linguistic form is true relative to some interpretation; one is saying that a certain (mind-independent) aspect of the world might have been otherwise. And I see no reason for denying that a moment ago, it was possible for my arm to have risen, in this same physical sense of 'possible'.[16] Of course, given that I have a corporeal nature, the details of that nature presumably impose many constraints (of which I may be unaware) on what I can do—and not

---

[16] I suspect, though will not try to argue, that genuine freedom of action requires at least some freedom to have done otherwise; where freedom to have done otherwise requires not only that there be a sense in which I have options, it requires that these options reflect genuinely possible ways the world might have been. We occasionally try to do that which we cannot do. But could there be a rational life in which (necessarily) all unsuccessful tryings were necessarily unsuccessful? Would such a life include genuine tryings, as opposed to mental counterparts of certain bodily motions? Quantum indeterminacy does not suffice for freedom; a free individual is not one whose bodily motions are random (and never the effects of reasons). But when I raise my arm, I affect a portion of the world that can be described without reference to any thinking subject. If I could have raised my arm a moment ago, a certain impersonal aspect of the world could have been different; and it would be cold comfort if the consequent of this conditional was not true in a sense of 'could' licensed by our best physical theories. If there is no mind-independent sense in which my arm could have risen, there is no mind-independent sense in which I could have raised my arm; and so to that extent, my self-conception (as an agent who can effect change in the world) is fraudulent. See Kane (1998) for defence of a sophisticated libertarianism that I find attractive. See also Wiggins (1973), Nozick (1981), cf. McCall (1994); Dennett (1984).

merely in the sense that I am not free to whisk off to Alpha Centauri and back before dinner. Perhaps I am even wrong, on a given occasion, when I say that I could have raised my arm, although the evidence we have strongly suggests that (at least often) normal adults can indeed raise their arms 'at will'.

Thus, we have reasons for talking about ways the world might have been, where these are not be understood as possible interpretations of syntactic structures. But one could retain the idea that model-theoretic possibility is possibility in the broadest sense, by biting the bullet (and denying that there is any other sense of possibility), or allowing for relativized notions of possibility in the broadest sense. The former position is grossly implausible, given other alternatives. So let us say that it is model-theoretically possible that P, even given that Q, if it is model-theoretically possible that P and Q. Someone might suggest that talk of physical possibility should be understood as talk of model-theoretic possibility, even given the laws of physics (and perhaps statements of certain particular facts). But this still provides at best a linguistic model of physical possibility. If an electron detected at point A could have been detected at point B, then the truth of this claim turns on (*inter alia*) features of the electron and where it might have gone—not on features of sentences (some of which are lawlike) and their possible interpretations. But there is a better way of getting at the intuition behind this suggestion.[17]

4.2

It is important to note that

(LF) a proposition P is logically possible iff P is true at some possible world

can be conjoined with various conceptions of what possible worlds are. If one combines (LF) with the idea that all possible worlds are possible arrangements of a single stock of objects, one will be led to postulate logically primitive objects, which are presumably distinct from the things we typically call 'objects'. Wittgenstein (1921) explored this option with

[17] If this is to believe in irreducibly *de re* modalities, then a mundane belief has a fancy name. Still, a theorist bent on unification might point to two facts in support of the claim that (what I am calling) genuine modality is a species of model-theoretic possibility: if proposition P is true at some way the world might have been, then it is model-theoretically possible that P; and if it is model-theoretically neccessary that P, then P is true at every way the world might have been. But these facts show little. If P is true at some possible world w, there is an L-interpretation relative to which the linguistic form 'P' is true at w; and if 'P' is true relative to every L-interpretation, then the truth of the proposition expressed by 'P' is a function of logical elements in 'P' (and its syntactic structure); hence, that proposition will be true at every possible world (given the meaning of its logical elements).

considerable ingenuity, but less success. Postulating logical atoms about which nothing can be said, apart from specifying their role in a system that allows for a certain description of logical possibility, is less than fully satisfying.

Moreover, Wittgenstein held that logical possibility was the only genuine kind of possibility.[18] We can focus on subregions of the space of logically possible worlds—subsets of the set of possible arrangements of the logical objects, possible arrangements of which are determined by the logical natures of these objects. Indeed, every contingent proposition (i.e. every genuine picture of the world) lets us do just this: divide the space of logical possibility in two. But apart from tautologies, no propositions are necessarily true. For the only necessities are those determined by the natures of the objects; and logical objects determine only logical necessities. (By analogy, one can speak of those possible worlds where the dice came up nine, but one does not thereby characterize a species of 9-ish necessity. All necessities—e.g. if the total was 9, then die A was at least 3—are determined by the natures of the dice.)

It is hard to believe, however, that there is no non-logical necessity. Surely there is a sense in which my dog cannot make a round trip to Alpha Centauri in a day, even though it is logically possible that she will make such a trip tomorrow. Lewis (1983*a*, 1986) offers a way of accommodating this intuition, while still retaining (LF), by rejecting the idea that all possible worlds are possible arrangements of the same stock of objects. Lewis countenances non-actual totalities of things, some of which include counterparts of my dog. Some of my dog's counterparts fly to (a counterpart) of Alpha Centauri at superluminal speeds. Indeed, for every logically possible proposition P, there is a Lewisian world at which P is true.[19] But unlike Wittgenstein, Lewis can also characterize many 'inner necessities', since logical necessity is not determined by (the logical natures of) any one stock of objects. Given all the Lewisian totalities, one can talk about all the possible worlds of type T, for various types T. In particular, one can talk about all the possible worlds that conform to the (actual) laws of physics—or some idealized theory of which our physics is (an approximation to) a special case. Similarly, one can talk about all the possible worlds that respect certain (fairly weak) metaphysical constraints. Perhaps some

---

[18] See Wittgenstein (1921: 6.37, 5.136, and surrounding passages). Ramsey (1929) offered a Humean proposal for how to understand causal necessity within a Tractarian metaphysics; see Pietroski (1995) for a development of this idea, in conjunction with appeal to *ceteris paribus* laws, and extend it into probabilistic contexts. But one needs to see how such proposals avoid objections of the sort discussed in the next chapter.

[19] There are Lewisian worlds where Hesperus/Phosphorus has *two* counterparts. And one can say that 'Hesperus might not have been Phosphorus' is true, relative to contexts where the two names are associated with *different* counterpart relations between the actual planet and objects at other worlds.

such world includes a Cartesian soul who is my counterpart at that world. Thus, Lewis can define notions of physical and metaphysical possibility, as well as many other notions of restricted possibility.

Moreover, the corresponding 'logically contingent necessities' can be nested. For one can say that every world of type T1 is of type T2 (but not vice versa). Perhaps physical and metaphysical possibility are related in this way, while other notions of possibility are not, as indicated in Figure 6.1. But as I have already noted,

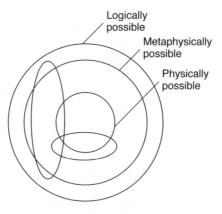

Fig. 6.1

(GS) if w1 and w2 are physically indiscernible, w1 and w2 are indiscernible in all respects

is false on any view that preserves (LF). If every logically possible proposition is true at some possible world, there are distinct but physically indiscernible possible worlds. And if (GS) is false, dualists do not owe an explanation for why it is true. But Lewis does not deny that there is *a* sense in which the mental supervenes on the physical. On the contrary, he holds that (GS) holds for all worlds *of a certain type*.

From this perspective, the task is to provide a restricted version of (GS). Lewis (1983*a*) proposes to characterize a notion of 'alien' worlds, such that if two possible worlds differ without differing physically, then at least one of those worlds is alien. Given such a notion, one can assert:

(GS*) if w1 and w2 are physically indiscernible non-alien worlds, w1 and w2 are indiscernible in all respects.

The idea is that while some possible worlds contain Cartesian souls, such worlds are alien to ours (given that there are no Cartesian souls). Similarly, a world counts as alien if it contains material objects that differ radically from the material objects of this world. In particular, the alien worlds will include those where certain material objects have some (intrinsic and irreducible) mental property Q, such that objects with Q can be otherwise just like objects without Q. (Jackson (1994) introduces the notion of a 'minimal physical duplicate' to restrict (GS); see also Chalmers' (1996) discussion of supervenience.)

This idea would be uninteresting if one characterized alien worlds as those worlds that provide counter-examples to (GS). For this would trivialize (GS*). This is especially important if the question is whether dualists are unable to explain some true supervenience thesis. If one adopts a conception of modality according to which (GS) is false, and a construal of 'alien' that makes (GS*) trivial, then one has yet to state a thesis that demands a non-dualistic explanation. Lewis, however, envisions a substantive characterization of 'alien'. He suggests that an alien *world* is one where some alien *property* is instantiated; and he thinks that we can characterize alien properties as properties not countenanced by (an idealized version of) our best theories. The idea is that alien properties are not merely not instantiated in the actual world, their instantiation is ruled out by certain (correct) theories of the actual world.

4.3

Internal to Lewis's conception of modality, this is a very good move. It lets one reconstruct the Kripkean notion of ways *this* world might have been, within Lewisian nominalism, by talking about logically possible worlds compatible with laws (and perhaps some especially important particular facts) that figure in the best theoretical description of the actual world. Lewis (1973) has also developed Ramsey's (1928) idea that the best theoretical descriptions are those that strike the best balance between simplicity (of the sort germane to explanation) and accuracy. Lewis thus exploits the familiar idea that universals are those properties posited by the best theories of how the (actual) world works (see Armstrong 1978). For the strategy is to characterize non-alien worlds in terms of universals, although for Lewis, 'universals' are world-relative. Since each world is actual relative to itself, many properties are alien with respect to some but not all possible worlds. For example, if world w contains Cartesian souls, then the best theory of w will countenance such entities; and relative to w, some properties instantiated at our world may count as alien. But the property *being a Cartesian soul* is presumably alien to our (wholly material) world; for presumably, any instantiations of this property would falsify the simplest most accurate theory of our world.

Unsurprisingly, there are complications. For example, the property *being a Cartesian soul or a mature human being* is instantiated at both our world and w. So this property is not alien to either world. But assume that such (Cambridge) properties are not 'natural' properties—at least not relative to the actual world. Then we can formulate the following logically contingent global supervenience thesis: among those worlds where no natural properties alien to our world are instantiated, no two worlds differ without differing physically. That is, physically indiscernible non-alien worlds are indiscernible in all respects (Lewis 1983: 364). If this non-trivial thesis is true, one can ask why it is true. Why do non-alien worlds satisfy this constraint? Given the logical possibility of individuals mentally different but physically indiscernible from me (in environments otherwise just like this one), why are such individuals confined to alien worlds? Why are there no worlds 'within the sphere of non-alien worlds' that differ without differing physically? Thus, Lewis offers a way of formulating a substantive supervenience thesis (which, if true, poses Kim's question) within a conception of modality that preserves (LF).

Of course, Lewisian supervenience presents no challenge for dualists if our best theory of the actual world includes a (modal) 'no difference without a physical difference' principle. For in that case, appeal to alien properties does not deliver a *substantive* alternative to

(GS) if w_1 and w_2 are physically indiscernible, w_1 and w_2 are indiscernible in all respects.

But let us grant that theories of the actual world need not presuppose supervenience. Dualists can also get off the explanatory hook if possible worlds are such that it follows from the physical indiscernibility of w_1 and w_2 that $w_1 = w_2$, so long as w_1 and w_2 are non-alien worlds. For in that case, one can still offer an 'individuationist' explanation for

(GS*) if w_1 and w_2 are physically indiscernible non-alien worlds, w_1 and w_2 are indiscernible in all respects.

There is, however, no reason to think that Lewisian possible worlds will satisfy the identity criterion relied on in such an explanation. From a Kripkean perspective, it makes no sense to speak of possible worlds that differ barely—i.e. without differing somehow with respect to features of the individuals at those worlds: to speak of two indiscernible arrangements of the basic objects is (at best) to speak of a single *way the world might have been* under two descriptions. But if possible worlds are Lewisian totalities, all but one of which contains individuals distinct from the individuals at this world (and properties are, to a first approximation, sets of possible individuals), perhaps there are endlessly many distinct but (otherwise) indiscernible possible worlds.[20]

[20] This is an instance of a familiar debate form, common to domains where one is led to ask whether the 'identity of indiscernibles' goes beyond the 'indiscernibility of identicals'.

I am inclined to regard this as another reason for being suspicious of Lewisian worlds. But perhaps, as Lewis suggests, there is no deep objection here. Whatever the modal facts, we can talk about equivalence classes of totalities, rather than individual possible worlds. And for present purposes, the important point is that given Lewis's conception of modality, a further assumption is needed to conclude that $w1$ *is* $w2$, given that $w1$ and $w2$ are 'internally' type-identical. For this reason, I am inclined to concede that a non-dualistic Lewisian could reasonably object if a dualistic Lewisian claimed to explain (GS*) by pressing the individuationist line of thought pressed in Sections 2 and 3. (Although the issues are complicated. Perhaps a clever dualistic Lewisian could argue that if $w1$ and $w2$ are physically indiscernible non-alien worlds, then $w1 = w2$, in which case the mental indiscernibility of $w1$ and $w2$ is no mystery; or $w1$ and $w2$ differ *barely*, in which case the mental indiscernibility of $w1$ and $w2$ is still no mystery— since worlds that differ barely do not differ with respect to the features of individuals at those worlds. On the other hand, this second kind of mystery-elimination may not *explain* any supervenience thesis.) But this is not an argument against non-Cartesian dualism.

It is an argument that non-Cartesian dualists ought not be Lewisians. And upon reflection, this conclusion is unsurprising. For consider just how demanding (GS*) is, given the Lewisian conception of modality. There is no *logically* possible world $w1$, such that $w1$ is a non-alien world physically indiscernible from another non-alien world $w2$ (say, the actual world), and $w1$ differs from $w2$ in some (say, mental) respect. Thus, mental properties are such that it is *logically* impossible for these properties to be instantiated differently at non-alien physically indiscernible worlds. So as a matter of *logical* necessity, two worlds differ mentally, only if they differ physically, or at least one of the worlds is alien. It is hard to see how this could be true, unless mental properties—and indeed, all properties— are logical operations on universals. If universals are world-relative, properties need not be truth functions of the properties posited by the best theory of *our* world. So Lewis can allow that mental properties are multiply realizable, and not just in the sense of being realizable by (truth functions of) various physical properties instantiated at this world. For example, the property of *thinking that five is a prime number* is instantiated at some worlds by Cartesian souls. Nonetheless, it seems that some analogue of Kim's view will be required, in order to explain why there is not even a *logical* gap between instantiating certain physical properties and instantiating certain mental properties.[21]

---

[21] See also Jackson (1994). Similar remarks apply to supervenient individuals. And it is no accident that Lewis (1971, 1986) has defended the idea that all objects are fusions of (time-slices of) physical particles. One can imagine a Lewisian token physicalist, who would say that there is some logical relation R, such that mental properties can bear R to

This is an elegant picture, in which certain theses in the philosophy of mind figure as part of an explanation whose general shape is forced by a conception of modality designed to accommodate the intuition that every logically possible proposition describes some way the world might have been. Physicalism, construed as Kim-style type identity, turns out to be the explanation for a logically contingent (but still modal) thesis of supervenience. But this picture is not mandatory. It relies on the Lewisian conception of modality, whose worrying features I noted above (Section 3.1). The motivations for event dualism, surveyed in Chapter 5, remain. And I have argued that modal concerns, having to do with overdetermination and supervenience, do not give us reason to abandon event dualism. For one can offer an 'individuationist' explanation of (GS), given a Kripkean conception of modality.

It is worth noting, however, that a deep irony has emerged. Lewisian physicalists countenance the genuine (but alien) possibility of Cartesian souls, while non-Cartesian Strawsonian dualists do not. I think those of us who want to resist the identification of persons with bodies should adopt a restrictive conception of modality, lest our generous conception of object make for trouble when it comes to explaining supervenience; while those who say that persons are actually bodies need a generous conception of modality if supervenience is to be characterized as a thesis explained by physicalism.

One is still free to combine a Kripkean conception of modality with a Kim-style identity theory. But then one cannot (as Kim does) appeal to the truth of

> (GS) if $w1$ and $w2$ are physically indiscernible, $w1$ and $w2$ are indiscernible in all respects

as the basis of an argument *for* physicalism. Absent reason for saying that (GS) is true on an ontological construal, Kripkean dualists can provide all the explanation for (GS) that is required. Thus, non-Cartesians need not view (GS) as an inexplicable 'emergent' truth to be accepted 'with natural piety' (cf. Kim 1993: 158). By way of conclusion, let me suggest that the same is true for a more local supervenience thesis.

A person's mental states supervene on her brain states, holding the environment fixed. But given (GS), two individuals differ mentally only if they differ physically in some internal respect, or there is a physical difference in the relevant worlds external to the individuals. If our thought experiment controls for differences of the latter sort, then any mental differences will coincide with physical differences, which may well be discernible as biochemical differences. If so, a certain mind–brain supervenience thesis is

(properties that are reducible to) physical properties, even if the former are not literally disjunctions of which the latter are disjuncts. But the burden is to describe R.

true.[22] This fits with the Strawsonian conception of persons. If persons have corporeal natures, then given certain facts about human bodies, it is hard to see how our rational natures could float free of our biochemistry. But it does not follow that rationalizing causes have impersonal descriptions. Supervenience does not imply neuralism.

---

[22] We may also discover relations between certain kinds of mental states and brain states—e.g. causal regularities between thinking about fearsome things, and brain states that tend to raise blood pressure. But if such regularities are discovered non-Cartesian event dualists can countenance them.

7

Natural Causes

In Chapter 5, I stressed the intuition that causation in the presence of freedom is special. But one might wonder how mental causation *can* be special, given that instances of mental causation must be instances of the *same* (extensional) relation as instances of causation that involve only non-mental events. One answer is that causation is the extensionalization of explanation. But this is not yet satisfactory, even though there are mental explanations, given the goal of defending event dualism. For one might think that mental explanations are causal explanations only if neuralism is true. I have said that whether or not neuralism is true, cp laws support explanations that license inferences to singular causal claims. But from a certain perspective, this will seem circular. For mental events are covered by genuine cp laws only if mental events are causes; and it will be said that mental events could not be causes, unless neuralism were true. It does no good to repeat that causation is the extensionalization of explanation. As we will see, this only invites an objection prompted by the very idea of characterizing causation in terms of explanation: either my proposal is circular, and so cannot be used to support the substantive thesis of event dualism; or it is based on a notion of explanation that is not sufficiently *objective* to license inferences from explanations to causal claims. Here, the needed reply is not a list of laws, but a different perspective on how our concepts of causation, explanation, and law are related.

An analogy may help to indicate the cluster of concerns I want to address in this chapter. The relation of causation to explanation is, in some respects, like the relation of truth to knowledge. In each case, the extensional notion reflects a mind-independent constraint on an intentional notion. A subject S knows that P only if P; so if S knows that P, then it is true that P. But this is not an interesting sufficient condition for truth. One can avoid triviality by replacing 'know' with something like 'would believe at the limit of rational inquiry'. But then the resulting sufficient condition for truth will rely on some objectionable (or at least tendentious) form of idealism. One might think that a similar fate—triviality or falsity—awaits any proposed sufficient condition for causation in terms of explanation (cf. Kim 1981, 1988a, 1994).

1. Avoiding Projectivism

Strawson (1985: 115) nicely expresses a view I endorsed in Chapter 3:

We sometimes presume, or are said to presume, that causality is a natural relation that holds in the world between particular events or circumstances, just as the relation of temporal succession does or that of spatial proximity. We also, and rightly, associate causality with explanation. But if causality is a relation which holds in the natural world, explanation is a different matter. People explain things to themselves or others and their doing so is something that happens in nature. But we also speak of one thing explaining, or being the explanation of, another thing, as if explaining was a relation between the things. And so it is. But it is not a natural relation in the sense in which we perhaps think of causality as a natural relation. It is an intellectual or rational or intensional relation. It does not hold between things in the natural world, things to which we can assign places and times. It holds between facts or truths.

At the end of his paper, Strawson hints at the kind of sufficient condition for causation (in terms of explanation) that I have offered explicitly. (See also Child (1994), who develops these remarks in a similar way.) But one might wonder how a natural relation can be characterized in terms of a rational relation without spoiling the mind-independence of the former.

1.1

Strawson uses 'natural', so that if relation R holds between entities that do not exist in space and time, then *ipso facto*, R is not a natural relation. Explanation holds between Fregean thoughts; hence, it is a non-natural relation. As we shall see, this comment on the relata of explanation tells us nothing about the mind-dependence of the relation, though one can slip into thinking otherwise. Nor do we think of every relation between spatio-temporal entities as natural. Contrast *is more massive than* with *is cuter than*. While both relations can hold between spatio-temporal particulars (like puppies), the latter relation seems to be mind-dependent or 'projected' in a way that the former is not. Specifying this distinction in any detail is hard. But presumably, saying what it *is* for one thing to be cuter than another requires reference to the dispositions of thinking subjects to make certain cuteness judgements, while one can say what it is for one thing to be more massive than another without referring to potential judgements at all. Correlatively, the claim that subjects can judge something to be cute *because it is* cute may require qualification, in a way that the analogous thesis about mass does not; and cuteness may be related to judgement (in a manner discoverable a priori) in a way that massiveness is not (see Wright's (1992) helpful discussion of the 'Euthyphro Contrast').

With these issues in mind, one might use 'natural', so that natural relations are *non-projected* relations between spatio-temporal particulars. I do not challenge the presumption that causation is a natural relation in this sense. But even if every natural relation is non-projected, it does not follow that every non-natural relation (and thus every relation between Fregean thoughts) is projected—and in that sense, less objective than natural relations. Thoughts have something to do with minds; but it does not follow that all relations between thoughts are, like the relation *is cuter than*, mind-dependent in a way that compromises objectivity. In particular, explanation is a relation between thoughts; but it does not follow that one thought explains another, only because thinking subjects are disposed to find certain facts 'explainy' of others. That one fact explains another may itself be an objective fact.[1]

Nonetheless, it is easy to worry that the mind-independence of causal relations has been slighted, given a condition of the form 'C causes E, if . . . C . . . explains . . . E . . .'. I have offered a sufficient condition for explanation in terms of *ceteris paribus* laws; and in my view laws (including those formulated in intentional terms) are objective truths. But one might doubt the objectivity of putative laws that would cover human mental events *whether or not* they are neural events. So note that my proposal has the following entailment: a singular event thought about C explains a singular event thought about E only if C causes E. Indeed, as Strawson (1985: 118–19) says,

[T]he power of one fact to explain another must have some basis in the natural world where the events occur and the conditions obtain and the causal relations hold. We must think this on pain of holding, if we do not, that the causal relation has no natural existence or none outside our minds; that the belief in such a relation is simply the projection upon the world of some subjective disposition of ours, the disposition, perhaps, to take some facts as explaining others.

---

[1] While many relations between non-spatio-temporal entities may be projected, this need not always be so. Mathematics suggests that there can be objective relations between objects that do not exist in space-time. Of course, as Strawson notes, 'the non-natural fact that the explaining relation holds between the fact that *p* and the fact that *q*' is at least intimately related to a certain natural fact, namely, that 'coming to know that *q* will tend, in the light of other knowledge (or of theory) to induce a state which we call "understanding why *q*"' (Strawson 1985: 117). Mental events occur in space and time. But in good Fregean fashion, Strawson goes on to say that 'we cannot report *these* naturally related events without reference to the non-naturally related objects'. That is, to return to a point made in Ch. 3, we individuate episodes of explaining in terms of ways of thinking about things (not the things themselves). There may be a trivial sense in which talk of thoughts presupposes the existence of thinkers. But similarly, any talk of mental states presupposes the existence of thinkers; yet this does not by itself establish that psychology is mind-dependent in a sense that compromises objectivity.

Saying that I want to avoid such projectivism, however, heightens the worry that my sufficient condition for causation is circular. If *ceteris paribus* laws support explanations, events are covered by such laws only when they are related as cause to effect. Neuralists will say that mental events can be causes only if they are neural events. So it can seem question-begging to use intentional cp laws in defending event dualism. But recall that our question is how mental causation is possible, not whether mental events are causes. The debate between neuralists and event dualists pre-supposes a positive answer to the latter question. So while it is true that mentalistic laws provide explanations only if mental events are causes, both sides get to assume that this condition is met. At any rate, *if* event dualists are begging a question here, this is hardly worse than insisting that intentional explanation requires the truth of neuralism. Hence, I see no special difficulty for event dualists on this point.

Still, a legitmate concern remains. As Mackie (1974: 20) notes, we are inclined to think that some objective feature distinguishes causal from non-causal sequences, *and* that this feature is 'an intrinsic feature of each causal sequence'. This inclination, which I do not challenge, conflicts with proposals according to which causation holds between events in virtue of these events being locatable in certain *patterns* of regularity (describable in non-causal terms). But I have said that intentional explanations, or at least those that invoke the practical syllogism, involve covering-laws; and part of my reason for saying this was that such explanations involve locating a particular action in a rationalizing pattern. If the acquisition of a belief causes a trying that causes some bodily motion B, the mental events are not mere causes of B; they *rationalize* B. And it is plausible that citing reasons is explanatory, at least in part, because events of the relevant intentional types fall into certain patterns (like those characterized by the practical syllogism).

In one sense, this feature of intentional explanation is innocuous: to acquire a belief is (*inter alia*) to be the subject of an event relevantly like other events that other agents have been the subjects of. Nonetheless, appeal to generalizations in a proposal about causation is bound to raise the following disjunctive suspicion (cf. the discussion in Chapter 4 of explanatory asymmetry): individual cause–effect pairs are treated as such, only because they constitute a pattern of regularity described by the generalizations; or the generalizations are mere summaries of particular instances of causation (i.e. 'F $\to$ G' just says that instances of F cause instances of G). If the first disjunct is correct, it seems that we must treat as illusory our view that each causal sequence exhibits an *intrinsic* feature distinguishing it from non-causal sequences (and so the illusion will have to be explained, perhaps by appeal to psychological mechanisms of the sort Hume posited). If the second disjunct is correct, my proposed sufficient condition for causation does not *explain how* mental causation is possible, since a law would just *say* that its instances are related as cause to effect.[2]

I need a third option. The trick is to show how cp laws can be non-trivially related to causation, without saying that what it *is* for one event to cause another is for the events to be suitably related (perhaps by virtue of belonging to a certain pattern) to still *other* events, and without treating laws as mere summaries of their causal instances (on pain of making the defence of event dualism circular).

I.2

In this context, it will be useful to focus on a question rightly emphasized by Hume: where do our ideas of 'power', 'force', 'compulsion', 'necessary connection', (and so on) come from? Like Strawson, I think Hume too quickly dismissed a possible answer: our experience of 'exerting physical force on physical things or having force exerted on us by physical things'. It takes a little care to say *what* we experience in such cases—as when we lift a heavy suitcase, or get pushed aside by someone hurrying past. But it is very plausible that our experiences of such causal transactions play an important role in shaping our views about causation. Of course, we do not restrict our idea of force

> to those mechanical transactions, the pushings and pullings, in which we our-selves, or our fellows, are engaged as agents or patients. We extend the idea to all such transactions. . . . In a great boulder rolling down the mountainside and flat-tening the wooden hut in its path we see an exemplary instance of force.

Moreover, these mechanical transactions (or 'manifestations of force') provide examples of

> natural relations, which, whether entered into by animate or inanimate beings, are directly observable (or experienceable) and which being observed (or experi-enced) or appropriately reported, supply wholly satisfactory explanations of their outcomes, of the state of affairs in which they terminate. (Strawson 1985: 123)

---

[2] In my (1994), I did not do nearly enough to dispel this worry. Mackie argues that Hume conflates two alleged senses in which causal connections involve necessity: necessity-1, which distinguishes causal from non-causal sequences; and necessity-2, which provides the alleged warrant for an a priori inference from cause to effect. I am inclined to follow Mackie in saying that our concept of causation demands necessity-1, but not necessity-2. Belief in necessity-2 is arguably an illusion, fostered by the following mistaken idea that the occurrence of a cause renders the effect *intelligible* in a very strong sense: if we knew the intrinsic characters of the events, we would see that the effect *must* follow the cause, in the sense that it would be *inconceivable* for something with the cause's nature not to be followed by something with effect's nature. And a certain kind of empiricist will see explanation as intelligibility *in this sense*. But appeal to cp-laws delivers only necessity-1.

I emphasize the two related points: we often observe (or experience) instances of causation; and we can often cite the occurrence of a cause in explaining the occurrence of its effect, without adverting to any further component of explanation, like a covering law. As Strawson puts it (ibid. 121), explanation often 'rests directly on observable relations in nature'. (In a similar vein, Woodward (1984) speaks of 'singular explanation', to capture the idea that sometimes the occurrence of a cause can explain the occurrence of its effect without further ado.) In the rest of this section, I elaborate on these twin points; Section 2 includes a suggestion about how laws enter the picture, given that the natural relation of causation is often an observable basis for explanation.

For simplicity, I speak of *seeing* instances of causation. But in this context, 'see' should be understood broadly, to cover a variety of non-inferential means of forming judgements—including, perhaps, certain judgements about own's mental events. I do not insist that thinkers can see one event cause another, as opposed to *seeing that* one event caused another (if there is a difference). But either way, one might resist the claim on semantic grounds. For the surface form of a typical perceptual report relates a *person* and an event (not two events), as in 'Nick saw Nora lift the suitcase.' Strawson takes this to show that we observe manifestations of causal powers, or exercises of an individual's *capacities*. I have no objection to this characterization of what we see. It can be useful to describe what Nora does, when she lifts the suitcase, as the manifestation of a capacity Nora has. But one can also say that we see liftings and pushings. In the formal mode, event sortals like 'lift' and 'push' belong to the observation vocabulary. Recall that the logical form of 'N_1 see N_2 lift the N_3' is:

$$\exists e \exists f \{ \text{Seeing}(e) \;\&\; \text{Agent}(e, N_1) \;\&\; \text{Theme}(e, f) \;\&\; \text{Lifting}(f) \;\&\;$$
$$\text{Agent}(f, N_2) \;\&\; \text{Patient}(f, \text{the } N_3) \}.$$

Indeed, we often see liftings *as* liftings—complex events (grounded by actions) whose parts stand in certain causal relations. So the semantics of perceptual reports does not conflict with the claim that we see instances of causation. Suppose one sees a complex event, whose parts include a bodily motion and some effect of that motion, *as* a complex event. Then one sees the bodily motion *as* a cause of the effect in question. This is especially clear with regard to event sortals like 'move' and 'raise'. If Nick sees Nora move$_T$ the suitcase, then Nick sees a complex event that culminates in a moving$_I$ (i.e. a motion) of the suitcase, and Nick sees some motion of Nora as a cause of the suitcase's motion. If Nick sees Nora raise the flag, then Nick sees a complex event that culminates in a rising of the flag, and Nick sees some motion of Nora as a cause of the flag's rising.[3] Similar points

[3] Nick also sees the suitcase's motion as having an intentional cause. But for now, I just want to show that seeing a moving$_T$ of y (as such) involves seeing some cause of y's motion

apply to 'push' and 'pull', even if these verbs are not semantically analysed as causatives.

I have no objection to saying that we often see the actions/tryings of others. But even if we do not, and thus do not see instances of causation involving the tryings of others, a thinker does not normally infer what she herself is trying to do. It seems that a thinker can see—or experience, or at least judge without engaging in theoretical reasoning that invokes gener-alizations—instances of causation involving her own tryings. In raising one's arm, one may not experience an isolatable event recognized as the mental cause of the arm-rising. But one experiences the raising, not just the rising of one's arm. I am not merely aware of a bodily motion isolated from its intentional causes; I know, and not by theoretical means, that *I raised* my arm. So an experience of 'exerting physical force on physical things' would seem to an experience *of* a complex event: the process of a trying having its effects on one's body; where the relevant bodily motion will have its own effects—including further effects on the body, like felt resistance from the object on which force is exerted.[4]

Such claims will not go unchallenged. A certain kind of empiricist will deny that we ever see instances of causation. He will insist that all we ever *see* is that certain events stand in certain acausal relations, which may indi-cate that the events fall into certain patterns of regularity. On this view, we always *infer* that two events are related as cause to effect, at least if we are not just guessing. Such an empiricist is likely to have a thesis about what it is *possible* to see. And one might well be suspicious that his thesis will be incompatible with the facts about what we do see. That is, one might have less confidence in the empiricist's thesis than in the claim that we do see

(as such). And I assume that one can see a Φ as a Φ without being aware of what is involved in so seeing a Φ.

[4] A certain scepticism about the inner might lead one to insist that the experience of rais-ing one's arm is only an experience of some bodily motion, but so much the worse for such scepticism. Note that the 'immediacy of inner sense' does not require infallibility or strange causal mechanisms. It requires only that our epistemic relation to some of our mental events be relevantly like our epistemic relation to observable external events. For reasons discussed in Ch. I (Sect. 1.3), one can allow that a thinker in the presence of an apple often sees the apple, without saying that (i) the thinker infers the presence of the apple from a prior judgement that there *seems* to be an apple, or (ii) the thinker is an infallible apple detector. One can identify seeings with seemings, while allowing for misleading seemings—i.e. events intrinsically like the event of seeing an apple, but in the absence of apples. Similarly, when a thinker tries to Φ, she may often see that she tried to Φ, where her seeing (that she tried to Φ) is also its seeming to her that she tried to Φ—even though on other occasions it might seem to her that she tried to Φ when she didn't. One might also judge that one tried to Φ by theoretical means if the usual (non-inferential) means of such judg-ing is unavailable. An 'unconscious' trying might be like a hidden apple: something whose presence can be detected, but not by just looking. In any case, one can resist excessive claims about inner sense, without saying that our epistemic relation to our own mental events is *less* secure than our epistemic relation to external events.

instances of causation. This is not to deny that the empiricist can, like the sceptic discussed in the Introduction, present us with a puzzle. Indeed, like the sceptic, the empiricist will emphasize the possibility of error. It *seems* that I lifted the suitcase. But perhaps I am the victim of a ruse: the suitcase was moved via an unseen string and I have been drugged to have the experience of a resisting force. Given the possibility of such error, various epistemological questions present themselves. But it does not follow that when I *do* lift a suitcase, I *infer* that the motion of the suitcase is caused by the motion of my arm. And prima facie, I do not infer that the motion of my arm has a causal antecedent in me (see n. 4). Luckily, though, defending my suspicion of contrary views may not be necessary for present purposes.

The imagined empiricist is likely to end up denying that causation is a natural relation, and/or endorsing a form of scepticism about causal relations (that will be no sharper with respect to mental events than with respect to other events). But many of us want to avoid such drastic conclusions; and in trying to show that a certain view of causation is acceptable, I am speaking to us. *We* should not deny that we see instances of causation, if such denial apparently leads to either projectivism or scepticism. Still, that is not much of an argument. So let me put the point this way. I will try to show that my proposal does not slight the objectivity of causal relations, *given* that we often see instances of causation. If someone does not grant this, but still thinks that my proposal slights the objectivity of causal relations, I can only suggest that he will have a hard time getting his intuitions about causation to hang together (without making causation into a metaphysical mystery). The challenge for the empiricist is to show how thinkers who lack any observable paradigms of causation could ever make trustworthy causal judgements, and to show this while also characterizing causal relations in a way that reveals why my proposal fails to properly capture their mind-independence. And I think this challenge is serious enough to motivate the alternative line of thought pursued below. (If it can be established that we can see instances of causation involving action only if neuralism is true, that would undermine my defence of event dualism. But I do not see how this could be established.)

I.3

If we do (and hence can) see instances of causation, this has an important implication for explanation. A thinker who sees an instance of causation can often cite the occurrence of the cause to explain the occurrence of the effect, *without* locating the relevant events in a pattern of regularity.

As I noted above, precisely because our observation vocabulary contains so many sortals for complex events grounded by actions, many explanations couched in terms of observable events do not cite a literal cause of the specified effect. Often, we cite a complex event that culminates with the very event whose occurrence is to be explained. But when we say that Nora *lifted* the suitcase and *put* it on the rack, we explain why the location of the suitcase changed, by reference to the *ground* of a complex event that has the suitcase's motion as a proper part. Many explanations take this form. Why did the window break$_I$? Nora broke$_T$ it. Why did her arm rise$_I$? She raised$_T$ it.[5] Indeed, our ability to see instances of causation may well be inseparable from our ability to classify events with sortals for complex events grounded by actions. In representing the world as containing events like liftings, we view the world as containing certain causal-explanatory connections. And I see no reason to suppose that this view is based on some acausal way of representing events.

This is not to say that *all* explanations in terms of 'perceived causation' cite complex events. Where non-persons are concerned, considerations of the sort discussed at the end of Chapter 1 are relevant. One can explain why a window broke$_I$ by saying that a rock broke$_T$ it. If Nick can see Nora break$_T$ a window, Nick can see a rock break$_T$ the window. But recall that if the rock broke$_T$ the window, the rock is the Agent of a breaking$_I$, not a breaking$_T$ grounded by an action/trying; the rock does not *act*. Correspondingly, there is more than one way to be an Agent. A rock is the Agent of a breaking$_I$ if it is the most *actor-like* participant in an event that causes the breaking$_I$. The extension of 'Agent' goes beyond the prototypical cases of persons, who bring about effects by acting/trying, to include other *salient initiators* of events. Similar remarks apply to Strawson's example of a boulder flattening a hut.

A common feature of these explanations, whether or not they involve complex events, is that they do not rely on generalizations that cover the particular instances of causation. (This is to be expected if such explanations are reflected in how we talk about events.) Even if there are laws about what happens to windows or suitcases in certain circumstances, this is irrelevant to the explanations given; the effect's occurrence is rendered comprehensible without adverting to any such laws (see Woodward 1984). Yet far from being defective or somehow second-class, these explanations are paradigmatic examples of rendering event occurrences comprehensible. If a thinker sees that C causes E, then a fortiori some singular event thought about C explains some singular event thought about E. If one sees that C causes E, one can think about C as the cause of E; that is, one can think about C so that its occurrence renders the occurrence of E comprehensible (in the sense of comprehensibility associated with causal expla-

---

[5] If Nora broke$_T$ the window, it *follows* that the window broke$_I$. And the presence of a semantic or logical connection does not preclude a causal connection: drinking plays a causal role in a drunken brawl; and the sun plays a causal role in sunburn (see e.g. Davidson (1963); Fodor (1975)).

nation). And in one sense, there can be no better explanations than those associated with perceived causation. There may be other explanations, which cite laws and/or underlying mechanisms that are more theoretically satisfying. But if one sees a cause of E as a cause of E, the occurrence of E is thereby rendered comprehensible; one knows why event E occurred.

2. The Extension of Causation

I have said that we often see instances of causation, and that when we do so, we can cite the cause in explaining the effect without further ado. If *all* explanations were like this, one might conclude that explanations are representations of antecedently given causal relations between events. That is, if *all* instances of causation were perceivable, one might conclude that our concept of causation is importantly prior to our concept of explanation; for of necessity, explanatory judgements would rely on causal judgements, but not vice versa. From this perspective, it will seem misleading at best to characterize the natural relation of causation in terms of explanation (involving singular event thoughts). The intentional relation of explanation will seem like a hybrid notion, factorizable into two components: a singular causal claim, whose truth can be perceived, or at least determined independently of distinctively explanatory concerns; and the epistemic residue—the ways of thinking about the relevant events, which may contribute to our *understanding* of causal relations. For when we do cite a law that covers a cause-effect pair $<C, E>$, one might think that we are really explaining *why C caused E*, and not E's occurrence (which is explained by the occurrence of C). But this factorizing view can and should be resisted.[6] While perceived instances of causation are paradigmatic instances of causation and explanation, it is not irrelevant that our concepts of causation and explanation extend beyond their paradigmatic (perceivable) instances.

2.1

Obviously, not all instances of causation are perceived. Nor is it plausible that all such instances are perceivable, even restricting attention to cases of (more or less) proximate causation. Some events are not open to view if only because many events involve very small objects. But in the context of showing how instances of mental causation can be instances of *causation*, it is worth stressing how grasping the concept of a person can lead any one

---

[6] *Pace* Kim (1988*a*), who provides helpful discussion of these issues. Compare Quine's (1953*a*) warning against factorizing meaning into convention and empirical content.

person to recognize that many instances of causation will go unperceived by her—and hence that the natural relation of causation has instances that go unperceived by any one person.

In Chapter 5, I reviewed Strawson's (1958) argument that our concept of person is primitive. A person is not the union of two things, but a special sort of individual, who can (justifiably, or at least not unjustifiably) self-ascribe mental traits without basing such ascriptions on evidence of the sort that would typically be required to justify a third-person ascription of the same traits. If someone says 'Nora believes that Fido barked' or 'I believe that Fido barked', the speaker ascribes the same property to the same sort of individual. In the course of discussing this point, Strawson draws attention to the fact that many *action* predicates, like 'writing a letter', have the following feature: they apply only to persons whose bodily motions have a certain sort of mental cause; they are typically ascribed to others on the basis of observable cues; yet one typically ascribes them to oneself without basing the ascription on such cues. One may have to infer that someone else is writing a letter. But as noted above, a person typically knows what she is up to. One does not typically *infer* (by means of generalizations) that one is trying to write a letter, or that one's hand motion has a mental cause. Again, many sortals for complex events belong to the observation vocabulary. Among the instances of causation a person perceives are some instances involving her tryings. And when one recognizes another person as another person, one recognizes her as the sort of thing that typically knows what she is up to.

Suppose that, on the basis of observable cues, Nick infers that Nora is writing a letter.[7] Then Nick should also conclude that, barring atypical circumstances, Nora is in a position to say of herself (independently of the observable cues) that she is writing a letter. Nick will not know what Nora is up to in the same way that Nora does. Even if Nick does not just *see* the trying that grounds the complex event of Nora's writing, Nick should allow that if Nora is writing a letter, then one of her tryings figures in an instance of causation that *she* can see. In general, given our concept of a person (and the semantics of action sentences), each person should allow for instances of (mental) causation that *he* cannot see. So while our conception of causation is importantly shaped by observable instances—the paradigmatic cases being (observable portions of) complex events that satisfy sortals used in describing actions—the fact that actions figure prominently in our thinking about causation already ensures that our concept of causation has an extension that goes beyond observable instances.

---

[7] Even if Nick can sometimes just see that Nora is writing a letter, and see the trying that is Nora's action, there will be other occasions on which Nick has to 'figure out' what Nora is doing.

Of course, any instance of causation must be *relevantly like* perceived instances, since all cause-effect pairs are instances of the same natural relation. Correspondingly, every instance of one singular thought explaining another is *relevantly like* instances of the explanatory relation that obtains between certain facts about events perceived as standing in a causal relation. In one sense, this is obvious. In another sense, much more needs to be said about how a thinker can begin to make (justified, or least not unjustified) causal judgements that go beyond her experience. We can label this phenomenon, by saying that thinkers engage in *theoretical* reasoning. As Strawson (1985: 125) remarks, using Sellarsian language:

To a first approximation, the search for causal theories is a search for modes of action and reaction which are not observable at the ordinary level (or not observable at all, but postulated or hypothesized) and which we find intelligible because we model them on, or think of them on analogy with, these various modes of action and reaction which experience presents to gross observation or which we are conscious of engaging in, or suffering, ourselves.

This is still a description of the phenomenon. But it points to a more substantive account, by suggesting (plausibly) that *theories* can relate us to unperceived instances of causation in a way that counts as analogous to the way that our perceptual capacities relate us to perceived instances of causation. At this point, I may be going beyond Strawson's intentions. But I read him as suggesting that we can understand what it is for an unperceived instance of causation to be relevantly like a perceived instance—and thus understand what unifies the various instances of causation as instances of a single natural relation—in terms of the theoretical tools we use in providing good explanations.[8] And I argued in Chapter 4 that one form of good explanation involves subsuming events under *ceteris paribus* laws. Since this is the main idea of this chapter, let me go slowly here.

The fact that causation and explanation go hand-in-hand does *not* show that one of these notions is somehow reducible (or always prior) to the other. Explanatory claims may ride piggy-back on causal claims, when the instances of causation are perceived. But we need not say this about instances of causation that go unperceived. On the contrary, I think this would make matters more mysterious than they need to be; that is, it would add to the difficulty of saying how theoretical reasoning could ever carry us (by analogies of the sort Strawson gestures at) beyond our own experience to anything like the range of causal judgements that we make.

---

[8] But I do not say that *only* theories so relate us to unperceived instances of causation. Unperceived instances of causation are like perceived instances, in being instances of causation. But this does not explain how we go beyond our own experience in making causal judgements without merely guessing.

When we correctly *infer* that one event causes another, this is often because
we have correctly judged that relevant facts stand in an explanatory relation. This is not a mere piece of psychology if there is no gap between (i)
certain facts standing in an explanatory relation, and (ii) the corresponding events being related as cause to effect. And there is no gap if the relevant concepts of causation and explanation are linked in the following
way: the former concept applies to pairs of events not perceived as
instances of causation, given which facts explain which.

   The idea is that the extension of our concept of causation is partly determined by the extension of our concept of explanation (since some
instances of causation are unperceived), even though the extension of the
latter concept is partly determined by the extension of the former (since
some instances of causation are perceived). While perceived causation
yields a paradigmatic form of explanation, our concept of explanation is
not limited to this non-theoretical kind of comprehensibility; we can and
do explain occurrences of events in other ways. In particular, one important way of rendering an event occurrence comprehensible is by citing
another event and a law that covers the events in question. On the traditional covering-law model, explanation via nomic subsumption involves
locating a given pair of events in a pattern of *strict* regularity. But I have
suggested that the occurrence of C explains the occurrence of E, making
it appropriate to infer that the former event caused the latter if <C, E> is
a Normal instance of a *ceteris paribus* law. Such explanation requires that
C and E be tokens of types that are nomically related. But not every token
of C's type must be paired with a token of E's type. It suffices that, for
every token of C's type, *either* it is paired with a token of E's type *or* there
is an (interfering factor) explanation for why not.

   That said, my view is not that locating events in *mere* patterns of regularity warrants causal claims. Again, it must be plausible that each alleged
instance of causation is like perceived instances; the same natural relation
must obtain between the relevant events. And events can belong to a pattern of regularity without being related as cause to effect. But a Normal
instance of a cp law is not a mere instance of some regularity (expressible
with lawlike predicates); it is an instance (in the absence of uncancelled
interference) of a nomic pattern of regularity, all of whose Abnormal
instances can be explained by citing interfering factors. Moreover, in
Chapter 4, I argued that *ceteris paribus* laws exhibit the asymmetry one
expects to find in generalizations that back singular causal claims. So
absent counter-examples, I think it is at least plausible that Normal
instances of cp laws are relevantly like instances of perceived causation.
Moreover, in focusing on nomic subsumption, I am *not* denying that other
theoretical forms of explanation can support singular causal claims. For
all I have said, other sufficient conditions for explanation (and thus

causation) are possible. I return to this point below, though for now, my claim is just that event occurrences can be explained via cp laws.

2.2

Even if this is true, though, one might wonder how appeal to cp laws can help account for mental causation. Laws are typically associated with changes in unobservable (or postulated) entities. But mental events are changes in persons. Moreover, on my own view, a person typically sees her own tryings; that is, a person typically knows what she is up to, without inferring this from observable cues. Similarly, one does not usually infer one's own reasons for action, especially not by noticing that one's actions are covered by a generalization. When Nora raises her arm, she can usually just tell why she did so.[9] In describing *others* as acting for reasons, the describer may posit causes that she does not see (and which are seen by at most one observer); and one's own reasons seem different from other perceived causes, since the characteristic experience of exerting a force (as when lifting a suitcase) is missing, when the onslaught of a belief causes a trying. Nonetheless, one does not usually invoke *generalizations* in explaining behaviour, especially not one's own. So even if I am right about how laws are related to mental causes, how does this help the event dualist?

It is tempting to reply, by treating all claims of the form 'Nora Φ'd because she wanted Ψ' as abbreviations for longer claims involving the practical syllogism. And there is independent merit in the idea that 'folk' explanations often reflect tacit theorizing (see Carruthers and Smith 1996). But my claim is that intentional cp laws support explanations that we could give, not that we regularly appeal to such laws in giving intentional explanations. So I need not say that *all* mental explanation relies on subsuming actions under (perhaps unstated) generalizations. Rationalizing the behaviour of others may require seeing their actions as belonging to more general rationalizing patterns. But if Nora explains why she raised her arm by saying 'I wanted to buy the painting', her claim is not obviously a stylistic variant on a third-person report noting that Nora is

---

[9] The ambiguity of 'tell' is intended. If Nora's judgement about why she raised her hand is typical, it will be non-inferential. And if her report of why she raised her hand is taken to be sincere, it will also be taken as authoritative in a way that third-person reports are not, even if Nora does not (and cannot) provide further evidence. But again, this does not imply that Nora is an infallible judge of her reasons; see n. 4 above. If some explanations rest entirely on observable relations in nature, perhaps some rest on relations observable only by the subject of the explanation. (Again, it is not implausible that our concept of a person ensures that the reasons and actions/tryings of others are relevantly like our own mental causes; one might say that having the concept of a person makes one a proto-theorizer.)

someone who acted on a certain means-end belief.[10] And while I think there are cp laws like 'if an adult human tries to raise her arm, her arm rises', my claim is not that one *must* rely on such generalizations in rationalizing bodily motions. Prima facie, Nora need not rely on a covering law if she explains why her arm rose by saying 'Because I raised it'.

If only to be clear about this, suppose that the intentional explanations we usually *give* do not rely (even tacitly) on any generalizations, and suppose that these 'bare' explanations are none the worse for being anomic in this sense. Then the fact that Nora acquired a certain belief explains why she tried to raise her arm, which explains why her arm rose, *whether or not* any laws cover the relevant events. But if there are such laws, facts about mental causes can also satisfy a sufficient condition for explanation stated in terms of laws. If citing mental causes is explanatory *absent* mentalistic laws, citing such laws may not deepen our explanations (or improve our predictive capabilities). Yet even if a law is uninteresting in this sense, it can do the kind of work I ask of it. For my goal is to provide a non-neuralistic account of mental causation, in part by appealing to covering laws, not to deepen our explanations of particular events. This raises the question, though, of why I appeal to cp laws at all.

If one can explain the occurrence of bodily motions by citing actions/tryings, whose occurrence can be explained by citing other mental events, can't event dualists move straight to the corresponding causal claims (without any song and dance about cp laws)? Even if instances of mental causation turn out to be covered by mentalistic laws, one might think that event dualists can (and hence should) avoid commitments to such laws if they are going to allow for mental explanations that do not *require* covering laws. But event dualists cannot just assume that facts about mental events are explanatory, whether or not mental events are neural events, even though it would be equally question-begging to just assume that facts about mental events are explanatory only if neuralism is true. For as we shall see, our *success* in giving theoretical explanations— and in discovering hidden causes—suggests an argument for neuralism. My response to this argument trades on the claim that rationalizing causes are covered by intentional laws, even if we do not cite such laws in giving rationalizing explanations.

2.3

I have said that, in terms of rendering the occurrence of event E comprehensible, one cannot do better than seeing an event C as a cause of E. But

---

[10] And *perhaps* some intentional explanations directed at others involve 'simulation'— where this is not another way of describing the application of a generalization that subsumes oneself and others. (See the essays in Stone and Davies (1996) for discussion.)

this leaves open the possibility that theorizing might have led to the claim that C caused E. And even if this instance of causation is perceived, theorizing might provide a deeper account of why E occurred, in part by describing C and E as tokens of types foreign to our means of perceiving events. This is not idle speculation. Where impersonal events are concerned, we have had amazing (if not universal) success in our theorizing. This makes it plausible that every instance of causation discoverable by us, and so every perceivable instance, is potentially within the scope of our theorizing. *Perhaps* we are 'tuned in' to causal connections that theorizing could not reveal to us. But I do not challenge the following thought: if we see that C caused E, there is a theoretical explanation—an explanation that does *not* rest entirely on the perceivable causal relation between C and E—that relates a fact about C to a fact about E. In this sense, our concept of explanation does not merely extend our concept of causation beyond perceptible instances. The theoretical means we use to go beyond our experience of causation are (or at least present themselves as being) *universal*, in that they also apply to the perceivable instances of causation.

At this point, premisses about theorizing can lead to dramatic metaphysical conclusions. For example, suppose the only legitimate explanatory tool is the strict law—or that every instance of a genuinely explanatory law must be covered by a strict law. Then every instance of causation, including those involving our own actions, is covered by some strict law. In my view, there is no reason to endorse this very restrictive premiss about legitimate theorizing, once we allow for (and see the need for) cp laws. But other restrictions lead to similar consequences. In particular, one might hold that the only legitimate explanatory tools are laws characterizable in non-intentional terms. On this view, mental causes would have to satisfy non-mental descriptions; and one could not show otherwise by appealing to explanations based on the practical syllogism, since it would be denied that such explanations are theoretical in the relevant sense. Stated so baldly, this begs the question against event dualists. But there is a strong intuition that theoretical explanations must be *impersonal*. And doesn't it follow from this that explanatory laws cover only events describable in impersonal terms?

This can make it seem that event dualists must either (i) insist that theorizing does *not* have the universal scope alluded to above, since mental causes lie outside its scope, or (ii) find an explanatory tool *other than laws* that can bring mental causes within the scope of theorizing. I see no plausible way of taking the second path, although this may be due to lack of imagination. And the first path, at least as described above, just bypasses a tension that we want to resolve. Similarly, it does no good to stipulate that intentional explanations are theoretical. We need to see how such explanations are *relevantly like* other theoretical explanations. This does not show that dualists cannot profitably pursue either of the two paths just mentioned. But my job is not to argue against other possible defences of event dualism. If it can be defended in several ways, so much the better.[11] My strategy, though, is to challenge the idea that intentional generalizations are not relevantly theoretical.

Here, it is crucial that one distinguish two senses of 'impersonal'. In Chapter 5, I used the term so that an event counts as impersonal only if it can be described without bringing a person (with her perspective and reasons) onto the scene. In this sense, laws characterized in rationalizing terms are not impersonal, given event dualism. A slightly different usage, though, is more closely connected to our notion of impartiality and the detached third-person perspective. Intentional cp laws can be impersonal, or objective, in this sense. Such laws apply to all persons; to grasp such laws is to see that they apply to all persons, oneself included. (First-person intentional explanations may not be impersonal in this sense; but as I have stressed, given our concept of a person, we each take our own experience to be generalizable.) So event dualists can grant that laws must be impersonal in this second sense.

By appealing to intentional laws, event dualists can thus grant that all causes are locatable from a theoretical (third-person) perspective in at least one important sense of 'theoretical'. On this view, principles of 'folk psychology' have an intellectual role to play, whether or not they deepen our explanations of particular event occurrences. Generalizations like the practical syllogism are abstractions over particular cases; they reflect (and give content to) the idea that any one action can be *relevantly like* many other causes. And given intentional cp *laws*, there is a substantive unity to instances of causation, even if mental events are not neural events. If causes are locatable from a theoretical perspective—if they belong to the 'space of law' (see McDowell 1994)—then mental events are *in this important sense* like causes describable without reference to persons.

There are other senses of 'theoretical'—related to other hallmarks of paradigmatic sciences (yielding quantifiable predictions, locatability within a broadly reductionistic framework, etc.)—in which intentional generalizations are not theoretical, or at least not obviously so. Dualists cannot concede that all causes lie within the scope of our theorizing in all these other senses. But I do not know of any *argument* that makes this an embarrassment. At this point, it may help to think of event dualism as an attempt to reconcile the Sellarsian manifest and scientific images, where a

---

[11] In particular, Rudder-Baker (1995) and Hornsby (1997) appear to reject neuralism (if not quite in these terms), while taking the first path, though Rudder-Baker's defence of a counterfactual approach to causation might be read as a (rather tendentious) proposal about how to go down the second path. But despite my sympathies with these authors, I still suspect that they fail to address an important source of motivation for neuralism.

reconciliation shows how the latter image emerges from *but does not displace* the former, even if the scientific image provides a view of the world that is complete in its own terms.

Sellars himself held that 'In the dimension of describing and explaining the world, science is the measure of all things, of what is that it is, and of what is not that it is not' (1963: 173). On this view, the manifest image can survive the successes of the scientific image only if the particulars presented in the former are locatable in the latter. Now if science includes all impartial generalizations—i.e. given a broad notion of science that includes intentional cp laws, whether or not neuralism is true—I have no objection to this kind of identity thesis: mental causes *are* causes locatable from within a theoretical perspective. But one might have (and I think Sellars had) in mind a more demanding notion of science according to which scientific generalizations are formulable without rationalizing terminology. Or one might characterize science in terms of a unity of science hypothesis, according to which intentional generalizations are scientific only if intentional properties satisfy some substantive constraint (e.g. that they be truth functions of properties reducible to physical properties). It can seem that rationalizing causes must be scientifically accessible causes in some such demanding sense of 'science'.

In this context, one often hears a story according to which prescientific thinkers viewed nature in *personal* terms: the wind wanted such and such; the trees believed that thus and so; Zeus was angry, but could be placated, etc. The idea is that our ancestors described—as we are often tempted to describe—various *im*personal phenomena as the products of reasons. This overextension of intentional explanation (and the concept of a person) precluded a serious understanding of nature; scientific progress has consisted in replacing rationalization with non-intentional ways of rendering comprehensible what happens around us. The scope of the manifest image has thus been greatly reduced. Metaphors aside, we now regard intentional explanations as being applicable only to a small portion of the universe—the individuals we now regard as persons, and only some of the events in which persons participate. One might take this as a success story. Rationalizing explanation was once overextended; now we have a better grip on its proper place. But the story is often told apocalyptically: on the latter day, true science will judge the manifest image, which will be saved or damned.

Either the scope of the manifest image will be reduced to nothing, and we will come to see that *all* putative intentional explanations were at best stand-ins to be replaced by scientific explanations, with the result that our very conception of ourselves as persons is undermined; or the manifest image will be vindicated when we see that reasons and actions are visible through the lens of the scientific image, despite initial appearances to the contrary. A philosopher who fears (or hopes for) the damnation ending will not say that rationalizing explanations are fine as they are; such complacency would amount to ignoring the very challenge that scientific progress presents to persons who conceive of themselves as persons. From this perspective, there is a sense in which we must earn the right to retain our view that reasons are causes, given that so many causes have turned out not to be reasons. But at no point have I seriously entertained the prospect that reasons are not causes. (This risks charges of complacency, rather like the charges I would be inclined to level against someone who saw no need to show *how* mental causes are relevantly like unperceived non-intentional causes.)

My view is not, however, that one can reconcile the manifest and scientific images without philosophical *work*. I have just suggested a different kind of reconciliation, according to which our concepts of causation and explanation have paradigmatic instances describable *only* with the intentional/rationalizing language of the manifest image, although the same concepts apply to events and facts describable from an arational point of view. If such a reconciliation can be given, one cannot insist that the real problem will remain, until reasons are shown to be causes that can be posited from within a wholly impersonal framework. If reasons and actions figure crucially in our thinking about causation, as I suggest, the mere fact that we have seemed to see reasons where there were none is no basis for doubting that reasons are among the actual causes.

Defending dualism can, however, seem like defending the last bastion of the spooky. Why should minds resist incorporation into a scientific conception of the world that contains us? But competing considerations about the nature of persons suggest an answer. Reasons are causes of a special sort, not apt for impersonal description. Such causes are still relevant to the scientific image, though. For without reasons, there would be no *descriptions*—much less confirmed scientific descriptions—of anything. (See Sellars (1963) on the methodological priority of the manifest image.)

2.4

I have made various claims about how causation and explanation are related, as part of an attempt to offer a view that coheres with my claims about mental causation. But of necessity, this discussion has been rather abstract. So let me try to summarize it with a picture. The suggestion is that we have concepts of causation and explanation that are interwoven, as indicated in Figure 7.1. We have a concept of causation that is a concept of a relation between events, and a concept of explanation that is a concept of a relation between facts. Instances of perceived causation provide paradigmatic examples of both relations; to see a cause of E *as* a cause of

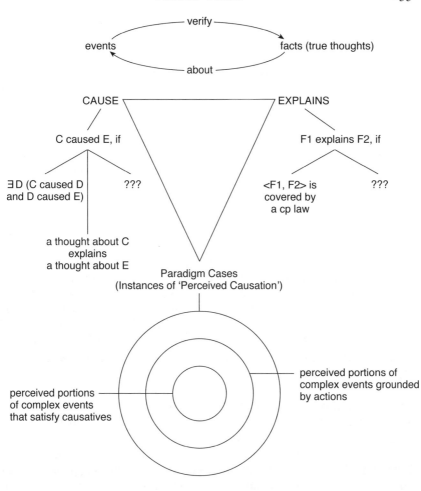

FIG. 7.1

E is to see why E occurred. An important subset of these paradigmatic cases are picked out by event sortals for complex events; and an important subset of these sortals are causatives like 'move$_T$', 'melt$_T$', and 'break$_T$'. But these verbs can also apply to events not grounded by actions (as when a rock breaks$_T$ a window). Correspondingly, not all instances of perceived causation are parts of complex events grounded by actions. This is not the only way, however, in which the concept of causation goes beyond cases involving action.

For one thing, causation is a transitive relation. More interestingly, the concept of causation is apt for application *via the concept of explanation* to event-pairs not perceived as instances of causation, where the relevant forms of explanation relate thoughts about event-pairs that are analogous to other event-pairs taken to be instances of causation. (This is at once a constraint on explanation and a claim about the nature of the analogy between perceived and unperceived instances of causation.) Assuming that covering laws support explanations, event-pairs covered by a law are instances of the same (natural, extensional) relation as every other instance of causation—from instances involving actions, to unobservable cases discovered by our best sciences. Finally, I have added the proposal that cp laws are laws, and that a Normal instance of a cp law is an explanatory instance.[12]

3. Forms of Causation

Even if one is sympathetic to the idea that intentional explanations are metaphysically neutral, with respect to the nature of mental events, it is not hard to think that my proposal involves some sleight of hand. For if M is a (non-neural) mental cause of some bodily motion B, which has some neural cause N, how can the *same natural* relation be instanced by <M, B> and <N, B>? I can just repeat: causation is the extensionalization of explanation; and mental explanations do not presuppose neuralism. But one might think that event dualism treats 'causation' as a label for a family of *different* explanatory relations (and thus treats causation as a *projected* relation). If neuralism is false, the relation between a reason and an action certainly seems different from (say) the relation between two topplings of dominoes. Indeed, I have said that causation in the presence of freedom is special, and that this is reason to be suspicious of neuralism. But it can also seem that event dualism fragments our notion of causation. Once again, a bald statement of this concern would be question-begging. Still, worries about the naturalness of causation are connected to the idea that event dualism will leave effects of mental causes *overdetermined*; and one might think that despite my claims in Chapter 6, concerns about overdetermination must have a role to play in arguing against dualism. So it will be useful to focus on an old anti-dualist argument that brings out this connection.

---

[12] And perhaps there are other sufficient conditions (not discussed here) for causation and or explanation. To say that our concepts have this contour is *not* to deny that tensions can arise. In a given case, it may seem that a thought about C explains a thought about E, though it seems that C does not cause E. In such cases, one appearance or the other has to give. If there were many such cases, that would be reason for doubting that our concepts have the suggested contour; or perhaps it would be reason for thinking that our concepts were somehow defective. But that is not our situation—at least not with respect to mental events, which *do* seem to be causes.

If only for the sake of discussion, suppose there is an interesting sense of 'physical' according to which neural events and bodily motions are physical events, but mental events are not physical events if event dualism is true. And consider the following argument: (i) the causation of a physical event requires a transfer, or a change in form, of some energy; (ii) total energy is conserved across time; and (iii) if event dualism is true, some physical events have causes distinct from their physical causes; so (iv) given event dualism, it should appear that total energy is *not* conserved if one considers only the physical causes of a physical event with mental causes. But (v) this prediction of event dualism is mistaken.

The obvious reply is that either (i) is false, or the inference to (iv) is fallacious, depending on how (i) is interpreted. The (non-Cartesian) event dualist grants that every physical event with a mental cause has a proximate physical cause; hence the mental causation of a bodily motion is always *accompanied by* an energy transfer. But it does not follow that every instance of causation is *itself* an instance of energy transfer; instances of psychophysical causation may be unlike instances of physical causation in just this respect. Equivocation can, however, blind one to this possibility. Intuitively, the process of a mental event M causing a physical event P counts as the causation of a physical event. And it is natural to count processes, so that if M is not a physical event, the process of M causing P is distinct from any process of any physical event causing P. On this way of counting causal processes, event dualism implies more processes than neuralism; but one cannot insist that *every* process of an event causing P is a process of energy transfer, in the sense that more processes entails more energy-transfers.

Correlatively, while event dualists can readily grant that some laws are stated in terms of energy transfer, they must deny that causation *is* the transfer of energy. If causation is the extensionalization of explanation, and not every explanation can be given in physical terms, then causation itself is multiply realizable. It may help to consider this point against the background of a cartoonish (but nonetheless compelling) picture of causation that bears a natural affinity to the idea of energy-transfer:

> Every event has a certain amount of *oomph*; one event *makes another event happen* by exerting its oomph; sometimes an event does not itself have enough oomph to make an effect happen; but a team of partial causes may *together* exert enough oomph to make an effect occur; and if each of two events exerts enough oomph to make an effect happen, then the effect is overdetermined, i.e. made to happen twice over.

I suspect that my own reservations about event dualism stem from attachment to this Metaphysical Oomph View of Event-causation (MOVE, for short) coupled with a tendency to identify oomph with energy transfer. So I take MOVE seriously, even though it is more a vague picture than a proper thesis.

Many homely analogies inspire MOVE. Imagine a weight on one end of a see-saw. A person can raise the weight by exerting her strength on the other end. Two people can raise a weight that neither person could raise alone. And two people, each of whom could raise the weight on their own, might still push on their end with all their strength. But in this last case, we expect the 'extra cause' to have some 'extra effect'. Perhaps the weight rose with greater force than it would have, given just one raiser (see Bunzl 1979). Similarly, if Bloggs were shot and poisoned, his death might have been overdetermined. But closer inspection will reveal that the poison may had a more specific effect (say, respiratory failure) that differed from the more specific effect of the bullet (say, internal bleeding). And MOVE encourages the idea that this feature of paradigmatic overdetermination cases—extra causes have an extra effect—stems from features of causation itself. (Typically, when two persons raise a weight, each person will have the characteristic experience of felt resistance—and each will know that the other is experiencing an instance of causation in much the same way.) Added effects may go unnoticed. But it can seem that a second dose of oomph *must* have effects that are in principle detectable. Conservation arguments bolster this intuition, since it is easy to think that energy-transfer *is* the natural phenomenon (in the mind-independent world) that answers to the conception of causation embodied by MOVE.

It can seem, therefore, that MOVE leads to neuralism. For suppose mental events cause bodily motions by exerting their oomph. Neural events exert enough oomph to make the motions happen. So either mental events are neural events, *or* the motions are 'overoomphed'; but no extra effect is observed. Burge (1992: 36–7) discusses a less cartoonish variant on this argument: unless mental causation was physical causation, the former would 'yield departures from the approximately deterministic patterns described by physical laws'; mental causes would somehow 'interfere with, disrupt, or otherwise "make a difference" in the physical outcomes'. (But this doesn't happen.) As Burge says, the idea that there is a problem here 'depends heavily on thinking of mental causes on a physical model—as providing an extra 'bump' or transfer of energy on the physical effect'. For on such a model, 'instances of "overdetermination"—two causes having the same effect—must seem to be aberrations'. And 'whether the physical model of causation is appropriate' is part of what is at issue.[13]

---

[13] One might think that Cartwright-style appeals to capacities—see Ch. 4—will support the idea that objects (like persons and brains) exert oomph, and hence that the exertion of

Nonetheless, MOVE is compelling; so simply rejecting it is bound to be unsatisfying. And once one allows that causation is a natural relation, one can hardly object to using 'oomph' as a name for this relation, whatever it turns out to be. So event dualists must say that causation—and hence, oomph, insofar as MOVE is an acceptable picture of causation—does not always make an aberration out of overdetermination. Given event dualism, the natural relation of causation is such that a single event can be 'twice caused' without the kind of 'extra effect' associated with paradigmatic cases of overdetermination (which are, after all, cases in which there are two *physical* causes). But this is tantamount to saying that causation is multiply realizable, in the sense mentioned above. (Owens' (1992) account of causation fits well with this claim; see also Tooley (1987).)

3.2

This is not to deny that some kinds of explanation are especially important to us. And, as Strawson notes, our ideas about *mechanism* surely influence how we think about causation.[14] Indeed, this may bear on a loose end earlier set aside: how can actions/tryings cause muscle contractions? Perhaps some cases are covered by psychophysical laws of the sort discussed in Chapter 3: cp, if a person tries to contract$_T$ her arm muscles, then her arm muscles contract$_I$. But in Chapter 1, I suggested that a person's actions/tryings can cause muscle contractions, even when the person does not try to contract$_T$ her muscles. So let me stress that the event pair <T, B> may be covered by a cp law, even if T is not a *proximal* cause of B. If Nora tries to clench$_T$ her fist (without trying to contract$_T$ the relevant muscles), the causal relation may be as depicted in either of the diagrams below, where C is the muscle contraction that causes the peripheral bodily motion B (i.e. the clenching$_I$ of Nora's fist), which has N as a neural cause.

$$T \searrow \quad\quad\quad\quad\quad T \searrow$$
$$C \to B \quad\quad\quad\quad\quad B$$
$$N \nearrow \quad\quad\quad\quad N \to C \nearrow$$

mental oomph must be the exertion of physical oomph (on pain of physical effects of mental causes being overoomphed). But event dualists can also be capacity dualists. And neuralists can hardly take as given that capacities are to be identified with *physical* bases (cf. Prior 1985).

[14] In science, we rightly prize theories that explain why events of type $T1$ often cause events of type $T2$, by revealing that: each $T1$-event is (or is constituted by) some cluster of events of type K; each $T2$-event is (or is constituted by) some cluster of events of type L; and when the relevant K-events stand in the relation they stand when a $T1$-event occurs, the K-events often cause the relevant L-events (with the result that a $T2$-event occurs). Event dualists need not deny this, although they will resist the idea that every instance of causation must be implemented by a non-intentional mechanism.

My account of mental causation would not be compromised if the second diagram often reflected the facts. For I used the claim that *some* tryings cause muscle-contractions to defend the idea that tryings could be in the head. And while it matters to me that tryings be causes of bodily motions, it does not matter if many tryings are not causes of muscle-contractions. If muscle-contractions are often part of the supervenience base for tryings, so be it. But since Nora can contract$_T$ the muscles that cause her fist to clench, Nora can bring about an event of C's type by trying to contract$_T$ her muscles; so events of C's type are not part of the supervenience base for at least some of Nora's tryings. This at least suggests that events of C's type are part of a mechanism whereby Nora's tryings result in a peripheral bodily motion. If we discovered that Nora could regularly bring about events of a certain neural type by trying to do so, that would be reason to treat even some neural events as part of this mechanism. But so far as we know, persons cannot 'move their brains' in any particular way. Brain-events do not lie within our control; they are what our tryings supervene on (see O'Shaughnessy 1980).

Similarly, event dualists can allow that mental episodes of perceiving may have biochemical events as proximal causes, as indicated below (where S is an external stimulus):

$$S \rightarrow N \rightarrow N \quad \begin{array}{c} \nearrow \ M \\ \searrow \ N \end{array}$$

This fits with the intuition that (modulo indeterminism) a molecular duplicate of me would form the same beliefs if his sensory peripheries were stimulated in the same ways that mine are stimulated, even if the distal causes differed; and correspondingly, I might be a brain in a vat. But mind–brain supervenience would also preserve these intuitions, even if stimuli did not cause mental events *via* biochemical events (say, those that occur in perceptual systems). And if the occurrence of S explains the occurrence of the mental event M, event dualists can adopt the following picture:

$$S \rightarrow N \rightarrow N \quad \begin{array}{c} \nearrow \ M \\ \searrow \ N \end{array}$$

I am here just briefly noting points that deserve much more attention. But once we allow that events can be overdetermined by rational and arational causes, the overdetermined events can include peripheral bodily motions, muscle contractions, and neural events.

Given supervenience, modal intuitions (even if true) will not establish causal relations between mental and biochemical events. But event dualists can allow that biochemical events cause mental events, and vice versa. If the occurrence of certain neural events explains why a patient undergoing brain surgery suddenly thinks of Paris, so be it; and, similarly, if thinking about Paris explains the occurrence of certain biochemical effects that cause a reduction in blood pressure. Of course, one must take care not to confuse coincidence with causation. But I see no reason to rule out the possibility of genuine explanations. One might discover biopsychological laws; and even independent of any generalizations, one might have good reason to think that the occurrence of *this* biochemical event B explained the occurrence *that* mental event M. (This is compatible with B causing another biochemical event that is part of the supervenience base for M.) From an event dualist's perspective, multiple explanations are not sources of difficulty—not even if the explanations relate singular event thoughts, and thus have implications for causation.

3.3

Let me end this section with one last pass at the central question. How can causation be a *natural* relation if different explanatory relations count as causal? The answer, I think, is that the extensionalization of explanation is a natural relation. Initially, this may seem unsatisfying. But bear in mind that a natural relation is an objective (non-projected) relation between particulars that exist in space-time; and events exist in space-time, while explanation is an objective relation (at least when based on laws). Recalling the discussion of Section 2, note that there is no special problem in saying how causation can be characterized as a *theoretical* relation, even if different explanatory relations count as theoretical. For we are used to the idea that there are different kinds of theories. No one expects the relation *is explanatory of* to be exhausted by what we discover in any *one* domain; trivially, every explanatory theory makes its contribution to what counts as explanatory. My suggestion is that we take a similar view of causation: while causation is a natural relation, it need not be a natural kind with an essence discoverable by engaging in some *one* theoretical enterprise; if causation has an essence discoverable by theorizing, the relevant theory is science as a whole, where 'science' is construed broadly enough to encompass *all* explanatory enterprises.

I cannot prove that there is no single science of causation in this sense. But note that physics is unlikely to play this role if causation conforms to anything like our ordinary picture of it. For one thing, physical laws seem to be symmetric in a way that at least many instances of causation are not. Moreover, the posits of our best physical theories are *weird*; they do not conform to any intuitive conception of causal relations. Whatever is going on in the quantum world—a domain of indeterminism, non-locality, and position/velocity uncertainty—it does not answer to the notions of power/compulsion/oomph that animate traditional notions of causation. This is, at least in part, why one feels queasy when hearing about slit experiments (EPR phenomena, quantum tunnelling, etc.).

Still, we all feel the pull of saying that physics describes the *real* movers and shakers in the world, and that *real* causation is to be found at the level described by physicists. But consider the epistemic implications of this view: if the real causal explanations are quantum mechanical, what kind of *comprehensibility* (if any) is associated with singular causal claims, in the absence of the detailed calculations required to subsume the relevant events under physical laws (assuming they can, in principle, be so subsumed)? We think of causation and explanation as intimately related, in part because we think that at least *some* instances of causation are distinctly *un*puzzling. Correspondingly, 'physics imperialism' with respect to causation would seem to threaten the claim that we sometimes *see* instances of causation; and if this claim is abandoned, one wants to know why the resulting position is not better described as *eliminativism* with respect to causation. If causation is characterized in quantum mechanical terms, then it is an open question whether our actions cause bodily motions and the motions of suitcases. Absent reasons for thinking that such questions will be answered affirmatively—i.e. absent reasons for taking the apparent instances of causation suggested by our perceptual judgements to be instances of the same relation characterized by our physical theories—one wants to know what justifies using the label 'cause' for both kinds of cases. (Compare the discussion of content in the appendix.)

On the other hand, the (Strawsonian) view urged here lets us see physics as a theoretical extension of our pre-theoretic views about what causes what. In the case of quantum mechanics, the extension is extreme. The relevant analogies have been stretched much farther than ever before. Perhaps they have been stretched too far, and explanation in physics should *not* count as causal. But once we engage in theoretical reasoning, we need not compare each alleged instance of causation directly with perceivable instances, ignoring the unperceived instances we have already discovered. We may come to see that certain instances of causation are relevantly like perceived instances, in part by noting that new instances of causation are relevantly like other unperceived instances. And increasing confidence in theorizing will be correlated with the increasing importance of detailed prediction and control as evidence for causal claims. So given the amazing precision made possible by physical laws, I see nothing wrong with saying that causation at the subatomic level can be very puzzling indeed. The naturalness of causation in no way guarantees that every singular causal claim is associated with an explanation closely analogous to those based on perceived instances of causation. Causation can be natural, without our finding every instance of it readily comprehensible.

Given that all events supervene on physical events, event dualists can also draw the following distinction: let an instance of physical causation be an instance of causation that holds between two events describable in the language of physics; let an instance of supervenient causation be an instance of causation that holds between two events, at least one of which is not describable in the language of physics. It is a substantive claim that there are instances of supervenient causation. For it is a substantive claim that some events are not describable in the language of physics. But it is no embarrassment to say that instances of mental causation are instances of supervenient causation in this sense. For if causation is multiply realizable, one need not say that causation is exhausted by physical causation, with supervenient causes being somehow epiphenomenal (cf. Kim 1993). It is not that there are two flavours of causation, physical and ersatz, with supervenient causes and effects being instances of the latter flavour. Instances of causation holding between supervenient causes and effects are just as good, *qua* instances of causation, as any other instances; though trivially, supervenient causes differ from physical causes, in that the former supervene on the latter.

If instances of supervenient causation are instances of the same natural relation as every other instance of causation, and if supervenient causes can have effects that have physical causes, then not every overdetermined event will be associated with extra effects as suggested by MOVE. (Mental events are sure to have physical effects if only because bodily motions can have physical effects. The motion of a physicist's finger can cause the motion of a particle through a slit. So if the finger motion has neural and mental causes, so does the particle motion.) Conservation of energy arguments reflect the confirmed belief that physics is a closed system; apparent cases of conservation failure are cases in which the relevant causes and effects have not yet been fully described. But supervenient causes of physical effects do not jeopardize conservation. And we can understand MOVE analogously.

Within any one explanatory framework, we expect extra causes to be associated with extra effects. If two lines of dominoes converge on a single domino, we expect each cause of the final toppling to have manifestations beyond the toppling itself. If the death of Bloggs is overdetermined, because of poison in his stomach and a bullet in his chest, each cause of death will have more specific effects. Similarly, a person with two sufficient reasons for moving to a new job (which offers better pay *and* a better location) will differ from an otherwise similar person with just one reason for moving. But if a single effect has causes that belong to different explanatory frameworks (like a bodily motion with mental and neural causes), this kind of over-determination will not be associated with extra effects in any framework. One might summarize the point by saying that *intra*level overdetermination is problematic in a way that *inter*level overdetermination is not. (Of course, one is not entitled to say this straight off, without begging the question against neuralists; one needs to defend a conception of causation that allows for interlevel overdetermination.) Alternatively, one might apply 'overdetermination' to only the intralevel cases; but then event dualism will not have the consequence that bodily motions with mental causes count as overdetermined.

Still, even if physics does not capture the essence of causation, one might think that treating reasons and actions as *sui generis* is bound to conflict with some plausible claim about the nature of causation. One might allow that our intuitive notion of causation must get its grip some-where, and that it gets its grip only given changes in objects large enough so that quantum phenomena can be ignored for all practical purposes. But perhaps with respect to these macroevents, the natural relation of causa-tion can be fully characterized (i.e. its extension can be exhaustively speci-fied) in the terminology of some *one* theoretical enterprise. Of course, this raises the question of which one. Any enterprise that focuses on relatively complex structures (like cells) will be insufficiently general; and a theory that deals with very simple structures (like atoms) will reflect the weirdness of the quantum world. It is tempting to say that every instance of causa-tion can be described in the terms of *some* non-intentional theory. But at least as it stands, this is blatantly question-begging; treating non-*intentional* theories as the relevant class for specifying causation just assumes that event dualists are wrong.

4. Concluding Remarks

When a person raises her arm for a reason, the arm rises as a result of causes internal to the person. Some of these causes will be describable in arational terms. But one of the causes will be the person's action; or so I argued in Chapter 1. This action will be an event of trying, an attempt by the person to achieve some end (e.g. raising her arm, which is perhaps a means to the further end of purchasing a painting). The person's action will in turn have mental causes, including the reason in question—say, coming to believe that she could purchase the painting by raising her arm. And as discussed in Chapter 5, I do not think that actions and their ration-alizing causes are describable in arational terms. In short, some events have *both* rationalizing causes *and* impersonal causes. I have tried to show how this could be so.

In Chapter 3, I sketched a picture of how the intentional relation of explanation and the extensional relation of causation fit together, drawing on a Fregean semantics of 'that'-clauses (from Chapter 2) and a Davidsonian event analysis (from Chapter 1). In this chapter, I filled in that sketch a little, by defending the claim that causation is the extensionalization of explanation. My aim has been to preserve the naturalness of causation while saying how reasons can be causes distinct from any biochemical causes. This is a fine line to walk. And I do not pretend to have characterized a fully satisfying way of walking it. But if appeal to *ceteris paribus* laws is independently motivated and defensible, as argued in Chapter 4, there is an alternative to the claim that reasons have impersonal descriptions. Denying this claim raises modal concerns, having to do with overdetermination and supervenience; though as I argued in Chapter 6, these concerns are far from decisive.

So I am inclined to think the issue is this: should we preserve our intuitive conception of ourselves as agents whose actions are distinct rational contributions to the causal order, even if this means adopting a relaxed metaphysics and a conception of causation that is perhaps 'thinner' than one might have expected; or should we adopt a more parsimonius metaphysics, and a conception of causation without any Humean spectre, at the cost of our natural self-conception? In my view, Humean spectres should be squarely faced; and Cartesian pretensions to immaterial souls are not the only metaphysical views that need taming. Some of our pre-theoretic views about causation may also be problematic. And parsimony does not require that we adopt an overly simple ontology. Sometimes, more is better than less. Human beings often act for reasons, and reasons are causes. But one need not identify our reasons and actions with biochemical events. If such identification is avoidable, there is reason for avoiding it.

APPENDIX

The Semantic Wages of Neuralism

In motivating event dualism, I focused mainly on three related ideas: rationalizing causes are causes of a special sort; persons are individuals of a special sort if only because we often act freely; and there is something distinctive about causation in the presence of freedom. But one might reply that rationalizing causes are simply causes with propositional contents; persons are individuals whose behaviour can often be explained by reference to their reasons; and because freedom is linked to reason, we regard subjects of rationalizing explanations as loci of freedom. So if some biochemical events have propositional contents, one can say that such events are distinctively mental, since they have contents, even though such causes have impersonal descriptions. Thus, one might hope to weaken the case for event dualism by arguing that biochemical events can have contents. (I assume that events can have contents; see Chapter 3. And for simplicity, I use 'event' broadly in this appendix to cover all eventualities, including states.)

One can, however, turn this line of thought on its head: (i) no neural events have contents; (ii) some mental events have contents; hence, (iii) neuralism is false. Given an independent argument *for* neuralism, (ii) would tell against (i). But absent such argument, (i) is prima facie plausible. Unlike Othello's coming to believe that Desdemona loved Cassio, biochemical occurrences do not seem to be meaningful.[1] Neuralists will say that some biochemical events have meanings nonetheless; and I cannot prove otherwise. Still, neuralists face a serious difficulty. They owe an account of content, according to which biochemical events can have contents. Thus, they appear to owe a *naturalistic* account according to which: e has proposition P as its content if e bears the right *non-intentionally specifiable* relation to P. For it seems that nothing less will explain how biochemical events *could* have the semantic properties of mental events; whereas event dualists can avoid this implausibly ambitious form of reduc-

---

[1] Burge (1979*b*, 1993) offers a modal variant: mental events have their contents essentially, but no biochemical events have contents essentially. I think the second premiss is plausible (*pace* Davidson 1986) if one does not conflate the thesis that distinct events have distinct causes with the thesis that an event's causes are essential to it. The first premiss is less secure; perhaps mental events have their 'wide content' properties only contingently (see Fodor 1987, 1991*a*). But prima facie, mental events have their rationalizing contents essentially; and it needs showing that 'narrow contents' rationalize.

tionism (cf. Dretske 1981, 1988; Fodor 1987, 1990; Millikan 1984, 1990). A thorough discussion of the issues at stake here would require another book, and even the cursory treatment below presupposes some familiarity with the literature on 'theories of content'. But I hope to show that considerations of mental content strengthen, rather than weaken, the case for event dualism.

I

Let me say at once that 'content' is a quasi-technical notion, and that there may be scientifically respectable senses in which biochemical events have contents of some sort. But the issue is whether neural events have the *same* kind(s) of content that mental events have. One cannot defend neuralism simply by arguing that biochemical events can bear some specified relation to certain states of affairs. The specified relation has to be the (rational) relation that mental causes bear to their contents; and the question is whether any biochemical events have contents in this demanding sense. On the other hand, it would be question-begging for me to insist that causes with content are special, because of their relation to a notion of human freedom that is foreign to biochemical events. So borrowing terminology from another debate, let us distinguish *conceptual* from *non-conceptual* content, where by stipulation: mental contents are conceptual; an individual can fail to be the subject of a rational perspective, yet still be the subject of events with non-conceptual content; and an event can have a non-conceptual content C, even if the event's subject bears no rational relation to C. Then events can have non-conceptual contents without rationalizing their effects; and if neuralism is true, certain biochemical events have conceptual contents. (Fodor (1998) offers an anti-Fregean argument that may be relevant here; but cf. Pietroski 1999*b*. For discussion of non-conceptual content, see Evans 1982; Davies 1987; Peacocke 1992.)

For reasons discussed in earlier chapters, I think there is an intimate relation between rational perspectives and Fregean senses. So I take conceptual contents to be Fregean thoughts: truth-evaluable structures, whose constituents are ways of thinking about things. It is a familiar idea that opacity is a mark of rationalizing explanation: mental events have properties, such that our usual way of describing those properties (i.e. via 'that'-clauses) does not respect substitutivity. In my view, this semantic phenomenon reflects the fact that rational beings are subjects of events that cannot be fully described in arational terms. (Recall that *ways* of thinking about things are individuated in terms of what someone could think without irrationality.) The alternative view is that some biochemical events have Fregean contents. But at least initially, it is hard to see how this could be true.

The problem is not merely that biochemical events would have to be related to abstract objects individuated in terms of how thinking subjects think about things. It is easy enough to describe a relation that my office light-switch bears to the sense of 'My office light is on': *ceteris paribus*, when the switch is up, the thought is true. But intuitively, there is no rationalization here. All the explanation is in the wiring. Correspondingly, since my office is room 1120, the light-switch is related just as well to the sense of 'Current is flowing through the bulb in room 1120.' Similarly, one can describe relations that hold between some biochemical event B in Nora and the thought that Fido barked. But it would take work to show that any of these was the intentional relation *has as its content*. At a minimum, one would need to show that B is not related just as well to the thought that Rex barked.

Since Nora believes that Fido barked (and not that Rex barked), *Nora* is suitably related to the sense of 'Fido barked'; unbeknownst to Nora, she thinks about one dog in two ways. From here, it is a short step to the claim that Nora has mental events with Fregean contents. But her biochemical events are another matter. Nora's *brain* does not think about any dog as the evening dog. On the contrary, it is hard to see how anything describable in impersonal terms could be just like a mental event with respect to bearing a *rational* relation to a Fregean thought. This point is often expressed in terms of semantic evaluability (see e.g. Fodor 1987), though the issue is not merely about assigning truth (or satisfaction) conditions to biochemical events. Having truth conditions may well be a symptom of having a sense, where only rationalizers (and things that express the content of rationalizers) have senses.

Nor is this worry dispelled by language of thought hypotheses. Event dualists can grant that belief formation often involves a relation to an internal representation with linguistic structure. There are familiar arguments for this claim, based on the systematicity (and apparent compositionality) of thought, that should appeal to Fregeans; see Fodor (1987) and Davies (1991). And one can reject neuralism, while saying that when Nora comes to believe that Fido barked, this mental episode consists partly in: Nora's coming to think about a certain animal in an evening-dog way; Nora's coming to think about the barkings as such; and the organization of these referential acts into a truth-evaluable structure that Nora affirms. (Recall that we need not grasp senses in the way we grasp cups; a thinker can be related to the sense of 'X' by thinking about the *Bedeutung* of 'X' in the right way.) If mental episodes have meaningful parts, so be it. The question is whether such episodes are biochemical.

Similarly, my concern is not that having truth conditions requires *syntax* that biochemical events cannot have. Grant that certain neural events exhibit structures like those of natural language sentences, and thus that certain neural events have syntactic parts in much the way that sentence tokens have word tokens as parts. (Chomskian linguistics at least renders this suggestion not implausible.) We still have no independent reason for thinking that any biochemical events have subsentential senses, like the sense of 'Fido'. One can see how a biochemical event B might be related (say, causally/historically) to a certain animal. But it is much harder to see how B could be related to an animal in such a way that B would count as an instance of thinking about Fido in an evening-dog (and not a morning-dog) way. So even if thinkers are sometimes related to neural sentences, that does not yet explain how biochemical events could be episodes of rational thought in which persons come to be related to senses.

Of course, one might draw distinctions among those biochemical events that bear some (say, causal/historical) relation to Fido. There will be various (say, functional) properties shared by some of these events. But for any such property P, it would be a leap to suppose that events with P are events of thinking about Fido in an evening-dog way. One can hypothesize that biochemical events have senses by virtue of (i) bearing a suitable relation to external *Bedeutungen*, and (ii) bearing a suitable relation to one another; where (i) is intended to capture the idea of thinking about something, and (ii) is intended to capture the idea of thinking about something in a certain way (cf. Field 1978; Fodor 1975, 1994). But no one endorses this proposal on inductive grounds. Even given the conception of sense suggested by (i) and (ii), it is a further claim that *biochemical* events satisfy this conception; and it is not implausible that the suitable relations in question are themselves intentional.

This is not to belittle the proposal. For the attractions of neuralism, as an account of mental causation, are considerable. So it is perfectly reasonable to explore the resources available to neuralists, when it comes to accounting for mental content. But I have tried to rebut the arguments for neuralism that I know of. And it is important to remember that there is nothing puzzling in the mere fact that *mental* events have contents. Episodes of believing are precisely the sorts of things that have contents. (Compare the triviality that persons have mental properties.) One can ask questions about contents, including the question of what it is to have a content. But the fact that mental events have content is not itself a fact that immediately calls for a reductive explanation (of how it could be true).

The claim that biochemical events have contents, however, does call for explanation if true. Thus, mental content does not merely present neuralists with a difficulty that can be set aside for future work. It seems that a biochemical event is the wrong *sort* of thing to have a (conceptual) content. So it seems that neuralism thus generates a question—viz. how *could* a biochemical event have a sense—to which there is no answer. We need to be told how such events, which can be described without bringing a person onto the scene, could bear an intentional relation to a proposition. In this sense, neuralism makes intentionality itself seem mysterious by turning an otherwise mundane fact into a puzzle: how could mental events have contents *if* mental events are neural events? If this question can be answered, that will be a point in favour of neuralism. (Sometimes, apparently mundane facts turn out to be puzzling.) But if the question cannot be answered, then so much the worse for the philosophical thesis that generated it.

Moreover, in saying how a biochemical event B manages to have a content, neuralists cannot assume that B has *any* intentional properties; or we would need an account of how B could have *those* properties. Put another way: it will not help to be told that B has a certain content, because B has some (perhaps relational) property, unless that property is characterized in an arational idiom. So it seems that neuralists cannot avoid the need for a naturalistic theory of content. For only such a theory offers the promise of discharging the neuralist's explanatory burden. Thus, neuralism turns the fact that mental events have contents into a puzzle that requires a particular kind of solution; and there is no guarantee that there is any solution of the required sort. If rational relations to propositions cannot be described in impersonal terms, that is what event dualists would expect. But given neuralism, this would call into question the very idea that mental events have contents—and hence that there are *reasons* for actions.

With this in mind, return to the idea that a biochemical event has a sense by virtue of bearing some relation R to a *Bedeutung*, and having some further (perhaps functional) property F. One might suspect a fallacy of division here: thinking about Fido in an evening-dog way need not be a species of thinking about Fido, in the way that knowledge is a species of belief; so why think that having a sense is a matter of having some property *in addition to* having a *Bedeutung*? But even setting this concern aside, neuralists would need to characterize both R and F in non-intentional terms. So even a naturalized aboutness relation R, which holds between (the mental analogue of) 'Fido' and the dog Fido/Rex, is not enough. Neuralists also need a naturalized account of the alleged relation F, which is effectively sense minus aboutness. Again, one might hypothesize that having F is having a certain causal role: if the mental analogues of 'Fido' and 'Rex' figure in different inferences, they can have different effects. But even if the difference in sense consists in a causal difference—and this is a big assumption—neuralists cannot assume that this causal difference can be characterized in non-intentional terms. (Even if senses *are* causal routes to referents, this will not help content naturalists, unless the causal routes can be specified without appeal to *intentions*; see Devitt 1981.) Moreover, believing that P may have different effects than believing that Q, because it is *reasonable* to infer R from P (but not from Q); and no one has yet provided an independently plausible naturalistic account of reasonable inference (cf. Putnam 1988).

2

Let me summarize to this point. Absent independent commitment to content naturalism, I see no reason to think that any non-intentionally characterizable relation F is such that: an event with F has the sense of 'Fido' as its content if the event bears a non-intentionally characterizable aboutness relation to Fido. If everything describable in manifest-image terms can be described in scientific-image terms, then content (and reasonable inference) can be naturalized, and this is a powerful source of motivation for the naturalistic project. Moreover, because neuralism can seem like the only option when it comes to accounting for the possibility of mental causation, one can slip into thinking that any costs of neuralism *must* be paid—and hence that neuralists only need to provide a naturalistic theory of content that is not demonstrably false. But given an alternative to neuralism, its defenders owe a plausible theory of content that shows how biochemical events could have (conceptual, rationalizing) contents. If such a theory can be provided, that would be good news for neuralists. But one cannot argue that content is naturalizable, by citing the very world-view that event dualists challenge. I grant that neuralism can be motivated by pointing to costs of event dualism. But in my view, we have no reason for thinking that the costs of neuralism can be paid; whereas if Chapters 6 and 7 are on the right track, the difficulties facing event dualists are less severe than initial appearances suggest.

It takes only one theory to rebut this more or less familiar kind of scepticism about naturalizing content. But in my view, none of the currently available naturalistic theories is plausible *independent* of commitments to naturalism, at least not if such theories are viewed as accounts of conceptual content, i.e. the kind of content that rationalizing causes have.[2] Perhaps one can argue that causal approaches are better (or worse) than teleological approaches, that a correct naturalistic theory will (not) include a historical component, or that appeal to functional role is (un)avoidable. But this would not provide reason for thinking that some naturalistic theory is correct.

Indeed, as Stich and Laurence (1994) note, it is hard to see how one is supposed to confirm theories in this domain. Intuitions about cases are

---

[2] I won't try to defend this claim here; though I suspect that few will deny it. See Kim (1991), Loewer and Rey (1991), and Pietroski (1992) for criticisms of leading naturalistic theories. The arguments for such theories typically presuppose that content needs naturalizing—the question being how. And as we have just seen, neuralists must do more than characterize a naturalistic aboutness relation.

not obviously reliable sources of evidence; and we cannot even identify the (alleged) content-bearing events in the head, much less determine their causal/informational/historical/teleological/functional properties. It seems that *all* one can do is muster intuitions, and some abstract theoretical considerations, for or against general naturalization strategies. This is bad enough if the general project is motivated. But Stich and Laurence doubt that we really need a non-intentionally specified sufficient condition for having a mental property. (It seems not to matter that we cannot give: a non-biologically specificied sufficient condition for having an biological property; a non-phonologically specified sufficient condition for having an phonological property; etc.) I share their scepticism, but suspect that neuralism is often the unstated source of motivation. *If* we adopt neuralism, we need to say how biochemical events could have propositional contents, and so we need a naturalistic theory of content. Again, the very existence of intentionality seems mysterious if *neural* events are the bearers of contents. So absent an alternative to neuralism, the naturalistic project can seem unavoidable. But the rhetoric has been that the project is mandatory (full stop).

In a widely cited passage, Fodor (1987: 97–8) suggested that eventually,

the physicists will complete the catalogue they've been compiling of the ultimate and irreducible properties of things. When they do, the likes of *spin*, *charm*, and *charge* will perhaps appear on their list. But *aboutness* surely won't; intentionality simply doesn't go that deep. It's hard to see, in face of this consideration, how one can be a Realist about intentionality without being, to some extent or other, a Reductionist. If the semantic and the intentional are real properties of things, it must be in virtue of their identity with (or maybe of their supervenience on?) properties that are themselves *neither* intentional *nor* semantic . . . indeed, the deepest motivation for intentional irrealism derives . . . from a certain ontological intuition: that there is no place for intentional categories in a physicalistic view of the world; that the intentional can't be *naturalized*.

This nicely articulates a desire, motivated by the threat of eliminativism, to locate the intentional within the scientific image. And while no one has ever offered a theory of content in terms of *spin* and *charm*, the thought seems to be that we can worry later about unreduced non-intentional notions; the big worry concerns the intentional. (If causation is the extensionalization of explanation, one might wonder if appeal to causation is legitimate in a naturalistic theory of content. But let this pass.)

The parenthetical remark about supervenience is also of interest. Later discussion suggests that Fodor simply wanted to allow for the multiple realizability of content: perhaps there are sufficient conditions for having a content besides the 'asymmetric dependence' condition he provided. But if the goal is to avoid lengthening the physicist's list, one does not need a non-intentionally specified condition for *having* a content; all one needs is a non-intentionally specified condition for there *being* contents. Consider a world that contains a body type-identical in all non-intentional respects to the body currently at location L, where L is my current location. Such a world, which I just described in arational terms, contains a person who is the subject of mental events type-identical to mine. For the mental supervenes on the non-mental. As we saw in Chapter 6, supervenience does not require the bearers of contents to be characterizable in non-intentional terms. So supervenience does not ensure the kind of sufficient condition (for meaning that P) that naturalists have in mind. Thus, one cannot move from Realism (non-eliminativism) to Reductionism without a premiss—e.g. that Realism requires neuralism, which requires content naturalism—that can be challenged. (While I have focused on Fodor (1987), let me again emphasize my agreement with Fodor (1989), who is less concerned with ontology.)

Rhetoric aside, though, much of the work in defending naturalistic theories of content takes the form of showing that such theories can accommodate the fact some beliefs are false. The reasons for this are partly historical: initial thoughts about how to naturalize content came to grief over this very point (see Fodor (1984) for discussion). For example, if a term 'F' is about those things that could cause tokens of 'F', then (on the assumption that every token of 'Fido' is caused by something) no token of 'Fido' is produced in the absence of something it is about; and this makes it hard to see how 'Fido is present' could ever be false.[3] But quite apart from attempts to naturalize content, false beliefs can seem puzzling. And one might complain that I have downplayed the extent to which intentionality generates puzzles, whether or not neuralism is true. At least since Plato, philosophers have been bothered by the following tension: a person's beliefs represent the world; yet how can one *re*present that which is not the case?

While it is not entirely clear just what the puzzle is, there is something here that wants explaining. And one might claim that only a naturalistic theory of content can provide a satisfying account of how error is possible. If this is true, then event dualists cannot object if neuralism requires a naturalistic theory of content as a companion. If everyone needs such a theory in order to explain the possibility of error, then neuralism carries no special cost. Put another way, if the possibility of error leads us to say that content is naturalizable, then we *do* have independent reason for thinking that content is naturalizable (even if we don't know how to

---

[3] This is the primary motivation for theories that specify content in terms of conditions that *should* obtain when symbols are tokened; where 'should' is cashed out (naturalistically) in terms of explanations for why the relevant symbol-producing capacities exist. But see Pietroski (1992) for an argument that such theories have a structure that is at odds with them being plausible theories of conceptual content.

naturalize it). It needs showing that the possibility of error leads us to say that content is naturalizable. But if event dualists cannot offer a non-naturalistic account of how error is possible, they are not obviously in the better position. Luckily, it is not hard to sketch an account of error, once one abandons the idea that theories of content must be naturalistic; though unsurprisingly, my aim in these last few pages is not to provide a complete theory of content, i.e. a theory that addresses all of the puzzles surrounding the notion of content. Rather, it is to supplement a familiar conception of intentional states with a highly simplified conception of content, by way of suggesting that event dualists really are in a better position to account for the possibility of error.

3

Let us assume that belief, desire, and action are functionally interrelated. This is especially plausible if (paradigmatic) actions are tryings. If a person desires that P, then to a first approximation she is disposed to perform actions that would, given her beliefs and other desires, be rational ways of trying to make it the case that P. And if a person believes that P, then (subject to a constraint discussed below) she is disposed to perform actions that would be rational ways of trying to satisfy her desires, given P and her other beliefs (but not given her other beliefs alone).

Let us take dispositions to be 'full-blooded' states of a system that can causally explain manifestations of the disposition, and not mere counterfactual facts (see Armstrong 1970; Evans 1981; Prior 1985; Dwyer 1995; cf. Ryle 1949). I assume that something can have a disposition that it does not manifest, even if the relevant 'triggering' condition is met. Salt is soluble, i.e. disposed to dissolve in water; and it has this property, even in the shaker, and even though there are abnormal cases in which a sample of salt fails to dissolve upon immersion. Since I have already appealed to *ceteris paribus* laws, and said that such laws can figure in causal explanations, a natural suggestion is that x is disposed to Φ given a suitable triggering condition C if cp(when C obtains, x Φ's). With respect to solubility, the relevant triggering condition is immersion in water; rational dispositions to action will typically be triggered by relevant mental episodes. If Nora wants a certain painting, she is disposed to act in certain ways; in particular, she will raise her arm (other things being equal) if she comes to believe that she can purchase the painting by raising her arm. (And even if she does not raise her arm, say because the price is too high, Nora's underlying desire may have other effects.) So as a first approximation, let us say that x is disposed to act in manner M if cp(given a suitable trigger, x acts in manner M). Then a person believes/desires that P if she is covered by a suitable cp-law. Given the view of intentional explanation urged above, this is not to say anything new; it just makes explicit the characterization of belief, desire, and action in terms of each other and the intentional cp-laws that relate them. And given the proposed account of cp-laws, such a characterization need not be trivial.

It is tempting to assert the converse theses as well: an individual with the right dispositions has beliefs and desires. But at least many beliefs and desires are associated with characteristic experiences of endorsement and longing. Having such experiences may be a necessary condition on having mental states, even if thinkers have some unconscious mental states; for perhaps an individual who lacked experience altogether could not have the relevant dispositions to action. Similarly, there may be inferential and/or normative constraints on intentional states, such that some of these constraints fail to be satisfied by certain dispositions to action (see Bilgrami 1992). On the other hand, an individual disposed to *act* (and not merely behave) satisfies the necessary conditions for acting. And perhaps if such an individual is disposed to act in the relevant manner, then she has the relevant mental states; there may be no further conditions that particular dispositions need to satisfy. But we need not settle such questions.

It is enough for present purposes if believing/desiring that P is a matter of having *the right kind* of disposition to act in the ways characterized above—so long as any further conditions on mental states are not peculiar to the propositional contents of such states. So suppose that a person desires that P if she has a disposition Δ to perform actions that would, given her beliefs and other desires, be rational ways of trying to make it the case that P; and Δ satisfies any further necessary conditions (which may be stated in intentional terms) on being a desire. Similarly, suppose that a person believes that P if she has a disposition β to perform actions that would, given P and her other beliefs, be rational ways of trying to satisfy her desires; and Δ satisfies any further necessary conditions on being a belief. This is to suppose that dispositions (to act) are the sorts of things that *can* satisfy necessary conditions on being beliefs and desires. But if this proposal—or a more elaborate variation—is correct, then to falsely believe that P is simply to be in a certain dispositional state (of the right kind) when P is false.[4]

As Stalnaker (1984) notes, however, a purely dispositional account will suffer from a fatal relativity. The *structure* of a person's rational dispositions will not distinguish plausible intentional explanations from bizarre

---

[4] This is a variant on a view discussed by Dennett (1971) and developed by Stalnaker (1984). For simplicity, I continue to ignore time-sensitive reasoning that involves intentions; and if thinkers can act/try without moving their bodies, this proposal is not behaviouristic in any traditional sense. Note also that actions are characterized as dispositions to *try to* satisfy desires. (And as noted in Ch. 3, it is not true in general that cp, trying to Φ, results in Φ-ing.) Actions based on false beliefs will not tend to bring about desired results, but such actions can still be rational.

(but structurally isomorphic) rationalizations. Consider two possible explanations for why Mary, a gifted cellist, is playing badly at 3 a.m.: Mary wants Fred to suffer, and believes that Fred will suffer if she plays her cello badly; or Mary wants *Albert* to suffer, and believes that *Albert* will suffer if she plays her cello badly. If Fred is Mary's neighbour, while Mary has never met Alfred (who lives far away),'one might find the second hypothesis less plausible—even perverse—since Mary has no reason to want Albert to suffer. And she has no reason to believe that playing her cello badly will cause him to suffer.' But let us elaborate the perverse hypothesis as follows:

Mary believes Albert, rather than Fred, to be her neighbour, believes that Albert, rather than Fred, insulted her, believes that Albert's name is 'Fred'. In fact, all the attitudes that a sensible observer would say Mary takes toward Fred, the defender of the perverse hypothesis says that Mary takes toward Albert. (Stalnaker 1984: 17)

The example illustrates a familiar point that dispositionalists need to capture (and incorporate into their theory): beliefs are somehow sensitive to the environment in a way that desires are not. Mental contents are constrained by a 'front end' relation between a person's environment and her beliefs that is independent of the back end relation between a person's desires and her environment.

Put another way, dispositionalists treat action as the primary intentional notion. Beliefs and desires are bearers of contents, because they are suitably related to actions. This is in keeping with the Cartesian (and Husserlian) intuition that intentionality arises from within, since actions/tryings lie within scope of our control. But our beliefs are still subject to constraints that lie outside the scope of our control. Indeed, a rational being wants beliefs that are responsive to external facts (see Wiggins 1973). And a theory that ignores these external constraints will be unable to distinguish plausible intentional explanations from *mere* rationalizations with the same structure. But as Stalnaker notes, there is an obvious strategy for providing the needed supplementation to a dispositional account.

Suppose that a person believes that P (as opposed to believing that Q) if the relevant disposition is appropriately sensitive to P (as opposed to Q). At this point, a content naturalist would have to cash out 'appropriately sensitive' in non-intentional terms; and Stalnaker needs to defend his view that propositions are sets of possible worlds. But my kind of event dualist faces the less ambitious task of saying what appropriate sensitivity might be, such that rational dispositions to action can be appropriately sensitive to Fregean senses. And once again, appeal to cp laws proves helpful. Suppose that a disposition β of some thinking subject is appropriately sensitive to proposition P if *ceteris paribus* (if P, then the relevant subject has β). An agent's dispositions will come and go; and beliefs—especially perceptual beliefs—are particularly sensitive to external conditions, at least when the agent is being appropriately responsive to evidence.

Again, to believe P falsely is to have the right sort of disposition when P is false. And N can have a disposition β, such that *ceteris paribus* (if P, then N has β), even though N has β when P is false. Suppose Nora acquires a disposition β to perform actions that would be rational ways of trying to satisfy her desires (taking Nora's other beliefs into account), given that a cow just went by. Nora may have acquired β, because a cow just went by and Nora perceived it as a cow; or Nora may have acquired β, because a horse just went by and Nora mistook the horse for a cow. But either way, it may be that *ceteris paribus*, Nora comes to have β when a cow goes by; while it is not the case that *ceteris paribus*, Nora comes to have β when a horse goes by. (As I argued in Chapter 4, not every true singular causal claim corresponds to a cp law stated in the same terms.) This model of error is highly simplified. But I think it helps show how error is possible; and content naturalists are not well positioned to press complaints of oversimplicity.

Let me emphasize, though, that the proposal does not assume or idealize to omniscience. For the claim is *not* that cp(if P, then a rational subject will believe that P). Rather, the 'cp-covariation' condition serves as a constraint on the basic dispositional account; it blocks the inference from having a rationalizing disposition to having a belief with a specific content (unless the disposition is sensitive to that content). If a subject α does not ever have a disposition that is a *candidiate* for being the belief that P, then the proposed account does not have the consequence that cp(if P, then α believes that P). For example, the mere truth of propositions about the distant past does not ensure that (other things being equal), rational agents believe such propositions; since most agents are not disposed to act in ways that would warrant ascription of beliefs about the distant past. So we need not seek a special explanation for each truth that anyone fails to believe. And given the proposed gloss of cp clauses, the cp-covariation condition is *not* that the relevant subject would have had the relevant disposition if only conditions had been epistemically ideal (cf. the *ceteris absentibus* readings of cp laws rejected in Chapter 4).

The cp-clause says that each abnormal case can be explained by citing some interfering factor. So if a subject α has a disposition that is a candidate for being the belief that P, then α believes that P if there is an explanation for each case of α not believing P when P obtains.[5] Returning to the

---

[5] See Stalnaker (1984). For my purposes, the explanation can be boring and overtly intentional, e.g. the subject was distracted. And this sufficient condition need not cover all beliefs; see below. Perhaps explanation is also be required if a thinker believes that P when not-P. But that is another matter.

earlier example, it might be that Nora is usually disposed to act in certain ways when a cow is present. This can be true, even if Nora is not disposed to act in these ways when a cow is present *and* there are interfering factors, e.g. bad lighting, or a horse-disguise placed on the cow. (That is, not only may Nora fail to act in the relevant ways, she need not even be disposed to act in those ways.) But external factors are not the only possible sources of interference.

Nora might fail to believe that there is a cow in front of her when there is, even when the lighting is perfectly good (the cow is undisguised, etc.), because Nora mistakenly *believes* that someone is playing a trick on her. Or perhaps Nora correctly believes that there are many horse-disguised cows in the vicinity, and so she withholds judgement. Here the interfering factor—the reason why the presence of a cow fails to cause a judgement (in the typically cow-savvy Nora) that a cow is present—is internal and *intentional*. So there is little hope of cashing out the 'cp-covariation' constraint in naturalistic terms, even if one could cash out the notion of a disposition to try in a naturalistic terms; see Cummins (1989).

One might worry that there will be more than one possible assignment of truth conditions to rational dispositions that satisfies the cp-covariation constraint (cf. the worry, briefly discussed in Chapter 4, about multiple systems of cp laws). But if there is *some* indeterminacy of content in this sense, that may not be the end of the world. Moreover, I do not exclude other sources of constraint on content. In particular, the dispositional account is compatible with the claim that rational dispositions have semantically evaluable parts, as considered above. Suppose that contents respect the compositional relations among: each rational disposition; its parts (if any); and other rational dispositions that share those parts. Then the cp-covariation constraint might consistently apply only to a subset of an agent's dispositions, though if these dispositions have parts, that may determine the specific contents of other dispositions with the same parts. Other dispositions might inherit their specific contents in still other ways—perhaps via deference to other thinkers. The proposal sketched here is only a sketch, and it could be supplemented in many ways.

Perhaps it will one day be shown that some naturalistic theory of content provides the best overall theory of content. For the notion of content is implicated in puzzles distinct from, though related to, the phenomenon of error. (I already hinted at indeterminacy, which is related to holism. There are also concerns about normativity, the relation between mental contents and sentence meaning, etc.) If some naturalistic theory offers a unified resolution of the family of somewhat bothersome facts in this domain, that will be reason to adopt such a theory. And sometimes, reduction does help resolve puzzles. (See Cummins' (1983) discussion of Einstein's account of the photoelectric effect.) But as things stand, there is no reason to think that insisting on a naturalistic theory will make it *easier* to provide a fully satisfactory theory of content. So I conclude that considerations of mental content do not weaken the motivation for event dualism. On the contrary, they make the costs of neuralism even more vivid.

REFERENCES

Anscombe, G. (1957): *Intention*. Oxford: Blackwell.

Antony, L. (1995): 'I'm a Mother, I Worry', *Philosophical Issues* 6: 160–9.

——and Levine, L. (1997): 'Reduction with Autonomy', *Philosophical Perspectives* 11: 83–106.

Armstrong, D. (1968): *A Materialist Theory of Mind*. New York: Routledge & Kegan Paul.

——(1970): 'The Nature of Mind', in C. Borst (ed.), *The Mind/Brain Identity Theory*. London: Macmillan.

—— (1971): 'Acting and Trying', repr. in *The Nature of Mind and Other Essays*. Ithaca, NY: Cornell University Press.

——(1978): *Universals and Scientific Realism*, ii. *A Theory of Universals*. Cambridge: Cambridge University Press.

Baker, M. (1988): *Incorporation*. Chicago: University of Chicago Press.

——(1997): 'Thematic Roles and Grammatical Categories', in L. Haegeman (ed.), *Elements of Grammar*, Dordrecht: Kluwer: 73–137.

Belletti, A. (1988): 'The Case of Unaccusatives', *Linguistic Inquiry* 19: 1–34.

Benacerraf, P. (1965): 'What Numbers Could Not Be', *Philosophical Review* 74: 47–73.

Bennett, J. (1988): *Events and Their Names*. Indianapolis: Hackett.

Bilgrami, A. (1992): *Belief and Meaning*. Oxford: Blackwell.

Block, N. (1997): 'Anti-Reductionism Slaps Back', *Philosophical Perspectives* 11: 107–32.

Bratman, M. (1987): *Intentions, Plans, and Practical Reason*. Cambridge, Mass.: Harvard University Press.

Brody, B. (1980): *Identity and Essence*. Princeton: Princeton University Press.

Bromberger, S. (1962): 'An Approach to Explanation', in R. Butler (ed.), *Analytical Philosophy*, ii. Oxford: Blackwell.

——(1966): 'Why Questions', in R. Colodny (ed.), *Mind and Cosmos*. Pittsburgh: University of Pittsburgh Press.

Bunzl, M. (1979): 'Causal Overdetermination', *Journal of Philosophy* 76: 134–56.

Burge, T. (1974): 'Demonstrative Constructions, Reference, and Truth', *Journal of Philosophy* 71: 205–73.

——(1979a): 'Individualism and the Mental', *Midwest Studies* 4: 73–121.

——(1979b): 'Frege and the Hierarchy', *Synthese* 40: 265–81.

——(1986): 'Sinning Against Frege', *Philosophical Review* 88: 398–432.

——(1989): 'Individuation and Causation in Psychology', *Pacific Philosophical Quarterly* 70: 303–22.

——(1990): 'Frege on Sense and Linguistic Meaning', in D. Bell and N. Cooper (eds.), *The Analytic Tradition*. Cambridge: Blackwell.

——(1992): 'Philosophy of Language and Mind: 1950–1990', *Philosophical Review* 101: 3–53.

—— (1993): 'Mind-Body Causation and Explanatory Practice', in Heil and Mele (1993).

Burzio, L. (1986): *Italian Syntax*. Dordrecht: Reidel.

Cappelen, H., and Lepore, E. (1997): 'Varieties of Quotation', *Mind* 106: 423–50.

—— (1999): In Marasugi and Stainton (eds.), 1999.

Carnap, R. (1950): 'Empiricism, Semantics, and Ontology', repr. in *Meaning and Necessity*, 2nd edn. Chicago: University of Chicago Press, 1956.

Carruthers, P., and Smith, P. (eds.) (1996): *Theories of Theories of Mind*. Cambridge: Cambridge University Press.

Cartwright, N. (1983): *How the Laws of Physics Lie*. Oxford: Oxford University Press.

—— (1989): *Nature's Capacities and Their Measurement*. Oxford: Oxford University Press.

Cartwright, R. (1971): 'Identity and Substitutivity', in M. Munitz (ed.), *Identity and Individuation*. New York: New York University Press.

Castañeda, H. (1967): 'Comments', in N. Rescher (ed.), *The Logic of Decision and Action*. Pittsburgh: University of Pittsburgh Press.

Chalmers, D. (1996): *The Conscious Mind*. New York: Oxford University Press.

Child, W. (1994): *Causality, Interpretation, and the Mind*. Oxford: Oxford University Press.

Chomsky, N. (1966): *Cartesian Linguistics*. New York: University Press of America.

—— (1995): *The Minimalist Program*. Cambridge, Mass.: MIT Press.

Church, A. (1951): 'A Formulation of the Logic of Sense and Denotation', in Henle *et al.* (eds.), *Structure, Method, and Meaning*. New York: Liberal Arts Press.

Cleveland, T. (1997): *Trying without Willing*. Aldershot: Ashgate Publishing.

Cornman, J., *et al.* (1987): *Philosophical Problems and Arguments*. Indianapolis: Hackett.

Costa, M. (1987): 'Causal Theories of Action', *Canadian Journal of Philosophy* 17: 831–54.

Coulmas, F. (ed.) (1986): *Direct and Indirect Speech*. Berlin: Mouton de Gruyter.

Crane, T., and Mellor, H. (1990): 'There is No Question of Physicalism', *Mind* 99: 185–206.

Creary, L. (1981): 'Causal Explanation and the Reality of Natural Component Forces', *Pacific Philosophical Quarterly* 62: 148–57.

Crimmins, M. (1992): *Talk about Beliefs*. Cambridge, Mass.: MIT Press.

Cummins, R. (1983): *The Nature of Psychological Explanation*. Cambridge, Mass.: MIT Press.

—— (1989): *Meaning and Mental Representation*. Cambridge, Mass.: MIT Press.

Davidson, D. (1963): 'Actions, Reasons, and Causes', repr. in Davidson (1980).

—— (1965): 'Theories of Meaning and Learnable Languages', repr. in Davidson (1980).

—— (1967a): 'The Logical Form of Action Sentences', repr. in Davidson (1980).

—— (1967b): 'Causal Relations', repr. in Davidson (1980).

—— (1967c): 'Truth and Meaning', repr. in Davidson (1984).

Davidson, D. (1968): 'On Saying That', repr. in Davidson (1984).
——(1969): 'The Individuation of Events', repr. in Davidson (1980).
——(1970): 'Mental Events', repr. in Davidson (1980).
——(1971): 'Agency', repr. in Davidson (1980).
——(1974): 'Philosophy as Psychology', repr. in Davidson (1980).
——(1979): 'Quotation', repr. in Davidson (1984).
——(1980): *Essays on Actions and Events*. Oxford: Oxford University Press.
——(1984): *Essays on Truth and Interpretation*. Oxford: Oxford University Press.
——(1985): 'Adverbs of Action', in Vermazen and Hintikka (1985).
——(1986): 'Knowing One's Own Mind', *Proceedings and Addresses of the APA* 60: 441–558.
Davies, M. (1987): 'Tacit Knowledge and Subdoxastic States', in A. George (ed.), *Reflections on Chomsky*. Oxford: Blackwell.
——(1991): 'Concepts, Connectionism, and the Language of Thought', in. J. Greenwood (ed.), *The Future of Folk Psychology*. Cambridge: Cambridge University Press.
Davis, L. (1979): *A Theory of Action*. Englewood Cliffs, NJ: Prentice-Hall.
Dennett, D. (1971): 'Intentional Systems', *Journal of Philosophy* 68: 87–106.
——(1984): *Elbow Room*. Cambridge, Mass.: MIT Press.
——(1991): 'Real Patterns', *Journal of Philosophy* 88: 27–51.
Descartes, R. (1641): 'Meditations on First Philosophy', in E. Haldane and G. Ross (trans.), *The Philosophical Works of Descartes*, i. Cambridge: Cambridge University Press, 1970.
Devitt, M. (1981): *Designation*. New York: Columbia University Press.
Dicke, R., Peebles, P., Roll, P., and Wilkinson, D. (1965): 'Cosmic Black Box Radiation', *Astrophysical Journal* 142: 414–19.
Dowty, D. (1979): *Word Meaning and Montague Grammar*. Boston: Reidel.
Dretske, F. (1970): 'Epistemic Operators', *Journal of Philosophy* 67: 1007–23.
——(1981): *Knowledge and the Flow of Information*. Cambridge, Mass.: MIT Press.
——(1988): *Explaining Behavior: Reasons in a World of Causes*. Cambridge, Mass.: MIT Press.
Dummett, M. (1973): *Frege: Philosophy of Language*. London: Duckworth.
Dupré, J. (1984): 'Probabilistic Causality Emancipated', *Midwest Studies in Philosophy* 9: 169–75.
——(1993): *The Disorder of Things*. Cambridge, Mass.: Harvard University Press.
Dwyer, S. (1995): 'A Disposition to Explain', in Marion and Cohen (1995: vol. 1).
——and Pietroski, P. (1996): 'Believing in Language', *Philosophy of Science* 63: 338–73.
Etchemendy, J. (1990): *The Concept of Logical Consequence*. Cambridge, Mass.: Harvard University Press.
Evans, G. (1978): 'Can There be Vague Objects? *Analysis* 38: 208; repr. in Keefe and Smith (1996).
——(1981): 'Semantic Theory and Tacit Knowledge', in S. Holtzman and C. Leich (eds.), *Wittgenstein, To follow a Rule*. London: Routledge & Kegan Paul.
——(1982): *The Varieties of Reference*. Oxford: Oxford University Press.

Feinberg, J. (1965): 'Action and Responsibility', in M. Black (ed.), *Philosophy in America*. Ithaca, NY: Cornell University Press.

Field, H. (1978): 'Mental Representations', *Erkenntnis* 13: 9–61.

Fine, K. (1975): 'Vagueness, Truth, and Logic', *Synthese* 30: 265–300; repr. in Keefe and Smith (1996).

Fodor, J. (1978): 'Propositional Attitudes', *The Monist* 61: 501–23.

——(1975): *The Language of Thought*. New York: Crowell.

——(1983): *Modularity of Mind*. Cambridge, Mass.: MIT Press.

——(1984): 'Semantics Wisconsin Style', *Synthese* 59: 231–50.

——(1987): *Psychosemantics*. Cambridge, Mass.: MIT Press.

——(1989): 'Making Mind Matter More', *Philosophical Topics* 17: 59–80.

——(1990): *A Theory of Content and Other Essays*. Cambridge, Mass.: MIT Press.

——(1991*a*): 'A Modal Argument for Narrow Content', *Journal of Philosophy* 88: 5–26.

——(1991*b*): 'You Can Fool Some of the People All of the Time, Other Things Being Equal; Hedged Laws and Psychological Explanation', *Mind* 100: 19–34.

——(1994): *The Elm and Expert*. Cambridge, Mass.: MIT Press.

——(1997): 'Special Sciences: Still Autonomous After All These Years', *Philosophical Perspectives* 11: 83–106.

——(1998): *Concepts: Where Cognitive Science Went Wrong*. Oxford: Oxford University Press.

——and Lepore, E. (1998): 'The Emptiness of the Lexicon', *Linguistic Inquiry* 29: 269–88.

——(1999): 'Impossible Words', forthcoming.

Forbes, G. (1987): 'Indexicals and Intensionality', *Philosophical Review* 96: 3–31.

——(1990): The Indispensability of *Sinn*. *Philosophical Review* 99: 535–63.

Francken, P., and Lombard, L. (1992): 'How not to Flip the Switch with the Floodlight', *Pacific Philosophical Quarterly* 73: 31–43.

Frankfurt, H. (1978): 'The Problem of Action', *American Philosophical Quarterly* 15: 157–62.

Frege, G. (1892): 'Sense and Reference', in P. Geach and M. Black (trans.), *Translations from the Philosophical Writings of Gottlob Frege*. Oxford: Blackwell, 1980.

——(1918): 'The Thought', trans. by A. M. and Marcelle Quinton, *Mind* 65: 289–311 (1965).

Ginet, C. (1990): *On Action*. Cambridge: Cambridge University Press.

Goldman, A. (1970): *A Theory of Human Action*. Princeton: Princeton University Press.

——(1986): *Epistemology and Cognition*. Cambridge, Mass.: Harvard University Press.

Goodman, N. (1979): *Fact, Fiction, and Forecast*. Cambridge, Mass.: Harvard University Press.

Grim, P. (1991): *The Incomplete Universe*. Cambridge, Mass.: MIT Press.

Guth, A. (1997): *The Inflationary Universe*. Reading, Mass.: Addison-Wesley.

Haegeman, L. (1994): *Introduction to Government and Binding Theory*, 2nd edn. Cambridge, Mass.: Blackwell.

Hale, K., and Keyser, J. (1993): 'On Argument Structure and the Lexical Expression of Syntactic Relations', in K. Hale and J. Keyser (eds.), *The View from Building 20*. Cambridge, Mass.: MIT Press.

Hanson, N. (1958): *Patterns of Discovery*. Cambridge: Cambridge University Press.

Hanson, W. (1997): 'The Concept of Logical Consequence', *Philosophical Review* 106: 365–410.

Hare, R. (1952): *The Language of Morals*. Oxford: Clarendon Press.

Harman, G. (1972): 'Logical Form', *Foundations of Language* 9: 38–65.

Hart, H., and Honoré, A. (1959): *Causation and the Law*. Oxford: Oxford University Press.

Haslanger, S. (1989): 'Persistence, Change, and Explanation', *Philosophical Studies* 56: 1–28.

Heil, J., and Mele, A. (eds.) (1993): *Mental Causation*. Oxford: Oxford University Press.

Heller, M. (1984): 'Temporal Parts of Four Dimensional Objects', *Philosophical Studies* 46: 323–34.

——(1990): *The Ontology of Physical Objects*. Cambridge: Cambridge University Press.

Hempel, C. (1965): *Aspects of Scientific Explanation*. New York: Free Press.

——(1988): 'Provisoes: A Problem Concerning the Function of Scientific Theories', *Erkenntnis* 28: 147–64.

Herburger, E. (forthcoming): *What Counts*, Cambridge, Mass.: MIT Press.

Higginbotham, J. (1983): 'The Logical form of Perceptual Reports', *Journal of Philosophy* 80: 100–27.

——(1985): 'On Semantics', *Linguistic Inquiry* 16: 547–93.

——(1986): 'Davidson's Program in Semantics', in Lepore (1986).

——(1991): 'Belief and Logical Form', *Mind and Language* 6: 344–69.

——(1993): 'Interrogatives', in K. Hale and S. Keyser (eds.), *The View from Building 20*. Cambridge, Mass.: MIT Press.

Horgan, T. (1993): 'From Supervenience to Superdupervenience', *Mind* 102: 555–86.

Hornsby, J. (1980): *Actions*. London: Routledge & Kegan Paul.

——(1981): 'Which Physical Events are Mental Events', *Proceedings of the Aristotelian Society* 81: 73–92.

——(1985): 'Physicalism, Events, and Part-Whole Relations', in Lepore and McLaughlin (1985).

——(1986): 'Physicalist Thinking and Conceptions of Behavior', in P. Petit and J. McDowell (eds.), *Subject, Thought, Context*. Oxford: Oxford University Press.

——(1993): 'Agency and Causal Explanation', in Heil and Mele (1993).

——(1997): *Simple Mindedness*. Cambridge, Mass.: Harvard University Press.

Jackson, F. (1994): 'Armchair Metaphysics', in M. Michaelis and J. O'Leary-Hawthorne (eds.), *Philosophy in Mind*. Dordrecht: Kluwer.

Joseph, G. (1980): 'The Many Sciences and the One World', *Journal of Philosophy* 77: 773–90.

Kane, R. (1998): *The Significance of Free Will*. New York: Oxford University Press.

Kant, I. (1956): *Critique of Practical Reason*, trans. L.W. Beck. Indianapolis: Bobbs-Merill.

Kaplan, D. (1989): 'Demonstratives', in J. Almog *et al.* (eds.), *Themes from Kaplan*. New York: Oxford University Press.

Keefe, R., and Smith, P. (1996): *Vagueness: A Reader*. Cambridge, Mass.: MIT Press.

Kim, J. (1976): 'Events as Property Exemplifications', repr. in Kim (1993).

——(1981): 'Causes as Explanations: A Critique', *Theory and Decision* 13: 293–309.

——(1984): 'Concepts of Supervenience', repr. in Kim (1993).

——(1988a): 'Explanatory Realism, Causal Realism, and Explanatory Exclusion', *Midwest Studies in Philosophy* 12: 225–39.

——(1988b): 'Supervenience for Multiple Domains', repr. in Kim (1993).

——(1989): 'Mechanism, Purpose, and Explanatory Exclusion', repr. in Kim (1993).

——(1991): 'Dretske on How Reasons Explain Behavior', in McLaughlin (1991); repr. in Kim (1993).

——(1992): 'Multiple Realization and the Metaphysics of Reduction', repr. in Kim (1993).

——(1993): *Supervenience and Mind*. New York: Cambridge University Press.

——(1994): 'Explanatory Knowledge and Metaphysical Dependence', *Philosophical Issues* 5: 51–69.

——(1995): 'What, me Worry?' *Philosophical Issues* 6: 123–51.

Kitcher, P. (1981): 'Explanatory Unification', *Philosophy of Science* 48: 507–31.

Kripke, S. (1963): 'Semantical Analysis of Modal Logic I', *Zeitschrift für Mathematische Logik und Grundlagen der Mathematik* 9: 67–96.

——(1971): 'Naming and Necessity', in D. Davidson and G. Harman (eds.), *The Semantics of Natural Language*. Dordrecht: Reidel.

——(1979): 'A Puzzle about Belief', in A. Margalit (ed.), *Meaning and Use*. Dordrecht: Reidel.

——(1980): *Naming and Necessity*. Cambridge, Mass.: Harvard University Press.

——(1982): *Wittgenstein on Rules and Private Language*. Cambridge, Mass.: Harvard University Press.

Kuhn, T. (1970): *The Structure of Scientific Revolutions*, 2nd edn. Chicago: University of Chicago Press.

Larson, R., and Ludlow, P. (1993): 'Interpreted Logical Forms', *Synthese* 95: 305–55.

Laymon, R. (1985): 'Idealization and the Testing of Theories by Experimentation', in P. Achinstein and O. Hannaway (eds.), *Observation, Experiment, and Hypothesis in Modern Physical Science*. Cambridge, Mass.: MIT Press.

——(1989): 'Cartwright and the Lying Laws of Physics', *Journal of Philosophy* 86: 53–72.

Lepore, E. (ed.) (1986): *Truth and Interpretation*. Oxford: Blackwell.

——and Loewer, B. (1987): 'Mind Matters', *Journal of Philosophy* 84: 630–42.

——(1989): 'More on Making Mind Matter', *Philosophical Topics* 17: 175–92.

Lepore, E. and McLaughlin, B. (eds.) (1985): *Actions and Events*. Oxford: Blackwell.

Lewis, D. (1966): 'An Argument for the Identity Theory', *Journal of Philosophy* 63: 17–25.

——(1971): 'Counterparts of Persons and Their Bodies', *Journal of Philosophy* 68: 203–11.

——(1973): *Counterfactuals*. Oxford: Blackwell.

——(1983a): 'New Work for a Theory of Universals', *Australasian Journal of Philosophy* 61: 343–77.

——(1983b): 'Introduction' to *Philosophical Papers*, ii. New York: Oxford University Press.

——(1986): *On the Plurality of Worlds*. Oxford: Blackwell.

——(1988): 'Vague Identity: Evans Misunderstood', *Analysis* 48: 128–30.

——(1997): 'Elusive Knowledge', *Australasian Journal of Philosophy* 74: 549–70.

Loewer, B., and Rey, G. (eds.) (1991): *Meaning in Mind: Fodor and his Critics*. Cambridge, Mass.: Blackwell.

Lombard, L. (1985): 'How not to Flip the Prowler', in Lepore and McLaughlin (1985).

——(1986): *Events: A Metaphysical Study*. London: Routledge & Kegan Paul.

Lycan, W. (1994): *Modality and Meaning*. Dordrecht: Kluwer.

McCall, S. (1994): *A Model of the Universe*. Oxford: Oxford University Press.

McCann, H. (1998): *The Works of Agency*. Ithaca, NY: Cornell University Press.

McDowell, J. (1994): *Mind and World*. Cambridge, Mass.: Harvard University Press.

Mackie, J. (1974): *The Cement of the Universe: A Study of Causation*. Oxford: Clarendon Press.

McLaughlin, B. (ed.) (1991): *Dretske and his Critics*. Oxford: Blackwell.

Marion, M., and Cohen, R. (eds.) (1995): *Québec Studies in the Philosophy of Science*, i and ii: *Boston Studies in the Philosophy of Science*. Amsterdam: Kluwer.

Mates, B. (1950): 'Synonymity', repr. in L. Linsky (ed.), *Semantics and the Philosophy of Language*. Champaign: University of Illinois Press, 1952.

Matthews, R. (1983): 'Explaining and Explanation', repr. in D. Ruben (ed.), *Explanation*. Oxford: Oxford University Press, 1993.

Mele, A. (1987): *Irrationality*. Oxford: Oxford University Press.

——(1992): *Springs of Action*. Oxford: Oxford University Press.

Mellor, H. (1995): *Facts of Causation*. London: Routledge.

Millikan, R. (1984): *Language, Thought, and other Biological Categories*. Cambridge, Mass.: MIT Press.

——(1990): 'Biosemantics', *Journal of Philosophy* 86: 281–97.

Moore, G. (1903): *Principia Ethica*. Cambridge: Cambridge University Press.

——(1925): 'A Defense of Common Sense', in J. Muirhead (ed.), *Contemporary British Philosophy*, repr. in *Philosophical Papers*. London: Allen and Unwin, 1959.

——(1955): 'Wittgenstein's Lectures in 1930–33', *Mind* 64: 1–27.

McGinn, C. (1982): *The Character of Mind*. Oxford: Oxford University Press.

Munro, P. (1982): 'On the Transitivity of "Say" Verbs', *Syntax and Semantics*, 15: 301–18.

Murasugi, K., and Stainton, R. (eds.) (1999): *Philosophy and Linguistics*. Boulder, Colo.: Westview.

Nagel, T. (1986): *The View from Nowhere*. New York: Oxford University Press.

Nozick, R. (1981): *Philosophical Explanations*. Cambridge, Mass.: Harvard University Press.

O'Shaughnessy, B. (1973): 'Trying (as the Mental "Pineal Gland")', *Journal of Philosophy* 70: 365–86.

——(1980): *The Will*, i and ii. Cambridge: Cambridge University Press.

Ormazabel, I. (1995): 'The Syntax of Complementation', Doctoral dissertation, University of Connecticut.

Owens, D. (1992): *Causes and Coincidences*. New York: Cambridge University Press.

Owens, J. (1995): 'Pierre and the Fundamental Assumption', *Mind and Language* 10: 250–73.

Parsons, T. (1981): 'Frege's Hierarchies of Indirect Senses and the Paradox of Analysis', *Midwest Studies in Philosophy* 6: 37–57.

——(1990): *Events in the Semantics of English*. Cambridge, Mass.: MIT Press.

Peacocke, C. (1979): *Holistic Explanation*. Oxford: Oxford University Press.

——(1992): *A Study of Concepts*. Cambridge, Mass.: MIT Press.

Penzias, A., and Wilson, R. (1965): 'A Measurement of Excess Antenna Temperature at 4080 Mc/s', *Astrophysical Journal* 142: 419–21.

Pesetsky, D. (1982): 'Paths and Categories', Doctoral dissertation, MIT.

——(1995): *Zero Syntax*. Cambridge, Mass.: MIT.

Pietroski, P. (1992): 'Intentionality and Teleological Error', *Pacific Philosophical Quarterly*, 73: 267–82.

——(1993): 'Prima Facie Obligations, Ceteris Paribus Laws in Moral Theory', *Ethics,* 103: 489–515.

——(1994): 'Mental Causation for Dualists', *Mind and Language* 9: 336–66.

——(1995): 'Other Things Equal, The Chances Improve', in Marion and Cohen (1995).

——(1996): 'Fregean Innocence', *Mind and Language* 11: 331–62.

——(1998): 'Actions, Adjuncts, and Agency', *Mind* 107: 73–111.

——(1999a): 'Plural Descriptions as Existential Quantifiers in an Event Analysis', *University of Maryland Working Papers in Linguistics* 8.

——(1999b): 'Compositional Quotation without Paratexis', in Murasugi and Stainton (1999).

——(2000): 'Euthyphro and the Semantic', *Mind and Language*.

——(forthcoming a): 'Small Verbs, Complex Events', in L. Antony and N. Hornstein (eds.), *Chomsky and his Critics*. New York: Blackwell.

——(forthcoming b): 'On Explaining That'.

——and Hornstein, N. (MS): 'Does every Sentence Like This Exhibit some Scope Ambiguity?' MS, University of Maryland.

Pietroski, P., and Rey, G. (1995): 'When Other Things Aren't Equal: Saving Ceteris Paribus Laws from Vacuity', *British Journal for the Philosophy of Science* 46: 81–110.

Prior, E. (1985): *Dispositions*. Atlantic Highlands, NJ: Aberdeen University Press (Humanities Press).

Putnam, H. (1988): *Representation and Reality*. Cambridge, Mass.: MIT Press.

Quine, W. (1953*a*): 'Two Dogmas of Empiricism', in *From a Logical Point of View*. Cambridge, Mass.: Harvard University Press.

——(1953*b*): 'Reference and Modality', in *From a Logical Point of View*. Cambridge, Mass.: Harvard University Press.

——(1969): 'Speaking of Objects', in *Ontological Relativity and Other Essays*. New York: Columbia University Press.

Ramsey, F. (1928): 'Universals of Law and of Fact', in H. Mellor (ed.), *Philosophical Papers*. Cambridge: Cambridge University Press, 1990.

——(1929): 'General Propositions and Causality', in H. Mellor (ed.), *Philosophical Papers*. Cambridge: Cambridge University Press, 1990.

Rey, G. (1997): *Contemporary Philosophy of Mind: A Contentiously Classical Approach*. Cambridge, Mass.: Blackwell.

Robinson, W. (1990): 'States and Beliefs', *Mind* 99: 33–51.

Rudder-Baker, L. (1993): 'Metaphysics and Mental Causation', in Heil and Mele (1993).

——(1995): *Explaining Attitudes*. New York: Cambridge University Press.

Ryle, G. (1949): *The Concept of Mind*. New York: Barnes & Noble.

Salmon, N. (1986): *Frege's Puzzle*. Cambridge, Mass.: MIT Press.

Schaffer, J. (1968): *Philosophy of Mind*. Englewood Cliffs, NJ: Prentice-Hall.

Schein, B. (1993): *Plurals*. Cambridge, Mass.: MIT Press.

Schiffer, S. (1987): *Remnants of Meaning*. Cambridge, Mass.: MIT Press.

——(1991): 'Ceteris Paribus Laws', *Mind* 100: 1–17.

——(1992): 'Belief Ascription', *Journal of Philosophy* 89: 499–521.

Schlick, M. (1949): 'Meaning and Verification', in H. Feigl and W. Sellars (eds.), *Readings in Philosophical Analysis*. New York: Appleton-Century-Crofts.

Segal, G. (1989): 'A Preference for Sense and Reference', *Journal of Philosophy* 89: 73–89.

——and Sober, E. (1991): 'The Causal Efficacy of Content', *Philosophical Studies* 63: 1–30.

Sellars, W. (1956): 'Empiricism and the Philosophy of Mind', in M. Scriven, *et al.* (eds.), *Minnesota Studies in the Philosophy of Science*, i. Minneapolis: University of Minnesota Press.

——(1963): 'Philosophy and the Scientific Image of Man', in *Science Perception, and Reality*. London: Routledge & Kegan Paul.

Seymour, M. (1994): 'Indirect Discourse and Quotation', *Philosophical Studies* 74: 1–38.

Shoemaker, S. (1984): *Identity, Cause, and Mind*. Cambridge: Cambridge University Press.

Slote, M. (1974): *Metaphysics and Essence*. Oxford: Blackwell.

Smart, J. (1959): 'Sensations and Brain Processes', *Philosophical Review* 68: 141–56.

Soames, S. (1987*a*): 'Direct Reference, Propositional Attitudes, and Semantic Content', *Philosophical Topics* 15: 47–87.

——(1987*b*): 'Substitutivity', in J. Thomson (ed.), *On Being and Saying*. Cambridge, Mass.: MIT Press.

——(1995): 'Beyond Singular Propositions', *Canadian Journal of Philosophy* 25: 515–50.

Sober, E. (1984): *The Nature of Selection*. Cambridge Mass.: MIT Press.

Stainton, R. (1999): In Murasugi and Stainton (1999).

Stalnaker, R. (1969): 'A Theory of Conditionals', in N. Rescher (ed.), *Studies in Logical Theory*. Oxford: Blackwell.

——(1976): 'Possible Worlds', *Nous* 10: 65–75.

——(1984): *Inquiry*. Cambridge, Mass.: MIT Press.

——(1996): 'Varieties of Supervenience', *Philosophical Perspectives* 10: 221–43.

——and Thomason, R. (1973): 'A Semantic Theory of Adverbs', *Linguistic Inquiry* 4: 195–220.

Steward, H. (1997): *The Ontology of Mind*. Oxford: Clarendon Press.

Stich, S., and Laurence, S. (1994): 'Intentionality and Naturalism', *Midwest Studies in Philosophy* 19: 159–82.

Stone, T., and Davies, M. (1996): 'Mental Simulation: A Progress Report', in Carruthers and Smith (1996).

Strawson, P. (1958): 'Persons', in H. Feigl and M. Scriven (eds.), *Minnesota Studies in the Philosophy of Science I*. Minneapolis: University of Minnesota.

——(1959): *Individuals*. Methuen: London.

——(1962): 'Freedom and Resentment', *Proceedings of the British Academy* 48: 1–25.

——(1966): *The Bounds of Sense*. London: Methuen.

——(1985): 'Causation and Explanation', in Vermazen and Hintikka (1985).

Taylor, B. (1985): *Modes of Occurrence*. Oxford: Blackwell.

Taylor, R. (1965): *Action and Purpose*. Englewood Cliffs, NJ: Prentice-Hall.

Thalberg, I. (1972): *Enigmas of Agency*. London: Allen & Unwin.

——(1977): *Perception, Emotion, and Action*. Oxford: Blackwell.

Thomson, J. (1971): 'Individuating Actions', *Journal of Philosophy* 68: 771–81.

——(1977): *Acts and Other Events*. Ithaca, NY: Cornell University Press.

——(1980): 'Parthood and Identity Across Time', *Journal of Philosophy* 80: 201–20.

Tooley, M. (1987): *Causation: A Realist Approach*. Oxford: Clarendon Press.

Van Fraasen, B. (1980): *The Scientific Image*. Oxford: Oxford University Press.

Vendler, Z. (1967): *Linguistics in Philosophy*. Ithaca, NY: Cornell University Press.

Vermazen, B., and Hintikka, M. (eds.) (1995): *Essays on Davidson: Actions and Events*. Oxford: Clarendon Press.

Vlach, F. (1983): 'On Situation Semantics for Perception', *Synthese* 54: 129–52.

Wiggins, D. (1973): 'Towards a Reasonable Libertarianism', in T. Honderich (ed.), *Essays on Freedom of Action*. London: Routledge & Kegan Paul.

——(1980): *Sameness and Substance*. Cambridge, Mass.: Harvard University Press.

Wilson, G. (1989): *The Intentionality of Human Action*, revised and enlarged edn. Stanford: Stanford University Press.

Wittgenstein, G. (1921): *Tractatus Logico-Philosophicus*, trans. by D. Pears and B. McGuinness. London: Routledge & Kegan Paul.

Woodward, J. (1984): 'A Theory of Singular Causal Explanation', *Erkenntnis* 21: 231–62.

Wright, C. (1992): *Truth and Objectivity*. Cambridge, Mass.: Harvard University Press.

INDEX